The
Consumer Reports
MONEY
BOOK

How to Get It, Save It, and Spend It Wisely

Janet Bamford, Jeff Blyskal,
Emily Card, and Aileen Jacobson

Edited by the Editors of
Consumer Reports Books and Jeff Blyskal

Consumer Reports Books
A Division of Consumers Union
Yonkers, New York 10703

The Editors of Consumer Reports Books give thanks and appreciation to Richard Greene for the contributions he made to this edition. And thanks to Greg Daugherty for his review.

Library of Congress Cataloging-in-Publication Data
The Consumer reports money book: how to get it, save it, and spend it wisely / Janet Bamford . . . [et al.];
edited by the editors of Consumer Reports Books with Jeff Blyskal.
p. cm.
"Originally published under the title Complete guide to managing your money in 1989" —Pp. verso.
Includes index.
ISBN 0-89043-465-4 (hc)
1. Finance, Personal. I. Bamford, Janet. II. Blyskal, Jeff.
III. Consumer Reports Books. IV. Complete guide to managing your money. V.
Title: Money book.
HG179.C6647 1992
332.024--dc20
91-26154
CIP

Design by Jeff Ward
First printing, January 1992
Manufactured in the United States of America
Originally published under the title *Complete Guide to Managing Your Money* in 1989 by Consumers Union of United States, Inc.

The edition has been revised and updated.

The Consumer Reports Money Book is a Consumer Reports Book published by Consumers Union, the nonprofit organization that publishes *Consumer Reports*, the monthly magazine of test reports, product Ratings, and buying guidance. Established in 1936, Consumers Union is chartered under the Not-For-Profit Corporation Law of the State of New York.

The purposes of Consumers Union, as stated in its charter, are to provide consumers with information and counsel on consumer goods and services, to give information on all matters relating to the expenditure of the family income, and to initiate and to cooperate with individual and group efforts seeking to create and maintain decent living standards.

Consumers Union derives its income solely from the sale of *Consumer Reports* and other publications. In addition, expenses of occasional public service efforts may be met, in part, by nonrestrictive, noncommercial contributions, grants, and fees. Consumers Union accepts no advertising or product samples and is not beholden in any way to any commercial interest. Its Ratings and reports are solely for the use of the readers of its publications. Neither the Ratings, nor the reports, nor any Consumers Union publications, including this book, may be used in advertising or for any commercial purpose. Consumers Union will take all steps open to it to prevent such uses of its materials, its name, or the name of *Consumer Reports*.

Contents

Foreword

As the last decade of the 20th century accelerates rapidly, consumers are increasingly confronted with disconcerting financial surprises. The stock market swings up and down with dizzying frequency. Real estate, generally a secure way to invest for the long term, fluctuates in value as well. Tax laws change almost every year on either the federal or state level. The financial health of insurance companies is threatened. Even banks, once thought of as the ultimate safe harbor for savings, go under with alarming regularity.

Such radical changes and uncertain times seem to inspire the get-rich-quick con artists who offer effortless solutions to money problems: quick and easy loans or instant credit cards for people who have never established credit; investment schemes that are guaranteed to triple your money overnight; real estate gambits that promise tons of cash for little or no money down. All are illusory.

The fact is, with no sign of calmer financial times on the horizon, it has never been more important to manage your money with prudence, reason, and logic. Using your money wisely in turbulent financial times requires no magic wand, but it does require patience, common sense, and perhaps most important, an unbiased source of facts, information, and advice.

The Consumer Reports Money Book is divided into six sections and twenty-six chapters, offering clear information and advice to help you with the most important financial decisions you will have to make, at any stage of life.

The first section, on banking, details the ins and outs of checking and savings accounts, loans, charge cards, and even alternatives to traditional banks such as credit unions.

The second, on money management, includes a complete system for budgeting and financial planning as well as a primer on credit ratings and details on dealing with bankruptcy—if all else fails.

The tax section provides you with the most recent general material for tax planning as well as tips and strategies for dealing with specific tax situations.

Section four, on insurance, is a complete buyer's guide to medical insurance as well as life, homeowner's, automobile, and other increasingly important categories of insurance, such as disability.

The investing section is not only a guide to stocks, bonds, mutual funds, your home, and other real estate, it also includes general principles of investing to guide you through the thicket of alternatives available.

Finally, the retirement planning section consists of chapters on IRAs and Keoghs, Social Security and pensions, wills, and trusts, as well as a general guide to planning for your retirement.

This one-in-all guide—reference source, practical adviser, and financial planner—gives you the information you need to meet today's needs while positioning yourself to realize tomorrow's goals.

The Editors of Consumer Reports Books

I

BANKING

1

Checking Accounts

Jeff Blyskal

CHECKING ACCOUNTS:
THE WORKHORSE OF PERSONAL FINANCE

Almost no one enters the world of personal finance without first passing through the portals of a bank to open a checking account. Like money, checking accounts are one of the necessities of financial life; they have been so since the end of World War II. Today, according to Federal Reserve estimates, some 50 billion checks are written annually to transfer more than $35 trillion in salary payments, tax refunds, utility bills, credit card payments, grocery bills, and other transactions.

Until the mid-1970s, checking accounts were relatively simple. They all did the same thing: transferred money from one party to another. And regular checking accounts were inexpensive. When *Consumer Reports* surveyed 35 bank checking accounts in 1975, it found that monthly maintenance fees ranged from 25 cents to 75 cents. Per-check charges, which may or may not have been imposed along with the above-mentioned monthly fees (depending on the bank), commonly ran from 10 cents to 15 cents. According to a 1973 American Bankers Association study, an estimated 13 percent of all U.S. banks offered totally free checking with no minimum balance requirements.

The middle of the 1970s, however, marked the beginning of a turbulent period of change for banking and created a multitude of new options for checking customers: Interest-bearing NOW checking accounts were born; savings institutions were allowed to offer checking; "overdraft checking" kept depositors from bouncing checks. Checking accounts were linked to other bank accounts and services. And technology brought such conveniences as automated teller machines (ATMs) and banking by telephone and computer.

The current confusing array of choices is reason enough for consumers to shop carefully for the checking account that best serves their needs. But there are also sensible financial reasons for learning about what the market has to offer.

Between 1980 and 1985, checking fees rose at a rate of 25 percent per year. By the mid-1980s, the Federal Reserve estimates, Americans were paying more than $10 billion a year in bank fees. According to a 1988 *Consumer Reports* survey of 120 banks, thrifts, and credit unions around the United States, depositors who kept an average daily balance of $500 and wrote only 10 checks per month paid an average $92 a year in fees on the account. In one unusual case, such a customer would pay an estimated $216 for the year.

Bank deregulation in the early 1980s brought on a host of other complaints: long lines to tellers, increased automation and decreased customer contact, and the growing perception that big banks no longer cared about the small checking account customer.

Although there is abundant evidence that that perception is accurate, all banks do not treat their customers the same way. Many smaller neighborhood commercial banks and savings-and-loan associations (S&Ls) charge some of the lowest fees and offer some of the highest interest paid on checking. The 1988 *Consumer Reports* survey also suggests that depositors frequently can obtain better checking account deals at a credit union than at a commercial bank. According to that study, the typical customer who kept a relatively low account balance of $500 paid about $16 a year for checking at the credit union.

Small community banks may also be more people-oriented than large urban and regional banks tend to be. One of the best examples exists in the tiny agricultural town of Cut Bank (population

3,329), located in north central Montana. The First National Bank of Cut Bank is reported to have friendly tellers who will call taxis and jump-start cars whose batteries have gone dead in subzero temperatures. They even use their own jumper cables.

KINDS OF CHECKING ACCOUNTS

During the last 10 chaotic years of consumer banking, depositors may have been overwhelmed by the many options available. But it is important to understand that all checking accounts boil down to two basic types: noninterest-bearing accounts and interest-bearing accounts.

Noninterest-Bearing Accounts

Also known as regular checking, noninterest-bearing accounts pay customers no interest on the amounts kept on deposit. You simply pay the banker to provide the checking services you need.

Because of various pricing methods, regular checking accounts are typically—but by no means always—cheapest for those who tend to keep modest balances ($100 to $500 daily) or who write a relatively small number of checks per month. According to various studies, however, statistically the average person writes 21 checks per month.

Interest-Bearing Accounts

As the name implies, interest-bearing accounts pay the depositor interest on balances kept in the account according to a number of balance-calculation methods. "NOW accounts" and "Super NOW accounts" are the generic names of interest-bearing checking accounts, but each bank often uses its own "brand" name—such as "High-Interest Checking" or simply "Checking with Interest."

Checking with interest came about in the early 1970s because of the way banking works. When you deposit $1,000 into your account, the bank does not place that money in the vault. Rather, it lends up to 85 percent of it to consumers, businesses, governments, and other banks to earn interest, which covers the cost of operating the bank and contributes to its own year-end profits.

Banks can lend out your money because they know that chances are you will not withdraw all, or even most, of that $1,000 deposit immediately. While some $1,000 depositors might very well write a $900 check the next day, most others do not; they leave the money there for days, weeks, or months. Meanwhile, other customers are writing checks and making withdrawals, and still others are making deposits.

In the cumulative ebb and flow of this money are certain relatively dependable patterns. Chief among them is: Most of the time, over the bank's entire customer base, less than 15 percent of total deposits is withdrawn each day. The Federal Reserve requires banks to keep in reserve a varying percentage, usually close to that 15 percent figure, of checking deposits. This reserve requirement, which may be increased or decreased by the Federal Reserve in accordance with its policy decisions on how much credit it wants in the economy, assures that banks always have enough money to meet their depositors' daily cash-flow needs. The other 85 percent, as mentioned, can be loaned out by the bank.

If the bank is not paying you interest on your $1,000 deposit, and if it is lending out 850 of your dollars at anywhere from 10 to 20 percent annually, the potential profit (even after expenses) can be huge. Consumers eventually called for their fair share of the profits that their money was generating.

Interest-bearing checking accounts were developed to give the depositor a portion of that fair share. In the 1970s, after the success of experiments with linked savings and checking accounts in New England, the Federal Reserve allowed banks nationwide to offer NOW accounts. They could pay a maximum of 5.25 percent interest to depositors. Later, in response to high interest rates and competition from money market mutual funds, banks were also allowed to offer Super NOW accounts (also known as money market checking accounts), which paid interest rates related to prevailing market interest rates. (Around the same time, money market savings accounts, or MMAs, were also introduced. Because one can write no more than three checks per month against a money market savings account without incurring steep charges, MMAs cannot be considered true checking accounts. We will cover MMAs in chapter 2, Savings Accounts.)

On the surface, an account that earns interest on deposits would appear to be more advantageous than one that earns no interest. Unfortunately, that is not always the case. Interest-bearing checking accounts also have monthly fees or other charges. If the total fees are higher than the total interest earned—as is often the case when a low balance is maintained—an account that was opened by the depositor with the expectation that it would earn money actually incurs a net loss.

As the above case demonstrates, what appears advantageous when examined superficially can prove costly to the consumer who is not aware of the complexities of banking. A preferable option is always available, but first you must know which factors to weigh carefully, which ones are less important, and which ones distract attention from the real issues.

CHOOSING AN ACCOUNT

In trying to determine which checking account is best for your needs and income, several factors warrant close evaluation. The relative importance of each will vary depending on your own financial needs and practices.

Factors to Consider

Pricing and Your Actual Cost   The monthly charge on your account is one of the most important dollars-and-cents aspects of checking. Unfortunately, it is also one of the most complicated.

In the not-too-distant past, if you kept only a couple of hundred dollars in your checking account, the bank gave you free checking in exchange for the lending power you gave it. Today, however, some banks require balances of $500 to $1,000 or more before they waive checking fees.

Banks employ several basic fee structures:

Flat fee. This is the simplest. You pay the bank a set monthly fee regardless of how much money you keep in the account or how many checks you write. Such accounts are often known as Special Checking or Budget Checking.

Minimum balance. Monthly fees are charged, based on minimum-balance requirements. For example, if you keep an average daily balance of $500 for a month, you may not have to pay any maintenance charge that month. If you fall below that, though, you trigger a certain set fee. In recent years, these minimum-balance thresholds have been rising.

But this pricing method can be confusing, depending on whether the bank figures your account on the basis of an average daily balance or the lowest daily balance for the month. The average daily balance is the preferred method from the customer's point of view because it works out to be a higher number than the lowest daily balance (unless the balance remains the same throughout the month). That gives you a better chance of hitting the balance target required to waive fees.

You could, for instance, wind up with an average daily balance of $500 and a lowest daily balance of $10 in the same month. If you must keep a $500 average daily balance to avoid the monthly fee, your checking is free. But if your lowest balance falls below $500 on any day, you will be charged.

Tiered pricing. This pricing method also relates fees to the amounts on deposit. However, instead of just one threshold and one possible monthly fee, there may be several tiers of each. Thus, if you maintain a balance of under $500 during the month, you might be charged a $7 monthly fee. If your balance is between $500 and $1,000, your monthly fee may be $4. If you keep $1,000 to $1,500 in your account, the fee may be $2, and if you keep more than $1,500 on balance, there may be no fee that month.

Per-check. In addition to a monthly maintenance fee, some banks also impose per-check (and possibly per-ATM-transaction) charges. Typically (but not always), such accounts have a lower monthly fee than accounts with a monthly fee alone. Obviously, if you write few checks, per-check fee structures could be less costly.

Free checking. While free checking is increasingly rare, some banks—usually smaller ones—still offer it with no minimum-balance or other requirements.

Discovering how and what your bank charges for checking gives you raw pricing data, but you cannot use that information alone to compare the total annual cost of accounts offered by various banks. For example, try to calculate which of the following accounts costs the least per year: Account A, which has a flat fee of $8 per month; Account B, which has a $5 monthly fee plus 25 cents per check; or Account C, which has a $10 monthly fee if the lowest balance falls below $500.

You cannot arrive at an answer until you know (1) how low the balance in your account typically falls; and (2) how many checks you usually write per month. Let's assume you write 15 checks per month and a reexamination of your last year's monthly checking statements reveals that your balance fell to $50 only three times and never fell below $500 the remaining nine months. Based on that information, Account A would cost you $96 per year ($8 × 12 months), Account B would cost you $105 per year ($5 × 12 months + 180 checks per year × 25 cents per check), and Account C would cost just $30 a year ($10 × 3 months below the minimum balance required). Account C, which at a glance appears to be the most expensive, is actually the cheapest in this particular instance.

Interest Paid To complicate matters, many checking accounts also pay interest. So your final cost of maintaining the account becomes a matter of subtracting fees and charges, then adding back any interest earned.

Many accounts now offer interest rates that may change periodically in relation to rates in the money markets. If interest rates in general rise, interest-bearing checking account rates may rise. If rates fall, interest-bearing checking account rates will likely fall.

Bank advertisements almost always claim that their interest-bearing accounts pay "market rates." Actually, while these rates bear a relationship to market rates, typically they are below the real market rate. For example, in spring, 1991, Super NOW accounts were paying an average 4.83 percent interest (before monthly fees, and subject to minimum-balance requirements). At the same time, the average money market fund yield—which is the true yardstick of "market rates"—was 5.35 percent.

You should not be too concerned about how much higher or lower your particular NOW or Super NOW interest rate is, compared with other bank offerings—unless your rate is unusually low. Chances are, your bank will not be more than a half-point or so higher or lower than other area banks, because they all monitor each other and adjust rates to remain competitive. A half-point rate difference on a $1,000 balance amounts to only $5 per year.

Sometimes, however, one bank will try to attract more customers by offering an exceptionally high rate. But once the new depositors are signed up, the promotional rates fall back to more "normal" levels. The inconvenience of moving money from bank to bank is frequently not worth these temporary gains.

As important as how much interest the bank pays is how the

bank pays interest. As with account fees, there are several methods used by banks to calculate interest earned by a depositor. Some methods are better than others.

All balances. Interest is paid on all balances kept in the account. This is the most advantageous system for depositors.

Minimum balance required. Interest is paid only if you maintain a certain balance level determined by the bank.

Within these two methods are further subsets:

Entire balance. The interest rate is paid based on the entire balance. If you have $1,000 in the account, your earnings are equal to the annual interest rate times $1,000.

Tiered rates (entire balance). With this method, depositors are rewarded with higher interest rates for keeping higher account balances. If you keep under $500 in the account, you may be paid 5 percent interest *on the entire balance*; if you keep $500 to $2,500, you earn 6 percent interest on the entire balance; and if you keep a balance of more than $2,500, your interest rate is 6.25 percent.

Blended rates. As with tiered rates, this method pays different interest rates at different balance levels. However, each rate applies not to the entire account balance, but to "slices" of the balance. Thus, using the above-mentioned tiered-rate threshold example, if you have $3,000 on deposit, you will earn 5 percent interest for the year on the first $500 in the account, plus 6 percent annual interest on the next $2,000, plus 6.25 percent annual interest on the last $500. That totals $176.25 for the year, compounded annually— or $11.25 less than the $187.50 you would have earned with the tiered-rate, entire-balance formula of $3,000 × 6.25 percent (compounded annually). Ask the bank you are considering if it uses a blended-rate formula on its interest-bearing checking accounts. If the answer is yes, avoid that bank.

Convenience   Most people shop for a bank the way they look for a mailbox: The nearest one will do. When one considers the importance of other factors, such as fees and interest rates, choosing a bank on convenience alone can be unwise. On the other hand, one should not ignore convenience. It has a real value.

First among these is time. If you have to travel halfway across town once a week to get to a bank that pays a slightly higher interest rate than the bank down the block, you may end up losing money. Consider the value of your lost time due to travel, as well as the actual costs of transportation.

Convenience also comes in the form of numerous branches. Bank of America has hundreds of branches scattered all over California. If you travel frequently around the Golden State, that easy access to your money can be very convenient. A bank that offers 24-hour ATM machines, or access to a regional or national ATM network, provides you with similar convenience (see p. 13).

Federal Insurance Make sure your bank or savings institution is federally insured. With the demise of the Federal Savings & Loan Insurance Corporation (FSLIC), both banks and savings institutions are now insured through the Federal Deposit Insurance Corporation (FDIC). The Bank Insurance Fund (BIF) and the Savings Association Insurance Fund (SAIF) protect each person's deposits at the same institution up to $100,000 (see p. 33).

Check-Clearing Policies Once a major issue, the unrestricted length of time that banks could deny you access to funds from a deposited check has been curtailed by federal legislation passed in 1987.

When you deposit a check, the bank has only a piece of paper—until it collects the cash electronically or otherwise from the bank on which the deposited check is written. This process usually takes about a day for local checks and rarely more than two or three days for out-of-state checks. But banks have typically made customers wait much longer before giving them access to the already-collected funds.

As of September 1988, the money from U.S. Treasury checks, state and local government checks deposited in the same state, and personal checks drawn on the same bank they are being deposited to must be available to the depositor no later than the next business day after deposit. Money from all local checks must be available no later than the third business day after deposit. All nonlocal checks must be cleared no later than the seventh business day after deposit. By 1990, the "check-hold periods" shrank; banks now have to credit local checks on the second business day after deposit and out-of-town checks by the fifth business day.

Tie-ins For several years, banks have been directing consumers toward so-called relationship banking, whereby one has a checking account, mortgage, savings account, IRA, credit card, and as many other accounts as possible at the bank. The inducement for consumers is that they can perhaps get a reduced-rate auto loan or mortgage if they also keep a checking account at the bank. Sometimes such bundled services actually reduce total costs, and consumers should consider the benefits of service tie-ins—but only after a careful analysis of all the costs involved. Some costs are well hidden.

For the banker, tie-ins sometimes offer an opportunity to mislead consumers with false economies. You may be lured into free checking at Bank A if you also keep $10,000 in an 8 percent CD there. But Bank B may offer free checking anyway, with no strings attached, while your $10,000 CD might earn 9 percent at Bank C.

Personal Relationship   Another kind of "relationship banking"—based on the genuine personal relationship between a particular bank officer and the customer—is potentially more beneficial to the consumer. Wealthy depositors and business people recognized long ago the value of personal banking, and they still demand it.

By knowing you and your special needs, by knowing that you are a valued customer, and by knowing that you bring the bank an abundance of good business, a banker is more likely to "bend the rules" for you. If you need an out-of-state check cashed immediately every so often, and if your banker is a "friend" who knows you, chances are he or she will approve the unusual request. If your check is about to bounce, he or she might alert you by telephone so you can make a deposit to cover it.

Establishing such a relationship is naturally less difficult at a smaller bank where there are fewer customers and there's more of a chance for bankers to get to know customers.

Although bank advertisements frequently imply that they maintain personal banking for the mass-market consumer, a true personal relationship does not start in a bank marketing department; it starts with you.

One way to establish a personal relationship is to utilize the relationship your employer already has with its bank. Because the company brings so much profitable business to a bank, the bank will sometimes offer the company's employees free or reduced-cost checking.

Another is to deal with the same officer in the same branch each time you do business with the bank, be consistently pleasant and businesslike, and bring them more business. Send a friend interested in opening an account to your banker—and make sure the friend mentions your referral. Also, assuming you cannot get a significantly better deal at another bank, bring as much as possible of your own financial business to your banker. Knowing that you have $2,000 in CDs, or $8,000 in an IRA, or a sizable mortgage that you never fall behind on, can make a banker very friendly. But, as suggested previously, never accept a tie-in that will cost you too much in terms of actual fees or reduced interest earnings.

Automated Teller Machines/Debit Cards   ATMs have both positive and negative attributes. On the one hand, they offer a major convenience in the form of numerous locations (there are an estimated 80,156 ATMs nationwide) and 24-hour access to funds. They also speed up routine banking transactions. ATMs can frequently be used to get cash advances from your Visa or MasterCard accounts. And with the rapid expansion of regional and national ATM networks, which allow a checking account holder of one bank to make withdrawals through the ATMs of another bank, more and more people now have access to hundreds or even thousands of these machines, depending on the network of which their bank is part.

But keep in mind that the machines limit your access to personal service. Thus, it is again most important that you assess whether a bank places its emphasis on efficient ATMs or on people.

Another potential negative is that ATMs and the estimated 138 million ATM cards Americans use to work these machines are laying the groundwork for a society of paperless financial transactions. Since 1981, some 200 banks, S&Ls, and credit unions in Iowa have used so-called point-of-sale (POS) transactions. Other banks around the nation—among them, Florida's Barnett Banks and Bank of America in California—have also been exploring the POS business. In a POS transaction, you present a store with your debit card when you make a purchase. The card is run through a card-reader, you punch in your personal identification number, and funds are instantly transferred out of your account and into the store's account.

Some banks are also issuing other debit cards under the Visa, electron Visa, and MasterCard names. These look just like the Visa and MasterCard credit cards, they are as widely accepted by the more than 4 million merchants who accept Visa and MasterCard credit cards, and they work the same way as the credit cards at the checkout (though they typically employ a paper-based charge imprinter at present). In reality, however, these debit cards are plastic, paperless checking accounts that do not extend credit.

Such technological capabilities are indeed fascinating, but there is a major disadvantage in POS transactions for the consumer. The so-called float, or the time it takes for the money from a check you've written actually to be withdrawn from your account, is eliminated. So you cannot write a check at the supermarket today knowing you'll deposit your pay tomorrow.

Furthermore, an estimated 1,300 debit cards are lost or stolen each day. While your loss liability is limited to $50 if you notify the bank within two days of discovering the loss or theft of your debit card, a criminal with access to your checking account can cause much more havoc than one who steals your credit card. With the credit card, you simply stop using it until a new one is issued. What do you do when your checking account is deactivated for several days while the bank straightens out the situation?

To protect yourself, keep your debit card in a safe place; never divulge your personal identification number (PIN) to anyone; don't write your PIN on the card or on a piece of paper kept in your wallet; and don't use your Social Security number, birth date, address, phone number, or other obvious number as a PIN, since an astute criminal might find those numbers written on other ID kept in your wallet.

Of course, one does not have to use—or even have—a debit card. However, banks are already providing incentives for POS and ATM usage by imposing no charge for those transactions but a per-check charge of 25 to 50 cents, and additional charges for human teller transactions in some places around the country.

To further reduce the use of paper, some bankers are also trying to convince depositors that they do not need their canceled checks returned to them with the monthly statement. "Truncation," as this is called, is a cost-cutting move by the banks—though banks call it "check safekeeping." In fact, the checks are not kept safely anywhere. They are destroyed after being microfilmed.

To force consumers to accept truncation, some banks impose

penalty charges if you want your checks returned; there are no extra charges if you agree to truncate. *Consumer Reports* advises most consumers to continue demanding their canceled checks. Canceled checks are a good legal record of transactions, and some banks are charging up to several dollars to produce photocopies of truncated checks. Having all your canceled checks in a safe place at home makes for very convenient verification of payments you have made.

Intangibles Last on the list of factors to consider—but nevertheless important to different people in varying degrees—are intangibles that are difficult to measure. Does your bank frequently have long lines? Some days of the month—such as the first and the fifteenth, Fridays, and the days before and after a holiday—are high-traffic times. Banks routinely monitor how many people come into the bank day by day and hour by hour for staffing purposes; the best of them bring in extra personnel to handle increased-volume days.

There are other important intangibles. Are the tellers friendly? (The job of bank teller is often a high-stress, relatively low-paying position.) How helpful are the bank officers? Are errors corrected quickly and to your satisfaction? How often are the ATMs out of service?

The best way to assess how well a bank provides these intangible benefits is to ask friends, coworkers, and relatives who use the bank you are considering. If their experience with the bank has frequently been frustrating or annoying, chances are yours will be too.

Factors to Ignore

It is almost as important to recognize what factors are not worth considering as it is to know what factors are important.

Gifts and Advertising Campaigns Some of the less important distractions are obvious: You should never open an account at a particular bank just because it offers free toasters, electric blankets, or other gifts as an enticement. You also shouldn't choose a bank based on its advertisements. Sometimes the ad will be overstated or will omit important details.

One large New York bank, admired in banking circles for its

marketing ingenuity, ran an ad campaign focusing on providing instant cash for any deposited check. What the ad copy failed to mention was that a depositor had to have other deposits at the bank—perhaps a savings account—to be able to get instant cash for a deposited check. A hold is placed on those other funds, and they cannot be withdrawn until the check they're covering actually does clear.

Yet another popular marketing omission involves the term *free checking.* Bank advertisements often neglect to mention (or hide in fine print) the conditions of free checking, such as, "if certain minimum balances are maintained."

Compounding Methods Often, banks will make daily and continuous compounding seem of great importance to depositors. The fact is, unless you have a five-digit balance—something that is, with rare exception, unwise for a checking account because your deposits can probably earn more interest in another financial vehicle—the dollar difference is insignificant. Even on a $1,000 daily balance, 5 percent annual interest pays $51.16 over a year when compounded monthly and $51.27 over the same period when compounded continuously. One must weigh the effort of searching for an account with continuous compounding against that extra 11 cents of interest.

Interest Calculation Methods Some critics of banks warn that depositors should pay close attention to the way a bank calculates both the balance on an account and, based on that, the interest earned. Various banks use a 366-, 365-, or 360-day year when calculating interest, but again, the disparity in total interest earned amounts to only pennies.

However, one way of calculating interest due the depositor, the *low-balance* method, should be avoided. It works like this: If you deposit $100 on April 1 and $10,000 on April 2, your interest for that month is based on the $100, not on the $10,100, because interest is paid only on balances that have been in the account for the entire month. Banks used the low-balance method in the past because it was easier to calculate the interest owed to depositors. Computers have made this method outdated, but be sure to ask any prospective bank whether it uses the low-balance method.

Miscellaneous Fees In the wake of bank deregulation, banks have begun charging for miscellaneous services that once were provided free. Such fees should not weigh heavily in your choice of bank unless you are likely to incur them or if the fee is for routine and frequent service. For example, Mellon Bank (East) in Philadelphia imposes a $30 penalty for a check returned because of insufficient funds in the account. Other banks will charge $25 if you deposit someone else's check to your account and it is returned. Stop-payment charges can be huge, too.

Some bankers claim that such large fees are necessary because of the expense of returning a check. However, according to Federal Reserve estimates, the real cost of returning a check is only about 12 to 35 cents. Thus, a $20 returned-check fine amounts to at least a 5,600 percent profit for the bank. More realistic is the idea that banks simply want to deter people from bouncing checks, a practice which is, after all, illegal. In any case, you may never have a check returned and thus will never incur a fine. On the other hand, charges for making withdrawals from an ATM—or from a human teller—should be weighed carefully and compared against charges at other banks in the area, in much the same way you would weigh a per-check charge. Some banks across the country are now charging for balance inquiries or for "excessive" numbers of visits to a human teller. Many more banks now routinely charge for ATM transactions. Small fees on such oft-used services can add up to a considerable amount.

Automated Services Technology-oriented services such as banking by telephone and computer may prove convenient to you, but you should not choose a bank based solely on their availability. Banks are constantly testing new "conveniences." If the innovation proves worthwhile, most banks eventually offer the service. Until then, you are part of an experiment that may be of questionable value and high cost. ATMs and ATM networks are the best examples of solid developments that not long ago were still in the experimental stage but spread rapidly because of strong consumer acceptance. Two other, more exotic, good ideas that are now utilized by most banks are preauthorized bill payments for loans— in which monthly payments are deducted automatically from your account and paid to the lender—and direct deposit of income checks, which are transferred electronically, directly from the payer's bank and into your account. One idea that has not yet proved itself is banking by home computer, though many such pilot programs are still under way at banks around the nation.

CLOSE-UP:
SPECIAL SITUATIONS IN CHECKING

While you are scrutinizing a bank, the bank is often doing the same to you. Banks clearly prefer certain groups to others. No group can be barred from a bank, but the favored ones can be attracted with such incentives as better services and higher interest rates for higher balances. The less favored groups can be provided with disincentives: high fees, high minimum-balance requirements before interest can be earned, and poor-quality service. Following are the four major groups most banks either love or hate.

The Wealthy   As one might expect, people with plenty of money are favorites of a bank—and for good reason. The wealthy individual has an abundance of what a bank needs—money. In recent years, banks have moved to provide wealthy customers— often defined as high-balance customers—with so-called priority services. For checking accounts, that has meant special, shorter teller lines, highly personalized service, and fee waivers. In some cases, banks will go to extremes in personal service to please a wealthy depositor. One New York banker helped a customer get a car into and out of the country; another intervened to rescue lost luggage from the clutches of an airline's bureaucracy.

If you are a wealthy depositor, be sure to use your advantage to the fullest. But be aware that some banks offering "priority services"—especially large, mass-market urban banks—do not always provide the levels of quality depicted in their advertisements. Wealthy depositors may be better off passing up such mass-market banks for an old-line institution that has a long history of dealing with a moneyed clientele.

The Middle-Income Depositor   The middle-income depositor is caught in a classic banking bind. Banks need the aggregate of this group's deposits, yet they often cannot treat the individual mass-market customer with the respect and service he or she deserves. Consequently, many such customers feel that they are serving the bank, not the other way around.

Here, then, is where the careful shopping outlined in much of this chapter can be most beneficial. Middle-income depositors must be aggressive in taking advantage of whatever strengths they do have; where they can exert little or no advantage over the bank, they must then shop wisely for the best of the available options.

The Poor Banks deny that they discriminate, but the fact is that the poor are being denied banking services because of the high cost. Low-income consumers—by the very definition—do not have $10,000 or even $500 to keep in a checking account all the time so that high monthly fees can be waived. Likewise, few can afford to spend $100 a year to have a checking account.

The alternative for these people has been to leave the bank altogether and to convert checks into cash at check-cashing storefronts found in some low-income urban areas. Such businesses exact a high price for their services: They take a percentage of the check's face value.

Lifeline banking legislation, which would require banks to offer special low-cost accounts to low-income individuals, has been proposed at the federal level. It was defeated, but probably will come up again. According to the American Bankers Association, many banks are already offering or are planning low-cost, no-frills checking accounts, but in some cases only if the customer uses ATMs instead of human tellers.

Low-income depositors who cannot find a low-priced checking account in their area should consider opening a free or inexpensive savings account to serve their check-cashing needs (see chapter 2) and use money orders from the same bank to pay bills.

The Elderly Many people over 65 may be surprised to know that they are desirable customers as far as banks are concerned. Why? Elderly depositors frequently have a deeply ingrained savings drive that dates back to the Great Depression. Consequently, they tend to let large amounts of money sit on deposit at the bank for very long periods of time. Other aged depositors, either because of fear or lack of knowledge of what to do with their money, will deposit money in a bank and literally forget about it.

Elderly checking customers should take advantage of such options as free checking for people over a certain age—many banks offer it, with varying age thresholds—as well as direct deposit of pension, Social Security, and dividend checks. Most of all, recognize your value to the bank and expect adequate compensation in return.

CLOSE-UP: WHAT'S IN THE FINE PRINT?

Most ordinary checking accounts do not have the kind of contractual fine print associated with loan agreements. There are few regulations governing checking accounts, so most of the details of the account are found in promotional brochures, pamphlets, and advertisements.

However, checking accounts with a debit card attached to them often have a page or two of fine print. Debit cards, also known as bank cards, fall under the regulations contained in the federal Electronic Funds Transfer Act. Look for several items in your bank-card agreement:

Your Liability for Unauthorized Transfers The agreement should outline your liability. By law, if you inform your bank about a lost or stolen card within two business days of your discovering its loss or theft—not two days from when it was actually lost or stolen—your liability is limited to $50. (Many banks have 24-hour phone numbers for reporting lost cards, making it even easier for you to meet the two-day deadline.) If you do not tell the bank within two days, your liability could be as high as $500. Beware of misleading phrases like this from one bank's agreement: "If you do not have overdraft privileges or a credit line for a particular account, you could lose all the money in that account if someone used your debit card and/or (personal identification number) without your permission." That statement is tricky; in most cases, the $50/$500 limits under the law will still apply. You *can* conceivably lose all the money in your account; however, you would have to fail to report the unauthorized transfers for more than 60 days after transmittal of the monthly statement. You would still only be liable for up to $50 of unauthorized transfers that occurred during the first 60 days, plus all unauthorized transfers that occurred after the 60-day period and before notification to the bank—if the bank can establish that those losses could have been avoided if you had notified it promptly. But if your failure to notify the bank within 60 days is due to such a matter as hospitalization or extended travel, the 60-day limit would be extended to "a reasonable time."

By law you also have 60 days to notify the bank if you find an unauthorized transfer on your monthly statement. The postmark on the statement mailing envelope starts the 60-day clock.

According to a report by the Comptroller of the Currency in Washington, not all banks follow the federal regulations regarding lost cards. Some banks have denied liability limits to customers who have either written their PIN on the card or have revealed the PIN to a friend or relative who later made an unauthorized withdrawal. Liability limits are based only on the time between discovering a card lost or stolen and reporting it missing; the limits still apply, no matter how an unauthorized user obtained your secret code number.

The fine print may omit the fact that your liability is zero if unauthorized transfers are made with a debit card you never received.

Limits on Transfers   Each bank sets limits on the amount of money you can withdraw on any one day. If you are planning to withdraw $2,000 from an ATM for a trip while on your way to the airport, a $400 daily limit can cause trouble. Find out what the limits are—especially for weekends, which some banks consider to be "one business day."

ATM Transaction Charges   What does the bank charge for various ATM transactions? According to the American Bankers Association, 14 percent of banks charge for ATM use at their own banks and 49 percent charge for using another bank's ATM. For those that charge for using their own machine, the average fee is 37 cents per transaction, while 85 cents per transaction is the average fee for banks that charge for using "foreign" machines. In the future, as banks decide to have these machines pay for themselves through transaction charges, such fees are likely to become more common.

Disclosure of Account Information to Third Parties   Even if you do not have a credit line, some banks reserve the right to provide credit bureaus with information about your checking account. This is an invasion of consumers' rights to privacy for which depositors receive nothing in return.

Correction of Errors   Your debit card agreement should outline what you must do if an ATM doesn't give you the $50 that it claims it did. The fine print probably will take you only as far as this: "If we decide that there was no error, we will send you a written explanation within three business days after we finish our investigation." What do you do if you disagree with the bank's final verdict? You can obtain a copy of the investigation report and sue the bank. You should also report the problem to the appropriate federal or state agency that regulates your bank, as well as to local consumer affairs offices.

In the area of disputed deposits, canceled checks are proof that you made an ATM deposit. When you make a cash deposit to a human teller, he or she will verify the amount and mark your deposit ticket in your presence, making it a legal receipt. According to a consumer finance handbook published by a subcommittee of the U.S. House Committee on Banking, Finance, and Urban Affairs, receipts from cash deposits at an ATM are equal to a canceled check.

Instant Cash for Deposited Checks   Some banks allow you to cash a check if the bank can put a hold on your other deposits—such as those in a savings account—until the check clears. Certificates of deposit (CDs) can sometimes be used for this purpose. But if the deposited check is returned because of insufficient funds and the bank has to pull funds out of your CD to cover that check, you could be charged a "substantial penalty for early withdrawal" on the CD.

Notices in the Mail   When you receive your monthly statement, other papers often are included in the envelope. Some of these are advertisements for loans or other services. Others, however, may be important notices about policies governing your account. Check all papers accompanying your monthly statement before throwing them out. Retain notices about account policies for your records.

2

Savings Accounts

Jeff Blyskal

Savings may be defined as the money that you set aside from your disposable income for future use instead of spending it immediately. The future use you anticipate may occur at the end of the month, when your mortgage payment falls due, at the end of the year, when you need to buy a new car, or 10 years from now, when you pay your child's first college-tuition bill. You may intend part of your savings to protect you against an unspecified rainy day— to pay for unforeseen emergencies like medical expenses or the loss of your job or to allow you to take a vacation or redecorate your home.

Whether you are saving for the short term or the long, however, you should be concerned with three factors: You want your savings to be *protected* against total or partial loss; you want them to *grow* by earning interest; and you want them to be readily *available*.

Unfortunately, there is no investment that will simultaneously satisfy your concerns for safety, yield, and liquidity. Whether you invest your money in a savings account, stocks, or real estate, the higher the safety, the lower the yield, typically—and the higher the yield, the lower the liquidity. This is why bank savings accounts, for example, which are both safe and liquid, offer lower yields than money market mutual funds (see p. 72), which are marginally less safe but as liquid.

The reasons for these triangular relationships are clear enough. Banks need deposits so that they can lend their depositors' money to loan customers and earn the difference between the interest they pay depositors and the much higher interest they charge borrowers. Because banks want to have long-term deposits that they can count on, they pay a higher rate for long-term certificates of deposit, which may carry penalties for early withdrawal, than they do for savings account deposits, which can be withdrawn at any moment. Because most banks have Federal Deposit Insurance Corporation (FDIC) coverage, they can pay less interest than money market mutual funds, which have no such insurance coverage and are theoretically less safe. Since the cost of maintaining a customer's account is virtually the same regardless of the balance, banks pay a higher yield on large balances than on small ones.

HOW MUCH LIQUIDITY DO YOU NEED?

Many consumers fail to realize the full earnings potential of their savings because they overestimate their need for liquidity and safety. Today the balance in the typical bank money market account—a safe and highly liquid form of savings (see p. 28)—ranges from $10,000 to $18,000, a sum far greater than most people actually need to keep liquid, because large expenditures almost always involve long-range planning. A large portion of such a balance could be invested to produce a much higher yield with only slightly less safety or liquidity.

Your first step in planning your savings strategy, then, is to estimate how much money you are likely to need in the near future, bearing in mind that some of the emergencies you anticipate—for example, sudden hospitalization or the total destruction of your automobile—are likely to be covered at least in part by insurance and will probably not require a next-day or even a next-week layout of cash. If you have a sizable amount of savings, you may want to put some into a regular savings or money market account, each of which has immediate liquidity; some into a three-month certificate of deposit, which has lower liquidity but a higher interest rate; and some into a one-year certificate of deposit, which has a still higher interest rate. You may also want to consider investments discussed in chapters 17 through 22, which offer a far wider range of safety, liquidity, and yield than anything a federally chartered bank or thrift institution can offer.

PASSBOOK AND STATEMENT SAVINGS ACCOUNTS

The traditional savings account—whether its activity is recorded in a passbook or a monthly statement—is safe and liquid. As a result, it pays the lowest rate of interest offered by banks. Prior to the changes brought about by the Depository Institutions Deregulation Act of 1982, the interest payable on such accounts was limited to 5.25 percent for commercial banks and 5.5 percent for savings banks. Although banks are now free to offer whatever rates they choose, these rates have not changed much. Instead, banks offer their customers higher rates for larger or less liquid forms of deposit, as discussed below.

With passbook accounts, all deposits, withdrawals, and other transactions are recorded in a book that the depositor holds and presents with each transaction. (Passbook account transactions are, of course, also recorded by the bank's computers.) Before the advent of computers, this was the standard type of savings account. Some consumers still prefer the passbook account—perhaps because it represents tangible evidence of their savings balance—even though the passbooks are easily lost or misplaced and passbook depositors do not have access to automated teller machines. (Some banks no longer even offer passbook accounts.)

The statement account is identical to the passbook account except that transactions are recorded solely by the bank's computer and the depositor receives a monthly or quarterly statement—often combined with his or her checking account statement—itemizing each transaction. Some banks encourage the use of statement accounts by offering slightly higher rates or by giving the depositors access to automated teller machines.

Advantages

Aside from safety, the sole advantage of either type of savings account is that your money is always available—moments after you make a cash deposit into a statement account and at any time, day or night—through an ATM. In addition, since there is normally no limitation on either frequency or amount for deposits or withdrawals, it is a convenient place for the deposit of small checks as well as for the periodic withdrawal of small amounts of money. It may also be a convenient place for a child's first savings or for a custodial account for minors (see p. 171), to which you plan to make periodic additions until it grows large enough for a higher-yield investment.

If your bank links a savings account with a checking account that pays no interest, you may find it worthwhile to keep most of your funds in the savings account and make transfers to the checking account only when its balance needs replenishing.

Interest and Fees

Although there no longer are any restrictions on the interest banks can pay, few if any of them have raised the earlier ceilings of 5.25 or 5.5 percent, and some pay an even lower rate. In addition, approximately 75 percent of banks have established a minimum balance requirement—between $25 and $400—and pay no interest on the account balance if it falls below the minimum. Some banks, moreover, have instituted monthly or quarterly account-servicing fees of $1 to $2, which further erode the interest you are likely to earn.

The method by which interest is compounded—quarterly, monthly, daily, or continuously—makes an insignificant difference. On a $1,000 balance, for example, monthly compounding at 5 percent interest would, at the end of a year, yield $51.16, whereas continuous compounding would yield $51.27.

Far more important than the frequency of compounding is the method used for calculating the interest. Whether the bank uses a 366-, 365-, or 360-day year in computing interest is insignificant, but the balance on which the interest is computed can influence your yield considerably. Some banks pay interest only on the lowest balance in your account during the month. Thus, if your balance since July 1 has been $1,500 but you withdraw $1,000 on July 29, your interest for July will be based on only $500. Before the advent of computers, banks used the low-balance method because it was easier to calculate. Computers are now able to handle interest payments on the basis of a daily balance, but some banks retain the old method to discourage small accounts.

Yield

Bank advertisements, whether for savings accounts, money market accounts, or certificates of deposit, often quote two figures: the annual interest rate and the effective yield, a slightly higher figure. The difference between these two figures stems from the frequency with which interest is credited to your balance and thus increases the principal on which subsequent interest is paid. A 5 percent interest rate will have an effective yield of 5 percent if the interest is credited annually, but its effective yield will be 5.094 percent if interest is credited quarterly and 5.116 percent if interest is credited monthly. This difference, too, is trivial unless the balance is very large (but, as we shall see, a savings account is no place for a large balance).

Is a Savings Account Worthwhile?

Before opening a savings account, you need to inquire about the interest rate, any minimum-balance requirements or service charges, and the method used for computing interest. In addition you should inquire about similar accounts in a credit union (see p. 69), which generally pays significantly higher rates than a bank.

Regarding any savings you invest, especially in a regular savings account, it is important to recognize the effects of inflation. If the inflation rate is a relatively low 5 percent and you deposit $1,000 in a 5 percent savings account that is compounded monthly, you will, as we have seen, have earned $51.16 at the end of the year. If you are in the 28 percent tax bracket, you are likely to pay about $14 in taxes on this interest. In real terms, then, your $1,000 will have increased to $1,037 after taxes. But the 5 percent inflation rate has reduced the purchasing power of your $1,037 to only $985—so you have actually lost money on your investment. You have fared only slightly better than you would have by keeping your money in your mattress (where inflation would have reduced your $1,000 to $950). Because neither interest rates nor the rate of inflation can be predicted, there is no alternative investment that can guarantee you a gain that is not eroded by inflation. But investments with a higher yield obviously are better than those with a lower yield.

Having recognized the disadvantages, you then need to ask yourself whether the convenience offered by a savings account is

worth the difference between its yield and a higher yield you might
earn with no loss of safety.

MONEY MARKET ACCOUNTS

The money market accounts offered by banks can be confusing for
three reasons. First, the same basic account is given a wide variety
of names by different banks: Money Management Account, Market
Plus Account, Investor's Choice Account, and so forth. Second, the
money market account is easily confused with the Super NOW
account, an interest-paying checking account (see chapter 1).
Third, the money market account is also easily confused with the
money market *mutual fund*, which is similar in some respects but
is not offered by banks (see p. 72). Regardless of its name, however,
the money market account available from banks has the following
characteristics:

Like a regular savings account, a money market account typically earns interest at 5.25 percent up to a specified balance—usually $1,000 to $2,500. Beyond that level, the interest rate rises to
what banks call the "market interest rate"—a rate that fluctuates
but normally is about one percentage point higher than the rate
paid on Super NOW accounts.

Like a savings account, the money market account is federally
insured, and there is no limit to the size or the number of deposits
or withdrawals that you can make. But while you are entitled to
write three checks per month on the account, exceeding this limit
can cost you a penalty of $5 to $10 per check. And, because its interest rate is higher than that of a regular savings account, some people use the money market account as a temporary parking place
for funds awaiting other kinds of investment. Keeping such funds
in a regular savings account or Super NOW account would earn
them less, and depositing them in a noninterest-paying checking
account would earn them nothing.

Unlike the fixed rate earned by a savings account, interest rates
on a money market account may fluctuate from week to week,
reflecting changes in the market rate. But, although the rate is
basically determined by the market interest rate, there is no legal
restriction on what banks can pay. Consequently, the rates paid by
individual banks are likely to vary slightly, depending on a bank's
need to attract new deposits and retain existing ones and on the

region in which a bank is located. Although such rate variations are unlikely to amount to more than one-half of a percentage point, there is no reason why you cannot open a money market account anywhere in the country you can find a better rate. But you will have to be willing to make deposits by mail, make withdrawals for a fee via an ATM network, limit checks to three per month, and forgo the convenience of a local branch.

Interest Computation

As important as the interest rate paid by a particular bank is the balance on which the bank computes the interest. Banks use one of two methods:

A bank that uses the *tiered* method pays the same rate of interest on your entire balance, the actual rate being determined by the size of that balance. Thus, a balance of less than $1,000 might earn 5.25 percent, but once you increased your balance to, say, $8,000, the entire $8,000 would earn the higher "market" rate.

Some banks, however, use the *blended* method to compute interest. Under this method, your first $1,000 might earn only 5.25 percent no matter what your balance, and only amounts above this minimum would earn the market rate. Thus, if your balance were $8,000, you would earn 5.25 percent on $1,000 and the higher rate only on $7,000. Because the blended method is obviously less attractive than the tiered, you should find out which method is used before opening a money market account.

Safety vs. Yield

Money market accounts had their origin in the 1970s after bank depositors were attracted by money market mutual funds (see p. 72). In those inflationary times, the money market funds were paying interest rates as high as 17 percent—in contrast to the 5.5 percent to which banks were restricted by law. Faced with the withdrawal of billions of their depositors' dollars, the banks lobbied successfully for permission to offer money market accounts.

In their competition with the money market mutual funds, however, the banks can offer potential depositors only two advantages: safety (because money market accounts are usually protected by federal deposit insurance, whereas money market mutual funds are not) and proximity (because a local bank may be more convenient for transactions than a distant money market fund).

Bearing in mind these differences, before deciding to open a money market account you should consider carefully whether a money market mutual fund, which is likely to pay you a significantly higher interest rate on your entire balance and which is regarded by most authorities as safe, might be a preferable investment, especially for substantial balances.

CERTIFICATES OF DEPOSIT

A certificate of deposit (CD) is a promissory note that you receive from the bank. In return for your loan, the bank promises to pay you a fixed rate of interest (or, sometimes, a variable rate) for the term of the loan and to return your principal and interest at the end of that period. While CDs pay higher interest rates than do regular savings accounts and provide the security of FDIC protection, they tie up your money for the term of the certificate.

Interest vs. Liquidity

The fact that the interest rate on a certificate of deposit is fixed and unchangeable may turn out to be either an advantage or a disadvantage. When interest rates are at a peak, a bank will have to offer certificates at a fairly high interest rate to attract buyers. If you buy a long-term certificate at that time, you will lock in a high rate, and continue to receive that rate even if interest rates drop precipitately. Conversely, if interest rates are low at the time of your purchase, you will lock in a low rate for the entire term of the certificate.

If you withdraw a certificate of deposit before its term ends, you are likely to pay a penalty. Federal law no longer mandates penalties, but banks have the right to impose their own, and some of these can be severe. The loss of three months' interest is not uncommon. You should check on the bank's early withdrawal policy before buying a certificate of deposit, and if you find the penalties too severe, look elsewhere. In some situations, if you find yourself locked in to a low-rate certificate of deposit, it may be worth paying a moderate penalty to free your funds for a more productive investment.

When a certificate of deposit matures, you have several choices. The bank can renew it automatically—*but at the rate prevailing at the time*—or deposit the proceeds into a regular savings account, or mail you a check. Since some banks choose one of these options automatically unless you instruct them otherwise, it is important to take action before the certificate matures.

Certificates of deposit are available with a variety of terms— from as short as seven days to as long as 30 years. But the most common terms are three months, six months, and one, three, and five years. Because banks are eager to retain their depositors' money over a long term, the interest rate rises with the length of the term. And because the banks profit more from large accounts than from small ones, the rates rise with the denomination of the certificate. A certificate of deposit for $2,000, for example, may command a rate half a percentage point higher than one for $500, and higher denominations may earn still higher rates.

Predicting Interest Rates

In the belief that they can predict interest rates, some depositors buy the largest long-term certificates of deposit they can afford when they think rates are peaking. They hope that they have locked in a higher rate than those that will prevail in the near future, when they anticipate that rates will decline.

Others, however, are convinced that interest rates are totally unpredictable over the long term. So instead of investing, say, $5,000 in a one-year certificate of deposit at a specific rate, they buy five $1,000 six-month certificates at intervals of three to six months. With this method, one certificate will mature every three to six months, at which time they can consider current interest rates and other investment options for each $1,000. This tactic precludes the possibility of locking in a high rate, but it also precludes the equal possibility of locking in a low one.

Some banks offer variable-rate certificates of deposit, but these sacrifice the advantage of locking in a high interest rate for a long term. In addition, the variable rate of some certificates is not tied to any specific index, and can be changed at the bank's discretion. In general, variable-rate certificates are a poor buy unless they incorporate a rate floor—that is, a minimum below which the rate will never fall.

Finding the Highest Rates

Rates on certificates of deposit vary not only with the term of the certificate and its denomination but also from one bank to another, and often from one region to another. There is no need to confine your purchase to the bank that handles your other accounts or even to a bank in your own community. Many banks advertise their certificates of deposit to a nationwide audience through the media, and sending $10,000 by mail or bank wire to a bank a thousand miles from your home is a relatively simple matter. However, some of the institutions offering unusually high rates are no longer in business; they closed in the giant shake-out of the thrift industry in the late 1980s and early 1990s.

Regional rate differences of as much as two percentage points are common because banks in some parts of the country experience a need for more funds—for mortgages, for example, in areas of high population growth. In addition, at certain times of the year—before the Christmas holidays and before income-tax deadlines—banks may need funds to replenish those withdrawn by their depositors. All banks, no matter where they are located, continuously compete with one another, as well as with the financial institutions discussed in chapter 5. One way of attracting new customers is through a certificate of deposit price war. In this struggle, it may be cheaper for a small bank to attract depositors by means of higher CD rates than by trying to match the expensive advertising campaigns of its larger competitors.

It is also possible, to some extent, to negotiate or bargain with your local bank. Because some banks give their officers a range of rates rather than a single rate for certificates of deposit, you might try bargaining for a better rate—or a waiver of withdrawal penalties—instead of accepting the terms posted in the bank lobby.

ARE BANK INVESTMENTS THE BEST FOR YOU?

There are several reasons why banks are the first alternative that people choose for the deposit of their savings. To begin with, banks provide many people with their earliest experience with any form of savings account. In addition, on the basis of a personal relationship with a pleasant teller or a friendly manager, some people develop a loyalty to their bank that discourages a cold, objective comparison of interest rates and investment options. Moreover, because they are reluctant to deal with strangers and mistrustful of the U.S. mail, many people prefer a relationship with a local bank they can visit at any time. And, finally, banks tend to emphasize the safety that FDIC insurance offers their depositors.

All of these factors predispose many depositors toward banks and cause them to overlook some attractive alternatives instead of considering them carefully and objectively. Before assuming that a bank offers you the best of all possible vehicles for your savings, you ought to consider the alternatives discussed in chapter 5 and in chapters 17 through 22.

CLOSE-UP:
LEGAL PROTECTION FOR DEPOSITORS

Deposit Insurance

Federal insurance coverage for bank deposits—through the Federal Deposit Insurance Corporation for commercial banks, many savings banks and savings and loan associations—protects depositors to a maximum of $100,000 at any one institution. All nationally chartered banks are required to be members of the FDIC; state chartered banks need not belong, but most do.

The $100,000 insurance ceiling applies to all moneys deposited in any one bank under the name (or Social Security number) of the same individual. Thus, a depositor with $30,000 in a money market account, $75,000 in one or more certificates of deposit, and $3,000 in a checking account would have coverage on only $100,000 of the $108,000 total.

A depositor can, however, extend this $100,000 coverage in several ways: by opening one or more accounts in a different bank (not just another branch of the same bank); or by opening a second set of accounts in the same bank in joint ownership with a spouse or a child, or in the name of a revocable trust. Each of these accounts, because they have different registrations, will enjoy the full $100,000 protection. (However, any one person's coverage for his or her total deposits in all joint accounts in the same bank is limited to $100,000.)

Although the federal insurance programs guarantee the safety of deposits, they do not guarantee that depositors will be able to withdraw their money on demand. The terms and conditions governing a regular savings account specify that the bank may require the depositor to provide advance notice—typically, 30 days—of the intention to make a withdrawal. In actuality, though, this requirement, which is designed to protect the bank in situations of unusual cash outflow or other crises, has been invoked very rarely, and only for periods of a few days. By contrast, some state insurance programs have been depleted in recent years by the failure of a number of savings-and-loan institutions, and depositors have experienced uncertainties and extensive delays in retrieving their deposits.

In general, depositors can rely on the protection offered by the FDIC. You can pick up the FDIC's question-and-answer pamphlet, "Your Insured Deposit," which should be available at any bank. Or, for more information on bank safety, send a stamped self-addressed envelope for "How Safe is Your Money After The Bailout," a booklet that explains how the federal insurance system operates, how to open a safe out-of-state account, and how you can determine the financial condition of a bank or thrift. The address is 100 Highest Yields, P.O. Box 88888, North Palm Beach, Florida 33408.

Investment Regulation

Consumers who use bank loans have been protected for several decades by the federal Truth-in-Lending Act, but no such federal protection extends to those who use banks as repositories for their savings, although proposals are before Congress. At this writing, nine states—New York, Massachusetts, Ohio, Illinois, Iowa, Maryland, Rhode Island, Texas, and Wisconsin—have enacted Truth-in-Savings legislation.

Consumers who bank outside those states can use the provisions of the New York law as a checklist for evaluating an individual bank. The New York law requires banks to disclose the basic annual interest rate, the periodic percentage paid at each compounding period, and the annual percentage yield—what your account would earn, with compounding, if it remained on deposit for one year. These basic figures should permit you to compare any bank with any other on equal terms.

In addition, potential depositors should check on other features that are not subject to regulation and are at the discretion of the individual bank: service charges on the account at various balance levels, minimum balances below which interest is not paid, the compounding and crediting of interest, the charges levied for the excessive use of checks drawn against money market accounts, the basis used to determine rate changes on variable-rate certificates of deposit, and the penalties for early withdrawal of time deposits.

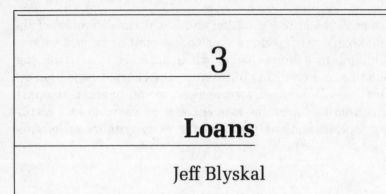

3

Loans

Jeff Blyskal

Repayments of borrowed money have become permanent items in the personal budgets of most Americans. Today the typical household debt totals more than $34,000, and the total consumer debt in the United States amounts to $3.3 trillion—about $2.6 trillion in mortgage debt, $277 billion in auto loans, $206 billion in personal loans, and $221 billion in credit card debt.

One reason for this high level of indebtedness is that before 1987 the interest on all consumer debt was tax-deductible, making the true cost of borrowing significantly lower than the actual interest rate of the loan. The Tax Reform Act of 1986, however, phased out the tax deductibility of interest on all consumer loans with the exception of mortgage loans (including home-equity loans) on first and second homes, and in 1991 the tax-deductibility of non-mortgage interest was eliminated entirely. As a consequence, borrowing has become increasingly expensive.

BORROWING: SOME PROS AND CONS

Although the traditional American value system views being in debt negatively, the fact remains that debt, undertaken prudently and rationally, can help the borrower achieve goals that would be unattainable otherwise. A mortgage loan may be used to acquire a home that can increase in value while providing the buyer with more comfortable living conditions. A loan for a college education or the purchase of an automobile may broaden the borrower's employment options. And a personal loan may permit the borrower to take advantage of an unexpected bargain in a major appliance or other big-ticket item. The fact is that very few Americans could enjoy their current standard of living without the use of some form of loan.

There are good and bad uses of loans—a mortage with affordable payments is a wiser use, for example, than a personal loan to finance an ill-affordable gambling expedition to Las Vegas. But it is also important to recognize that any one type of loan—a mortgage, an automobile loan, or a cash advance through a credit card—is available in good and bad forms, and that the choice you make within any one type can affect your financial welfare just as powerfully as your choice of how the borrowed money is to be spent.

Basically, there are five types of consumer loans: mortgages, automobile loans, personal loans, home equity loans (actually a new form of mortgage), and credit cards.

MORTGAGES

You need to exercise special care in choosing a home mortgage, because it differs from other loans in several important respects. Most often, a mortgage is the largest loan that you will undertake. A seemingly small difference in interest rates can therefore involve a very large amount of money. In addition, its term—often as long as 30 years—saddles you with a payment schedule almost as long as your working life. And last, since the home serves as collateral, mortgage loans are extremely secure from the lender's point of view.

Traditionally, banks would not write a mortgage for more than 80 percent of the appraised value of a home, reasoning that a buyer who contributed the remaining 20 percent had a large enough investment to motivate him or her to avoid foreclosure if at all possible. In recent years, however, as escalating home prices have made a 20 percent down payment less affordable for many buyers, banks have stretched mortgages to 90 or 95 percent of the home's appraised value, provided the buyer purchases mortgage insurance to protect the bank in case of default.

The borrower must, of course, satisfy further financial criteria. Banks are unlikely to write a mortgage unless the total of monthly mortgage payments, property taxes, and homeowner's insurance does not exceed 25 to 28 percent of your monthly income (which includes salary, profits from a business, investment income, and alimony and child support payments). Furthermore, the bank is unlikely to offer a mortgage if your total monthly debt obligations (the mortgage payment plus installment payments on other debts) exceed 36 percent of your monthly income. The bank will probably insist on a good credit record and a history of stable employment as well.

Although these criteria may vary slightly from bank to bank, they are generally consistent. The reason is that many banks do not hold mortgages themselves but sell them to the Federal National Mortgage Association (FNMA) and the Federal Home Loan Mortgage Corporation (FHLMC) in order to obtain working capital. For the mortgages to be eligible for sale, they must meet FNMA or FHLMC standards.

Until the mid-1970s, the typical mortgage term was 20 to 30 years at a fixed rate of interest. Since then, however, as both home prices and interest rates have escalated at a rate that made these mortgages unaffordable to many potential buyers, new forms have appeared. The adjustable-rate mortgage, for example, offered lower initial interest rates and down payments. And various forms of "creative financing" were developed for buyers unable to afford either the conventional or the adjustable-rate type. These alternatives, however, can best be evaluated by comparing their rates and terms with those of the conventional fixed-rate mortgage.

Conventional Fixed-Rate Mortgages

While the conventional fixed-rate mortgage has to some extent been replaced by other types, it has by no means disappeared. Although the fixed-rate mortgage may appear to be more expensive than some of the alternatives, it is in many ways the most desirable kind of mortgage for most home buyers.

Interest Rate and Terms As its name implies, this type of mortgage carries a fixed interest rate for its entire term, which may be as long as 30 years. Generally each payment remains constant and includes interest and a portion of principal. As the payments continue, the proportion applied to interest diminishes and the proportion applied to principal increases correspondingly.

This type of mortgage illustrates dramatically not only the total cost of mortgage interest but also the importance of seemingly small differences in interest rates over a long period of time. If you borrowed $80,000 for only one year at 10 percent with monthly repayments of interest and amortization of principal, your total interest cost would be $4,339.36. If, however, you stretch the loan period to 30 years, your total interest cost would rise to $172,741.60—more than twice the principal amount originally borrowed. In addition, a reduction of the rate to 9 percent would reduce your monthly payments by about $60 and save you almost $22,000 over the 30-year term. Even a difference of one-quarter percent can save $5,000 over the life of the mortgage.

This is why it pays to shop around for the lowest available interest rate. Some differences in interest rates, even if small, can be found in almost any community, so careful comparison shopping can pay off.

The rate you pay on the mortgage is essentially governed by the banks, but the term of your mortgage may to some extent be under your own control. Invariably, the shorter the mortgage term, the less costly it will be, because you will be using the bank's money for a shorter period of time. As our example illustrates, the 30-year loan's total interest cost is almost 40 times the one-year loan's total interest cost. Thus, a 15- or 20-year term, if you could afford the higher principal amortization, would save you a substantial amount. An $80,000 mortgage at 12 percent would require a monthly payment of $823 on a 30-year basis and $960 on a 15-year basis. But if you could afford the $137 difference, you would save a total of $123,480 in interest over the life of the mortgage. (Of course, you might find another way to invest the $137 at a rate of return higher than 12 percent.) In addition, many banks charge lower rates on shorter-term mortgages.

As an alternative, you can reduce total interest costs if you agree to make more frequent mortgage payments—for example,

$411.50 every two weeks instead of $823 monthly. If your cash flow permits it, this has the effect of shortening a 30-year 12 percent mortgage to 19 years, because you pay off more principal with each payment by making 26 biweekly payments each year instead of 12 monthly payments.

Points   Any rate comparison must take into account the points that banks generally add to mortgages. A point is a fee that must be prepaid, equal to 1 percent of the principal borrowed. It represents the bank's commission when it sells the mortgage to the Federal National Mortgage Association or the Federal Home Loan Mortgage Corporation, or provides the bank with additional profit if it decides to retain your mortgage. Because the points represent the bank's profits and have nothing to do with the salability of the mortgage, they may, in some situations, be negotiable.

Points have the effect of raising the actual cost of your loan, but the Truth-in-Lending Act requires banks to include points in calculating the annual percentage rate of fixed-rate mortgages. Thus, the larger the number of points—which may range from zero to as many as four—the higher the annual percentage rate will be above the note rate or contract rate specified on the mortgage note.

Prepayment   Although interest rate, term, and points are the three most important considerations in your choice of a mortgage, a prepayment clause is also a valuable feature. Ideally, such a clause permits you, at any time during the term of the mortgage and as often as you choose, to make cash payments that are applied to the principal. By reducing the principal, you simultaneously shorten the term of the mortgage and reduce the portion of your monthly payment that is applied to interest, thus accelerating the amortization, or gradual repayment of principal, and increasing your equity. In some states, a prepayment clause is required by law in a mortgage.

The prepayment privilege is also very useful if there is a significant drop in interest rates during the life of the mortgage. If, for example, your mortgage rate is 10.5 percent and interest rates fall to 8.5 percent, a prepayment clause allows you to borrow money at the lower rate and pay off the mortgage on which you are paying the higher rate.

A prepayment clause is desirable even if you don't currently anticipate using it. You are never obligated to use it, but, with the clause in place, an unexpected windfall, gift, or inheritance can help you shorten the term of your mortgage and reduce its overall cost.

Some banks refuse to write a prepayment clause; others limit the number and scheduling of prepayments or assess a penalty charge for each prepayment. But this may be negotiable.

There may be some disadvantage to paying off the mortgage as quickly as you can afford to. If, for example, interest rates rise substantially to 15 percent and your mortgage rate is only 8 percent, your cash could be "earning" more if invested elsewhere than it would if used for prepayment.

Assumability Although you may plan to spend 10 or 20 years in your home, the fact is that all sorts of circumstances—a job-related move, for example, or a change in your family situation—may require you to sell in five years or less, possibly at short notice or in a slow real estate market. For this reason, another very useful feature of a mortgage is assumability—that is, the right of a buyer of your home to take over your mortgage—especially if your interest rate is below prevailing rates.

Adjustable-Rate Mortgages

The fixed-rate conventional mortgage is almost always preferable to any other kind. But, alarmed by wild fluctuations in interest rates during the past two decades, many banks prefer to offer a mortgage with rates that are adjusted every year, three years, or five years to reflect changes in market interest rates. Whether the longer or the shorter adjustment period is preferable depends entirely on the direction of market rates. If rates begin to climb shortly after you have taken the mortgage, a long adjustment period locks you into a low rate, but just the opposite occurs if rates begin to drop when your mortgage is only a month old.

Regardless of the adjustment period, most banks do not change the rate arbitrarily. Instead, the mortgage specifies that rates will be based on some widely publicized index—for example, the rates paid on one-year U.S. Treasury securities—plus an additional two or so percentage points.

Since you assume some of the risk of future interest-rate fluctuations, initial rates are invitingly low—especially at times of high interest rates. Often, in fact, the initial rate may be as much as 2 percentage points below that of fixed-rate mortgages. But this type of mortgage can be hazardous unless it incorporates two kinds of caps, or limits, on how much interest rates may rise or fall—one cap for the rise each year and one for the rise over the life of the mortgage. Usually, the caps limit rate changes to two percentage points between adjustment periods and six percentage points for the life of the mortgage.

A cap allows you to calculate your approximate payments in a worst-case situation. Caps on all adjustable mortgages are now required by federal law.

A rate cap is a good safeguard, however, only if it applies to the rate at which you initiate the mortgage, and often this is not the case. To attract borrowers, many banks offer a first-year teaser rate that may be as much as two percentage points lower than their regular rate for adjustable-rate mortgages. In such a situation, a 2 percent cap will apply not to the introductory rate but to the already higher regular rate and thus increase the interest payments substantially more than you anticipated.

Within any one adjustment period, monthly payments remain constant, consisting of interest and the amortization of principal. To protect the borrower against sudden increases, some adjustable-rate mortgages may cap the amount by which the monthly payment can be increased between one adjustment period and the next. If, however, the rise in interest rates is higher than the rise permitted in the monthly payment, an increasing proportion of the monthly payment must be applied to interest and a correspondingly lower proportion to amortization. If interest rates rise sharply, and each adjustment period sees an increase in the limit of the cap, it is even possible that your monthly payments will become insufficient to cover the entire interest charge. In such a situation you could conceivably find yourself owing more on your mortgage after five years than you did when you initiated it.

Creative Financing

Creative financing, which differs radically from the conventional types of home financing, tends to become popular when there are high interest rates, high housing prices, a recession, or a population shift and potential buyers cannot afford housing or potential sellers cannot find buyers. In such situations, creative financing, although hazardous, may be the only route to home ownership. When interest rates and the housing market are normal, it is wise to avoid this option.

Creative financing is available in the four distinct forms described below, all of them in one way or another linked to changes in interest rates or property values. They promise the borrower some very attractive advantages if interest rates should fall or housing prices should rise. But, unfortunately, interest rates are almost completely unpredictable over the long term, and the value of a specific community may, for a variety of reasons, fall sharply even though housing in general is appreciating steadily.

For these reasons, instead of optimistically assuming that the conditions governing both interest costs and housing values will either remain unchanged or improve, you should try to visualize a worst-case scenario when considering creative financing. This kind of caution may lead to the conclusion that conventional financing is far safer—or that current market conditions make the purchase of a home simply not feasible.

Graduated-Payment Mortgages　Graduated-payment mortgages enable you to buy a house sooner than you can afford to by making the monthly payments low at the outset and increasing them gradually for five to ten years before stabilizing them at the higher level.

The rationale behind these mortgages is that your income will rise during this period and thus make the increasingly higher payments affordable. But if, in fact, your income does not rise, you are still faced with payments that inexorably increase. Because payments are low at the outset, the total interest cost will also be higher than with a traditional mortgage.

If you are anticipating a gradually rising income, you would be wiser to choose a conventional fixed-rate mortgage with a prepayment clause. Under this arrangement, you can, if you wish, use that additional income to prepay the principal but you retain a comfortable level of monthly payments and the freedom to spend or invest your income in other ways.

Graduated-Equity Mortgages　Like a graduated-payment mortgage, the graduated-equity mortgage involves a steady increase in the size of the monthly payment. Under this arrangement, however, payments begin at the level of a conventional fixed-rate 30-year mortgage, and the payment increments are applied against principal. As a result, your equity in the home increases more rapidly, total interest cost is lower, and the mortgage is paid off sooner than would be the case with the conventional mortgage. In addition, because the term of the mortgage is shorter, banks tend to charge an interest rate somewhat below that charged for conventional mortgages.

This kind of mortgage is advantageous only if your income rises at a rate sufficient to meet the increasing payments. Although the increases in mortgage payments are automatic and predictable, however, increases in your earnings are not. Here, too, a conventional mortgage with a prepayment clause offers you much greater flexibility.

Shared-Appreciation Mortgages The adjustable-rate mortgage, as we have seen, makes the borrower share the risk of fluctuations in the interest rate. The shared-appreciation mortgage makes the borrower and the lender partners in the appreciation of the mortgaged property. In return for a lower interest rate, which may permit the purchase of a more expensive home, the borrower agrees to give the bank as much as 50 percent of the increase in the value of the property when it is sold, or five years later. Thus, if in five years the value of a $125,000 home increases to $175,000, the borrower would owe the bank one-half of the $50,000 appreciation.

This type of mortgage is likely to appeal to borrowers who foresee a rising market and plan to sell the home within the five-year period. There is, however, no certainty that within this period the value of housing in general or the mortgaged home in particular will appreciate. If for any of a variety of reasons, you are forced to sell the property below market value, you will have to make up the shortfall from other funds in order to meet your obligation to the bank.

Balloon Mortgages Usually offered by the seller of a home rather than by a bank, the balloon mortgage requires the payment of interest (with, in some cases, a very small amount of principal) only for a given period—for example, five years—at the end of which the principal must be repaid in one large balloon payment. Because they do not include any amortization of principal, monthly payments tend to be substantially lower than those on a conventional mortgage.

The balloon mortgage has two serious disadvantages. First, if it calls for payments that cover interest only and no amortization of principal, you will, at the end of the term, have paid a substantial amount of interest without increasing your equity in the home beyond your original down payment and any appreciation. Moreover, if interest rates do not fall during the term, but rise further, refinancing with a conventional mortgage may be very expensive.

Balloon mortgages are likely to be offered by owners who are eager to sell but don't need a large amount of cash immediately and who are content to earn a higher rate of return from the mortgage than alternative investments would provide. They may be attractive to buyers because both the down payment and the interest rate may be significantly lower than what a bank would require, because no points are involved, and because mortgage origination costs are likely to be minimal. Moreover, if you assume a balloon mortgage at a time of high interest rates, you have some breathing room of perhaps several years during which time interest rates may fall so that you can refinance the home with a conventional mortgage.

In certain circumstances, the advantages of the balloon mortgage can outweigh its disadvantages. Because it is a private arrangement, a good deal of bargaining is possible—especially with an owner who is eager to sell. The seller is more likely than a bank to accept a low down payment, a low interest rate, and the inclusion of prepayment and assumability clauses.

AUTOMOBILE LOANS

A loan for the purchase of an automobile is similar in most respects to an unsecured personal installment loan (see p. 47) but the interest rate is likely to be lower—perhaps by as much as two or three percentage points. The percentage rate is lower because the automobile serves as collateral and can be repossessed by the lender in case of default.

As automobile prices have continued to escalate, the term of an automobile loan has been extended from the traditional three years to four and as long as five years for new models. Used-car loans are available for shorter terms and at rates as much as two percentage points higher.

Interest and Other Costs

As is true of all loans, the longer the term, the lower the monthly payment but the higher the interest cost. For example, on an $8,000 loan at 11 percent, the total interest charges would amount to $1,429 for a 36-month term but would rise to $2,436 for a 60-month term. Obviously, the most economical plan is to take the shortest loan term you can afford and use as much of your own cash for as big a down payment as possible, since you are unlikely to earn nearly as much interest on your cash as you are being charged for the loan.

Regardless of the term of the loan, interest rates within the same community may vary by 1.5 percentage points or more. Some conscientious comparison shopping is likely to be worth your trouble. Most automobile loans carry a fixed rate, but some banks offer variable-rate loans that may carry lower initial rates but present the same risks as adjustable-rate mortgages (see p. 41). Because federal law doesn't require rate caps on nonmortgage adjustable loans, caps on variable-rate auto loans are rare.

Some banks, in an effort to reduce paperwork and prevent late payments, offer a reduction in interest rates if you authorize the bank to deduct the monthly payment automatically from a checking or savings account. This is a worthwhile economy if the bank offers competitive terms on such accounts. But if you have to sacrifice yield on a substantial balance in order to maintain an account at the bank that issues your loan, the interest-rate discount you gain may be more than offset by the interest you forgo by keeping your account in the lender bank instead of placing your money where it could earn more. Of course, you may be able to qualify for the lower loan rate by opening a very small savings account and depositing your monthly payment into it instead of mailing it to the bank.

Unlike mortgages, automobile loans do not involve points, but some banks charge the borrower an initial fee—sometimes called a "processing" or "document" fee. This charge can range from $20 to more than $200 if the bank bases it on 1 or 2 percent of the amount of the loan.

Another hidden cost of loans may be the premium for the fire and theft insurance coverage that the bank insists on in order to safeguard the value of its collateral. Not all owners of new vehicles buy this coverage voluntarily, some preferring to self-insure. But even those who choose to buy it should have freedom of choice as to the insurer and the coverage. If the bank does not permit you such freedom, your insurance premiums may be higher than you anticipated.

Other Sources of Automobile Loans

A bank loan is not the only way of financing the purchase of an automobile. Savings-and-loan associations, credit unions, and some insurance companies offer automobile loans. Automobile manufacturer and dealer financing is yet another source that, under certain conditions, can be far less costly than a bank loan. Alternatively, you may be able to obtain the money through a home equity loan, which provides for tax-deductibility of interest charges but has other major disadvantages (see p. 49). In general, however, using your own funds for as large a down payment as possible and paying the balance with a loan for as short a term as possible—even if it requires adjustment of your overall budget— may be the least expensive way to finance the purchase of an automobile.

PERSONAL LOANS

A personal loan is generally taken out to pay for a specific expenditure—a vacation, for example, or a major appliance, or perhaps a wedding. It is usually not secured by collateral and carries a higher rate of interest than an automobile loan, but it is often still a less expensive form of loan than a credit card.

Because banks make greater profits with credit card loans, they tend to discourage personal loans—in part by raising the cards' credit limits to $5,000, $10,000, and even $50,000. But compared to a personal loan, a credit card loan costs approximately two percentage points more in interest.

Since a personal loan is made to you in a lump sum that you have specified, it is likely that you have given some thought to what the money will be used for and have carefully assessed your need for the loan as well as your ability to repay it. In addition, if you meet the schedule of monthly payments, you are certain to be free of the debt within a fixed period of time. A credit card loan, by contrast, is not fixed either in its amount or in its repayment schedule.

In most other respects, a personal loan is like an automobile loan and justifies careful comparison shopping for the best rates, because rate differences within the same community are likely to be even greater than they are for automobile loans. Variable-rate loans are available at somewhat lower initial rates, but they entail the risks that have been described in connection with adjustable-rate auto loans (see p. 46).

As in the case of automobile loans, some banks offer a rate reduction for personal loans if you authorize the automatic deduction of payments from your checking or savings account. But, aside from the fact that this arrangement may force you to maintain an account that yields less than a similar account at a competing bank, it presents a further problem. Unlike an automobile loan, a personal loan is unsecured, and the bank may have the right to seize funds from your checking or savings account in the event that you default on your loan payments—an action it could not take if these accounts were held in a different bank. A careful reading of your savings and checking account agreements will disclose whether the bank has this "right of offset."

Another type of loan—the savings-secured or passbook loan—may be offered at a rate only two percentage points above the rate paid on your savings account because the account serves as collateral for the loan. This loan, however, does not cost you only the 2 percent, because you must forgo the interest payments on your savings account. Thus, if your savings account pays 5 percent and your loan interest is two percentage points above this rate, your actual interest cost is 7 percent. If, in fact, your savings balance is large enough to secure your loan, you could save on interest simply by using the balance instead of taking a loan.

The administrative costs for large and small loans being the same, banks prefer to make large loans, and typically offer reductions in interest rates with increases in the loan principal. This should encourage you to borrow all you need at one time instead of negotiating a series of small loans, but it should not lead you to borrow a sum larger than you need simply because the interest rate may be lower.

HOME EQUITY LOANS

The home equity loan—a loan secured by the equity you have in your home—has become increasingly popular in recent years. These loans use your home as collateral and carry variable or fixed interest rates. They should be avoided.

There are several reasons these loans remain popular. For one, you are able to borrow a larger amount of money at a lower interest rate than would be available through a personal or automobile loan. More enticing is the fact that the interest on a home equity loan remains largely tax-deductible, whereas the tax-deductibility of all other forms of non-mortgage consumer loan interest has been phased out. These attractions make a home equity loan extremely tempting, but the dangers of foreclosure in case of default must be considered very carefully.

The equity loan is based on the market value of your home and your current equity in it. That is, if your home is worth $100,000 and you have paid off all but $20,000 on your mortgage, your equity is $80,000, and you are likely to be able to get a loan amounting to about 80 percent of this figure.

Home equity loans are available in two forms—the traditional second mortgage and the much more recent type of loan advertised under the term "home equity loan." Although both are based on your equity in the home, they differ in a number of important respects.

Second Mortgages

One form of equity loan—the second mortgage—has been in use for decades, but its reputation has been tarnished ever since the Great Depression, when homeowners were forced to use it as their only source of cash to pay for daily necessities. In many ways, however, it is the preferable form of home equity loan.

Like a first mortgage, the second mortgage provides you a specified sum of money at a fixed rate (although some variable-rate second mortgages are available) and provides for repayment in a number of monthly installments that include amortization as well as interest. Although it is likely to involve points and other closing costs that can amount to from $500 to $1,000, its lower interest rate and tax-deductibility make it preferable to a large, long-term personal loan. It does, however, expose your home to the risk of foreclosure, a danger that will be elaborated further in connection with home equity loans.

The New Home Equity Loans

Unlike the second mortgage, the newer form of home equity loan, developed in the mid-1970s, has proliferated widely since 1987, when the interest on other forms of consumer credit was no longer fully tax-deductible.

Whereas a second mortgage or a personal loan specifies a fixed principal and a fixed schedule of repayment, the home equity loan need not specify either. Instead, as in the case of a credit card, you are given a credit limit on which you can draw at any time for any purpose. Repayment requirements vary widely. Some require a scheduled repayment of interest and principal. Others require interest payments only for a specified term, followed by payments that include principal and interest. Still others involve payment of interest only with a balloon payment at the end of a specified term.

Although the interest rate on this kind of loan—as low as four percentage points below the rate for personal loans and seven percentage points below that for credit cards—may be attractive, origination costs are likely to be high. Aside from closing costs— for appraisal, paperwork, and so on—each point on a home equity loan is calculated as 1 percent of the credit limit that the lender establishes and not of the money actually borrowed. On adjustable-rate home equity loans, lenders are not required by law to include such costs in calculating the annual percentage rate, and the quoted rate may be misleadingly low. Even if the true rate is attractive the additional costs make a home equity loan worth taking only if the amount of the principal is substantial and the term of the loan relatively long—but in such circumstances the threat to your home may be considerable.

Risks Inherent in the New Home Equity Loans

The kind of home equity loan that offers you a revolving line of credit can easily tempt you to use it irresponsibly for unnecessary or unaffordable goods and services—much as some borrowers use credit cards—or for high-risk activities, such as going into business or investing in the stock market. The important distinction between home equity debt and credit card or other forms of debt, however, is that the home equity debt exposes your home to foreclosure, whereas other forms of debt do not.

If you default on an automobile loan, the lender can repossess the automobile. If you default on personal or credit card loans, the creditor can place a lien against your home or even force you to declare personal bankruptcy. Although a lien prevents you from selling your home before satisfying the debt, it does not dispossess you of it, and most state bankruptcy laws protect the bankrupt person's home against the claims of creditors.

But home equity loans do not afford the borrower any such protection. If, for example, you have a $25,000 first mortgage and a $75,000 second mortgage or home equity loan and you default on your payments at a time of severe weakness in the real estate market, foreclosure and a forced sale may not yield a net price of more than $90,000. In that circumstance, after the first mortgage (which has priority) is paid off, you will still owe the lender an additional $10,000. And you will be homeless.

The Home Equity Loan Consumer Protection Act of 1988 now provides some safeguards for consumers. Previously, lenders could base an equity loan's variable rate on the bank's own cost of funds index or other internal index. Since the bank controlled that index, it could manipulate the home equity loan's variable rate. Now banks have to base a variable equity loan rate on an outside public index not controlled by the bank. The Act also requires that ads trumpeting very low (and temporary) introductory or "teaser" rates on equity loans also display the regular rate as prominently. In addition, lenders must disclose certain information about rates, fees, and any limits on the consumer's borrowing rights.

CLOSE-UP:
HOW TO SHOP FOR A LOAN

Many consumers in need of a loan sometimes assume that the bank will be doing them a favor. But loans constitute the major source of income and profit for banks, so most often they are as eager to sell you a loan as your local appliance store is to sell you a refrigerator. It is important that you have an objective understanding of what you can afford to borrow and what you regard as its legitimate and affordable price.

Your Personal Situation

Before even considering a loan, you should review your assets to determine whether or not you have a savings account, securities, or some liquidatable property that is yielding you less than what you would pay in loan interest. If, for example, you have $5,000 in a money market fund that is paying you three or four percentage points less than the current rate charged for personal loans, you can save money by withdrawing from the fund, either to eliminate your need for a loan or to reduce your loan principal.

Once you have determined the minimum loan you need, review your current debt obligations (including mortgage and credit card payments) and estimate the additional outlay for the new loan payments, based on the size of the loan, the interest rate, and the repayment period. These estimates can be obtained either in the course of your loan shopping or from readily available handbooks that include tables of loan repayment.

After estimating the monthly cost, you should make a realistic decision as to where the extra money will come from. You can safely use your current level of income only if your job is secure. If your income is jeopardized by threatened layoffs, a looming recession, or maybe more personal reasons, you would be wise to forgo the loan. If you expect a raise or a promotion, you should nevertheless use your current income as a basis rather than the one you anticipate.

The next step is to obtain a copy of your credit report (see p. 141) to make certain that it is up-to-date and in good order. If it contains errors or if it omits pertinent information, have it corrected before making your loan application.

Determining Costs

Your comparison shopping can be done most expeditiously by telephone, since most lenders are quite willing to quote rates and terms. A half-dozen telephone calls can give you a reasonably firm impression of the prevailing rates in your community. The only problem in such telephone comparisons is making certain that you are comparing rates on loans whose terms and conditions are identical in every respect. A casual telephone conversation may not disclose the full information that would be available from a longer visit in person and from brochures.

For some areas of the country, computerized data bases are available to provide the current rates and terms for mortgages offered by scores of banks. For automobile loans, car dealers have access to computerized data on rates. Although you can use the computer data for a general picture of prevailing rates, you should still do some local comparison shopping on your own, since there is always the possibility that the lender offering the very lowest rate may not appear on the computer listing. In addition, you should consider the alternative loan sources described in chapter 5.

Applying for the Loan

Some loan applicants, like those seeking college admission, try to play it safe by making more than one application. This is not a sensible policy. Since all banks use the same credit information, they are all likely to view your application in the same light. Worse yet, since each credit application is recorded on your credit report, the fact that you seem to be making more than one application may prejudice the bank against you. In addition, a mortgage application, because it usually involves appraisal fees, is not inexpensive. A sounder policy is to make the application to the one bank that offers you the best combination of rates and terms.

When you visit the bank to file your application, take with you as much information as possible to document your financial condition: brokerage, bank, and mutual fund statements; W-2 forms; your last year's federal tax filing, especially if you are self-employed; current paycheck stubs; account numbers for your credit accounts; and any other evidence that might not appear on your credit report.

4

Charge Cards

Jeff Blyskal

Although advertisements try to convey the impression that a charge card will enhance your social status and give you access to glamorous and exotic restaurants and resorts, the fact is that it is hardly an admission ticket to membership in the elite class. Americans carry more than 830 million charge cards in their wallets (with more than $230 billion owed on them), and the annual income requirements for the most widely used cards may run as low as $12,000. Stripped of their glamour, the advertisements for charge cards are really selling credit—in a sometimes insidious and most expensive form. Far from constituting an elite group, many cardholders are severely pressed to meet either the minimum payments on their monthly credit card statements or the entire balance due on their charge card bill.

In addition to credit, however, a charge card offers you convenience—at relatively low cost if, like some 35 percent of all cardholders, you pay your monthly bill in full. Whether they pay their bills in full or use their cards as a source of credit, all cardholders can enjoy this convenience, but it comes at a price—often an exorbitant price for the credit users.

Many cards also offer extras—discounts at some retailers,

extended warranties on items purchased with the card, and rental car insurance. Those add-ons are largely marketing gimmicks designed to distract attention from the important dollars-and-cents elements of every charge card: interest rates, fees, retailer acceptance, and terms and conditions of the credit card agreement.

TYPES OF CARDS

There are several types of charge cards and significant differences within each type. Strictly speaking, a *credit card* offers its holders a line of credit and makes provision for monthly payments of principal and interest unless the balance is paid within a set grace period. A *travel and entertainment (T&E) card*, by contrast, offers a grace period but requires full repayment before the grace period expires; interest is charged on late payments. With a credit card, you may pay part of your bill plus interest over several months; with a T&E card, you must pay your entire bill by the end of the month (or whatever the grace period is) or incur the interest charges. Issuers of credit cards make money on the interest charges; issuers of T&E cards make money from the annual membership fees they impose. The distinctions between credit and T&E cards are becoming increasingly blurred, and they function identically with respect to purchases, though the latter are less widely accepted by retailers than the former.

Bank Credit Cards

Although MasterCard and Visa are widely recognized as brand names, neither organization issues credit cards. Instead, they provide advertising, credit-authorization systems, and some record-keeping services for member banks, which actually issue the cards. Because these banks can, within broad limits, establish whatever charges and terms they wish, the widespread notion that all credit cards are alike is clearly unfounded. MasterCard and Visa are alike, however, in that both are widely accepted in the United States and abroad. Hence, a choice between them should be governed by the terms offered by individual competing banks.

Both MasterCard and Visa cards produce income for the issuing banks from three sources: the annual fee, the interest paid by cardholders, and the commissions they charge merchants for converting their credit card charge slips into cash. When these cards were first issued, no annual fee was imposed, and cardholders who paid their monthly statements in full were charged nothing for the service. Subsequently, most banks, pleading high administrative costs, imposed an annual fee; a few banks did not, but these may charge a higher interest rate for installment payments.

Interest rates also vary from one bank to another, but virtually all are significantly higher than the rates the banks charge for personal loans. Although a few states impose a ceiling on the rates banks can charge, many banks evade the limit by moving their credit card operations to a less restrictive state.

As the prime rate dropped to more than 10 percentage points below the average credit card rate of 18.8 percent in the mid-1980s, several attempts were made to establish federal regulations limiting credit card rates. At the time of this writing, however, no such federal legislation has been successful. The banks claim that administrative costs and a high default rate justify the high interest charges. Those who would regulate the rate argue that the default rate (as well as consumer financial difficulties) could be sharply reduced if the banks were to issue cards less indiscriminately. The threat of regulation did not produce a general or precipitous drop in the rates, but in 1987 it did set off a small flurry of rate competition that produced rates as low as 11.5 percent.

Another credit card—issued only by a single bank—is somewhat different from MasterCard and Visa. The Discover card, issued by the Greenwood Trust Company of Wilmington, Delaware (a subsidiary of the Sears financial network), charges no annual fee and also offers the cardholder a small annual rebate based on the total amount charged. These tiny rebates may be attractive to cardholders who charge large amounts annually and pay their monthly balances in full, but the interest rate on this card is very high, and its acceptance is not nearly as widespread as for MasterCard and Visa.

Travel and Entertainment Cards

Travel and entertainment (T&E) cards—issued primarily by American Express and also by Diners Club and Carte Blanche—generally do not offer cardholders a credit arrangement and require payment in full (except for travel-related charges) at the end of each billing period. The issuers of T&E cards derive their income from a substantial annual membership fee (ranging from $35 to $250) and commissions from participating merchants.

Traditionally, T&E cards were used primarily for travel and entertainment expenses by business people who needed to keep separate records for business expenses. Self-employed individuals also have found them helpful in calculating their tax deductions. Today, of course, T&E cards are being used for all kinds of purchases. American Express has also recently introduced Optima, a credit card that does offer installment payments at a relatively low rate of interest, but applicants for this card must also hold the regular American Express card.

T&E cards are heavily advertised as status symbols, and some restaurants honor no other credit cards (see p. 62, Acceptance). But if you have no great need to impress waiters and have no tax-deductible travel or entertainment costs to document, you may find that they offer little, if any, advantage, short of an interest-free grace period between the time of purchase and the due date of your payment.

Premium Cards

For many, a charge card of any kind once served as a status symbol, but as the cards proliferated, their symbolic value dropped. Premium cards are supposed to bring it back. American Express has a premium gold and a platinum card, both of which have more stringent eligibility standards. MasterCard and Visa also offer premium cards. Because these cards impose higher annual income requirements—from $20,000 to as high as $100,000—displaying them conspicuously may advertise the cardholder's affluence, but they offer few advantages to justify the typically higher annual fee. Generally they carry a lower interest rate on unpaid balances (presumably because their cardholders are good credit risks), but since most high-income cardholders pay off monthly balances right away, the lower interest rate offers little actual savings.

Secured Credit Cards

For people who have not established a credit rating or have one that is inadequate to qualify them for any charge cards, some banks provide what is known as a secured credit card. Under this arrangement, the applicant deposits a sum of money—$2,000, for example—in a savings account for use as collateral to ensure that the cardholder will meet his or her monthly payments. Although the cardholder collects interest on this deposit, he or she may not withdraw it without surrendering the card.

This plan is not without its costs, because the required deposit might be earning a considerably higher rate of return if invested elsewhere. Moreover, individuals whose credit ratings would not qualify them for a regular credit card would probably be wise to forgo it. But in some cases, it may be a useful interim arrangement, because regular payments on such an account will help establish a good credit rating. If you do want to make this kind of arrangement, go directly to a bank. Do not use third-party marketers, who advertise heavily that they "guarantee" credit cards to anyone, no matter what their credit rating. They charge $35 to $50, and all they do is pass on an application from a bank with which they have no affiliation. To get a screened list of banks that perform this service, send $3 to Bankcard Holders of America, 560 Herndon Parkway, Suite 120, Herndon, Virginia 22070.

Debit Cards

Although a debit card is neither a credit nor a T&E card, it is often confused with a charge card because it is similar in appearance and can be used in the same situations. A debit card offers you no credit whatever. Instead, when the merchant processes your transaction, the charge is electronically deducted from the card's associated checking account balance. The only advantage offered by this type of card is that it frees you from having to write personal checks and persuade merchants to accept them. On the other hand, if your checking account earns interest, this instant deduction will lose you interest for the two or three days that are required for a personal check to clear.

YOUR PERSONAL CHARGE-CARD PORTFOLIO

The typical cardholder carries eight cards, which probably were accumulated haphazardly rather than selectively and which undoubtedly duplicate one another to some extent. Cardholders who use this entire collection actively may find themselves writing more checks than necessary and risking more difficulties should the cards go astray. You should keep the number of cards to a minimum and make certain that each card meets particular needs or provides specific advantages not available with the others.

Because spending patterns vary widely, it is impossible to suggest a typical portfolio. But, in general, no more than three or four cards should adequately serve your needs.

Both MasterCard and Visa are so popular and so widely accepted that there is no need to carry both of them. Your choice between them should depend almost entirely on the terms offered by the banks to which you apply. A standard—not premium—card should fulfill your needs adequately.

Some consumers carry two credit cards in order to increase the amount they can charge—for example, $1,500 on each—in the event that they buy, for example, $3,000 worth of airline tickets. This is quite unnecessary, because the issuer of any one card will willingly raise your card limit to $5,000 or more if your credit rating justifies it. If it does not, you would be very unwise to raise your credit line with a second card.

Whether you want the Discover card, which offers rebates, depends on its acceptance in your community and by other merchants with whom you deal. The rebates it offers have some slight value, but if you charge excessively on the account to rack up rebates, you may find you've lost more (thanks to the card's high interest rate) than you've gained in rebates.

Among T&E cards, American Express is accepted at more locations than either Diners Club or Carte Blanche. If you pay your charge-card bills in full each month, you may prefer a T&E card to a bank credit card, particularly if the annual fee of the T&E card is lower than the annual interest you accumulate using a credit card.

Whether or not a department store card is worth having depends largely on your shopping habits. If your local department stores accept the usual charge cards, a card limited to one store (or chain) is of little value, although some department stores send their cardholders advance notice of special sales, and the threat to cancel a department store card may give you some leverage in settling disputes about returns or other problems. If you use department store charge cards, pay off the monthly balance in full to avoid the typically high interest rates associated with these cards.

CONVENIENCE AND ITS COSTS

A major convenience of a charge card is that it allows you to buy merchandise, meals, and even theater tickets without carrying a substantial amount of cash in your wallet or purse. The cash you would otherwise have to carry would be subject to theft or loss. Even if it were not lost or stolen, it would lose the interest it could be earning in a savings account until your monthly payment is due.

Merchants who might balk at accepting your personal check have no hesitation about allowing you to use your charge card, thus giving you at least two or three weeks before you have to pay for your purchase. Charge cards can also permit you to take advantage of special sales that you encounter when your checking balance is low or you are not carrying enough cash.

Charge cards are especially useful in expediting a purchase by mail. Instead of mailing a check for a catalog item, you can usually reduce effort and delay by using a toll-free telephone number and paying for your purchase with your card. In addition, ordering by card rather than by check expedites refunds for unsatisfactory merchandise and provides you with effective recourse against non-delivery or defective merchandise (see p. 67).

Charge cards can also serve as proof of identity and, to some extent, of financial stability, in check cashing and other transactions. Renting an automobile without a card is extremely difficult—often impossible.

A charge card is also convenient if you travel frequently—not only because it permits you to carry less cash but also because it enables you to guarantee hotel reservations for late arrival. It is especially useful when you travel abroad, because it reduces the sum you need in traveler's checks (which you pay for in advance), as well as your need to make frequent currency exchanges—sometimes at unfavorable rates. Because the card issuer makes such exchanges in very large amounts, your charges in other currencies are generally converted to dollars at the wholesale rather than the retail exchange rate—although this advantage depends to some extent on the stability of the U.S. dollar against a specific foreign currency.

Charge cards do not offer you all these conveniences for free. In addition to the interest charges and annual fee on most major charge cards (see below), there may be hidden costs that some cardholders fail to recognize. Since the bank handling each merchant's account collects a commission of 2 to 5 percent for processing each card transaction, charge cards have a broadly inflationary effect, raising prices because merchants must compensate for this commission. As a consequence, many items may be priced lower in shops that do not accept plastic, and if you need a fairly costly item, you should forgo the convenience of credit for the sake of a substantial price difference.

This principle is also applicable to routine purchases. When, for example, a service station offers a four-cents-per-gallon price reduction to cash customers, the use of a charge card is a rather extravagant convenience. Another strategy to consider when buying a high-ticket item such as a television set or a refrigerator from a merchant who accepts charge cards would be to negotiate a discount (3 to 5 percent) by offering to pay by check instead of by card. This transaction costs the retailer nothing but provides you with a substantial saving.

SHOPPING FOR CHARGE CARDS

When shopping for charge cards, you should weigh several factors:

Interest Rate   The finance charges should be your first consideration. To get the best rate, shop around by telephone to compare rates in your area. Keep alert for articles in newspapers and personal finance publications that list especially low rates. Some state banking authorities and consumer organizations periodically survey credit-card rates.

Annual Fee   Most, though not all, banks that issue credit cards levy an annual fee, as do the major T&E companies. Department store and oil company charge cards usually cost nothing but have, of course, very limited acceptance.

Some cards advertised as free, however, are in fact not free at all. Although they make no annual charge, some levy a prepayment fee on accounts that are paid in full each month and some charge the cardholder $1.50 for each month in which the card is used—in short, an $18 annual fee collected in installments. Credit cards that carry low fees or none at all may—and often do—charge very high interest rates on unpaid balances. When, for example, the Missouri legislature prohibited an annual fee for credit cards, the issuing banks immediately raised their interest rates. Although interest rates need not concern you (assuming you have a 30-day grace period) if you intend to pay your account in full, other features of a card need to be considered before you sign up for the card that has the least expensive annual fee.

Acceptance Charge cards have no value if merchants refuse to accept them. Both MasterCard and Visa are the most widely accepted, not only in the United States but also abroad. Some restaurants accept only American Express cards. Discover is accepted at roughly one-fourth the number of locations that accept MasterCard and Visa.

Grace Periods Another factor to consider is the card's grace period. Some cards provide no grace period but begin calculating interest on all charges as soon as they appear on the statement, as in the case of cash advances. Other card issuers allow 25 to 30 days after purchase for you to pay off the balance in full and incur no interest. The difference can add up. A 30-day grace period could save you $7.50 in interest on a $500 purchase, assuming an 18 percent annual interest rate. It should be noted, however, that grace periods are only operative if you pay in full. If any of the balance remains unpaid at the due date, you will find yourself losing the benefit of the grace period.

Cash Advances As automated teller machines and regional or nationwide ATM networks have proliferated, the availability of instant cash has become a recurrent theme in charge card advertising. The advertisements point out that a cardholder can get cash just by inserting his or her charge card in an authorized automated teller machine. Many cardholders think these cash advances enjoy the same grace period as their ordinary charges. In fact, interest is charged from the moment you receive the cash advance, whether or not you pay your account in full during the grace period. Many banks also charge cash advance fees of 2 to 5 percent, capped at $15 to $20. At least one card, Discover, offers a 25-day grace period on cash advances, but charges a 2.5 percent cash advance fee up front, with a minimum of $2 and a maximum of $10.

Fringe Benefits In their competition for cardholders, some issuers of charge cards offer a number of minor benefits: for example, flight insurance coverage for cardholders who charge their tickets to their card, collision coverage on rental cars, purchase protection—a kind of insurance policy to replace or repair broken, stolen or lost items, discounts on travel charges that exceed a specified amount, discounts on long distance telephone calls, or registration for all your charge cards so that you can report their loss with a single telephone call. Some banks that issue credit cards will automatically deduct your full payment from your checking account on its due date; others will accept payment by telephone—practices that eliminate the need for you to write and mail checks. For most cardholders, however, these benefits are less important financially than a lower annual fee or a lower interest rate.

The Dangers of Plastic Money

As we have noted, charge cards offer some conveniences at relatively low cost to cardholders who consistently pay the charges in full each month. But for those cardholders who are less orderly in managing their finances they can be extremely hazardous. The net loss for MasterCard alone, resulting from cardholders' inability to pay, is more than half a billion dollars annually, dramatic evidence of the overspending and the very serious indebtedness that cards can produce. The vast proportion of personal bankruptcies precipitated by the irresponsible use of charge cards provides further proof of the danger of their uncontrolled use.

There are several reasons why a charge card can easily lead its holder into financial difficulties. Purchasing an item with a piece of plastic does not give the buyer pause, as it might if he or she had to use actual cash or determine the bank balance before writing a check. The card makes impulsive—and unnecessary—buying all too easy, allowing many to disregard budgetary restraints and to use the card for restaurants, travel, and clothing they they cannot afford.

Perhaps most important, whereas a bank loan is often used to buy tangible, long-lasting goods that provide long-term satisfaction and increase the buyer's net worth, for the most part charge cards tend to be used for items that are consumed immediately or depreciate very rapidly.

A bank credit card, even though it provides a grace period, is a loan—at an interest rate *much higher* than you would pay for an unsecured loan from a bank. But there is another difference that makes credit cards more worrisome. Whereas a bank loan is for a specified amount and specified purpose and has a specified repayment schedule, a credit card has none of these restrictions. To the limit of your credit line (usually $1,500 but often much higher), you can be in debt continuously as long as you pay the interest and enough of the principal to reduce your debt below your limit so that you have further buying power. And many consumers apparently manage their budgets so ineffectively that they are chronically indebted to the limit of their card.

Surveys indicate that only 40 percent of cardholders choose their credit cards on the basis of the interest rate charged on unpaid balances. Nevertheless, if you plan to use your credit card as a revolving loan—or if you are concerned about the possibility of temporarily running short of cash during the holiday season or when income tax payments come due—the interest rate should be your prime consideration. Although virtually all credit card rates are higher than the rates charged for bank loans, there are some significant differences among banks, and if you can find a rate of 15.5 percent instead of 21.9 percent—both of which are currently charged by different banks—the lower rate can provide a substantial advantage.

In general, however, this mode of personal finance should be avoided at all costs. In some circumstances, a cardholder seriously indebted on his or her credit card should consider a short-term personal loan in order to pay the credit card debt in full. The interest on the loan will be lower than the rate on the credit card debt. But this tactic is useful only if the cardholder can reform his or her pattern of card use and pay each month's total charges when due.

LOSS AND FRAUDULENT USE

Although MasterCard and Visa report annual losses of about $250 million resulting from the counterfeiting, theft, or fraudulent use of their cards, your personal responsibility as a cardholder is strictly limited.

If your card is lost or stolen, you are expected to report its loss promptly to the issuing bank through the 24-hour telephone hotline number the bank provides. If you report the loss before a finder has made any use of the card, you are not responsible for any charges. If unauthorized use has been made before you report the loss, you are responsible for a maximum of $50, although some issuing banks will waive the charge. If, however, unauthorized use of your card was made without actual presentation of the card—as in the case of a telephone order—you are not liable for any amount. Because of these limits, the various credit card insurance policies, which cost several dollars a year, may not be worth buying.

Although loss of a card will do you no major harm financially, it can inconvenience you seriously, because as soon as you report the loss, the bank cancels your card and may take as long as two weeks to set up a new account for you. In the interim, your card is unusable, even if it should turn up at home or be returned by the finder. For this reason, and to protect yourself against other unauthorized uses, we suggest you take the following precautions:

- Sign your new cards as soon as you receive them, and cut all expired cards in two before discarding them.
- Keep a record of your account numbers and expiration dates in a safe place. One easy way to do this is to photocopy them.
- Avoid signing blank charge slips if possible. If this is not possible—as in the case of some automobile rentals—make sure that you are dealing with a reputable firm.
- Destroy all incorrect charge slips and all carbons, since the latter may be used to retrieve your name and account number, which can then be used for fraudulent telephone purchases.
- If possible, keep your card in sight during a transaction and be sure to retrieve it.
- Do not disclose your account number over the telephone unless you have initiated the transaction, and do not write it on an envelope that you plan to mail.
- Save your charge slips for checking against your statement, and open each statement promptly to check for unauthorized transactions.
- Never lend your card to anyone.

· Keep a record of the hotline telephone number provided by the issuer to report a lost or stolen card.

CLOSE-UP:
LEGAL PROTECTION FOR CARDHOLDERS

The Fair Credit Billing Act of 1974 offers cardholders significant protection against billing errors made by the card issuer or the merchant and limited recourse if you are dissatisfied with the goods or services you have charged on your card.

Billing Errors

Billing errors for which the issuing bank is responsible include failure to record payments that you made and mathematical errors made in totaling your charges or calculating the finance charge.

Billing errors for which merchants are responsible include charges for items you did not order or never received; items delivered to the wrong address, in the wrong quantity, or so much later than promised that the bill arrived before the item; and items that turned out to be different from what you had ordered.

When either type of error occurs, you must notify the issuing bank *in writing* within 60 days of receiving the statement containing the disputed amount. By law, you must write to the address on your statement for billing errors or inquiries. Your letter should include, in addition to your account number, a description of the error, the amount of the error, and, if possible, some explanation of why the error may have occurred. If the error involves a merchant, you should attach copies of any bills, sales receipts, or other supporting documents.

Pending resolution of the dispute, you may withhold payment of the disputed amount, but you must pay the undisputed balance. Until the dispute is resolved, the card issuer is not permitted to close your account or to threaten your credit rating by reporting you as delinquent.

The card issuer must respond to your statement within 30 days and must, within 90 days, conduct an investigation to determine the basis for your complaint. If your claim turns out to be justified, the charge is canceled; if not, you must pay the amount plus whatever interest charges may have accrued.

Defective Merchandise

Although your state consumer-protection laws may help you in the event that merchandise you buy proves defective, the Fair Credit Billing Act offers you scant protection. If permits you to withhold payment on an unsatisfactory card transaction only if it meets all three of the following requirements: the purchase must have amounted to more than $50; the purchase must have been made in the same state as your card billing address or, if outside the state, within 100 miles of your billing address; and you must have made an effort to clear up the problem with the merchant or supplier involved.

Even if your problem satisfies these conditions, the law does not prevent the supplier from suing you, although in that event your defense may specify the card issuer as the seller of the defective goods or services.

A preferable tactic is to define your problem as a billing error, since presumably you were billed for a satisfactory product and received a defective one. Most banks seem willing to accept this kind of claim—presumably because they have more to gain by retaining your long-term goodwill than that of the supplier who is the subject of your complaint.

5

Banking Alternatives

Jeff Blyskal

NEW COMPETITION FOR BANKS

In the area of personal finance, the substantial changes that took place in the 1970s in the structure and functions of financial institutions prompted a proliferation of alternatives for consumers. Perhaps nowhere have the changes been felt more than in banking. Early in the decade, federal laws limited banks in regard to the maximum interest they could pay and the services they could provide. As these restrictions gradually were lifted, banks gained more freedom to compete for depositors' accounts, but—even more important—so did a number of competing institutions that had previously been barred from providing consumer financial services.

As a consequence, you are no longer captive to the low interest rates and high service charges of traditional banks and can take your savings accounts elsewhere: to credit unions, money market funds, brokerage houses, and even your local Sears, Roebuck store. The banks' new nonbank competitors are also vying successfully for a share of the loan and credit card business, and many provide their customers with checking accounts.

No one institution—bank or nonbank—is ideal for everyone.

Each has its advantages and disadvantages. Your choice of one or more institutions should be governed by your personal needs. For most consumers, the following considerations are relevant:

- *Proximity and convenience.* Does the institution have to be close to your home or business, or can most of your transactions be done by mail or by use of automated teller machines?
- *Interest rates.* Are you primarily concerned with earning a high rate on your savings or with paying a low rate on your loans? The same institution may not satisfy both these needs.
- *Credit.* Which forms of credit—credit card, auto loan, home mortgage, etc.—are you likely to need?
- *Other services.* Unless you need a safe deposit box, signature guarantees, a financial reference, traveler's checks, direct deposit of payroll and pension checks, bill-payment services, electronic fund transfers, notary service, and similar amenities, you may be better off at a no-frills institution that provides none of these services and translates the resulting economies into higher interest rates.

Of course, there is no reason why you should confine your financial activities to a single institution—bank or nonbank. You may want to use several types of institutions in order to take advantage of the special features of each.

CREDIT UNIONS

A credit union is essentially a nonprofit financial cooperative that offers its members many, if not most, of the services provided by banks. In theory, because credit unions are operated for the sole benefit of their members and have relatively low overhead expenses, both loan rates and savings interest rates should be more attractive than those offered by profit-making financial institutions. A 1988 survey of banking services by *Consumer Reports* confirmed this.

Small credit unions provide their members with basic services: loans and savings accounts. Large ones may be full-service operations, offering checking and savings accounts, certificates of deposit, automated teller machines, direct payroll deposits, auto and personal loans, bill-payment service, and credit cards. About 10 percent of credit unions also offer mortgages.

Credit unions can assure their members of a high level of safety, because more than 90 percent of them are covered by the National Credit Union Share Insurance Fund (NCUSIF), a federal agency that insures deposits in the same way that the FDIC does for banks. Approximately 62 million Americans maintain accounts in some 14,350 credit unions, and, according to a recent survey, credit union members were more than twice as likely as bank customers to be satisfied with the services they received.

For most consumers, however, a major drawback of credit unions is eligibility for membership. Although a few credit unions are open to the general public, most are sponsored by an employer or an association, and membership is generally limited to employees or members and their families. Consequently, only about 50 to 60 percent of American consumers have access to a credit union.

This limitation of access virtually precludes shopping among credit unions for the best rates, since normally your choice would be limited to those sponsored by your employer, union, church, or a community group or other association. Nevertheless, you should consider carefully any credit union for which you are eligible, because it may offer you advantages not available from traditional banks.

Credit unions are able to offer low loan rates and high interest rates not only because they are nonprofit organizations but because they are not saddled with high overhead costs. Their administrators are not paid as highly as bank executives, their staffs are often made up of volunteers, their office space typically is donated or subsidized by their sponsors, and they are the beneficiaries of federal tax exemptions. Most of their earnings from loan interest can be paid out as savings interest to the depositors. In addition, credit unions, like banks, invest their depositors' funds in certificates of deposit, U.S. Treasury instruments, and other investments but do not charge their members the profit margin (3 to 8 percent) that is usually built into bank-account interest rates. Some credit unions, in addition, offer their members automobile and group life insurance at economical rates, and some arrange for membership discounts with local merchants.

In reality, however, these benefits are not always realized. Not all administrators and directors of credit unions have financial credentials and expertise, and the union's investment policy may not yield optimal returns. In addition, since depositors' funds are the source of loans, and since loan interest is the source of interest payments to depositors, it may not be possible for a credit union to offer both low-interest loans and high-interest savings accounts.

As a consequence, at some times auto loans cost less from a credit union than they do from local banks, but at other times the reverse is true. Although credit unions tend to charge a lower interest rate than banks on credit cards, many credit unions allow no interest-free period on their cards—that is, interest charges begin the moment the credit card purchase is recorded.

On mortgages, credit unions are likely to offer few advantages with respect to interest rates. Because, like banks, credit unions sell their mortgages to the Federal National Mortgage Association or the Federal Home Loan Mortgage Corporation (see p. 38), the rates on these mortgages must be similar to those banks are charging if the mortgages are to be salable. In addition, the kind of mortgage that you can choose is likely to be limited. On the other hand, loan origination fees and points (see p. 40) are likely to be lower, and the down payment required may be as low as 5 percent instead of the 10 to 20 percent demanded by most banks.

On savings accounts, certificates of deposit, and interest-bearing checking accounts, credit unions have been shown to pay higher rates than banks, but these findings come from surveys of large numbers of credit unions and do not necessarily hold true for the one for which you may be eligible. Some 66 percent of credit unions calculate account interest by the low-balance method, either for the month or for the quarter. Thus, if your balance is $100 on January 1 and on January 6 you deposit $10,000, your interest for the period will be calculated on the basis of $100.

Before opening an account, ask about the method used for interest calculation. Credit unions use the low-balance interest calculation to encourage depositors to maintain stable balances on which the credit union can depend for making loans. But if you use your account actively for frequent deposits and withdrawals, low-balance interest calculation is almost certain to penalize you. If you keep a substantial balance inactive for a long period of time, however, the low-balance method will have little impact, but you might enjoy a higher yield from a certificate of deposit.

Some further disadvantages may be important to you. Credit

unions do not return your canceled checks along with your statement. Instead, each check you write has an attached carbon copy, which you are expected to retain for your records. Although this copy can help you verify your statement, it cannot serve as proof of payment, and getting a copy of your original check may involve delay, extra charges, or both. Some credit unions issue statements quarterly rather than monthly. And not all credit unions are equipped to handle electronic fund transfers—a consideration that may be important if you use a money market mutual fund (see below). Moreover, most credit unions have only one branch, and although some of them have joined regional bank networks of automated teller machines, this single location may be an inconvenience for both deposits and withdrawals.

Credit unions as an alternative seem to offer a number of advantages over conventional banks, and you may find the concept of a nonprofit cooperative congenial, but it is important to check whether the credit union that is accessible to you offers the specific advantages you want or need. You may find it advantageous for loans but not for a savings or checking account. Some of the largest credit unions—those sponsored by large universities or associations of government employees—focus on low-cost loans rather than high-yield savings accounts.

MONEY MARKET MUTUAL FUNDS

If your banking needs include a liquid savings account that offers a relatively high yield and limited check-writing privileges, a money market mutual fund may be a very attractive alternative to the savings or money market accounts offered by banks (see p. 28). Money market mutual funds are in many respects similar to bank-sponsored money market accounts. Indeed, the latter were established to stem the outflow of funds from traditional savings accounts to the money market mutual funds. Although money market funds are not protected by federal insurance, most experts regard them as a safe investment, and they almost always offer lower fees and a higher interest rate than bank money market accounts. The spread between the two changes depending on the economy. A few years ago, the average money market fund paid more than two percentage points higher than the average bank money market account. In spring 1991, the difference was much slighter—the seven day compound yield for a money market mutual fund was 5.74 percent; the equivalent yield for a money market account was 5.35 percent. Should interest rates rise, however, the money market fund will respond much more quickly to the increase.

Money market funds are operated by private investment companies that use their depositors' money to invest in a variety of short-term (usually under 30 days) high-denomination debt obligations. In return, the funds pay their depositors the interest thus generated, after deducting a small amount (usually less than 1 percent per annum of the fund's asset value) for administrative expenses and profit.

You invest in a money market fund by buying shares at the fixed price of $1 each. (There is no load or other charge when you buy or sell shares, as there is with some other types of mutual funds.) Once the fund has acknowledged your deposit and your check has cleared, your balance is liquid and can be withdrawn by telephone, letter, or checks that the fund provides. Additional deposits can be made by check, by bank wire, or by authorization of systematic withdrawal from your local bank account. Deposits made by check are usually frozen for a week to 15 days to allow your check to clear, but they earn interest during this period.

Although most funds require a minimum initial investment of $500 to $2,000 and minimum subsequent investments of $100 or more, there is wide variation in these requirements. Checking privileges also vary from one fund to another. In general, free checks are provided and there is usually no limit to the number you can write, but there is a minimum amount, generally ranging from $250 to $500, for which each check can be written.

These minimums on check writing and deposits prevent you from using a money market fund as your sole checking account, because you will almost certainly have occasion to write small checks, make cash withdrawals, and make small deposits. But you may want to use your money market fund as your major depository for funds that you want to keep liquid, maintaining a minimal-cost local checking account for small transactions. For example, you can arrange to have your salary, pension, and large investment-

income checks deposited directly into your money market fund
account and then write money market fund checks to your local
account whenever its balance requires replenishment. You can
then use your local account to pay small bills but write money market fund checks to pay large bills. Your money market fund balance
continues to earn interest until the day each check actually
clears.

Because their balances are entirely liquid, it is possible to use
a money market fund as a temporary parking place for money that
is between investments—for example, the proceeds of a stock sale
or the sale of a home pending a further investment in stock or the
purchase of another home, or a windfall that you plan to invest as
soon as market conditions become more favorable.

Unlike the fixed rate on a certificate of deposit, the interest rate
on money market accounts can change daily, reflecting changes in
the fund's portfolio of debt instruments, which, in turn, reflect general interest rates. Indeed, over the years, the average yield from
money market funds has gone as high as 17 percent and as low as
4.1 percent as the prime interest rate has fluctuated. Although
there is no way of locking in a high rate with a money market fund
investment, there is no way of getting locked in to a low one—two
occurrences equally possible with certificates of deposit. And
money market funds consistently pay a higher rate of interest than
bank money market accounts.

Interest on your account is calculated daily and posted monthly.
Money market fund accounts earn the maximum on all balances,
no matter how low. Most depositors instruct the fund to reinvest
dividends—by buying additional shares at the $1 price—but if your
balance is large enough, you can instruct the fund to mail a
monthly interest check to you or to your local bank. You will
receive a written acknowledgment for each transaction and a
monthly or quarterly statement of your account. In addition, most
money market funds have toll-free telephone numbers through
which you can find out the current rate as well as the status of your
balance.

Not all money market funds make the same types of investments or provide the same kinds of services. Some issue credit
cards. Some belong to a family of mutual funds (see chapter 20,
Mutual Funds) and permit depositors to make telephone exchanges

between funds within the family. Some invest only in government securities; others invest in tax-exempt bonds.

Because of differences in their investment portfolios, not all funds produce the same yields. Although the yield of any fund will fluctuate from one week to the next, some funds perform consistently better than others. You can compare the performances of money market funds by consulting *Donoghue's Money Fund Report* or the weekly performance data published in major newspapers. A listing of money market funds, including toll-free numbers, is available free of charge from the Investment Company Institute, 1600 M Street NW, Washington, DC 20036. Using these telephone numbers in conjunction with the *Donoghue's* performance data, you can get information and prospectuses that will help you choose the funds best suited to your own needs.

Despite the obvious advantages of money market funds, many consumers hesitate to invest in them for two reasons. First, they are concerned about safety, pointing out that deposits in bank money market accounts are federally insured, whereas deposits in money market funds are not. Second, they prefer the convenience of a local institution and hesitate to invest through a company that may be 2,000 miles away.

Concern about safety is largely groundless, because money market funds invest in widely diversified debt obligations of only the most stable corporations and banks or federal government obligations. Since these obligations are short term, any signs of insolvency on the part of a specific corporation or bank are likely to become apparent in enough time to warn the fund against further investment. No money fund has ever failed, and only one has paid its depositors slightly less than they invested. On the other hand, in recent years scores of banks and S&Ls have failed annually.

The remoteness of a money market fund is also not a serious drawback, since you can use your money market fund checks at any time and place and for any purpose, and also since deposits can be made by bank wire instead of by mail if necessary. In fact, consumers who insist on depositing their money locally often fail to realize that bank interest rates vary regionally and that they may be penalizing themselves if they live in an area in which interest rates are chronically low.

ASSET MANAGEMENT ACCOUNTS

Asset management accounts, offered by brokerage houses in the hope of attracting customers for securities transactions, provide comprehensive financial services in a single account: the buying and selling of securities; a free checking account (with no limits on the number or size of the checks); a money market fund for your cash balance; the safekeeping of your securities, with interest, dividends, and sale proceeds paid directly into your account; a credit card; automatic payment of mortgage and other constant-figure payments; and telephone payment of any other bills you specify. Each monthly statement covers all these activities, and the year-end statement provides you with most of the information needed for your tax return. If you own a wide variety of securities or write large numbers of checks, you may find these accounts both convenient and economical, since the higher interest they earn on their cash balance usually offsets the service charges.

Eligibility requirements for these accounts, however, are fairly stringent. The minimum balance required ranges from $5,000 to $25,000, although some firms will waive the minimum balance if the depositor transfers into the account $20,000 in securities. In addition, annual service fees range from $25 to $100. The minimum balance earns relatively high money market rates, and the other services—especially the bill-payment feature and the comprehensive statements—may be well worth the fee in terms of the time and postage they save depositors.

The term *asset management* gives some potential customers the impression that the brokerage house actively manages the assets in the account. This is not correct. The brokerage house is involved in the account only with respect to the purchase and sale of securities—and only on explicit instructions from the depositor. If the brokerage firm charges full commissions, buying and selling securities will cost you more than a discount broker would charge, and this difference should be added to the true cost of your account. But some asset management accounts are offered by discount brokers, and consumers who maintain asset management accounts with full-service brokerage firms can nevertheless use discount brokers for buying and selling securities by depositing into the account securities they purchase elsewhere and by transferring securities that they plan to sell from the asset management account to their discount broker.

"NONBANK" BANKS

As we have noted, a number of investment companies and other corporations have, in recent years, begun offering certain kinds of banking services to the general public. Although these nonbanks are insured by the FDIC, they are not true banks because they do not offer commercial loans or accept commercial accounts. Instead, they concentrate on serving the individual consumer and compete actively for his or her business.

The Dreyfus Corporation, for example, an investment company that manages a wide variety of mutual funds, has established the Dreyfus Consumer Bank, which offers credit cards, automobile and personal loans, and second mortgages at rates it claims are significantly lower than those charged by commercial banks. Sears, Roebuck & Company has taken over the Greenwood Trust Company, which currently offers money market accounts and Discover credit cards without an annual fee. In addition, charges incurred with the Discover card earn an annual rebate based on the amount charged. No rebates apply to cash advances, however.

LOAN ALTERNATIVES

Banking alternatives are available not only for savings and checking activities but also for various kinds of loans. But whereas the terms and conditions for savings and checking alternatives are relatively simple and straightforward—and hence readily comparable—the terms governing loans can be quite complex. Any nonbank loan arrangement needs to be scrutinized with the greatest care. In general, only one or two of the alternatives offer distinct advantages over a bank loan.

Insurance Policy Loans

If your life insurance policy has a specified cash surrender value— that is, a cash reserve that is available to you on the termination of your policy—the insurance company may be a source of a low-cost loan. In their eagerness to sell policies, some companies incorporate in the policy a presumably attractive rate at which the insured may borrow funds against the policy's cash surrender value. These rates vary from policy to policy, and some policies do not specify a rate, but policies that predate the 1970s, before interest rates reached unprecedented heights, specify a rather low interest rate. For example, until a few years ago, insurance policies sold to servicemen by the Veterans Administration carried a loan rate of only 5 percent. Many veterans borrowed at this rate and earned a much higher rate by investing the loan in money market funds.

Aside from its competitive interest rate, the great advantage of an insurance policy loan is that the principal need not be repaid by any specified date. As long as interest is paid, the insurance company is not concerned about repayment of the principal, since, in the event of your death, the outstanding debt can be deducted from the face value of your policy. This advantage is also a disadvantage, since nonrepayment of whatever loan you make reduces the benefits payable to your beneficiaries.

Brokerage Firms

Many stock brokerage firms will make personal or real estate loans to customers who are willing to use the stocks and bonds they own as collateral. Such loans are made at rates only one or two percentage points higher than the call rate—the relatively low rate that brokers themselves pay to borrow money. (The current call rate, which fluctuates regularly, can be found in the financial pages of any major newspaper.) As a result, interest on such loans may cost two to three percentage points less than a similarly secured loan obtained from a bank.

Brokerage loans can be risky for the borrower. If stock prices should drop to the point at which the value of your collateral no longer protects the broker against the possibility of your default, you will be asked to provide additional collateral, and failure to do this can result in the forced sale of your stock—almost by definition at a time when the market prices are low. If, however, you borrow a sum that represents only a small fraction of the value of your portfolio, a brokerage loan can be extremely economical.

Consumer Finance Companies

Advertising heavily through television commercials, consumer finance companies offer personal loans and, more recently, home equity loans and second mortgages at interest rates consistently and significantly higher than those charged by banks. Many consumers believe that the higher rates are necessary because these companies make loans to borrowers whose credit ratings are not good enough to qualify them for a bank loan, and to some extent television commercials reinforce this impression. But a recent study indicates that this is not true: A loan application has at least as good a chance of approval by a bank as by a loan company. The higher interest rates are due in part to the finance companies' higher costs in obtaining money to lend, and perhaps also to their high expenditures on advertising. They cannot draw on low-cost depositors' funds in savings and checking accounts but must obtain funds from commercial sources at money market rates. Given their consistently higher rates, finance companies should be a last resort for any kind of loan or mortgage.

Reverse Mortgage Companies

Many elderly people own their homes free and clear but have low cash income, even though their home, having appreciated in value in recent years, represents a substantial but nonliquid asset. Reverse mortgages, offered by a number of firms that specialize in them, can provide such homeowners with an increase in their current cash income.

The reverse mortgage is essentially a home equity loan in reverse—that is, the home serves as collateral for monthly payments that are made *to the homeowner* and the loan is repaid from the estate of the borrower after his or her death. Under a typical arrangement, a couple at least 62 years old may borrow up to $700 a month for as long as they live. Moreover, the monthly payment, because it constitutes a loan rather than income, is tax-free. Upon death, the loan is repaid through the sale of the home, but usually no other assets of the estate can be used for repayment.

Although a reverse mortgage can be a very useful way of enhancing retirement income, it obviously reduces the value of the

estate you may wish to pass on to heirs. Moreover, it must be negotiated very carefully. It must provide, for example, for payments
to continue for the life of the surviving spouse. Some reverse mortgages provide payments for a set number of years that exceeds the
borrowers' life expectancies as determined by actuarial statistics.
Borrowers who outlive the term may find themselves dispossessed
of their home.

CLOSE-UP:
SHOPPING IN THE FINANCIAL SUPERMARKET

As we have noted, the dramatic changes that have occurred in the
financial marketplace offer consumers some very attractive opportunities to increase the yield on their savings and to reduce their
costs for checking services, credit cards, and loans. But consumers
will fail to realize these potential advantages if they assume that
all banks are more or less alike or that a bank is doing them a favor
by offering them a loan.

In reality, a proliferating number of institutions are competing
for a relatively fixed number of potential customers, and each of
them can compete successfully only by providing services that are
superior, more versatile, or less expensive than what the competition has to offer. You have much to gain from carefully analyzing
your financial needs, comparison shopping the markets to satisfy
them, and continuously monitoring the market for new, better, or
less expensive services. You can also try to negotiate for better
terms in any given transaction—for a better rate on a certificate
of deposit, for example, or a lower rate on a loan.

You need also be aware, however, that institutions competing
with one another often use advertising that stresses the advantages of a service while glossing over its costs or other disadvantages or by offering specials that appear to be bargains but prove
to be costly. Both banks and nonbanks, for example, have been
known to lure depositors with certificates of deposit or money market accounts promising yields significantly higher than those prev-
alent at the time. But, as the fine print of the advertisement indicates, these rates are subject to change, and they tend to decline
as soon as a sufficient number of customers have been signed up.

Perhaps the best way to find the services you need and to avoid
paying for those you do not use is through a careful review of your

overall financial needs and activities. For example, once you have analyzed your past year's checking account and stock market activities, you may conclude that an asset management account (see p. 76) is a bargain, despite its $35 annual fee and high minimum balance requirement. Then, too, you may decide that a free checking account, an $18-per-year credit card, and a money market account are all you really need.

A thorough review of your assets can also save you money. You may find, for example, that getting the money for a new car by dipping into your savings or by selling some shares of stock will cost you far less than a loan, even at the most favorable rate. Or you may discover that you have far too much money earning a low yield in a traditional savings account at your local bank and that shifting it into another form (or another institution) can increase its yield significantly with no loss of safety or liquidity.

CLOSE-UP:
WHAT'S IN THE FINE PRINT?

The cautions related to checking accounts, savings accounts, loans, and credit cards—to be found in chapters 1 through 4—are, of course, equally applicable to those services when offered by a banking alternative. But banking alternatives, because they are less strictly regulated than banks, warrant some additional caveats.

Checking and Savings Services

Before investing in a money market mutual fund, read the prospectus carefully. Although money market funds have an exemplary safety record, those that invest solely in government securities enjoy a small margin of safety over those that invest, for example, in bank repurchase agreements. Those that invest in tax-free instruments will give you a lower yield in return for the tax exemption, but only a careful estimate of your tax obligations can tell you whether or not the lower yield is desirable for you.

Before committing yourself to a checking account at any banking alternative, find out if your canceled checks will be returned with your statement and that charges for account maintenance, stopping payment on a check, or incurring an overdraft are competitive. You should make certain, too, that you understand the additional service charges that may be levied if your balance falls below a specified level.

Although most credit-union accounts are insured, company-sponsored credit unions may experience serious cash-flow problems in the event of a strike, a plant closing, or another event affecting the credit union's members. In such situations, your money is likely to be safe, but you may experience serious delays in withdrawing it.

Loans

Consumer finance companies have been known to make loans on either an add-on or a discount charge basis, each of which increases the borrower's cost significantly.

Here's how the add-on rate cheats you: As you pay off a loan, you are gradually reducing the amount of money you have borrowed. Thus, in the first month after you have borrowed $1,000, your interest charge should be ($1,000) × (.01, the monthly percentage rate) = $10. If you made a payment of $93.33 after the first month, you've paid $10 in interest and $83.33 of the principal. So, the second month of your loan, you're not really borrowing $1,000, you're only borrowing $916.67. The month's interest charge on that amount should be only $9.17. But with the add-on loan, you still pay $10 a month in finance charges the second month and for each of the remaining 10 months.

Most loans take into account the declining principal owed, and interest charges each month decline accordingly. With those loans, a 12 percent annual interest rate works out to be a 12 percent annual interest rate. A 12 percent add-on rate, adjusted for the declining balance, actually works out to be a 21.46 percent annual interest rate. This fact should become readily apparent when the legal annual percentage rate (APR)—which reveals the true cost of borrowing—is calculated for the add-on loan. Make sure any add-on rate quotes are converted to the APR rate, as required under the Truth-in-Lending Act.

The discount charge basis works in much the same way. When you borrow the $1,000 for one year at 12 percent, the interest is deducted in advance and you actually receive $880. On this basis, your actual annual percentage rate would be 24.28 percent rather than 12 percent.

When dealing with a consumer finance company, ask for the APR in writing. This can give you legal recourse if the add-on or discount charge bases are used covertly.

Because loans from a stockbroker use your stocks as collateral, be sure to find out in advance not only the basis for the interest rate but also the conditions under which your loan can be called in for full payment or your collateral would have to be increased by the addition of cash or stock.

II

MONEY MANAGEMENT

6

Budgeting

Emily Card

THE ADVANTAGES OF BUDGETING

Who wants to budget? Maybe no one. For nonbudgeters, the term often evokes feelings of anxiety and fear about the constraints of limited financial resources. But those who do maintain the discipline of a budget understand well its benefits.

A budget is a plan for spending and saving money. The major reason for making a budget and sticking to it is to save for future goals while meeting present ones. The budget itself serves a number of useful functions in money management.

Planning A budget provides a plan that ensures that your total income meets your total expenditures. It also helps you to manage cash so that the timing of income and expenditures matches. If cash-flow problems are likely to occur, a good budget can anticipate them and allow you to prepare necessary adjustments, either by postponing expenditures, obtaining income sooner (if possible), or using credit to smooth out the cycle.

Although a budget is a plan, budgeting must be distinguished from long-term financial planning. With financial planning, major long-term decisions are made for several years or even a lifetime.

With a budget, you look at the immediate future—usually a month, six months, or a year—and decide how these long-term plans will be refined and implemented. Without a budget, it's unlikely you'll meet the goals set in financial planning, because immediate resources are rarely adequate to meet competing demands (see chapter 7).

Communication   A budget is a concrete expression of monetary plans and a device for codifying and communicating the details of those plans. A budget communicates many kinds of information, from amounts to be spent on utilities, transportation, and restaurants to savings for future education.

Motivation   A budget can help motivate you to reach your goals by creating realistic objectives and showing how they will be achieved.

Control   A budget can help you control your finances because it enables you to measure *actual* performance against *planned* performance. Analysis of the differences between planned and real results can reveal areas of weakness that need attention, opportunities to save money not foreseen in the initial budgeting process, or unrealistic planning in the original budget.

Evaluation   At the end of a budget period, you can compare actual and budgeted results to evaluate your overall performance in meeting your goals.

Self-education   Budgets show how money is spent and how it might be spent.

Although budgeting can tell us much about our spending and earning habits, a significant number of people *do not* budget. According to one psychologist who has studied the financial attitudes of 12,000 Americans for twenty-five years, only 60 percent of those surveyed kept budgets. That same psychologist reports that the two most common reasons people start a budget are the birth of a child and a move to a new home. The next three catalytic events are a major medical expense, divorce, and retirement.

Another reason people begin to budget is to rectify financial problems caused by overspending or abusing credit. In our consumer-driven economy, constant media messages to spend, spend, spend—coupled with pressure to keep up with the Joneses—tempt us to spend more than we have planned.

Easy credit, although a boon for purchasing large-ticket items and managing financial emergencies, can play havoc with a budget.

About 10 percent of consumers overextend routinely. Credit experts suggest that if you spend more than 20 percent of your salary, not including mortgages, on credit purchases before your paycheck arrives, it's unlikely you'll have any discretionary income to budget. Once a family or an individual recognizes that overspending and credit abuse impede financial success, a budget can become the key to a financial turnaround.

Analyzing your expenditures is simply a matter of assigning spending categories or "accounts" for each check written over a period of time and then totaling the checks for each category as explained below. The appropriate category for each check is usually self-evident (phone bill, mortgage payment, alimony), unless the check was written to pay a credit card bill. In that case you would need to use the statement to assign charges to accounts that month, whether or not you paid in full.

Whatever the immediate motivation—whether the contemplation of a more ordered financial life or relief from overspending—the decision to begin budgeting is only the start. Next comes the difficult work, which, if carried out with persistence, will produce the desired rewards.

STEP ONE: CASH-FLOW ANALYSIS

The first step in making a budget for future income and expenditures is to look back at how past income and expenditures flowed through your pocketbook. This cash-flow analysis—as it is called technically—is not a budget, since it implies no goals and represents no plan. Rather, it is a financial snapshot that tells you how you presently behave. Budgeting or planning will come after a thorough cash-flow analysis.

To gather data about expenditures, start with information you already have. Even if you are not particularly well organized, you will have a surprisingly good collection of data on hand in the form of canceled checks and credit card receipts. If your checkbook is up to date, if your bills are organized either by function, alphabetically, or by date paid, and if your tax worksheets are kept with your completed returns, the task of organizing for the budget analysis will go much more quickly.

Set up a ledger book, a yellow legal pad, or a computerized spreadsheet, and add up figures for each category into monthly amounts for the previous six-to-twelve-month period. (See figure 6-1.)

Income Write down the gross income you receive during each month. If you receive your income weekly, list the total for each month. For income received annually or quarterly, list it in the month you actually receive it. Alternatively, add up your gross income on an annual basis.

If you currently pay directly into a credit union monthly savings plan, or a qualified deferred-income plan [such as a 401(k)], include this amount under gross income but deduct it later as an expense—a savings payment. If you have income other than a monthly paycheck, such as dividends, rents, or interest, be sure to list these as well. Income categories will include the following:

- Salary or wages
- Self-employment income
- Pension, disability, unemployment, or Social Security income
- Interest
- Dividends
- Alimony
- Child Support
- Rents and royalties
- Trust and annuity income
- Cash gifts received
- Net gambling earnings

Expenses List your monthly or annual expenses by category. If you prefer, you can group these expenses under two subcategories: fixed expenses, which remain pretty much the same month to month (such items as mortgage or rent payments, installment loan payments, and insurance premiums); and variable expenses, which change each month (such items as food expenditures, phone bills, and entertainment costs).

If grouping by fixed and variable expenses is too confusing or unsuitable for you, keep it simple. Start with major functional categories. Later refinements can be added when the budget itself is prepared.

At the top of your expense list will be federal, state, local, and Social Security taxes withheld. These figures appear on your pay statement. After that, you might employ the categories used by the

FIGURE 6-1 Cash-Flow Analysis

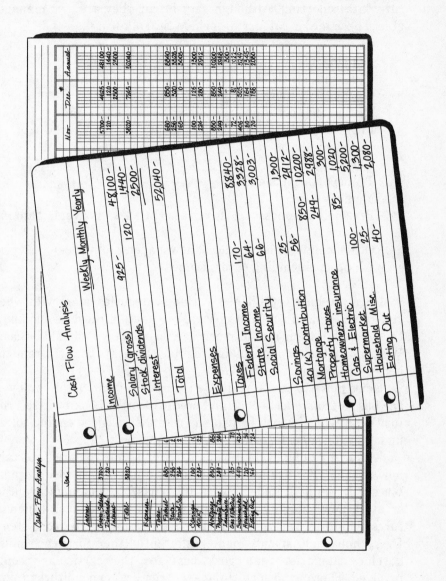

Cash Flow Analysis

Income	Weekly	Monthly	Yearly
Salary (gross)		925-	48,100-
Stock dividends		120-	1,440-
Interest			2,500-
Total			52,040

Expenses			
Taxes			
Federal Income		170-	8,840-
State Income		64-	3,328-
Social Security		66-	3,003-
Savings		25-	1,200-
401(k) contribution		56-	2,912-
Mortgage		850-	10,200-
Property taxes		249-	2,988-
Homeowners insurance			300-
Gas & Electric		85-	1,020-
Supermarket		100-	5,200-
Household Misc.		25-	1,300-
Eating Out		40-	2,080-

Department of Commerce in its Personal Consumption Expenditure data reporting. Although very broad, they are also manageable. These major categories include the following:

- Housing
- Food and beverages
- Clothes and shoes
- Household operation
- Furniture and household equipment
- Autos and parts
- Gas and oil
- Transportation services
- Medical
- Personal business services (accountants, lawyers, banking fees)
- Other nondurables (tobacco, newspapers, toiletries)
- All other, including entertainment

Once you have established working categories, start with what you know to build your data base. For example, most people know the amount of their rent or mortgage, so entering it should be easy. Write down the amounts of any regular payments that you remember in the appropriate category.

Next, move to easily available records. You can obtain many of the basics from checkbooks and credit records. Look over records for the previous month or two and establish basic spending totals under the broad categories.

As you go along, you may identify items that you are uncertain how to label. For example, where should automobile insurance be placed? It would fit under "autos and parts," or you might want to create a new category for "insurance." Categorize such expenditures whatever way is comfortable for you—but be consistent. Every household spends money differently; therefore, each must develop categories that work best for the particular people involved. There is no such thing as a "correct" expenditure grouping. But, out of the process of attempting to organize existing recorded expenditures, natural groupings will tend to emerge. (See figure 6-2.)

Existing expense records, of course, only go so far. Beyond that are still plenty of miscellaneous expenses of which few people keep

FIGURE 6-2 Sample Expenditure Categories.

track: meals at a fast-food restaurant, newspapers, cigarettes, the $10 bill slipped into a nephew's birthday card. Such expenses can go into an account called "cash." If any single type of cash expense seems high or out of control, it should be broken out and given its own category. You can keep a diary of such expenses for a short period to see how they add up.

Be prepared for some surprises. Some people learn for the first time how much they spend on newspapers, magazines, and other sundries. One man in a *Consumer Reports* survey reported that the diary process revealed he spent more than a dollar a day on doughnuts. That's $30 a month, or $350 a year!

Another source of expense data is your tax return. It should be reviewed at this stage, since many expense items are identified there by broad groupings if you file Schedule A, "Itemized Deductions," or Schedule C, "Profit or Loss from Business."

Using the categories you have established for working on the monthly diary, set up a page to group all income and expenses by yearly amounts. Convert fixed-income and fixed-expense items from monthly, quarterly, and semiannual amounts into annual figures. If you have listed actual variable income and expenses for each month, convert those amounts into annual totals.

With all of your income and expenses on one annual statement—called a summary of cash receipts and disbursements for the year, or, informally, a cash-flow statement—you should have a good picture of where all of your money goes. The value of an annual figure is that it does not reflect cyclical differences in spending and gives you a total picture of the period. The budget you prepare will be based in good part on these past real annual expenses.

Once your figures have been converted to an annual amount, you may want to compare your results to the spending habits of others, because it could reveal potential areas for making changes in your habits. If you spend $100 per week on food, for example, while the average per-person weekly food expenditure is $57, you might explore whether you are buying more food or more expensive food than is necessary.

Note, however, that income level and geographic location play a role in how much you spend, as does age. Spending by people living in urban and rural areas is significantly different. The survey of *Consumer Reports* readers (see table 6-1) illustrates spending pattern differences by income level.

Over the decade, many changes have occurred in our economy; according to Department of Commerce figures, however, the percentages of expenditures by consumers on various items remained surprisingly similar. Although some changes are certainly evident, as amounts tripled, the percentages remained recognizable. For instance, in 1973, spending on housing accounted for 14.2 percent of personal consumption expenditures; in 1986, housing accounted for 15.9 percent. In 1973, food and beverages stood at 20.1 percent; in 1986, 17.8 percent.

STEP TWO: SETTING BUDGET GOALS

Cash-flow analysis gives you a picture of where you are; a budget gives you a picture of where you are going—the goals you want to achieve. To make a true budget, you must set goals for growth and establish plans with specific targets that will help you meet your goals.

Goals should be broad sweeps of the brush—purchasing a home; planning for education, trips to Europe, or early retirement; or even just making ends meet. Every family member who spends money should participate. These goals, once committed to paper, become guideposts. If your goal is to retire in five years, you can analyze your cash flow to see whether sufficient funds are being— or can be—set aside to reach the projected amount needed.

The Department of Agriculture's *Guide to Budgeting for the Family* suggests listing goals in three categories: long-term goals, goals for the next five years, and goals for this year. To a certain extent, the kinds of goals set will reflect your life stage. In general, goals at specific life stages tend to run as follows:

Young single. Start a savings habit; begin to build investments; consider purchasing property.

Young couple. Plan for wedding expenses; work to save for a home; save for purchases of furniture.

Family with young children. Establish plans to ensure that enough money is available for food, clothing, day care, and other expenses of having a child or children in the home; obtain life insurance to ensure income in case of loss of one or both income earners.

Family with children in school. Establish college funds for the children; begin retirement funds.

TABLE 6-1   Annual Expenditures:
Consumer Reports Readers' Survey

	Readers Overall		Percent of Income Spent		
	Average Amount per Year	Percent of Income	$15,000–$30,000	$30,000–$50,000	$50,000–150,000
Taxes					
Federal income [1]	$5039	12%	7%	11%	15%
Social Security [1]	3100	7	7	8	7
State and local	2833	7	6	6	7
Housing					
Mortgage or rent	4291 [2]	10	11	11	9
Other housing costs [3]	4930	11	13	12	11

Food and groceries [4]	5850	14	20	15	10
Transportation [4]	3955	9	12	10	7
Vacation, recreation	1958	5	5	4	5
Health care, insurance [5]	1578	4	5	4	3
Clothing	1252	3	3	3	3
Savings and investments [1]	3600	8	5	8	12
Other, specified	1895	4	5	4	5
Other, not specified	3019	7	1	4	8

[1] Estimated.
[2] Average would be $5786, eliminating the 23 percent who own their homes free and clear.
[3] Includes utilities, furnishings, home improvements, and insurance.
[4] Includes auto insurance.
[5] Includes life, health, and disability insurance.

Couple with children nearly grown. Complete financial arrangements for retirement years; plan for the children's wedding(s);
help children to buy a first house; plan for early retirement or a
career change.

Retired persons. Budget for reduced and often fixed incomes;
allow for travel or other pleasures and unexpected medical
expenses; provide help for children or grandchildren.

STEP THREE: ALLOCATING RESOURCES

There are three basic methods of budgeting to allocate your available resources: the expenditure budget, the accounts system, and
the bank-account budget.

The Expenditure Budget

The expenditure budget groups the data you have gathered by
broad categories and smaller subcategories so that you can keep
track of as much detail as your bookkeeping time will permit. It
resembles the cash-flow analysis ledger you set up, but this ledger
is for future expenses, not past ones.

Whether you lead a relatively simple life with a few major
expense categories, or a complicated existence calling for many
payments per month, the format of the expenditure budget should
be the same as that illustrated in table 6-2. Down the left side of
the page, list the expenses you plan to incur by groups. List past
expenses as well as your new spending or saving goals.

Across the top, you should have four columns per month. The
first column should indicate the actual or estimated amount spent
on this item during this month last year. The next three columns
should reflect the budgeted amount for this year, the amount spent
in the current period, and the difference or variance from the budgeted amount.

Next, fill in the estimated expenses, month by month, for the
period being budgeted. To estimate monthly expenses, divide your
annual expenses, figured previously, by 12. If there are cyclical
variations—for example, if you spent more to heat your home in
winter—adjust estimates accordingly. Add in any new items you
plan, and adjust projected expenses until your total income and
expenses are equal.

TABLE 6-2   The Expenditure Budget:
Month of January

Expense	Last Year Actual	Budget	Actual	Variance
Housing				
Rent or mortgage	_____	_____	_____	_____
Real estate taxes	_____	_____	_____	_____
Homeowner's insurance	_____	_____	_____	_____
Water and sewer	_____	_____	_____	_____
Heat	_____	_____	_____	_____
Electricity	_____	_____	_____	_____
Gas	_____	_____	_____	_____
Telephone	_____	_____	_____	_____
Total	_____	_____	_____	_____
Food and beverage				
Home	_____	_____	_____	_____
Restaurant	_____	_____	_____	_____
Total	_____	_____	_____	_____
Clothing and shoes				
Husband	_____	_____	_____	_____
Wife	_____	_____	_____	_____
Children	_____	_____	_____	_____
Total	_____	_____	_____	_____
Household operations				
Laundry/dry cleaning	_____	_____	_____	_____
Repair	_____	_____	_____	_____
Housekeeper	_____	_____	_____	_____
Gardener	_____	_____	_____	_____
Total	_____	_____	_____	_____
Day care	_____	_____	_____	_____
Life insurance	_____	_____	_____	_____
Medical				
Doctor	_____	_____	_____	_____
Dentist	_____	_____	_____	_____
Prescriptions	_____	_____	_____	_____
Total	_____	_____	_____	_____

TABLE 6-2   The Expenditure Budget:
Month of January (*continued*)

Expense	Last Year Actual	Budget	Actual	Variance
Automobile				
Payments	_____	_____	_____	_____
Insurance	_____	_____	_____	_____
Maintenance	_____	_____	_____	_____
Repair	_____	_____	_____	_____
Total	_____	_____	_____	_____
Gas and oil	_____	_____	_____	_____
Household equipment				
Furniture	_____	_____	_____	_____
Appliances	_____	_____	_____	_____
Tools	_____	_____	_____	_____
Total	_____	_____	_____	_____
Transportation				
Taxi	_____	_____	_____	_____
Carpool	_____	_____	_____	_____
Total	_____	_____	_____	_____
Personal business				
Lawyer	_____	_____	_____	_____
Accountant	_____	_____	_____	_____
Banking fees	_____	_____	_____	_____
Total	_____	_____	_____	_____
Investments				
Education fund	_____	_____	_____	_____
Savings	_____	_____	_____	_____
Total	_____	_____	_____	_____
Nondurables				
Travel	_____	_____	_____	_____
Entertainment	_____	_____	_____	_____
Organization dues	_____	_____	_____	_____
Magazines	_____	_____	_____	_____
Newspapers	_____	_____	_____	_____
Toiletries	_____	_____	_____	_____
Total	_____	_____	_____	_____

TABLE 6-2   The Expenditure Budget:
Month of January (*continued*)

Expense	Last Year Actual	Budget	Actual	Variance
Miscellaneous				
Husband	————	————	————	————
Wife	————	————	————	————
Children	————	————	————	————
Total	————	————	————	————
Grand Total	————	————	————	————

At this stage, you may have to revise your plan in order to attain your newly targeted goals. For example, if you have been wanting to start a fund to purchase a boat, you may find you have to allocate money from other expense items in the budget to do so. If you haven't budgeted before, you may want to start with a three-month period, but the final product eventually should be an annual budget.

Now comes the part requiring time and discipline: doing the bookkeeping necessary to see whether actual expenses match the projected ones. For most people, it's easiest to fill in a ledger, whether manual or computerized, as the expenses are paid. For example, if you pay your bills at the beginning and the middle of the month, take time to log the expenses in the budget sheet as well as in your checkbook balance record. Or, if you pay bills as they come in, record the payments in the appropriate budget category as well as in your checkbook.

Not every expense will be paid out as a response to a bill. Many will be made at the point of purchase by cash or check. Record check purchases when you write the check or review your checkbook log from the past week or two-week period, and mark them in the budget record by the appropriate category.

For cash purchases, either continue recording amounts in a notebook or diary or form the habit of asking for receipts. If you obtain receipts, keep them in an envelope or file until they can be entered into your expenditure budget.

Of course, not every penny can be tracked, nor should it be, because of all the record-keeping that would be required. A category should be established for "personal allowance" or "petty cash," which allows each individual in the household to spend some money without needing to report it, other than by total amount.

Table 6-3 illustrates another system. The affluent professional two-income couple in our example has the necessary time, resources, and inclination to carry out the most useful budget exercise. The family has made the commitment to prepare a complete budget projection that includes last year's expenses as well as variance analysis.

To start saving for their children's college educations, the family decided to cut back restaurant meals and travel from the amounts spent the previous year. The money reflected in the "Budget" column for these items has been adjusted so that the education fund can be created. But even with these changes, the family needs to add more into its budget for savings and investments. This first budget effort will have to be revised with the objective of cutting down on their high current expenditures and allocating more resources toward the future.

The budget system described above is the ideal for serious budgeters, because all the information required will appear in one location. Those with little time or inclination to account for their expenses in such detail may want to consider one of the other methods.

Expenditure budgeting can be made simpler with a computer. Another couple developed the version shown in figure 6-3. Since both receive commissions from their sales jobs, recording the variable income as well as expenses on a monthly basis is vital to make their budget work. To provide budgeting flexibility, the couple decided to divide their expenses into "fixed" and "variable." Each month, their first priority is to see that their fixed expenses are met. Then variable expenses are handled. In months in which commissions are low, variable expenses can be cut back.

Rather than keep a running total of variances by item, the couple can scan the two columns headed "Budget" and "Actual." That quick review, coupled with a look at the fixed and variable totals budgeted and spent, provides enough information to make necessary adjustments. For example, in January, variable expenses of $1,145 were less than the total budgeted amount of $1,208. But in February, variable expenses came to $1,685—$502 above the budg-

TABLE 6-3　The Family Expenditure Budget:
Month of January

Expense	Last Year Actual	Budget	Actual	Variance
Housing				
Rent or mortgage	1250.00	1250.00	1250.00	0.00
Real estate taxes	175.00	175.00	175.00	0.00
Homeowner's insurance	125.00	125.00	135.00	−10.00
Water and sewer	27.00	27.00	29.00	−2.00
Heat	150.00	150.00	175.00	−25.00
Electricity	35.00	35.00	37.50	−2.50
Gas	12.00	15.00	14.00	1.00
Telephone	150.00	175.00	210.00	−35.00
Total	1924.00	1952.00	2025.50	−73.50
Food and beverage				
Home	350.00	400.00	420.00	−20.00
Restaurant	250.00	100.00	100.00	0.00
Total	600.00	500.00	520.00	−20.00
Clothing and shoes				
Husband	125.00	140.00	135.00	5.00
Wife	140.00	150.00	140.00	10.00
Children	25.00	30.00	35.00	−5.00
Total	290.00	320.00	310.00	10.00
Household operations				
Laundry/dry cleaning	125.00	130.00	130.00	0.00
Repair	50.00	65.00	95.00	−30.00
Housekeeper	200.00	220.00	220.00	0.00
Gardener	160.00	180.00	180.00	0.00
Total	535.00	595.00	625.00	−30.00
Day care	260.00	260.00	320.00	−60.00
Life insurance	85.00	85.00	85.00	0.00
Medical				
Doctor	25.00	45.00	55.00	−10.00
Dentist	110.00	125.00	130.00	−5.00
Prescriptions	35.00	45.00	45.00	0.00
Total	170.00	215.00	230.00	−15.00
Automobile				
Payments	245.00	275.00	275.00	0.00
Insurance	170.00	185.00	195.00	−10.00
Maintenance	20.00	30.00	30.00	0.00
Repair	50.00	50.00	50.00	0.00
Total	485.00	540.00	550.00	−10.00

TABLE 6-3   The Family Expenditure Budget:
Month of January (*continued*)

Expense	Last Year Actual	Budget	Actual	Variance
Gas and oil	110.00	130.00	135.00	−5.00
Household equipment				
Furniture	125.00	130.00	145.00	−15.00
Appliances	75.00	95.00	105.00	−10.00
Tools	35.00	45.00	40.00	5.00
Total	235.00	270.00	290.00	−20.00
Transportation				
Taxi	30.00	35.00	30.00	5.00
Car pool	20.00	25.00	25.00	0.00
Total	50.00	60.00	55.00	5.00
Personal business				
Lawyer	150.00	175.00	165.00	10.00
Accountant	125.00	150.00	160.00	−10.00
Banking fees	35.00	45.00	40.00	5.00
Total	310.00	370.00	365.00	5.00
Investments				
Education fund	0.00	150.00	150.00	0.00
Savings	0.00	50.00	75.00	−25.00
Total	0.00	200.00	225.00	−25.00
Nondurables				
Travel	200.00	150.00	125.00	25.00
Entertainment	175.00	185.00	190.00	−5.00
Organization dues	300.00	350.00	350.00	0.00
Magazines	40.00	50.00	50.00	0.00
Newspapers	30.00	30.00	30.00	0.00
Toiletries	55.00	60.00	65.00	−5.00
Total	800.00	825.00	810.00	15.00
Miscellaneous				
Husband	200.00	225.00	250.00	−25.00
Wife	175.00	195.00	190.00	5.00
Child	35.00	45.00	45.00	0.00
Total	410.00	465.00	485.00	−20.00
Grand Total	6,264.00	6,787.00	7,030.50	−243.50

FIGURE 6-3   A Computerized Spreadsheet

	January Budget	January Actual	February Budget	February Actual	March Budget	March Actual	YTD Budget	YTD Actual	% of income
Income									
Lee--gross salary	1680	1680	1680	1680	2100	2100	5460	5460	44.2%
Lee--commission	200	141	200	253	200	115	600	509	4.1%
Cindy--gross salary	960	960	960	960	1200	1200	3120	3120	25.2%
Cindy--commission	150	156	150	136	150	133	450	425	3.4%
Interest	35	36	35	39	35	52	105	127	1.0%
Miscellaneous	700	949	700	981	700	788	2100	2718	22.0%
TOTAL INCOME	3725	3922	3725	4049	4385	4388	11835	12359	
Less taxes withheld--Lee	-404	-404	-404	-404	-505	-505	-1313	-1313	10.6%
Less taxes withheld--Cindy	-168	-168	-168	-168	-210	-210	-546	-546	4.4%
TOTAL NET INCOME	3153	3350	3153	3477	3670	3673	9976	10500	
Fixed expenses									
Mortgage	990	990	990	990	990	990	2970	2970	24.0%
Insurance: Mortgage	30	30	30	30	30	30	90	90	0.7%
Homeowner's	200	200	200	200	200	200	600	600	4.9%
Auto	0	0	60	62	0	0	60	62	0.5%
Property tax	108	108	108	108	108	108	324	324	2.6%
Student loan	179	179	179	179	179	179	537	537	4.3%
Savings--Lee	100	100	100	100	100	100	300	300	2.4%
Savings--Cindy	100	100	100	100	100	100	300	300	2.4%
Savings--joint	200	200	200	200	200	200	600	600	4.9%
TOTAL FIXED EXPENSES	1907	1907	1967	1969	1907	1907	5781	5783	46.8%
Variable expenses									
Medical	20	0	20	5	20	15	60	20	0.2%
Drugs	10	0	10	6	10	5	30	11	0.1%
Auto/gas	100	66	100	71	100	49	300	186	1.5%
Food	200	124	200	225	200	246	600	595	4.8%
Meals out	100	104	100	76	100	135	300	315	2.5%
Home supplies	350	344	350	822	350	177	1050	1343	10.9%
Electric	30	47	30	43	30	22	90	112	0.9%
Gas	15	12	15	9	15	16	45	37	0.3%
Water	0	0	20	21	0	0	20	21	0.2%
Telephone	35	49	35	28	35	56	105	133	1.1%
Clothing	20	7	20	0	20	0	60	7	0.1%
Cleaners	10	0	10	7	10	0	30	7	0.1%
Recreation & travel	50	46	50	20	50	17	150	83	0.7%
Beauty	18	18	33	33	18	18	69	69	0.6%
Miscellaneous	50	28	50	219	50	17	150	264	2.1%
Pocket money--Lee	100	150	70	50	200	100	370	300	2.4%
Pocket money--Cindy	100	150	70	50	200	100	370	300	2.4%
TOTAL VARIABLE EXPENSES	1208	1145	1183	1605	1408	973	3799	3803	30.8%
TOTAL EXPENSES	3115	3052	3150	3654	3315	2880	9580	9586	
OVER/UNDER	38	298	3	-177	355	793	396	914	7.4%

eted amount—bringing February's total expenses to $177 over income. In March, the couple cut back variable expenses to $973, so that income exceeded total budget by almost $800.

Computerized spreadsheets can make the work of doing a formal expenditure budget much easier. Columns can be established and programmed automatically to add and subtract the figures you enter. You can also program the computerized spreadsheet—which is simply an electronic ledger page—to calculate the difference between what you intended to spend and what you spent. This calculation, called a *variance analysis*, will be made each time you enter an expenditure, thus providing a running tally for the serious budgeter. Several home-accounting software packages are also available.

Computers can simplify calculations and reorganization of your budget. So even though it may take time to turn on the computer system, boot a program, and key in data, in the long run they can save time. Especially if financial affairs are sufficiently complicated to require an accountant, computerized records can save money as well, since presenting professionals with well-organized records will lower expensive hourly fees.

The Accounts System

The accounts system can be compared to budgeting with envelopes, an old-fashioned method used when few people had checking accounts or credit cards. Every payday, the income was divided among a set of envelopes, one for each budget category. Each category's expenses were paid out of that envelope; when the envelope was empty, spending stopped in that category. Economies one month in one category might finance an extra expenditure in that category the next month, or the surplus might be siphoned off to a savings account. Of course, "borrowing" from one envelope to another might occur, but doing so consistently could ruin the budget.

If we take the labels off the envelopes and make them headings on a notebook or ledger page, we have the modern version of an envelope system—called an accounts system. Accounts kept on paper serve to divide up income as the envelopes did. Each paycheck is apportioned to the various accounts, just as you'd dole out cash from a set of envelopes. When money is spent in a particular category, the amount is subtracted from the account balance (just as with the envelope), giving a running total to serve as a corrective for further spending. Balances or deficits in an account carry over from one month to the next, allowing the same sort of flexibility that people found valuable in the old cash system.

For the couple represented in figure 6-4, this simpler method works best. In their late fifties, they have only 10 expense categories and can maintain a running sense of their expenses by category. For example, their mortgage payment is $330 a month. Each month, $330 of their total income is allocated to the "Mortgage" column. When the mortgage is paid, the amount is subtracted and the balance in that account is noted. Everything that doesn't fit one of the major categories is put in a "Miscellaneous/Remainder" category, and the couple feels free to spend liberally from this category, since savings have been taken out routinely.

Accounts Ledger

Date	Savings $200	House Expenses $55	Food $80	Utilities $55	Mortgage $330	Car Payment $150	Car Expenses $52	Medical $20	Clothes $25	Misc. Remainder
Previous Balance	10,027.17	47.53	143.21	120.11	347.31	151.70	300.67	25.25	199.88	300.50
June 12										-180.00 / 120.50
June 14 Deposit	+200. / 10,227.17	+55.00 / 102.53	+80.00 / 223.21	+55.00 / 175.11	+330.00 / 677.31	+150.00 / 301.70	+52.00 / 352.67	+20.00 / 45.25	+25.00 / 224.88	+362.16 / 482.66
June 17				-21.28 / 201.93						
June 21			-78.06 / 24.47	-133.23 / 68.70	-13.71 / 161.40	-657.74 / 19.57	-300.49 / 1.21	-27.12 / 325.55	-16.00 / 29.25		-215.69 / 266.97
June 22 Cash										-125.00 / 141.97
June 28 Deposit	+200. / 10,427.17	+55.00 / 79.47	+80.00 / 148.70	+55.00 / 216.40	+330.00 / 349.57	+150.00 / 151.21	+52.00 / 377.55	+20.00 / 49.25	+25.00 / 249.88	+281.15 / 423.12

FIGURE 6-4   Family Accounts Budget

Bank-Account Budgeting

Even a written "accounts" method may be too complicated for some people to maintain. A husband wrote *Consumer Reports*, "My wife and I have tried several budgeting methods. The more complex a budget, the quicker we'd drop it." If you have made up and dropped many budgets, the solution may lie in instituting controls through a simplified "accounts" system using more than one bank account.

Many people use bank accounts to serve two broad budget categories—current expenses and long-term investment. With a checking account for monthly bills and a money market fund for long-term goals, a single individual can do a fairly decent job of budgeting by simply depositing the planned amount to each account. Then, within the current expense account, moneys can be spent until the next deposit is made.

A slightly more complicated version of the same arrangement is needed when a couple wants to engage in informal bank-account budgeting. In addition to the current expense account for bills and the investment account, each spouse will need an individual account for personal expenses. It might seem complicated and more expensive to have four accounts, but if the couple writes discretionary spending checks on the family expense account, coordination and control will be difficult; therefore, this method may well be worth the extra effort and expense. If you establish several accounts, shop for a no-fee or interest-bearing account (see chapter 1).

This method also prevents the temptation to dip into family funds for impulse spending, and it allows each spouse a degree of control and independence.

STEP FOUR: YEAR-END REVIEW

The final step in your budgeting process is the year-end review. When a budget year is complete, add up the monthly totals by category. Then compare these totals with your annual budgeted amounts and with the previous year's expenditures. In addition, you'll want to look at the overall total of money spent and be sure annual income, not counting savings, exceeds annual expenditures.

The review provides a chance to see how you have done and to set goals for subsequent years. You may want to graph debt repayment and savings so that you can actually see the debt line fall and the savings line rise.

CLOSE-UP:
BUDGETING FOR THE UNEXPECTED

Experts recommend that you maintain an emergency reserve of from two to six months' income. Budgeting thus can help you plan for job loss, illness, or other emergencies. Set up a special contingency fund when you budget, and add to it every week or month.

Job Loss Losing a job ranks high on stress scales. In the 1970s and 1980s, layoffs in major industries and the failure of small businesses accompanied news reports of unemployment compensation "running out." Even in the midst of the economic recovery of the mid-1980s, the foreclosure rate on farms throughout the Midwest and South regularly made the headlines. Then a downturn in the economy began to spread. In the early 1990s, many high-tech and professional jobs were lost. Even large accounting and law firms laid off scores of employees. Good times may be around the corner, but, with a cyclical economy, it's wise to stay prepared for the possibility that income sources always can erode.

If you have included savings as an expense and if you have saved the requisite income, freeze that amount in an account that provides liquidity without instant (and possibly tempting) access. Where you keep the money and how much you need to shield it from your own temptation depend entirely on your own practices. Treasury bills or certificates of deposit can be used for part of the reserve. You can earn high interest and pay a penalty for early withdrawal in the event trouble occurs. The rest of this cushion can be kept in a separate interest-bearing account. (See chapters 1 and 2.)

Medical Emergencies and Accidents Setting aside money for emergencies could mean the difference between having peace of mind during a difficult period and worrying about how bills will be paid, or even losing your home and other savings.

During the past few years, many companies have entered the supplemental insurance business. But do not take on extra coverage promoted by scare tactics. If you have made steady savings, your investments—coupled with the coverage you have through

TABLE 6-4 Record-keeping

Document	Where to Keep	How Long
Canceled checks and bank statements; records of itemized deductions (interest, medical, etc.) and depreciated equipment	Current file Dead storage	One year Five years
Credit card numbers	Current file	Keep current
Contracts	Safe deposit box and lawyer	Until expiration
Household inventory	Safe deposit box and current file	Keep up to date
Insurance policies	Current file (policy number in safe deposit box)	Indefinitely for life insurance; until expiration for others
Loans and promissory notes	Current file	Until paid off
Medical records	Current file	Keep up to date

Mortgage records and home-improvement receipts	Safe deposit box and current file	As long as you own home or roll over profits into new home
Net-worth statements	Current file	Indefinitely
Personal records—birth certificates, marriage and divorce papers, military service papers	Safe deposit box	Indefinitely
Real estate deeds	Safe deposit box	Until property is sold
Receipts for major purchases	Current file	As long as you own the item
Stock or bond certificates	Safe deposit box or broker	Until sold
Tax returns	Current file Dead storage	Three years Three years or more
Vehicle titles	Safe deposit box	Until vehicle is sold or junked
Warranties	Current file	Until expiration
Will	Safe deposit box and lawyer	Indefinitely

health insurance, homeowner's insurance, and automobile insurance—should be sufficient in the event of a major medical emergency. You'd be better off putting the money you'd pay for extra insurance into your savings.

CLOSE-UP: KEEPING YOUR DOCUMENTS

As you budget, you keep better records. Your current financial papers should all be in one place, easy to get to and easy to use. When records are no longer current, you can remove them to a dead-storage file in a closet or the attic. You also need a safe place to keep important papers—a safe deposit box or at least a fireproof strongbox. A master file showing how you have arranged your records can also be useful. (See table 6-4.)

Many records eventually can be thrown away—Internal Revenue Service rules will often determine when. Only the previous three years' records can be requested by the IRS for routine audits; six years if income was significantly underreported; indefinitely if fraud is involved.

The more complex your financial affairs, the longer you should keep records. And any records related to capital improvements on your home should be saved indefinitely. You'll need them to establish how much, if anything, you owe in capital-gains tax when you sell the house. (If you move into a house of equal, or higher, value, the tax is deferred.)

CLOSE UP:
MAKING YOUR BUDGET WORK

Here are some tips that should make budgeting easier.

- Invest "extra" paychecks. If you budget on four weekly paychecks per month, every thirteenth paycheck is an "extra." If you are paid biweekly, there's an extra check every quarter. But do not treat this "extra" money as a windfall; either include it in your regular budget or invest it.
- Make impulse buying difficult. Start leaving your checkbook or credit cards at home. Deposit savings in a bank that's hard to reach.

- Pay bills when due—not before. To make the most of a minimum balance, write out the bill as soon as it comes in, but don't mail it until it's due.
- Treat "windfalls" with care. Don't trust unexpected amounts such as bonuses, tax refunds, and dividends as windfalls to be spent freely. Such money should be earmarked for special spending rather than impulse purchases.
- Make savings a regular "expense."
- Allow some expenditures that require no accounting for "fun" money or personal allowance.
- Don't try to keep track of every penny.
- Don't try to divide a couple's paychecks functionally, with one paying the mortgage and the other the auto, and so forth. Instead, pool the funds and set up a separate expense payment account and an investment account.

7

Financial Planning

Emily Card

Working out a budget (see chapter 6) is a short-term project. It involves little more than adjusting your expenditures to your income for the next year or so. Continuing the process is relatively simple because neither expenses nor income is likely to change very much in any one year. Financial planning, by contrast, is more complex. The time span it must take into account may be as long as 40 years—a period during which almost every element of your spending pattern, as well as the sources and amount of your income, will inevitably change. But, difficult though it may be, financial planning enables you to choose the changes you prefer and to prepare for those that are inevitable.

Because this seems exhausting and time consuming, many people simply neglect to do it, often with the justification that the future is unpredictable and that planning for it is a futile exercise. But the very fact that the future is to some extent unpredictable is a strong argument in favor of financial planning because a carefully worked-out plan can protect you against the contingencies, emergencies, and uncertainties that the future may hold.

No matter what may lie ahead for you, planning can enable you to use your income most effectively. It can help you to accumulate assets more rapidly, to cope with whatever emergencies may arise, to enjoy the lifestyle you prefer at various ages, and to spend your money not only on what you need but also on what you enjoy. A relatively small amount of time devoted to financial planning once a year or so can pay enormous dividends for the rest of your life— not merely in dollars but also in peace of mind during both your working years and your retirement.

Good planning involves two processes: setting your goals and arranging your finances so that these goals can be realized. A matter only you can undertake, the setting of goals is a continuous, incremental process rather than a one-time measure. Early stages are likely to be simple because you will have relatively few assets to allocate among relatively few alternatives; as you continue your planning, your sophistication about investments will inevitably grow. Eventually you may well find that your do-it-yourself planning is not only effective but actually enjoyable because it challenges you to make optimal use of limited resources.

SETTING YOUR GOALS

If you have a savings account, a life insurance policy, or a will, you have, in fact, done some financial planning, because all of these items are future-oriented. The first makes possible your plans for future spending, and the last two protect you against future contingencies. Once you understand this, you can see that financial planning is simply a more detailed and more systematic version of what you have already begun.

Anticipating Change

One of the limitations of an annual budget is that it may tempt you to believe that your current pattern of spending will continue almost indefinitely, even though the actual dollar amounts will change. This belief is totally misguided, because over the years your needs and wants, as well as your discretionary income, are likely to change.

At age 30, if you have dependents, you need enough life insurance to support them to maturity. At age 60, you usually need less because your children are more self-sufficient and your other assets have probably increased.

At age 35, because your increasing income may be taking care of your routine expenses, you may choose to invest in growth stocks in the hope that they will increase in value by the time you retire. At age 60, with your earned income less likely to increase sharply, you will probably prefer safer investments that yield generous dividends rather than those that promise growth.

At age 35, you may have to forgo travel and other recreation to meet your mortgage payments and to provide for your children's education. At age 60, however, your mortgage payments might well have terminated, your children's education will probably have been paid for, and you may take a profit by selling your home and buying a smaller one—but you may want to spend more on travel and recreation, and you may have to prepare to meet higher medical costs.

At age 25, a spouse may leave the work force to bear or rear children, and the family budget will need to be readjusted for the loss of one income. At age 40, the spouse may return to work, once again requiring a revision of the budget.

Table 7-1 provides a sample timetable that indicates some of the adjustments you might consider making at different stages of your life. Although the examples we have cited and the actions suggested in this table are fairly typical, none of them is preordained, and your own life experiences and family circumstances may follow a very different pattern. Your course may, for example, be disrupted by divorce or other changes in family structure, by a drop in earnings in middle age instead of the typical gradual increase, by a child's continuing dependence into adulthood, and by other unpredictable events. For such reasons, your plan should be as spe-

TABLE 7-1   Sample Goals and Benchmarks
at Specific Ages

20–30 Years
    Establish credit
    Open bank accounts
    Purchase health, life, and auto insurance
    Begin to formulate tax strategies
    Set aside one-tenth of income in savings
    Invest in an IRA or pension plan
    Make a will

TABLE 7-1   Sample Goals and Benchmarks
at Specific Ages (*continued*)

30–40 Years
  Purchase a primary residence
  Review net worth and analyze cash flow
  Establish children's education fund
  Review life insurance
  Formulate strategies to save on taxes
  Open a fund for emergencies
  Accumulate a reserve to start a business
  Invest discretionary income
  Budget and reorganize finances

40–50 Years
  Take stock of your assets
  Plan for income to increase and expenses to decrease
  Invest in a vacation home or income property
  Invest in tax-free vehicles such as municipal bonds
  Review and revise your will
  Plan to travel

50–65 Years
  Look for weak spots in retirement plan
  Check with Social Security on benefits
  Sell some assets and reinvest for future income
  Evaluate whether to retain your home or purchase a
    retirement home
  Think about relocating
  Review life insurance
  Check your health insurance coverage
  Consider early retirement
  Revise your will

Retirement Years
  Have adequate medical care and emergency funds
  Continue working part time if possible or necessary
  Shift assets and reinvest in income-producing vehicles
  Enjoy activities you have put off for years
  Review and finalize your will and your estate planning
  Consider establishing a living trust
  Consider ways to avoid estate taxes

cific as possible for the first three years, more general for the next five or ten, and still more tentative as it proceeds further into the future. But it should at all times reflect your personal goals and values, even if they differ radically from those of your friends or neighbors. Your aim, after all, is not just to be able to pay your bills but to have your bills represent goods and services that give you satisfaction and pleasure.

Putting It on Paper

Even when you recognize the need for financial planning, you may do little more than think about it at odd moments. But this kind of sporadic attention is more likely to culminate in a vague resolve to do something about it one of these days rather than in a specific plan. A far more effective approach is to set aside some uninterruptible time and commit your goals and their timetable to paper.

The goals you set down should be a combination of realities and dreams. If you limit yourself to the realities that your current budget dictates, you are unlikely to realize any of your dreams. But if you include your dreams, you may find ways of modifying your budgetary constraints so that you can obtain them.

As we have noted, your goals, no matter how personal, are inevitably related to your age; a young two-income couple will set up very different goals from those of a single person approaching retirement age. This is why the plan you set down must be revised every few years. Each review offers you an opportunity to check your progress, recalculate your net worth, and revise your goals accordingly.

Although planning involves thoughtful discussion with your spouse, the point at which you draft your goals is not the time for it. Each of you, separately and independently, should prepare your own draft, and then you should bring them together. Although your two sets of goals may be generally compatible, there will inevitably be some differences, major or minor, in both the timing and the goals themselves. Serious conflict can usually be resolved if both partners are committed more to finding solutions than to scoring a victory. Deft negotiation of differences may even serve to improve and enrich the plan or to make it more feasible. Successful negotiation can, for example, improve your financial situation by affecting a spouse's initial decision about entering or returning to the work force. Or it may lead to a better decision on the issue of starting up a business or taking early retirement.

ACHIEVING YOUR GOALS

Fine-Tuning Your Budget

Once you have reached agreement on your goals and their timing, your next step is to examine your current budget to see whether your spending pattern is likely to lead toward their realization, even though they may be years away. Usually some changes are necessary. If, for example, a young two-income couple plans to buy a home in five years but is currently saving nothing, both should cut down on some of their expenditures.

Although adjusting your current budget will not by itself enable you to realize your long-term goals, it will certainly move you in that direction. And if you make these adjustments periodically as your earned and unearned income increases and as some of your expenditures decrease, you will be well on your way—provided, of course, that your goals are reasonable and possible to achieve.

Calculating Your Net

Once you have made adjustments in your budget, your next step is to calculate your net worth—that is, the amount you have left after subtracting your liabilities (everything you owe at the moment) from your assets (everything you own). This simple bookkeeping procedure is illustrated in table 7-2.

Your purpose in calculating your net worth is to determine how much money you actually have, how much of it can be dedicated to the achievement of your goals, and whether that money is at all times earning as much as it can earn without undue risk.

You may discover, as many people do, that you are keeping too much money in a low-interest savings account for the sake of its liquidity. Once you realize that most of the emergencies you contemplate are covered by insurance or can be met temporarily with a credit card, you may decide to transfer your emergency fund from the savings account into a more profitable form of investment that is as liquid as a savings account but pays a higher return. Sim-

TABLE 7-2 Net Worth Worksheet

What You Own
(Assets)

Cash and Cash Equivalents	Dollar Amount
Cash on hand	_____
Cash in checking accounts	_____
Cash in savings accounts	_____
Life insurance cash value	_____
Savings bonds	_____
Money owed you	_____

Personal Property	Estimated Current Market Value
Household furnishings	_____
Special items (car, boat, jewelry, furs, antiques, tools, art, etc.)	_____
Miscellaneous personal property	_____

Real Estate	
Your house	_____
Other properties	_____

Investments	
Stocks	_____
Bonds	_____
Government securities	_____
Mutual funds	_____
Other investments	_____
Equity interest in your own business	_____
Vested interest in pension or profit sharing (money now owed you, even if you leave the firm)	_____
Keogh or IRA retirement savings	_____
TOTAL ASSETS	_____

What You Owe
(Liabilities)

Current Bills	Dollar Amount
Charge account balances	_____
Credit cards	_____
Utilities currently due	_____
Rent currently due	_____
Insurance premiums	_____
Other bills	_____

TABLE 7-2   Net Worth Worksheet (*continued*)

Amount Owed on Loans
   Mortgage _____
   Auto loan _____
   Personal loans _____
   Installment loans _____
   Life insurance loans _____

Taxes Due _____

Other _____
TOTAL LIABILITIES _____

Your Net Worth

Total assets _____

Total liabilities _____

Net worth (assets minus liabilities) _____

© Emily Card

ilarly, you may discover that you are overpaying for life insurance policies your agent assured you were a splendid investment. By changing your insurance program, you may be able to invest the overpayment more profitably.

Investing Your Liquid Assets

If your calculation of your net worth indicates that you have liquid assets distributed across a number of investments that you made at random or on impulse or for the sake of convenience—savings accounts, certificates of deposit, a mutual fund—you should set out deliberately to maximize your yield on them, in the form of dividends, appreciation, or both. This is the juncture at which many people, confused by the alternatives available and understanding little about any of them, are tempted to seek the help of a financial planner.

If your liquid assets do not amount to a substantial sum, you won't have enough to use the more sophisticated types of investments. More important, no investment counselor or stockbroker will welcome you as a client because the commissions to be earned on your small account will be negligible. At this point, your best plan might be to put the money into one or two conventional investments—a money market fund or a certificate of deposit— and, while it grows through further deposits and interest payments, to familiarize yourself with the basic principles of investing and the various alternatives open to investors. Since no adviser, broker, or investment company has been able to demonstrate consistent outstanding performance over the long term, you may be encouraged to undertake a do-it-yourself investment program.

Managing your own investments does require you to apply yourself and to monitor them closely and regularly. Here again, people with neither the time for this nor a head for figures may consider delegating responsibility to a "professional" financial planner.

During the past several years, the proliferation of investment opportunities—life insurance, annuities, mutual funds, certificates of deposit, and a confusing variety of securities—has led to a parallel growth in the population of professional planners. Unlike medicine or law, this profession is almost entirely unregulated, and in many states virtually anyone can adopt the label of financial planner, no matter how flimsy his or her qualifications.

Financial planning has become a popular occupation because the incomes of many planners include not only the fees their clients pay but also the commissions from the various financial products they incorporate into their client's plans. Planners who work for financial institutions that market a wide variety of products and who earn commissions on sales of those products stand to make more money by steering you toward investments that reap them commissions. An informed consumer can almost certainly find for himself or herself better financial products at a lower cost than the ones sold by a planner whose income derives partly or wholly from commissions.

Planners who are unconnected with any institution and rely entirely on clients' fees are more likely to be unbiased, but you pay for protection against bias in the form of more expensive hourly charges.

If your income is in the middle range, an affordable and reliable planner may be hard to find. Until recently, financial planning was used only by the very rich, and consequently many of the most experienced and sophisticated planners are accustomed to dealing with sums of money far beyond the dreams of the people who are now seeking their services. Some of these planners refuse to deal with people with annual incomes of less than $100,000. Others cater to those with incomes of $25,000 to $90,000, but this range is so broad that only the most exceptional planner is likely to serve the needs of every client who falls within it equally effectively. Some firms attempt to resolve this difficulty by providing computer-generated plans that are activated by the financial information the individual inputs. These are generally without value.

For the consumer, then, using a "professional" financial planner usually involves a choice between a luxurious service for millionaires and financial products marketers with misleading titles.

In fact, few people need a financial planner. Setting goals, revising them as needed, and investing assets according to sound principles (see chapters 17 through 22) is safer and more sensible for most families.

CLOSE-UP:
REGULATING FINANCIAL PLANNERS

Despite the phenomenal growth of financial planning services and the enormous influence that planners can exert over the investment of their clients' resources, there is virtually no enforced national regulation of the industry or any uniform system of earning credentials. Indeed, there is no agreement about either the functions of a planner or the training needed to perform them responsibly.

As concern mounts about the growth of the industry in both size and influence, a number of governmental and private groups—Congress, the Securities and Exchange Commission, and some industry organizations—are looking at ways of regulating it with a view to protecting the clients. At least one substantial bill to regulate the profession was wending its way through Congress in 1991. However, as of the summer of that year, no federal standards had been set. A number of states, however, have established a variety of laws governing the regulation of financial planners within their borders.

Meanwhile, the professional preparation of financial planners leaves much to be desired, especially when compared to the far more rigorous preparation of lawyers and accountants. The Institute for Certified Financial Planners awards the title of Certified Financial Planner to anyone completing the series of correspondence courses—equivalent to about six semester courses at the upper undergraduate level—offered by the College for Financial Planning in Denver. The American College, in Bryn Mawr, Pennsylvania, offers the title of Chartered Financial Consultant to those who complete its series of courses. Whether training of this sort equips a planner to cope with any but the simplest planning issues is an open question, and many potential clients who have completed the exercises in this chapter may find sounder and less biased advice from an accountant or an attorney experienced in financial matters.

8

Credit Rating

Emily Card

If you are steadily employed and you manage your money sensibly, you probably devote no more thought to your credit rating than you do to your car's spare tire. But because you may need it unexpectedly—for getting a credit card, raising the limits on the one you have, or applying for a personal loan or a mortgage—you should make sure it provides potential creditors with accurate information about your creditworthiness. Your rating is especially important if you have moved to a new community or if you are a married, divorced, or separated woman seeking credit in your own name.

A credit rating is essentially a record of your past performance in paying your bills. If your record is consistently good, automobile dealers, mortgage lenders, department stores, and others who sell on credit will assume that your future performance will be equally reliable. But there are several reasons why some people's performance may be far better than their credit rating reflects. If you have been paying your creditors conscientiously but your application for a charge account is rejected because you have no credit rating or a poor one, there are, as we shall see, a number of steps that you can take to make certain your credit rating accurately reflects your credit history.

HOW CREDIT RATINGS ARE BUILT

If you have ever had to fill out an application for a department store charge account or a credit card, you have probably diligently answered the numerous questions about your age, income, employment, length of residence in the community, and so forth. But processing this application by verifying every one of your answers is far too expensive a procedure for the potential creditor. Instead, the creditor sends your name to the credit bureau to which the company subscribes and obtains, in response, your credit report (see p. 142). Indeed, some retailers that advertise "instant credit" have a computer link with the credit bureau that allows them to call up your credit report on their screen in a matter of seconds.

The likelihood of your getting the credit you need depends, then, not only on your past bill-paying record or on the potential creditor's willingness to trust you but also on the record—or lack of one—you have built in the files of the credit bureau.

The credit bureau's file begins with your demographic characteristics, most recording only your Social Security number, birthdate, and address. Some keep more extensive information, such as your age, education, and marital status.

Unlike the Dun and Bradstreet credit ratings of corporations, which take the form of a letter grade, your credit report consists simply of an ongoing financial biography, built on data provided by the credit bureau's subscribers—the department stores, banks, and other establishments where you use credit. These subscribers report back to the credit bureau regularly on how punctually you pay your bills and on your current indebtedness. A potential creditor receiving a copy of your report makes decisions on the basis of what this record shows and on individualized criteria or a credit score.

Your record, however, may be distorted by several factors. First, there is the matter of accuracy. Because credit bureau reports are entirely computerized, the kind of ridiculous error that a human being would detect immediately may pass unnoticed into your permanent record. In addition, a bill you have legally refused to pay because of a dispute over the quality of the goods or services it represents may be illegally reported to the credit bureau as a nonpayment. Moreover, if you are a married woman, much of your credit performance may be reported under your husband's name, even though the Equal Credit Opportunity Act makes this practice illegal.

More important, a large proportion of your bill-paying activity is never reported because your creditors are not subscribers to the credit bureau. Among the bills that are unlikely to be reported are your telephone and utility bills, your rent payments, your medical and dental bills, and similar routine payments for which you have been extended short-term or long-term credit. Hence, your faithful payment of these bills will not enhance your credit report. Court actions—suits, judgments, and liens—may or may not show up on your report, because the credit bureau is not routinely notified about them but must check them individually.

Mortgage payments are increasingly being reported to credit bureaus and more and more lenders themselves are relying on credit reports. (They also look at income and your previous mortgage performance.)

The information most likely to appear on your report comes from bank cards such as MasterCard and Visa, charge accounts at national department stores such as Sears and J. C. Penney, and some travel and entertainment (T&E) cards, such as Diners Club. (When you are short of cash, paying the minimum due on these bills should receive top priority so that you can preserve your credit rating.)

Despite the possibility of error and distortion, the system leaves you—the pivotal figure in credit transactions—with little control over what goes on.

The credit bureau derives both its income and its information from subscribers. It will sell you credit information about yourself, but takes no responsibility beyond what is required by federal law for the accuracy of the information it maintains on you—even though misinformation can have serious consequences for you. Moreover, false credit records can be difficult and time consuming to correct. (See page 133 for information on how to request changes.)

Such incorrect information is alarmingly common. A Consumers Union Report in 1991 demonstrated that 48 percent of the credit reports it reviewed were inaccurate in some way. Moreover, nearly one out of five contained a significant inaccuracy, of the sort that could prevent an individual from getting deserved credit.

Such problems with accuracy led the House Banking Committee to hold hearings in 1991 to consider tightening the Fair Credit Reporting Act of 1970, which governs the bureaus.

Some consumer advocates are also concerned about the issue of privacy as it relates to credit bureaus. At present, virtually any potential creditor—or anyone able to provide credentials which appear to fit into that category—can obtain your credit records. As a result, consumer advocates have recommended that individuals should be able to state, in advance, who may get access to their credit records.

What's more, Consumers Union has recommended that consumers get easier access to their own data than is currently the case. CU has proposed that consumers get yearly access to all their reports without charge.

A credit bureau does not actually score your credit performance. That chore is left to the individual potential creditors, who interpret the record sent by credit bureaus according to criteria that matter most to each. A mortgage lender, for instance, looks at your mortgage-to-income ratio to determine whether a monthly mortgage payment will be in the range of 25 to 30 percent of your gross monthly income. Issuers of charge and bank cards use formalized scoring systems designed to take the guesswork out of granting credit.

Creating scoring systems is a multimillion-dollar business, and such systems are custom tailored for each creditor. While the components that make up this score, the weight that each is given, and the "passing" score are closely guarded industry secrets, table 8-1 provides a general approximation of how a typical scoring system works.

Although federal law requires the scoring system to be race- and gender-neutral, the neutrality is not perfect. For example, the scoring for length of employment is likely to disadvantage women whose employment may be interrupted by child rearing.

As table 8-1 illustrates, the score is composed of a number of items, some of which will counterbalance others. A move to a new

TABLE 8-1   Credit Scoring

Characteristics

Have home phone	+36
Own your residence	+34
Indebtedness	−12
Have bank credit card	+29
Have checking or savings account	+13
Have checking and savings account	+19

Occupation

Professionals and officials	+27
Technicians and managers	+ 5
Proprietors	− 3
Clerical and sales workers	+12
Craftsmen and nonfarm laborers	0
Foremen and operators	+26
Service workers	+14
Farmworkers	+ 3

Age

30 or under	+ 6
Over 30 to 40	+11
Over 40 to 50	+ 8
Over 50	+16

Years on Job

Less than 5	0
5 to 15	+6
More than 15	+18

community or a new job can damage your rating, but other factors may bolster it. For example, a university professor who moves to a new job in a new community may get a low years-on-the-job score, but his or her occupational status will earn a far higher score than a lab technician in the same position. An executive is likely to get a higher score than a salesman, even though both of them may be renters rather than homeowners.

DEALING WITH THE CREDIT BUREAU

Most people who have an unjustifiably negative credit report discover it only when their application for further credit is rejected. You can avoid an unpleasant surprise by checking up on the current status of your report before you intend to make a credit application. Although the law requires credit bureaus to disclose your report to you, getting it may require some persistence.

To begin with, you need to identify the bureau or bureaus that maintain reports on you. This is not easy, because no single credit bureau dominates the national market. Three large companies are national in scope. Trans Union Credit Information Company has five regional offices around the United States. The company suggests you look its name up in your local yellow pages under credit bureaus to find the appropriate one for you. Addresses for the other two are:

TRW Information Services
Attention: Consumer Assistance
P.O. Box 749029
Dallas, Texas 75374-9029
(214) 235-1200, ext. 251

Equifax Credit Information Services
P.O. Box 4091
Atlanta, Georgia 30302
(404) 885-8000

There are also hundreds of small firms that concentrate on local markets. Your best plan is to ask your bank or a local merchant for the names of the major credit bureaus that serve your area. If these turn out to be one or two of the major firms, you can consult the telephone directory or write to the national headquarters for the addresses of the local offices.

Credit bureaus are required by federal law to allow you to *see* a copy of your report, but they are not obligated to provide you with a copy unless your state law requires it (although most do in practice). They are entitled to charge you for a copy (a fee usually under $25), but if you have been denied credit on the basis of the report within the previous 30 days, the charge must be waived. If the bureau is not required to provide a written copy, make an appointment to see your report. You are entitled to take along one other person—as an adviser or for moral support.

Once you have called the bureau to determine the fee, you can usually order a copy of your report by using the form shown in figure 8-1 or by writing a letter that includes your Social Security number, any other names you have used, and your addresses for the previous five years. Although credit bureaus claim that they process these requests promptly, people seeking this information report that there have been long delays. If you get no response within 10 days or so, send a copy of your letter with the notation Second Request.

It should be noted that the major credit bureaus now do have additional services that you can purchase for a fee. These may include credit tips, increased access to your credit reports, analyses of your financial standing, or easier-to-read versions of the credit report.

Such services are probably unnecessary to most people, but may be beneficial to those whose credit files are problematic—someone whose name is very common, for example, is a junior, or has been the victim of fraud.

Interpreting Your Report

Credit reports do not make easy reading; designed for computer processing, they are cluttered with abbreviations and symbols that you can decipher only by scrutinizing the fine print on the back of the form. (See p. 142 for a sample report and its interpretation.)

Once you understand the code, you can see that the report will record any delinquency in paying an account (balance due and amount past due), the credit limit for each of your accounts, the date on which each account was most recently updated, and similar information relevant to your current financial condition. Some credit reports are updated monthly; others are not.

If your report reflects a history of regular payments and no financial delinquencies, it is in good order and you need do nothing further. If it is negative as a consequence of errors or omissions, you will need to take further steps.

FIGURE 8-1   Sample Credit Report Order

Your Name

Address

City, State, Zip

Date

XYZ Credit Bureau

Address

City, State, Zip

Dear Sir or Madam:

Please send me a copy of my credit profile. Following is

the pertinent information:

Name: _____

Social Security: _____

Birthdate: _____

Present Residence: _____

_____

Past Residences (the last five years): _____

_____

_____

Signature

Check one:

— Check enclosed

— I have been denied credit within the past 30 days as a

result of information from your credit file.

132

Correcting Reporting Errors

If an error has been made either by the credit bureau or by one of your creditors, the Fair Credit Reporting Act requires that it be corrected. But since the bureau relies on the reports of your creditors, any error for which a creditor is responsible must be rectified not by the bureau but by the creditor.

Once you have identified the error—for example, a failure to report a payment that you made, or a charge for merchandise that you never received or was not what you ordered—you must deal with the creditor responsible for it. Your request for correction, which must be made within 60 days of your receipt of the bill, should specify that you are writing under the provisions of the Fair Credit Reporting Act—or, for billing errors, the Fair Credit Billing Act, which requires the creditor to respond within two billing cycles or, at most, 90 days. (See figure 8-2.) If you receive no response within this time limit, your follow-up letter or telephone call should point out that the delay has placed the creditor in violation of the law.

Your rights to withhold payment for defective merchandise purchased with a nonmerchant card such as a bank or T&E card are somewhat more limited. The charge must be at least $50, and the purchase must have been made in your own state or within 100 miles of your home. If the dispute is settled in your favor, you owe no interest on the payment you withheld. If the merchant's view prevails, however, you are liable for the interest.

PROBLEMS ENCOUNTERED BY WOMEN

Although most young single women, having entered the financial arena in an era of credit equality, readily recognize the need for a satisfactory credit report, many older married women do not. Even a happily married woman should have a credit report in her own name because of the possibility, no matter how remote, of divorce, and because of the statistical probability that her husband will die before she does.

Before the passage of the Equal Credit Opportunity Act, women were subject to considerable discrimination—generally on the grounds that pregnancy might interfere with their income from employment, that their employment history was irregular, or that

FIGURE 8-2   Sample Letter to Credit Managers

Your Name

Address

City, State, Zip

Date

Credit Manager

Company Name of Creditor

Address

City, State, Zip

Dear Sir or Madam:

    I'm writing under the provisions of the Fair Credit Billing Act to request that you correct your entry in my file at the XYZ Credit Bureau. The entry incorrectly states that I was late paying my account when in fact the monthly bills reflect a perfect payment record.

    Please make this correction and confirm same to me within 90 days as required by law.

Signature

divorce or widowhood would reduce their incomes. Although it is now illegal, sex discrimination still exists to some extent. A loan officer may, for example, tactfully steer a woman away from one kind of loan application on the grounds that a rejection would look bad on her record. Of course, if she fails to apply, she will not get the loan, but if she applies and is denied a loan, her rejection becomes part of the statistics that the federal agencies monitor for evidence of sex discrimination.

Nevertheless, the Equal Credit Opportunity Act has made credit more accessible to women in several ways. For example, earnings from part-time employment, pensions or other retirement income, and alimony or child support payments must be counted as income that meets the potential creditor's criterion (although with respect to alimony and child support, the creditor is permitted to check on the financial stability of the ex-spouse). In addition, after age 62, age may not be used negatively as a factor for the granting of credit—a rule especially important to widows.

Many married women discover, when applying for credit, that no record exists in their own names. Although the Equal Credit Opportunity Act has required creditors to maintain separate reporting for each person's credit activities since 1977, this rule is frequently disregarded, and a woman's credit activities are still reported in her husband's name only—a problem commonly encountered by people who were married prior to the 1977 change. When a couple applies for a credit card that both of them expect to use, they usually apply for it *jointly*, with both parties responsible for the debt and hence both entitled to a credit report reflecting their payments. Too often, however, the records are maintained in the husband's name alone.

In such circumstances, you can send the form shown in figure 8-3 to each of your creditors when you next pay their bills. Once your creditors have complied with your requests, you should check your credit report again to make certain that the corrections have in fact been entered.

In connection with credit card reporting, the Equal Opportunity Credit Act created an additional category for reporting a spouse's participation, that of "user." This category was designed to help women who do not enjoy joint accounts. If you use cards but your use is not reported, ask the creditor to do so. The law defines "use" as charging on an account or paying the bill.

FIGURE 8-3   Sample Credit Reporting Request

Your Name

Address

City, State, Zip

Date

Credit Manager

Company Name of Creditor

Address

City, State, Zip

Dear Credit Manager:

    Please report all information concerning the account

listed below in both of our names, as provided for by the

Equal Credit Opportunity Act, Regulation B.

Name: _____

Spouse's Name: _____

Name in which account is listed (name on the billing

statement): _____

Account Number: _____

                         _____

                         Signature of either spouse

Often a wife who holds a joint account (and hence is fully legally liable) is listed only as a "user," a lesser category of involvement. If you are the holder of a card, not just a user, make sure your report says so.

If you were married before 1977, when the Equal Credit Opportunity Act was passed, your credit activities may still be reflected in your husband's report and you may have little or nothing reported under your own name. The following checklist shows the steps you can take to ensure that you have a credit history of your own:

- Have a bank account in your name.
- Check your credit report.
- Ask that all credit you use be reported in your given name and surname: "Lizzie Butler," not "Mrs. Bill Butler."
- Obtain at least one bank card (MasterCard or Visa) in your own name—Lizzie Butler, not "Mrs. Bill Butler."
- If you are not married but plan to be, consider leaving your credit in your own last name because many women discover that linking their financial identity to that of their husband leads to trouble later.
- If you are married now but your marriage is not secure, consider building a separate credit identity in your birth name (maiden name) now. The law provides for your right to credit in your birth name if you so choose, and having credit of your own will make separation or divorce, if necessary, easier.

IF YOU ARE AT FAULT

An unfavorable credit report is relatively easy to correct if the credit bureau or a creditor made an error. But if you are at fault— by having been delinquent on your payments, for example—the process may be more difficult. In that case, you have two options. First, if you have paid the overdue amount, you can ask the creditor to notify the credit bureau that your delinquency has been rectified. Second, you are entitled by law to write a 100-word comment explaining the reason for the delinquency. This comment, which will appear in your credit report in the future, should offer an explanation that is likely to be acceptable—loss of job, for example, or business failure, illness, or a death in the family. Marital problems should probably not be included, because there is some evidence that discrimination against divorced persons still exists, although the law prohibits it.

The law specifies that negative information must be removed after 7 years (or 10 in the case of bankruptcy). If your more recent performance is satisfactory, past delinquencies, especially if they are accompanied by your explanatory comment, may not discourage potential creditors. And if you are applying for credit, offering an explanation in advance or forewarning your creditor about past problems may offset his or her negative reaction to your unfavorable credit report.

IF YOU ARE DENIED CREDIT

Credit is not an inalienable right, and every creditor is permitted to establish company guidelines for extending credit provided they are nondiscriminatory and in compliance with federal regulations. The Federal Reserve Board [Regulation B, Sect. 202.9(b)(2)] lists the following as the lawful grounds on which you may be denied credit:

- Credit application incomplete
- Insufficient credit references
- Unable to verify credit references
- Temporary or irregular employment
- Unable to verify employment
- Length of employment
- Insufficient income
- Excessive obligations
- Unable to verify income
- Inadequate collateral
- Too short a period of residence
- Temporary residence
- Unable to verify residence
- No credit file
- Delinquent credit obligations
- Garnishment, attachment, foreclosure, repossession, or suit
- Bankruptcy

· We do not grant credit to any applicant on the terms and conditions you may request

If your application for credit is rejected on the grounds of your past performance, you may be tempted by classified advertisements or direct-mail solicitations that promise to get you a credit card or to clean up your credit report in return for a fee. The "credit" card promised in the advertisements is actually a secured card. A secured card requires you to put a deposit in the bank equal to your credit line. Your deposit will be frozen as long as you have the account. Such cards are a legitimate alternative for those who have lost their credit, but not if they are obtained through a newspaper ad. Many people have paid deposits only to learn later that their funds have disappeared. Companies that pledge to clean up your credit report fulfill that promise by filing a false claim that all the negative information in your credit report is incorrect. In theory, you can apply for a credit card while the negative entries on your credit report are removed for review. In practice, however, this ploy is unlikely to work, because when your creditors review your report, as they do periodically, the negative information will reappear as soon as it is found to be correct. And, although you may obtain temporary use of a credit card, you may have engaged in acts that could potentially be construed as fraudulent.

Many companies that offer special services to persons without credit prey on consumer fears. Unless the firm promising a debit card is highly reputable, proceed with extreme caution. Steer clear of credit rating "fix it" firms altogether. Otherwise, you may pay exorbitant rates and receive little or no actual help.

A more effective way to enjoy credit when your rating is poor is to obtain a secured credit card, or debit card, from a bank or brokerage house (see pp. 57–58). Under this arrangement, you deposit a certain amount of money in the bank as a form of collateral and are issued a card with a line of credit not exceeding the amount you have on deposit.

Many individuals, however, may be denied credit even though their financial condition is exemplary. People who have lived overseas for a number of years may be turned down simply because they have no recent credit history. People who move frequently may have fragmentary credit reports in credit bureaus in various parts of the country. For such people, credit credentialing may be of help (see p. 143), but before using it they should avail themselves of their significant rights under federal legislation.

The Equal Credit Opportunity Act, although it was intended to eliminate credit discrimination against women and minorities, serves to protect all applicants. A major part of the law flatly prohibits discrimination. While recognizing a creditor's right to decide who is creditworthy and who is not, the law requires that the decision be made without regard to sex, marital status, color, race, religion, or national origin. Age cannot be used except in certain carefully prescribed circumstances, and after age 62 it can only be counted positively.

The law entitles every credit applicant to a response within 30 days of the application date. This requirement is intended to discourage reluctant creditors from withholding credit simply by not responding to the application.

Because the law spells out acceptable reasons for a creditor's adverse action (see list on p. 138), a creditor may not tell you simply that you failed on a credit scoring system. If you are denied credit or if you are offered less credit than you applied for, the potential creditor must either specify the reason or tell you that you have a right to know it. In the latter case, you have the right to file a request for the reason within 60 days, and the creditor must respond within 30 days. All the creditor is legally required to provide is one of the 20 or so general reasons approved by the Federal Reserve Board.

On the other hand, if your personal circumstances are such that you are unlikely to meet most of the criteria of the scoring system (see table 8-1) but are otherwise qualified, you may be able to persuade a potential creditor to evaluate you on a personal rather than a bureaucratic basis.

Some creditors attempt to discourage marginal applicants by suggesting that too many inquiries to the credit bureau will look bad on a credit report. Although a large number of inquiries may lead creditors to suspect that you are overextending yourself, rejections are not recorded as such, and inquiries more than six months or a year old, depending on the bureau, are dropped from your report.

CLOSE-UP:
A SAMPLE CONSUMER CREDIT REPORT

Figure 8-4 illustrates how to read a credit report. In this sample, the name has been changed and all other details have been simplified.

Going from left to right across Mrs. Jones's report, you will first see a column headed Account Performance. In this column, one of three abbreviations is used: POS for positive, NEG for negative, or NON for not evaluated. Note that Mrs. Jones had no problems with her department store account, so the account performance shows POS.

In the next column to the right, under the creditor name, which in this case is F. C. Bradfords, a department store, is the abbreviation CURR ACCT, for current account. This simply indicates that the account is still active and has not been closed.

To the right again, we see the date, 5/89, which is the date on which the account was last reported. The next date, 10/78, refers to the month and year the account was first opened. To the creditor reading this report, this information indicates that the account has been open for approximately 10 years and that the last information received on it was in May 1989.

Under the next column, TYPE OF ACCOUNT, you will see the abbreviation REV, which stands for revolving; this describes the type of charge account Mrs. Jones enjoys at the department store. Next, the AMOUNT column shows the charge amount authorized and BALANCE shows what is owed now—nothing.

The next column is divided into BALANCE DATE and AMOUNT PAST DUE. These are of particular interest to you because if you have ever been late in paying an account, it is here that the details of the delinquency will be recorded.

Assuming there were no other entries in Mrs. Jones's report (which would make it shorter than the normal report of a credit-active consumer), her overall performance is positive. While there is no rating per se, she shows timely payment of her bills over the previous 12 months and the account itself is ranked positive.

Had Mrs. Jones not paid her bills on time, eventually the report would have reflected that fact. Although being one month behind

FIGURE 8-4   Sample Credit Report

Mrs. Jane Jones
1100 Sample Blvd.
Anytown, U.S.A.

PAGE	DATE								
1	6-01-89	MRS. JONES				12-345678/9			

ACCOUNT PER-FORMANCE			CREDITOR NAME			TYPE OF ACCOUNT					
POS	NON	NEG	STATUS COMMENT	STATUS DATE	DATE OPENED	TERMS	AMOUNT	BALANCE	BALANCE DATE	AMOUNT PAST DUE
A			F C BRADFORDS							
			CURR ACCT	5-89	10-78	REV	$200	0.00	5-25-89	
---	---	---	-END							

Confidential

will not necessarily affect a person's standing, repeated lateness or lateness stretching beyond a month will begin to erode a good standing.

Any married person reviewing a credit report (especially a woman) should check to see whether accounts on which he or she is a user are also reported. Remember, in addition to the standard designations of individual and joint accounts, the Equal Credit Opportunity Act provides for the creation of a user designation. This category was added to give a married person (usually a woman) credit for accounts used regularly even if the account is actually recorded in the spouse's name. Some credit reports have a separate column to indicate the user category, or the category is denoted by a code.

CLOSE-UP:
CREDIT REPORT CHECKLIST

1. Find major credit bureau(s) in your area.
2. Order your credit report or go see it.
3. If married, order your spouse's report.
4. Review the report for errors.
5. If accounts are missing from your report for reasons other than marital status, including a recent move, ask the credit reporting bureau whether you can pay a fee and have them added. There's no legal provision for this, so it will be up to the discretion of individual credit bureaus.
6. Review the report for omissions of joint and user accounts or accounts for which you are liable by virtue of state property laws. Residents of community-property states are liable for their spouse's accounts, so they should make sure both accounts appear on a report.
7. Request that credit managers of each account make corrections and additions. Use the "Sample Letter to Credit Managers" shown in figure 8-2 as a guide.
8. Recheck your credit report after 90 days to see whether your request was honored. If not, remind creditors they are in violation of the Fair Credit Reporting Act for not responding in "a reasonable amount of time," and of the Equal Credit

Opportunity Act, Regulation B, Sect. 202.10(a) if marital accounts aren't reported as requested.

9. If creditors refuse to adjust past negative reports, insert your 100-word "consumer comment" explaining your side of the situation (see p. 140).

9

Bankruptcy

Emily Card

BANKRUPTCY:
PROTECTION FROM CREDITORS

Bankruptcy is a legal state in which:

1. Your responsibility for repaying certain debts is at least temporarily suspended while you and a bankruptcy trustee work out a plan for meeting all or part of your credit obligations.
2. Your liability for certain debt obligations may be limited to an amount significantly smaller than the actual amount of debt you owe, and you may be freed from repaying certain debts.
3. You repay some or all debt obligations according to the repayment plan worked out by you, the court, and the trustee—either out of sale of your assets or from income after living expenses.

When you borrow money, you normally enter into a contractual agreement in which the terms of the loan, including the manner and time in which the money is to be repaid, are spelled out. If you fail to live up to the terms of the loan contract—as you might when you have more debts than income to pay them with—the lender can file a lawsuit against you to make you repay the debt in whatever way possible. (A successful suit against you may also make you liable for damages and legal costs.) To repay the debt, you may be forced to sell assets you own.

When you file for bankruptcy, the bankruptcy court temporarily halts the lender's legal actions. This is one of the first protections from creditors that bankruptcy provides. (Several other protections afforded by bankruptcy will be explained shortly.)

Bankruptcy law has its roots in eighteenth-century England, where laws allowed bankruptcy as an alternative to debtors' prison. With the Bankruptcy Act of 1841, voluntary bankruptcy became part of U.S. law.

The first U.S. bankruptcy laws were written with creditors, not debtors, in mind. The intent of these laws was to ensure that the creditors had an equal chance of being paid in the event that the debtor had insufficient assets to pay off his or her debts in full. But the focus of bankruptcy law, as well as collection laws such as the Fair Debt Collection Practices Act, has moved toward protection of the debtor by barring creditors from harassing uncooperative debtors.

In 1978 the Bankruptcy Reform Act broadened the debtor's exemptions—those assets exempt from sale to repay debt in bankruptcy—making bankruptcy more advantageous to consumers. The law allowed state bankruptcy laws either to follow their own exemption rules or to follow the more liberal federal system. Even states that opted out of the federal system, though, broadened their exemption rules. You should fully understand both state and federal bankruptcy laws and their differences, for the system under which you file may have a major impact on how much of your assets you can retain.

The 1978 legislation also gave debtors more power to keep creditors at arm's length by broadening the rules regarding automatic stays—actions that freeze any attempt by creditors to seize property of the bankrupt person(s).

Finally, reform removed some of the discredit previously attached to bankruptcy, which had been considered an embarrassing last resort that told the world you couldn't handle your finances. Now, bankruptcy is viewed in slightly more positive terms. The Bankruptcy Reform Act, for example, changed some wording to identify the petitioner as "the debtor" rather than as "the bankrupt" in order to promote the idea that bankruptcy is a chance for a fresh start. Consequently, bankruptcy carries less of a stigma than it used to, although inquiries about past bankruptcies are still made regarding everything from purchasing a house to adopting a child.

In 1984, Congress amended the laws again, taking back some of the gains debtors had made six years earlier. A debtor who declares so-called Chapter 13 bankruptcy must now devote all of his or her excess earnings to pay off debts. Rules for other types of personal bankruptcy were revised to eliminate abuses.

Despite the changes in 1984, bankruptcy is still more attractive than it was before 1978. That, creditors claim, has led to an explosion in bankruptcy filings. In 1978, 172,414 nonbusiness bankruptcy petitions were filed; by 1990, the number had climbed to 718,107—more than a 300 percent jump.

Lenders must also share responsibility for the rise in bankruptcies because banks and other creditors—eager to take advantage of high loan interest rates in the late 1970s and early 1980s—added as many loans to their portfolios as possible. As a result, consumer debt has risen dramatically over the past several years. In December, 1990, total consumer debt (including mortgages) stood at $3.3 trillion—up 154 percent from $1.3 trillion in 1980.

In 1970, about half of all American families were in debt of some kind. By 1984, the number reporting that they owed money in the Consumer Expenditure Interview Survey was 58.5 percent, and in 1989, it was up to 60.3 percent. Individual consumer debt outstanding (not including mortgages) now averages $7,660 per household. Not surprisingly, the ease with which many people have received credit has created the opportunity for more people to receive too much credit.

Further eroding the argument that more liberal bankruptcy laws are the sole cause of more bankruptcies is the fact that most Americans in financial trouble do not run to the courthouse to find a solution. At any given time, as much as 10 percent of our population is overextended with debt or unable to keep bills current. Many reduce their debt by simply cutting back their spending and paying off their bills.

Lenders and bankruptcy lawyers also know that most bankruptcies are triggered by unemployment, divorce, catastrophic illness, or business failure. In such cases, a reasonable amount of debt quickly becomes too much debt in times of crisis. Problems with the U.S. economy in the late 1970s and early 1980s obviously created increases in unemployment and business failures, making conditions ripe for more bankruptcies. The high incidence of divorce in the United States has also caused more bankruptcy.

While the laws make bankruptcy more attractive, the evidence seems to suggest that people in legitimate need—not opportunists—make up the bulk of those debtors who end up in bankruptcy court.

As valuable and sometimes necessary as bankruptcy can be, it should be explored very carefully before being undertaken. It is important to consider both negative and positive aspects of such a step.

Although it should never be considered an easy way out, for the consumer who feels overwhelmed by the burden of debt, bankruptcy offers relief from persistent creditors and allows a debtor to avoid total financial ruin and begin anew. For debtors who own homes, bankruptcy may preserve their equity. It may also prevent any garnishment of wages or other income once the petition is filed.

On the negative side, a bankruptcy is recorded in your credit file for 10 years and may affect your ability to obtain credit in the future; even after the ten years, many potential creditors ask whether you have ever filed for bankruptcy. Obviously, creditors prefer that debtors pay back what they owe in accordance with their loan agreements. However, bankruptcy means that the creditor will usually recover at least part of what is owed through the liquidation of the debtor's assets. That, at least, is preferable to recovering nothing.

PERSONAL BANKRUPTCY

Most consumer bankruptcies have fallen under Chapter 7 or Chapter 13 of the Bankruptcy Code. In mid-1991, the Supreme Court also permitted Chapter 11 to be used by some—in the past, it was primarily a corporate device. The chapter a consumer chooses will be determined by income, the property owned (whether it is exempt or nonexempt from asset liquidation) and the type of debts owed (secured or unsecured). In a Chapter 7 bankruptcy, the debtor's assets are liquidated to pay creditors. By contrast, in a Chapter 13 or Chapter 11 bankruptcy, the debtor must adhere to a court-approved budget; creditors are paid only what is left over from that budget and cannot take the debtor's assets.

In a Chapter 7 or "straight bankruptcy," the most widely used form, debtors are freed from their obligations if they agree to relinquish most of their assets. The assets are liquidated by a court-appointed trustee, and money from the sale is then used to pay off creditors' claims. Secured debtholder claims—those with property as collateral—are paid first. If any money remains after that, unsecured debtholders are paid proportionally, based on the percentage they hold of the bankrupt's total unsecured debt. A Chapter 7 bankruptcy is filed for people without any income, with debt too high to qualify for Chapter 13, or with few assets. However, neither Chapter 7 nor 13 can be filed more frequently than once every seven years.

Under a Chapter 13 filing, the debtor agrees to pay back part of what he or she owes over a three-year period following a court-ordered plan that is adminstered by a court-appointed bankruptcy trustee. After that period, remaining debts are discharged (or forgiven), thus effectively limiting what the debtor actually pays. The plan requires payment only from disposable income left after living expenses are met. Thus, if a debtor's allowable living expenses (those expenses determined by the debtor's previous standard of living) are $1,800 a month and net income is $1,900 a month, only the remaining $100 a month will be distributed among all the creditors each month for three years. The courts will "discharge" or dismiss the rest of the debt after three years. Up to a total of $100,000 in unsecured debts could, for example, be dismissed with only $3,600 paid.

To file under Chapter 13, a consumer must have an income, either from employment or from self-employment. There are also limitations on the amount of debt a person can owe. You cannot file under Chapter 13 if you and your spouse have more than $100,000 of *unsecured* debts (such as credit card debts) or more than $350,000 of *secured* debts (such as a mortgage). For amounts exceeding these, you would file under Chapter 11. Chapter 13 is used by debtors who have a large number of nonexempt assets—

those that would have to be sold off in a Chapter 7 filing. The debtor can keep nonexempt property in a Chapter 13 bankruptcy, although he or she may be required to pay off the creditor for the present value of the property.

A Chapter 13 may be used to stop the repossession of a car or foreclosure on a house. Some debts that are not dischargeable under Chapter 7 may be forgiven under Chapter 13—primarily, student loans more than five years old that the court deems would be an excessive burden for the debtor, and tax obligations more than three years old.

Consult an attorney to find out which type of bankruptcy would apply to you. Any consumer seriously considering bankruptcy should obtain legal help if at all possible before taking this serious step.

AVOIDING BANKRUPTCY

Since a large proportion of your debts, depending on their type, may be nondischargeable (in other words, you will have to pay them back in spite of bankruptcy), it may be wise to avoid bankruptcy. But if your debt burden becomes so great it inhibits your ability to earn a living or to keep your health, then filing is the right course of action. To make that decision, you must first assess your situation.

Make a list of all your debts, including the total balance due, the monthly payments, and due dates for monthly payments. Then draw up a list of your assets, including income, property owned, dividends, cash surrender value of insurance policies, and so forth.

After you have completed your financial profile, you can do the necessary analysis to determine whether or not your debts would make bankruptcy worthwhile. There is no hard-and-fast rule to determine when bankruptcy is advisable. It is a judgment you must make, preferably in consultation with an attorney specializing in bankruptcy.

Although overextended, the family in tables 9-1 and 9-2 is not a good candidate for bankruptcy, as long as the income of $60,000 remains steady. Only if they had suffered both a loss of income and a drastic increase in debt should this family consider bankruptcy, because in their current situation, bankruptcy would not serve to eliminate most of their debt. The majority of the family's debt is

TABLE 9-1   Example of Financial Analysis

Debts Creditor	Total Due	Monthly Payment
Bank card	$ 1,953.19	$ 112.00
Dept. store S.	239.22	39.00
National bank	1,164.29	78.00
Dept. store N.	328.97	40.00
Oil card	120.00	60.00
Insurance company home insurance	525.00	43.75
Insurance company car insurance	1,000.00	83.33
Doctor	2,600.00	200.00
Furniture	1,750.00	72.91
Bank car loan	10,996.00	228.75
Savings bank home mortgage	123,345.80	1,204.00
National direct student loan	3,885.49	57.18
Total Indebtedness (col. 1) and **Total Monthly Payments** (col. 2)	$147,907.96	$2,218.92

not currently owed but made up of a mortgage against the home; and the student loan would not necessarily be discharged. If the income were suddenly interrupted, and the family could not meet mortgage payments, a bankruptcy could be used to save the family home, so it should be considered.

TABLE 9-2   Total Personal Equity and Liabilities

Equity		Liabilities	
Equity in home	$25,000	Total (from table 9-1)	$147,907.96
Equity in car	1,000	Nonmortgage	24,562.16
Savings	1,000	Not dischargeable (student loan)	3,885.49
Total Equity	$27,000	**Total Dischargeable**	$20,676.67
Annual Income	60,000		

TABLE 9-3   Summary of Equity and Liabilities

Equity		Liabilities	
Household furnishings/ personal effects	$10,000	Business loans	$38,000
Car	1,200	Debts owed to vendors	26,000
	$11,200		$54,000

If the picture were different, as in table 9-3, Chapter 13 bankruptcy might be contemplated but should still be avoided. In this case, a family business went under in an unpredictable market. The family home has already been sold, and the remaining assets are exempt. Two considerations might tempt this debtor to weigh bankruptcy: a desire to stop the fearful pressure of creditors, and the belief that he or she is judgment-proof because there are no assets to protect—meaning that if the creditors go to court and win a legal right to collect, the judgment will be meaningless, since there are no real assets to sell. Such thinking, however, is folly. In a Chapter 13 bankruptcy judgment, the creditors can still collect for up to 10 years or longer, depending upon the state, when the debtor is once again financially solvent.

Instead of opting for bankruptcy, both debtors should talk to their creditors, either directly or through an attorney or consumer credit counselor, to let them know they are experiencing financial difficulties and to propose an informal plan to pay all or part of their debts. Creditors are sometimes willing to work with you if they sense you are sincere in wanting to repay them.

Some debtors may have the energy and stamina to work out their own plan to pay back some portion of each debt every month. If the debtor can manage it, a good starting point might be 6 percent of the total of each debt owed. For example, if a debtor owed $1,800 on a charge card, 6 percent would amount to $108 a month. However, this do-it-yourself payment plan is not for everyone.

If you try to hold off your creditors and pay your bills, you will face months of discussion with adversaries. On the other hand, preparing for bankruptcy and dealing with attorneys and the court also takes its toll in time and effort. But the most stressful course of action is to ignore your problems, because they will not go away. For the person with too many debts, too little money to meet day-to-day living expenses, and too much emotional stress, it may be time to let someone else intercede.

If you are in serious financial trouble—or headed in that direction—you might consider seeking assistance from a community agency, such as Consumer Credit Counseling Services, an accountant or from an attorney.

In theory, community agencies must remain neutral. Although they are usually nonprofit organizations, you should realize they are primarily funded by the lending industry, so one of their goals is to encourage you to repay something rather than declare bankruptcy. That may not necessarily be bad; if you can avoid bankruptcy, you should. But this might also mean that the agency would discourage bankruptcy while your attorney might advise you to file for it, and you might have to choose. That aside, because community agencies generally have good standing in the areas they serve, they can usually help you work out a repayment plan along the lines of 3 to 6 percent-of-total-balance-due per month. Most federal government credit counseling agencies are not set up to provide individual assistance to debtors, so try to seek nonprofit, community-oriented legal assistance if you cannot retain a private lawyer.

If you can't afford to spend much for an attorney (which is usually the case in such circumstances), check with the legal services organization in your area to find out about low-cost attorney services. Or look for one who will work for you and be paid out of the proceeds of your bankruptcy estate (nonexempt assets). Bankruptcy attorneys are paid first under the law, so they often will work on a deferred basis if you have any assets. If you have previously used an attorney who does not specialize in bankruptcy, ask for the name of a reliable attorney who does. Choose your attorney wisely. Many run a high-volume business and don't have much time to spend on individual cases; such an attorney may not fight your creditors as hard as he or she could, or may put together a carelessly thought-out or unworkable payment plan if you decide on a Chapter 13 bankruptcy.

The attorney can draw up an informal repayment plan for each of your debts and then communicate this information to creditors, negotiating if necessary. The attorney can also act as a wall between you and angry creditors. Under the Fair Debt Collection Practices Act, if you are being represented by an attorney, all communication with you must be directed through him or her.

Whatever you work out with your creditors, do not sign any papers that admit to mismanagement of your financial affairs. In fact, it would be wise not to sign anything before seeking legal counsel.

Avoid a debt-consolidation loan—one large loan used to pay off all other debts. Such a loan will probably turn unsecured debt into secured debt and, in addition, you may have to pay a higher interest rate.

If the attorney has analyzed your debts and assets and determined that you will not be able to pay off all of them, then he or she may recommend a formal reorganization of your finances—otherwise known as bankruptcy.

THE BANKRUPTCY PROCESS

If you are going to file a simple Chapter 7 or straight bankruptcy, it may be possible—although not advisable—to file without an attorney, depending on whether you have assets to protect. However, if you have any assets or are planning to file a Chapter 13, obtaining the services of a reputable attorney specializing in consumer bankruptcy is most important. Timing in such a filing is often critical to prevent foreclosure on property or repossession. A good attorney will know when to file the papers and, before you file the bankruptcy, can help you formulate an exemption plan to help you keep as many of your assets as possible. But whether or not you have legal help, you need to understand the process, since the steps to be followed are the same, and your participation is required throughout the process. When you have an attorney, he or she will file papers on your behalf and make court appearances. If you decide to file your bankruptcy without a lawyer and represent yourself instead, it is called *in pro per*. Do-it-yourself bankruptcy books are available on the reference shelves of most libraries.

Once you have determined that you are insolvent—i.e., that your debts exceed your assets, with no hope of paying them off—you should halt all credit purchases. Any purchases above $1,000 made during the 20 days before you file bankruptcy must be paid back. If you continue to charge while insolvent, you could be accused of fraud. Stop using your checking account, and once checks have cleared, close it. Before filing the petition for bankruptcy, some lawyers advise prebankruptcy planning, including converting nonexempt assets into exempt assets. Although the trustee, or person who sells the debtor's property, may later challenge your actions, many legal experts regard this procedure as within the debtor's rights. The general rule is that any assets so converted within 90 days of filing the petition are subject to challenge.

The advice of an attorney is important because you could be accused of fraudulent conversion of nonexempt assets into exempt ones, and the transaction could be reversed. This is an area in which there is considerable legal controversy, so these transactions should be handled carefully. For example, if you have several hundred dollars in cash, it would make sense to purchase something for your home that would fall under the exempt category. (See page 160.)

After the prebankruptcy planning stage, the next step is to file a petition for voluntary bankruptcy. If you don't have an attorney, obtain the forms from the bankruptcy court clerk or a law library. These forms include a voluntary bankruptcy petition, schedules of assets and liabilities (a schedule A statement of debts and a schedule B statement of property), and a statement of financial affairs for a debtor not engaged in business. (Forms may vary from state to state.)

If you have decided to fill out the forms yourself, do so slowly and carefully, making sure you include everyone you owe. If you inadvertently omit a creditor, you will have to pay back that debt even after all of your other debts have been discharged.

After you have filled out and signed all of the forms, make copies of each, file the originals with the court clerk, and pay the filing fee. Check with the court clerk for state and local rules to find out how many copies are required, as well as other regulations.

Once the petition has been filed, you may legally stop paying debts that fall under the unsecured or dischargeable category, although by the time you file, you've probably done so anyway. As for your mortgage, during this period you may gain time to work out a payment plan. According to one nationally recognized bankruptcy expert, and depending on the state where you live and the stage of foreclosure, you could delay mortgage payments up to nine months. Renters may be able to obtain a shorter delay, again depending upon the exact circumstances.

About a month after the petition is filed, you will receive a summons to a meeting with your trustee and the creditors. At this meeting, be prepared to answer questions about your income, what you own, and what you owe. Take along supporting documents such as checkbooks and tax returns.

Over the next few months, you could receive several notices from the trustee that may threaten your discharge from being granted on specific debts. If you should receive any of the following papers in the mail, contact your attorney: "Objection to Debtor's Claim of Exempt Property," "Complaint to Deny Discharge and Determine Debt to Be Nondischargeable," or "Notice of Intended Dismissal." All of these documents challenge your right to dismiss a debt.

About six months after you have filed the bankruptcy petition, you should receive a notice of the discharge hearing, at which you should receive the discharge from all debts that were not secured or exempt.

The following is the average length of time it takes to complete each stage of bankruptcy proceedings:

1. Petition is filed.
2. Three to five weeks later, creditors meet.
3. Six months later, discharge hearing takes place.

What Will You Owe?

The purpose of bankruptcy is to discharge debts in order to give the debtor a fresh start. However, not all debts are dischargeable, and the rules for dischargeable debts differ according to whether the debtor opts for Chapter 7 or Chapter 13 bankruptcy.

Debts fall into two major categories: secured (those backed up by property) and unsecured (those not backed up by property). If your debts are secured and there is no other means with which to repay, you have promised to pay off the debt by liquidating the property backing up that promise. Some typical secured debts would include an automobile loan or a home mortgage. With secured debt, the usual rule if you can't repay the debt is that you must pay the creditor the dollar value of the property pledged or the balance owing, or turn over title of the collateral property to the creditor—even though you declare bankruptcy.

The Bankruptcy Code does allow exceptions to the rule—for example, when the property you pledged is exempt household goods. Another exception is secured loans that are in fact under-secured, which is to say that the security amount is less than the amount of the loan.

Unsecured debts will not have to be paid back upon completion of the bankruptcy. In fact, the usual aim of bankruptcies is to rid the debtor of most unsecured debts. But until a bankruptcy petition is filed, unsecured creditors may try to seize some of your property as reimbursement for the debt, and bankruptcy is often the only way to protect it.

Although many debts are dischargeable, a number of them are nondischargeable, so you will have to pay them back even after the bankruptcy is completed. Chapter 13 offers a broader discharge than Chapter 7.

The following are some types of nondischargeable debts:

· Alimony
· Child support
· Student loans (only dischargeable if they became due at least five years earlier, or if they impose an undue hardship on you or your family)
· State or federal income taxes due within the previous three years, or fraudulent income taxes; taxes that may be discharged include those filed on time and those that were nonfraudulent
· Automobile accident claims in which you were drunk or reckless
· Traffic tickets and fines for violating the law in criminal cases
· Debts incurred by using false financial statements, unless the lender told you to make these statements
· Debts obtained fraudulently
· Credit purchases for $500 or more for services or luxury goods made within 40 days of filing the bankruptcy petition
· Loans or cash advances of $1,000 or more made within 20 days of filing the bankruptcy petition
· Debts you forget to list

Some of the items in this list, such as some taxes and some student loans, may be dischargeable under Chapter 13. Even if you can't get out of paying your old taxes, you may be able to arrange a longer period of time to pay them off.

If you have a large number of nondischargeable debts, bankruptcy may not be the answer to your problems. Don't sign any papers reaffirming debts that will be dismissed; such signing will legally bind you to repayment after bankruptcy. Some creditors may attempt to have you sign such papers, so once you are in bankruptcy, have no further contact with creditors.

What Will You Own?

Even though you go bankrupt, you may keep some of your property, called *exempt property*, as provided for under the Bankruptcy Code. This provision is included in the law to help you recover and begin anew after your discharge is granted. The more exemptions you have, the more you will own in the end. All *nonexempt property* must be turned over to the bankruptcy trustee, who then sells it and pays back a portion of what is owed to each of your creditors. Some of your nonexempt assets may actually be converted to exempt assets *before* the bankruptcy by a legal maneuver called *prepetition exemption planning*, as discussed earlier. A knowledgeable attorney who specializes in bankruptcy can help you with prepetition planning. For example, if you purchased an auto worth less than the exempt amount of $1,200 allowed, you could keep the car, whereas, depending on your total assets, you might lose the equivalent amount if you kept it in the form of cash.

As mentioned earlier in this chapter, the Bankruptcy Code is more liberal regarding exemptions than it was in the past. In some states, you can choose from one of two types of exemption systems, federal and state. The systems differ in what you're allowed to keep. Of course, you'll want to review your state's system of exemptions and compare it with the federal system before deciding which one best fits your situation.

Legally speaking, there are two types of property: real and personal. Real property is any type of real estate; personal property is everything else, from cars to refrigerators. Under the federal system, you are allowed a homestead exemption of $7,500. This exemption may be used for real or personal property such as a residence, burial plot, land, trailer, motor vehicle, or even business inventory. Thus, even if you don't own a home or other real estate, you can use the federal exemption by applying it to other property, such as business inventory. You can combine the $7,500 exemption under the applicable section of the Bankruptcy Code [11 USC Sec. 522(d) (1)] with the $400 exemption allowed under 11 USC Sec. 522(d) (5), also called the "wild card," to create a total exemption of $7,900 that can be applied to any property (see table 9-4).

For example, a California couple owning a home might decide to take the California system of exemptions, which is far more generous to homeowners than is the federal system. California offers a basic $50,000 homestead and dwelling house exemption, but many people qualify for additional exemptions that can bring the total to $75,000 and in some cases as much as $100,000. In contrast, if a California couple took the federal homestead exemption, the total would amount to only $15,800. Obviously, this couple would be wiser to choose the state exemptions. However, if they didn't own a home, they might be better off taking the federal exemption system, which could allow more generous exemptions in other areas. The only way to know is to sit down and make a list comparing state exemptions with federal exemptions.

A married debtor faces some choices partially dictated by state law. In a separate-property state, either spouse can file. In community-property states, it's harder for only one spouse to declare bankruptcy because of the community nature of the system of property. If only one of you needs to file, and if it's possible in your state, it's better to leave one spouse with credit intact.

Also, both spouses do not have to choose the same system of exemptions; the wife can choose the state system of exemptions, for example, while the husband chooses the federal. However, the chosen system for each must be followed all the way through. If you like your state's homestead exemption, but the federal exemption for motor vehicles would be more beneficial to you, you must go ahead and take the federal motor vehicle exemption if you have chosen the federal system for homesteads.

In addition to the homestead and burial plot exemptions, there are exemptions for other types of personal property. Under federal law, you may exempt up to a $1,200 interest in your car or other vehicle. If you didn't use up all of your homestead exemption, you may add to your exemptions any leftover amount from that category, up to $3,750. In addition, there is a provision for a further exemption of $400, the "wild card," to be used however you want.

TABLE 9-4   The Federal Bankruptcy Exemptions

Homestead
Each debtor may claim a $7,500 homestead exemption, i.e., in equity over and above mortgages and liens on the home.

Motor vehicle
Each debtor may claim up to $1,200 in one motor vehicle.

Household goods
A $4,000 aggregate limit.

Jewelry
Each debtor is allowed up to $500 worth of personal jewelry.

Any property
Sometimes called the "wild card," the amount of this exemption is $400 per debtor plus any unused amount of the homestead exemption, up to $3,750 per debtor.

Tools of the trade
Each debtor can exempt up to $750 worth of professional books and tools of the trade.

Life insurance
Life insurance policies that have a cash value of up to $4,000 per debtor may be exempted. In addition, term life insurance receives a separate exemption.

Health aids
A debtor may exempt an unlimited amount of professionally prescribed health aids for a debtor or a debtor's dependent.

Disability, retirement, and other benefits
Social Security, unemployment, welfare, disability, and illness benefits are generally exempt, but this is a very complex area and you should consult your attorney for particulars.

Compensation for injury or losses
Certain types of injury or loss payments are exempt. For example, $7,500 received for personal bodily injury would be exempt.

Source: Federal Bankruptcy Code

Thus, you could keep a car worth $5,350 ($1,200 + $3,750 + $400) if you didn't have a home or other property qualifying under the homestead provision.

Declaring bankruptcy does not mean you'll end up with only the shirt on your back. In fact, you can keep items such as household furnishings, apparel, appliances, books, animals, crops, or musical instruments that you or your dependents use, up to a $200 interest per debtor, per item. For example, if you own a television worth $400, and you and your spouse take the federal household exemption, you are each allowed a $200 exemption on that television, so you will be able to keep it. The total amount you may exempt under the household exemption is $4,000, or $8,000 if both spouses file for bankruptcy.

In addition, there is some leeway under federal rules as to how you categorize your possessions. With jewelry, for example, you may keep up to $500 per debtor; if you have a great deal of jewelry, and some of it is worth less than $200, you might want to count it among household items in order to keep it.

Up to $4,000 of accrued dividends, interest, or loan value of any unmatured life insurance contract may be exempted. This exemption does not apply to a "credit life insurance contract." If you have borrowed against your property to pay the premiums, the $4,000 maximum may be reduced to the extent that you have borrowed.

Some exemptions are mandated in the federal bankruptcy law. These include Social Security payments, alimony, pensions, and annuities. However, such payments that you have already received and not spent may not be covered by this exemption if they exceed the amount of savings allowed. And if you expect future payments for properties that were acquired before filing, these might be put into your bankruptcy estate (i.e., the pot of assets creditors can get). Here again, you need to seek legal advice about the specifics of your situation.

Effect on Credit

Once your bankruptcy has been recorded by the court, it is automatically picked up on your credit report by one of the major consumer credit reporting agencies. The type of bankruptcy you chose, either Chapter 7 or Chapter 13, is specified too. The information will remain there for 10 years.

What this means to you is that every time you want to make a purchase on credit, the creditor will check your file and see the record of bankruptcy. Naturally, most creditors look unfavorably on bankruptcies because they indicate poor credit performance in the past. However, you may be able to talk to the creditor where you are applying and explain why you had to file for bankruptcy, particularly if you had a good reason, such as a major illness. If you have a good, steady income at present and your bank account is healthy, with no overdrafts, you may actually be able to persuade the lender to extend credit to you.

The type of bankruptcy you chose, Chapter 7 or Chapter 13, will also have an impact on your ability to obtain credit. If you took a Chapter 7, which completely discharges all your debt, you will not be able to file another Chapter 7 for another six years. Ironically, you may therefore be a *good* credit risk, since you cannot go bankrupt again in the near future. If you filed a Chapter 13 bankruptcy and paid back a major portion of your debts, creditors will look even more favorably upon you than if you'd taken the Chapter 7. One study found that 70 percent of those interviewed had made major purchases on credit since bankruptcy and only about one-third of that number found credit harder to get. One-third found no difference in their ability to get credit, and 8 percent found it easier.

CLOSE-UP: WHAT IS TOO MUCH DEBT?

Lenders and bankruptcy attorneys report that most bankruptcies are triggered by unemployment, divorce, catastrophic illness, or business failure. These life events make a level of debt that was appropriate under normal conditions too onerous under crisis circumstances. Other bankrupt-bound individuals simply overextend themselves and borrow more than they can handle.

No matter how you get into debt, you should know the warning signs of being overextended. If you answer yes to two or more of the following six questions, you may be headed for credit trouble:

1. Are you constantly behind in paying your bills?
2. Do you tend to earmark all or most of your paycheck for debt servicing, leaving little or nothing for current living expenses?

3. Does a significant portion of your monthly income go to pay interest?

4. Do you routinely have to go to more expensive restaurants and stores because they accept a charge card and you are short of cash?

5. Do you dread opening your mail for fear of finding bills or past-due notices?

6. Do you frequently receive calls from creditors and/or bill collectors?

III

TAXES

10

Tax Planning

Aileen Jacobson

The last five years have seen a number of dramatic changes in tax policy. The Tax Reform Act of 1986, a number of smaller changes over the rest of the decade and the Omnibus Budget Reconciliation Act of 1990 changed the way many taxpayers had been planning for decades. We shall begin this chapter, therefore, with a description of some of the major areas in tax law which have been altered in that time span. Then, we'll deal with some general planning strategies to help you reduce your tax bill.

THE NEW RULES OF THE GAME

In general, the recent tax changes have eliminated the large number of tax brackets and replaced them with three—15 percent, 28 percent and 31 percent. There's also an alternative minimum tax aimed at high-income taxpayers who may be able to reduce their tax liability through the use of several types of deductions, including tax-shelter losses.

Starting in 1991, deductions for itemized items will be reduced by 3 percent of the amount the taxpayer's adjusted gross income exceeds $100,000 (or $50,000 apiece for married couples filing separately). Medical expenses, casualty and theft deductions, gambling losses and investment interest expenses are not subject to the limit.

RULES THAT YOU SHOULD CONSIDER

Consumer Interest

The Rule Until the 1986 law took effect, all interest on consumer debts—on credit cards, charge accounts, personal and automobile loans, and mortgages—was deductible. Currently, mortgage interest on first and second homes remains deductible in most cases, but deductions for all other consumer-debt interest have been phased out.

Strategies If you have been accustomed to paying interest on credit card and charge accounts, the new law makes an already expensive habit even more costly. The solution is to use credit cards and charge accounts only if you regularly pay your account in full within the interest-free period.

Because deductions for the interest on automobile, personal, and other such loans have been phased out, you should consider paying them off with your own money from a savings account or other source and then paying yourself back in the same installments that the loans required. The interest you lose on your own money will amount to far less than what you would pay on the loan.

The tax law was modified in 1987, and under the new rules, home mortgage interest is deductible up to a total of $1 million for the acquisition, construction, or substantial improvement of a home (or of a first and second home combined). There is also a $100,000 limit on the deductibility of loans secured by a home (such as a second mortgage or a line of credit) but used for another purpose, such as to pay college or medical bills.

The deductibility of home mortgage interest has led lending institutions to market aggressively home equity loans—which are essentially second mortgages on your home.

If you are buying a new home and are strapped for cash, you may want to obtain a mortgage that extends for as long a term as possible. In this situation, low monthly payments, which are largely deductible in the early years because they consist of much more interest than principal, may ease your budget so that you can pay cash for such items as clothing and furniture instead of buying them on credit and paying the interest that is no longer deductible.

IRA Accounts

The Rule The earnings on all IRA accounts are tax-exempt until withdrawal. You may contribute a maximum of $2,000 per year to an IRA account, or $2,250 for a worker and nonworking spouse. But your contribution is not deductible if you are eligible for an employee retirement plan and if your adjusted gross income exceeds $35,000 on an individual return or $50,000 on a joint return. (Individuals with adjusted gross incomes of $25,000 to $35,000 and couples with $40,000 to $50,000 may take a partial deduction, as explained in chapter 24.) If neither you nor your spouse is covered by another plan, you may take the deduction no matter what your income.

Strategies Even if you do not qualify for deduction of your contribution, it is important to recognize that the IRA's yield is not taxable until you withdraw it. It remains an investment sound enough to warrant your further contributions, even if they are not deductible, in cases in which your tax-deferred earnings, compounded each year, would outstrip other investments. You should compare your IRA's potential yields with those from other tax-deferred investments and from tax-free investments, such as municipal bonds. Also compare the relative safety and liquidity of each type of investment (see chapter 25). On the other hand, if you have a 401(k) or other pension plan to which you may contribute at work, you might consider investing your surplus cash there instead of in your IRA. Contributions to a 401(k) plan are tax-deferred to an annual maximum of $8,475 (for 1991, and adjusted for inflation in future years), compared to the $2,000 limit for IRAs.

If you operate a business of your own, you may want to consider setting up a Keogh or Simplified Employee Pension (SEP) plan, which allows a deduction for contributions and the deferral of tax on their yield until retirement.

Capital Gains and Losses

A combination of changes have left many investors with no tax advantages from long-term capital gains—that is, the profit you realize from the sale of property you have owned for more than one year. However, married couples with taxable income over $82,150 or a single person making $49,300 pay a top capital gains tax rate of only 28 percent while they pay 31 percent on ordinary income. Below those income levels, the rates for capital gains and ordinary income are parallel. Capital losses can be used to offset capital gains and then, to a maximum of $3,000 to offset ordinary income.

Strategies These changes cast a new light on many kinds of investments. For those with incomes high enough to pay only 28 percent on capital gains as opposed to 31 percent on ordinary income, it may make sense to hold onto an investment for a year in order to save tax dollars. But for those who do not qualify for the preferential top rate, there is no longer any need to hold an appreciated investment long enough to qualify profit as a long-term gain. Instead, you may sell it at any time with the same tax consequences. Because you owe no taxes until you sell it, however, you may decide to postpone its sale to a year in which you anticipate lower income from other sources.

In addition, the elimination of favored treatment for capital gains for many may heighten the attractiveness of investments that promise immediate income rather than future appreciation.

Whether or not there are tax advantages for you at the time of sale, you always have the advantage of deferring taxes while your capital asset appreciates—no taxes are due until you sell. And there's some possibility that the law may change, so that capital gains will once again have more broadly favored status.

Capital gains on the sale of your principal residence will also be taxed at ordinary income rates unless you reinvest the money in another principal residence within two years. If you are 55 or older, however, you have the right to a one-time exclusion of as much as $125,000 in capital gains—whether or not you invest the money in another home.

A few years ago the IRS clarified what is meant by "one-time exclusion," which usually applies to both spouses in a couple. The IRS held that if an individual uses the exclusion and then later marries or remarries, the new spouse may not use the exclusion.

So if an older couple plans to marry, and both own homes, they should consider selling one home and taking that exclusion before they marry. That way, each may take the exclusion on the home owned solely by one.

If you are eligible for this exemption and own a second home that has appreciated more than the one you regularly occupy, you might consider transferring your primary residence to the second home before selling it (see p. 458). IRS Publication 523, *Tax Information on Selling Your Home*, explains the residence requirements you must satisfy to do this.

Because you may be paying the full tax rate on profits realized on your home, it is especially important to keep a record of all improvements, since they can be added to your cost when determining your actual gain. For each year in which you occupy the house, you should keep a careful record of all disbursements you make for such items as the addition of a room, the construction of a patio, or other expenditures that are not classifiable as routine maintenance. *Always* retain your original purchase records so you can figure your cost.

Children's Taxes

The Rule   Children who file a tax return cannot take a personal exemption if they are claimed as a dependent on another return.

A more important concept with respect to a child's return, however, involves tax liability for unearned income. On the first $550 of such income, a child is permitted to use $550 of the standard deduction to offset income. (The $550 figure will be revised to account for inflation.) A child under the age of 14 pays tax at his or her rate, which is presumably lower than that of the parents, on the next $550. On unearned income beyond the $1,100, children under age 14 must use their parents' tax rate, regardless of who provided the principal that produced the income. A child aged 14 or older is taxed at his or her own rate on the entire amount.

Strategies   The taxability of custodial accounts and other assets owned by children affects only children who have enough investments to produce a yield of more than $1,100. At a rate of 10 percent return, that means about $10,000. If the account stays below this limit, transferring assets to your children may still result in a tax saving if the child's rate is lower than your own. It is important to bear in mind, however, that all funds transferred to the child belong permanently to the child, that they may not be used by you personally or for the child's ordinary expenses, and that the child, on reaching the age of majority, can dispose of them in any way he or she chooses without your consultation or consent. If your children are already earning $1,100 on their investments, you might consider tax-free or tax-deferred investments for them, such as U.S. savings bonds or zero-coupon municipal bonds (see chapter 19), or investments in stocks or stock mutual funds with high potential growth but small dividend payments (see chapter 20).

Medical Expenses

The Rule Medical expenses have remained deductible, but only to the extent that they exceed 7.5 percent of your adjusted gross income.

Strategies In the year in which you incur heavy medical expenses, you should do everything you can to reduce your adjusted gross income so that the nondeductible expenses amount to 7.5 percent of the lowest possible figure. You might, for example, invest in a CD that does not pay interest until the following year; or, if you are withdrawing from an IRA account, you might postpone the withdrawal until the following January.

Alternatively, if you are planning to have expensive elective surgery or dental work done, you can try to schedule it either for a year in which you anticipate a lower adjusted gross income or for a year in which your other medical expenses are already approaching the 7.5 percent floor. If you are short of cash, you can, in some cases, charge your medical costs at the end of one year to your credit card (the date of the charge is the date used to establish the deduction) and not pay it off until the following year—provided, of course, that the interest charges don't outweigh any tax saving.

Two-Earner Deduction

For 1991, the basic standard deduction is $5,700 for a married couple filing jointly, $5,000 for a head of house and $3,400 for a single filer.

Charitable Contributions

The Rule Deductions for charitable contributions are now restricted to those taxpayers who itemize. In addition, any gift of appreciated property may subject a high-income donor to the alternative minimum tax (see p. 198).

Strategies If you don't always itemize, you should, where possible, schedule your charitable contributions for years in which you do—an estimate you can best make in December. A December contribution is also advantageous in general because it gives you use of the money or other property for the longest possible time without loss of the deduction for the tax year. Because the postmark date is the official date of the contribution, some people wait until December 31 before mailing it. If you are donating articles to be picked up by a charitable organization, the date of your contribution is the date of your call, even if the pickup is delayed until the next calendar year. You may also use a credit card to make a donation, and the date of the charge—not of your payment to the credit card company, even if it's in the following year—is the one that applies for deduction purposes.

If your donation to a charitable organization or thrift shop consists of miscellaneous discarded items, you should keep a list and ask the recipient to sign it and, if possible, assess its value. If your total donation is worth more than $500, you will need to file Form 8283 with your tax return.

If the value of your donation is worth more than $5,000, you must have the item appraised and attach the appraisal to your return, and you must file Form 8283, signed by the recipient, in connection with it. Of course, publicly traded securities do not require appraisal, since their value on the date of your donation is a matter of public record.

Donating items that have appreciated significantly—stocks, for example, or real estate, or artwork—is an effective way to reduce your tax liability because you take the deduction for the full value of the item and avoid paying tax on its appreciation. It may, however, subject you to the alternative minimum tax.

Miscellaneous Deductions

The Rule The category of miscellaneous deductions includes a variety of expenses you incur in connection with earning your income but for which you are not reimbursed by an employer. It includes dues to professional organizations or unions; work-related educational costs; subscriptions to professional journals; fees to accountants and investment advisers; IRA custodial fees; safe deposit box rentals; the cost of work uniforms, travel, and other business expenses for which your employer has not reimbursed you; and similar income-related expenses. They are now deductible only to the extent that they exceed 2 percent of your adjusted gross income.

Strategies You may be able to maximize your deduction by bunching your expenses in a single year—preferably a year in which your adjusted gross income is likely to be low. But the IRS restricts the bunching you can do. If, for example, in an attempt to bunch expenses, you buy a five-year subscription to a professional journal or a three-year membership in a professional association, according to the IRS you can deduct only that portion of it that extends to the next year, and your deduction must be prorated on the total cost of the subscription or the membership fee.

Similarly, it is not always possible to pay for services not yet rendered, although you may be able to pay an accountant in December for tax-preparation services to be performed the following April if you retain the accountant on a year-round basis. Check with your own accountant on this.

Travel for educational purposes—to Spain, for example, by a teacher of Spanish—is no longer deductible. Costs related to attendance at investment seminars are deductible only by taxpayers who are investment counselors, tax advisers, and other professionals, and not by investors.

Exemptions for the Blind and the Elderly

The Rule The extra exemptions formerly allowed to taxpayers who were blind or over the age of 65 have been eliminated and replaced by additional standard deductions of $850 for single and $650 for married individuals—and double these amounts for those who are both blind and over 65.

Strategies The extra standard deductions are available only to those who do not itemize. If you generally itemize, you might consider bunching your expenditures that result in deductions in one year so that in the next year you can omit itemizing and gain the advantage of the additional standard deductions.

Business Losses

The Rule If you operate a business of your own, either as a part-time or full-time occupation, and you do not show profits in any three out of five consecutive years, or two out of seven for a farm, the IRS will consider your business a hobby. You may not deduct your losses and claim a full deduction for your expenses unless you can convince the IRS that your occupation is not a hobby, even though you're losing money on it. Although expenses can be deducted against hobby income, the deduction must be combined with your other miscellaneous expenses and hence can be taken only to the extent that the total exceeds 2 percent of your adjusted gross income.

Strategies If you qualify under the tightened rules, you can, as the self-employed operator of a business, even if it is part-time, enjoy a number of tax advantages. For example, in two out of five years, you can allow your expenses to outstrip your income and then deduct the excess losses against other income. Moreover, you can establish a Keogh or SEP account in addition to whatever retirement plan you may have at your regular place of employment—an especially valuable advantage if your IRA contributions are no longer deductible. (Remember, though, that your Keogh or SEP contribution is based on your *net* income—minus expenses.) You may deduct all expenses attributable to your business—a home office or a computer, for example—which otherwise would have to be deducted as miscellaneous expenses and limited to their excess over 2 percent of your adjusted gross income.

Finally, you can take advantage of income shifting by employing your spouse or your children and deducting their wages as a business expense. Your spouse may be able to shelter this income by contributing $2,000 of it to an IRA account (if you are not covered by another pension plan and meet the income limitations discussed on page 169, The Rule) and your child will pay a lower tax rate on it. This employment must, of course, be bona fide and not simply "on paper"—that is, family members must receive no more than the prevailing rate of pay, and they must render their services on a regular basis.

More details of business-related deductions are discussed in chapter 11.

Investment Interest

The Rule   Investment interest generally includes the interest paid on stock margin accounts. If it is to be deductible as investment interest, the IRS requires you to prove that your borrowing went into investments, and not to pay for consumer expenses. For example, if you borrow from a stock margin account or a cash management account, you should use that money promptly for an investment. To be safe, don't place the funds in a checking account with which you also pay consumer expenses.

As of 1991, interest is deductible only to the extent that it does not exceed net investment income—that is, income derived from stock portfolios, investment properties, and some businesses in which you are not an active participant. Any excess of interest over income can, however, be carried forward to offset future investment income.

Strategies   You must keep very careful records if you do borrow to make investments—a strategy we do not generally recommend.

Tax Shelters

The Rule   The use of tax shelters—investments that produce losses to offset income—has been sharply curtailed. Although abusive shelters—those that were structured virtually only for tax losses with little or no profit motivation—have been the targets of IRS scrutiny for many years, the new laws provide that losses from passive investments can be used to offset only income from passive investments (see p. 451).

Strategies   If you are already involved in a tax shelter, you should consider investing in limited partnerships that produce passive income, which can be used to absorb the losses still being generated by your existing tax shelters. Be sure that the limited partnership actually generates passive (not portfolio) income (see p. 462). The prospectus will tell you.

Make sure, too, that the investment is worthwhile from an economic standpoint. Never invest in a partnership for tax purposes alone.

MAINTAINING TAX-RELATED RECORDS

With all of the foregoing complexities fresh in your mind, you may decide to reorganize and refine your existing file of tax-related documents, or you may resolve to start one. Your choice of a fire-resistant file drawer or one of the various styles of tax organizers available from office-supply firms (preferably to be kept in a fire-resistant safe) will depend, of course, on the extent of your documentation. The various documents you should preserve are listed below, along with some explanations as to why you need them and how to use them when filing your return.

Paycheck stubs for the entire year. If you work for a large company, the stub is likely to include such tax-related information as Social Security tax; withholdings for federal and state (and possibly city) taxes; deductions for health insurance, union dues, and contributions to a 401(k) plan; and perhaps your reimbursement for employee expenses. The year's totals on union dues can help you determine whether they exceed 2 percent of your adjusted gross income along with other "miscellaneous" items and are therefore deductible. Some of this information will be available on your W-2 form, but it is useful to compare the two sources and check for discrepancies.

W-2 forms. These forms must be sent to you by your employer(s) by January 31 of each year and must be submitted with your tax return. Check them against your paycheck stubs not only for accuracy of the income and withholding figures but also for the accuracy of your Social Security number.

Copies of these forms should be kept for at least three years, and preferably for your entire working life. They are useful if you should have to file for Social Security disability or survivors' benefits.

Form 1099. This form records your income, both earned and unearned, from sources other than your regular employer, such as interest, dividends, or distributions from retirement plans. Since the payers report this income directly to the IRS, the 1099 is your best protection against errors, which are not uncommon now that the IRS uses computers to cross-check your return. If you receive a notice from the IRS claiming that you overlooked or underpaid on income shown on a 1099, an explanatory letter from you, accompanied by a photocopy of your 1099, may resolve the issue promptly.

Investment-related documents. All statements from brokers, mutual funds, banks, or other financial institutions should be kept for checking against their 1099s. Get a corrected 1099 if your check reveals an error, and remind the institution to send a corrected 1099 to the IRS. You should also retain all brokers' confirmation slips on your purchase and sale of securities and records of your purchase and sale of mutual fund shares so that you will have documented information for computing gains and losses.

Tax returns. The previous year's tax return can be very helpful to you when you prepare your return for the current year. In addition, you may find older returns useful as a record of your sale of stocks, a home, or other assets. They can also be useful in negotiating a settlement in divorce proceedings. Many taxpayers retain all tax returns throughout their lives.

Expense-account records. The discussion of deductible expenses in this chapter and in chapter 11 should convince you of the importance of keeping detailed records of your expenses, whether for your employer or for a business of your own. If your employer's reimbursement for expenses is included as income in your paycheck, you will have to pay tax on the full amount unless you can document the portion that represents expenses.

Automobile log. The log should record not only the mileage at the beginning and end of each year but also the purpose and length of each trip that can be deducted as a business expense. Using these figures, you can either deduct business mileage on a per-mile basis or calculate the percentage of business use if you are prorating on a total-expenses basis (see p. 191). In the former case, you should retain all receipts for tolls, parking, and other easily overlooked expenses that can be added to the mileage charge; in the latter case, you should also retain all receipts for maintenance, repairs, insurance, fuel, and other operating costs.

Records of charitable contributions. You will need to keep canceled checks or receipts for all charitable contributions, whether in the form of cash or of goods of some kind. Receipts for goods should carry an assessment of their value.

If your volunteer work for a charitable organization involves the use of your automobile, your mileage is deductible at a rate specified by law: 12 cents as of early 1987. Alternatively, you can deduct the actual cost of the travel in terms of oil, fuel, tolls, and parking fees, but not maintenance, insurance, or depreciation.

You should retain ticket stubs or other evidence of your attendance at a charity event, but you are entitled to deduct only the contribution portion of the admission price, not including the admission charge for the event if it were not a charity benefit.

Medical expenses. If you are covered by health insurance, you are unlikely to qualify for a deduction, because the premiums and the costs you must pay are unlikely to add up to more than 7.5 percent of your adjusted gross income. Nevertheless, it is useful to keep careful records of all your costs, including those for copayments, prescription drugs, dental work, and ophthalmological and optometric services, hearing aids, and living expenses incurred while seeking medical care at a hospital or similar facility in another city, since these are not covered by all health insurance policies and the total may exceed 7.5 percent of your adjusted gross income if they are great enough.

Casualty and theft records. Losses resulting from accident, fire, a natural disaster (such as a flood or lightning), theft, or vandalism are deductible but only to the extent that they are not covered by insurance and that they exceed 10 percent of your adjusted gross income *after* you have absorbed $100 of the loss. In addition, you can deduct only the cost of the items involved or the decline in market value due to casualty or theft, whichever is less.

This means that you need to keep records to document your deduction. These records are essentially the same as those you would use to support an insurance claim: photographs or videotapes of your major household possessions; recent appraisals of such valuable items as antiques, jewelry, or silver; bills of sale; inventories; and repair bills.

In all cases, you are required to seek payment first from your insurance company, and you can claim as a deduction only the value for which you are not reimbursed. In cases of theft, make an immediate report to the local police, specifying what has been stolen and what was damaged if the thief made a forcible entry. Keep a copy of the report, or its file number, with your other records.

In case of extensive damage caused by a tornado or a hurricane, you should photograph the scene in detail immediately after the event and perhaps have an appraisal of the amount of damage done, especially if part of the destruction involved large, old trees that cannot be replaced. In most cases, however, repair bills constitute sufficient proof, provided that they cover only work done to restore the property to its original condition and not improvements or additions.

Moving expense records. Retain all documents connected with a household move related to your employment. If you change jobs and move to be closer to work, your new place of work must be at least 35 miles farther away from your former residence than your old place of work was for you to be entitled, within limits, to deduct moving expenses. Such expenses as house-hunting trips, temporary housing, realtors' commissions, attorneys' fees, escrow fees, mortgage points that are not deductible as interest, moving, packing, storage, and travel to your new home are generally deductible if these costs are not reimbursed by your new employer. The deduction is limited to an overall amount of $3,000. Of that, not more than $1,500 may be for house-hunting trips and temporary living quarters. Under the new law, moving expenses must be included under miscellaneous deductions, so not all taxpayers will be able to take advantage of the deduction.

Miscellaneous deductions. Although most miscellaneous deductions are permitted only to the extent that they exceed 2 percent of your adjusted gross income, you cannot determine your eligibility unless you keep careful account of them. Hence, you should keep records of such expenses as investment and tax advice (and books on the subject), professional journal subscriptions, safe deposit box rentals, custodial fees for IRA accounts and other income-producing assets, postage related to unearned income, and education related directly to your job. The cost of work uniforms is deductible, but other work clothing is not if you can wear it outside of work.

Travel expenses. Although travel is deductible if you operate your own business and deductible as a miscellaneous expense if you are not reimbursed for it by your employer, such travel must be for business purposes, and the records you keep must reflect this. If you take your spouse along and he or she is not involved in the business, you must subtract from your expenses those incurred by having your spouse along, such as the difference between single and double room accommodations. Meals and entertainment expenses incurred while traveling are only 80 percent deductible—the same as if you incurred them at home.

To ensure accuracy and completeness, you should keep all receipts and use a travel calendar, available from office-supply firms, to record not only airfares, taxi fares, tips, meals, entertainment costs, and similar expenses, but also the dates and purpose of each trip.

All of these documents should be retained for at least three years, because the IRS may audit the return you filed three years ago—or six years ago if you underreported your income by more than 25 percent, or indefinitely if fraud is suspected.

A TAX-PLANNING CALENDAR

Effective tax planning is a year-round activity. This does not mean that you must be preoccupied with it 12 months of the year. It means, rather, that a few hours devoted to it each month can prevent you from overlooking important deadlines, can help you take full advantage of the strategies outlined earlier in this chapter, and can help you avoid hasty and ill-considered decisions at the end of the year, when you and your tax adviser both may be under pressure. The following calendar can be used to schedule your activities:

January Buy a record book or calendar to keep a day-by-day log of your deductible expenses.

As you pay bills, make regular notations in your checkbook of those that may be tax deductible—for example, a health insurance bill or the interest part of a mortgage or loan payment.

Start thinking about your individual retirement account, particularly if you are eligible for the deduction. It is never too early to start sheltering the income from taxes. If you haven't made your previous year's contribution, then you should act now if you plan to make one. If you can't make up your mind about how to invest it, park the money in an IRA bank account or money market mutual fund until you decide on something that may be a little more advantageous or have a higher yield (see chapter 24).

If you have contributed to an IRA during the course of the year and then find that your contributions are no longer deductible because you earned too much or became a participant in a pension plan, you can, if you wish, withdraw the nondeductible portion of your IRA without penalty, provided you act before you file your return for that year and also withdraw earnings on the contribution (which must be reported as taxable earnings).

At this time of year, review all your previous IRA investments to make sure that they are earning maximum yield at the level of risk with which you feel comfortable.

If you anticipate a refund, file your tax return for the previous year as soon as you receive all your W-2s and 1099s. Filing electronically will speed the refund, but authorized tax preparers often charge a fee for the service.

If you expect a substantial refund, consider readjusting your W-4. Even if you like the idea of getting money back, bear in mind that you're not getting it back with interest. But beware of under-withholding. The amount withheld this year must be at least 90 percent of this year's tax liability (which may be hard to predict) or at least 100 percent of your actual tax liability for the previous year. If you are unsure, use the figure of 100 percent of last year's income.

Your estimated quarterly payment is also due, if you have taxable income not covered by withholding. Estimated taxes are generally paid by those who have income, such as from investments, that are not covered by withholding. If you pay estimated taxes, you should also consider readjusting those payments so that they accurately reflect taxes due. However, estimated payment must be accurate (90 percent of this year's liability or 100 percent of the previous year's) on a quarter-to-quarter basis, while W-4 withholding must be within the right bounds only by year end—that is, you can increase your W-4 withholding at the end of the year to make up any shortfall and still escape a penalty.

February   If you earn tips as income and received $20 or more last month, you must report them to your employer, usually by the tenth of the month. You can use Form 4070 for reporting and Form 4070A for daily records. Both are contained in IRS Publication 1244. Publication 531 explains the rules.

If you did not earn enough last year to have to pay taxes, you may be able to claim an "exemption from income tax withholding" on your W-4. Even if you filed a W-4 last year, you need to file a new one this year. The deadline is usually February 15.

If you have not received a W-2 or one of the 1099s you expected (including one from your state if you received a tax refund), contact the appropriate institutions or, if you get no satisfaction, your local IRS office. If you do not receive a W-2 by April 15, you have to file your return with a statement explaining how you arrived at the missing wage and tax information.

March This is the month in which most people collect the forms and other information they need to file their taxes. If you owe taxes, you might as well wait until April 15 to mail your return. But you should not wait until then to have it ready.

Review your credit card receipts and your checkbook for deductions you may have overlooked, including medical bill payments and charitable contributions. Sometimes items slip by, no matter how meticulous your record-keeping. If you have noted deductible items in your checkbook or on your credit card bills during the year, this task will be easier. But go over everything again. A tax guide can help to remind you of deductions you may have overlooked. An accountant or other tax preparer should remind you, too, but the person you hire prepares your form based on the information you supply, and you should not rely entirely on a professional tax preparer to remind you.

April April 15 is the deadline for filing your return, except when it falls on a weekend, as it will in 1995, in which case the deadline is the following Monday (April 17 in 1995). The same deadline also applies for making contributions to last year's IRA, even if you receive a filing extension. If you have already established a Keogh plan, you can wait to fund it if you get an extension. If you haven't established a Keogh but you own your business, consider a Simplified Employee Pension (SEP) which must be set up and funded by April 15.

By filing Form 4868, the application for an automatic extension, you can get an automatic four-month extension to file your return—that is, you don't need to offer an explanation and the IRS cannot refuse the extension—if, by April 15, you have paid an amount equal to the full amount of the previous year's tax liability or 90 percent of the current year's. These payments can be a combination of withholding during the year, estimated tax payments, and a mid-April payment. You can request an additional two-month extension—until October 15—by filing Form 2688 and telling the IRS why you need more time. The IRS may accept or reject this request.

If you have not set up record-keeping files yet, do so now, when you are very much aware of your tax situation.

If you pay estimated taxes, your first installment is due, using Form 1040-ES. Your estimated taxes and withholding combined must cover at least 90 percent of the current year's tax bill or 100 percent of last year's.

May If you have made a mistake on your return, you can file Form 1040X to correct it.

June If you were living abroad on April 15, your filing deadline is June 15. If you are a student starting a summer job, you may be exempt from withholding tax if you will not owe taxes this year. Request the exemption on Form W-4 and file it with your employer.

If you are a newlywed, report your new marital status to your employer and readjust your W-4.

Your second installment of estimated taxes is due June 15.

July If you have a Keogh retirement plan, you must file a Form 5500 or one of its variations if you are the sole proprietor. (See chapter 24 for details.)

August If you were granted an automatic four-month extension, your return is due on August 15 (or if you have paid in full, you can wait to file until October 15). If you've taken an extension and have a Keogh plan, you must fund it now.

September The third installment of estimated taxes is due September 15.

October Begin your year-end tax planning. This is the time to determine whether you are close to exceeding the floors for deducting medical expenses or miscellaneous expenses. If you will exceed them, or have already done so, then try to pay as many of these expenses as possible this year. Unless you face the alternative minimum tax or have some other reason for not wishing to do so, you should also try to postpone as much income as possible, such as end-of-year bonuses or, if you are in business for yourself, payments that might be made to you.

You should also start thinking about stock transactions that could balance out your gains and losses. Review your other investments again to see whether everything is earning or appreciating as you expected. If you want to make adjustments, now is probably a better time than in December, when many end-of-year transactions may affect prices of stocks, bonds, and other investments.

November Continue your year-end planning. Begin to organize the items you want to give to charities and decide how much money you want to donate to which group.

If you were uncertain about whether you could qualify for a deductible IRA, you should be able to tell by now. If you find you do qualify, deposit the contribution now.

If you were unsure about whether you were having the right amount withheld, check your withholding again and make adjustments if you are substantially overpaying or underpaying.

December If you wish to have a Keogh account, you must set it up by the end of this month, although you may wait until next year to fund it.

Any donations to charity that you were waiting to make should be made by December 31, either by credit card or by check.

You may also want to prepay estimated state and local taxes and real estate taxes (which you may have to arrange through your bank if the bank pays your taxes) that are due in January. This will entitle you to deductions a year sooner, even though you are paying bills only a month in advance.

If you will save money by getting married and filing jointly, schedule the wedding before the end of the year so that you can file jointly for the whole year. But if you are better off filing as an individual, you may want to postpone your marriage to the new year.

Make sure you keep all end-of-year pay stubs and documents from banks and other financial institutions.

CLOSE-UP: WITHHOLDING

Many people prefer overwithholding because they see it as a method of enforced savings and they look forward happily to their refund. They fail to recognize, however, that their "savings" earn no interest whatever. They would be considerably better off to have minimum withholding and to have any "excess" from their paycheck deposited into a payroll savings plan or a savings account. In this way, they would have more than enough to pay any tax that might be due with their return and would have the use of (as well as the interest on) their money during the year.

Although the only "penalty" for overwithholding is the loss of interest on the excess, there are severe penalties for underwithholding. For this reason, you should fill out your W-4 conscientiously and review it periodically.

If you plan to use the figure of 90 percent of the current year's taxes as the basis for your withholding, monitor your income carefully and ask your employer to increase or decrease your withholding as time goes on. To determine whether your current withholding is correct, you can use IRS Publication 919, *Is My Withholding Correct?*, which includes a worksheet that takes into account your year's withholding to date and projects your correct withholding for the balance of the year.

If you are required to pay estimated tax quarterly because you own income-producing investments or you are self-employed, you cannot be as flexible, because each of your estimated tax payments must be accurate for each quarter for which it is filed.

11

Special Tax Situations

Aileen Jacobson

The preceding chapter dealt with general tax-reduction strategies most taxpayers can use. The present chapter will describe strategies applicable to specific groups: people with home offices, investors, individuals who are divorced, people involved in barter transactions, and taxpayers subject to the alternative minimum tax.

BUSINESS DEDUCTIONS

Home Offices

Though there has been no new tax law in the last several years pertaining to home offices, the IRS has clearly been tightening up in this area. There has been more controversy over what qualifies as a home office than virtually any other area of tax law. To further complicate matters, there are even a number of areas in which the IRS and the Tax Court disagree. Unless you are self-employed, you may find it impossible to deduct the costs of maintaining an office in your home, no matter how convinced you are that you are entitled to the deduction. In fact, claiming a home-office deduction may trigger an audit, because the IRS has kept such deductions under close scrutiny.

Is Your Office Necessary?   You can deduct the costs of a home office only if you maintain it for the convenience of your employer. This test applies whether or not an employer provides office space. But if an employer does so, that suggests that your home office is for *your* convenience, not the employer's. Maintaining a home office merely for your convenience, even if you use it extensively after hours, does not justify a tax deduction.

Only occasionally have the courts considered an employee's home-office expenses deductible when an employer also provided an office. In 1986, for example, an appeals court allowed a college professor to deduct home-office expenses because 80 percent of his required research and writing was done there each week and because the college did not provide him with a suitable office. In the same year, however, a tax court (which is lower than an appeals court) ruled that another college faculty member did not qualify for the deduction for the home office she used for preparing lectures and grading student papers because the college provided her with an office and did not require that she have another. Hence, the court ruled, she was using her home office only for her convenience and not as a condition of her employment.

Of course, if you conduct a business—either as a full-time activity or as a sideline unconnected with your regular employment— you may qualify for the deduction, provided that the IRS recognizes your activity as a bona fide business. Managing your investments, for example, is not considered a business by the IRS. Managing rental properties ordinarily is, but you should consult your tax adviser before claiming a deduction for this purpose.

Qualifications   In general, to qualify for a deduction, the office for the business you run must be used regularly and exclusively for business purposes; and it must be the principal place of business, a place to meet people for business purposes, or a structure detached from your residence.

The "principal place of business" criterion has been interpreted variously and inconsistently. In one case, the tax court ruled that the proprietor of a hot dog stand was not entitled to a deduction for the home office where she kept her business records and accounts because the stand itself was the "focal point" or principal place of business. In another case, the tax court ruled that a woman who owned a laundry with her husband could not claim a deduction for the home office where she spent two hours daily on business activities. A higher court, however, overturned this ruling, arguing that both the time she spent in the office and the importance of the work she did there justified the deduction.

If you are uncertain about the legitimacy of your deduction, you would be wise to consult a tax adviser. As the foregoing examples indicate, you may or may not prevail in court, but even a victory may not be worth its costs in time and legal expenses.

If you and your tax adviser decide that your claim for a deduction is legitimate, be careful to adhere to the following practices:

- If the office is a room of your home, make certain that it is used exclusively for business. Do not furnish it with a bed, a television set, recreational equipment, or anything else not directly related to business.
- If the office occupies only part of a room, keep that part isolated from the rest of the room by setting up bookshelves, file cabinets, or other barriers.
- Using the office for meetings with clients, suppliers, customers, and other business-related contacts can make your claim stronger than using it merely for paperwork and telephone calls. This is especially important if your employer requires you to maintain the office.

Additional Tax Considerations If you own your home, deducting the costs of office space may not be worth the trouble. To begin with, you face the complex task of prorating many of your housing costs—from utility bills to maintenance expenses and interest on mortgage payments. The prorating may be based on room count or square footage. Perhaps more important, when you sell the house, the proportion of capital gains attributable to the office is immediately taxable and may not be postponed if you reinvest in another home within two years. You may be able to salvage this tax advantage by converting your office space to personal use before the beginning of the year in which you sell the house, but the law on this is unclear.

Even if your home office does not qualify for a deduction, any items you buy in connection with your business—file cabinets, ledgers, stationery, and other office supplies—are deductible either as business expenses or expenses unreimbursed by your employer. Unreimbursed employee expenses, however, are lumped together with other miscellaneous expenses, such as tax preparation, and the total is deductible only to the extent that it exceeds 2 percent of your adjusted gross income. If you maintain an office for the convenience of an employer, the expense is considered a miscellaneous expense.

If your home office is legitimately your principal place of business, you can deduct travel expenses whenever you go out for business purposes—even if you visit your employer. Ordinarily, the cost of travel to and from work is not deductible, but in this situation the deduction is legitimate. One final note: the home office deduction can only be used to offset profit; it cannot be used to create a loss.

Home Computers

The principles governing deductions for home computers are basically similar to those applied to a home office. If you work for someone other than yourself, the computer must be used for "the convenience of the employer," and not simply for your own. It must, in addition, constitute a "condition of employment"—that is, you must have it in order to perform your work properly.

A letter from your employer might help, but only if it can provide sufficient support for your deduction. If an employer can attest that the computer was purchased for the convenience of the employer as a condition of employment and that no computer facilities were available at work, the IRS might be persuaded to let you deduct the cost. But if any of these conditions is missing, the computer is probably not deductible. In a 1987 ruling, the IRS disallowed a deduction by an aerospace engineer for a computer he had bought exclusively for his employer's work because the computers at the company offices were often used by others during working hours. Although a letter from his employer claimed that the computer was a condition of the engineer's employment, the IRS disregarded this claim, arguing that he could have used the computers at work.

Those who have their own businesses or who qualify for the home-office deduction as employees are not subject to the condition-of-employment test. In addition, the computer need not be used exclusively for the business, provided a log is kept to document the proportion of such use. If more than 50 percent of the computer's use is for business purposes (excluding its use in managing your personal investments), it can be depreciated more advantageously. Unlike other expenses, the computer must be installed before year end—not just purchased—to qualify for a deduction.

For tax purposes, a computer can be depreciated in two ways. You can "expense" it—that is, deduct its entire cost or a large part of its cost in the year of its purchase up to a maximum of $10,000. Any excess over the $10,000 can be carried over to the following year, but if you are self-employed, you may not deduct more than your net income from self-employment to produce a loss.

The alternative is to depreciate it generally over five years—a strategy that may be preferable for equipment costing more than $10,000, or for firms showing a low level of profit.

Automobiles Used for Business Purposes

If you use an automobile in a business of your own, the costs are deductible to the extent that they are incurred for business as distinct from personal use. Automobile expenses are also deductible if incurred for investment purposes, such as a trip to inspect your real estate properties. If you use your own automobile as an employee but are not reimbursed for its use, you may claim its costs as unreimbursed expenses, but only to the extent that they exceed 2 percent of your adjusted gross income—and only to the extent used for business purposes, not commuting or other personal use.

The operating costs may be calculated either on a per-mile basis or on the basis of actual operating expenses. On a per-mile basis, the IRS allows a deduction of 27.5 cents per mile in 1991.

Even if you use the standard mileage rate, you may deduct costs of parking and tolls. Keep receipts and records.

Although the total-expenses basis may give you a larger deduction, it is more complicated because it requires you to maintain not only complete records of all operating costs (including insurance, repairs, and tune-ups as well as fuel) but also a log in which you record the length and purpose of each trip and the total mileage at the beginning and the end of each year. The mileage log must be kept even if you use the IRS's standard allowance.

If your employer provides you with a company car, the value of your personal use of it is counted as part of your gross income and is therefore taxable. The IRS provides rules for assessing this value and it offers the employer several options for the tax treatment of this fringe benefit, but the procedure is complicated, so you should consult your employer about how to handle it.

INVESTMENTS

If you invest actively, moving frequently from one security or mutual fund to another, you need to be concerned about the tax consequences of your investment activity, particularly about balancing gains and losses. All investors should understand the rules about deducting investment-related expenses.

It is never advisable to allow tax considerations alone to govern your investment decisions; the fundamental soundness of the investment is a far more important criterion. Nevertheless, the timing of any transaction can have significant tax consequences, and occasionally, all other things being equal, tax considerations may be the deciding factor that motivates you to choose one investment over another.

Capital Gains and Losses

Capital gains and losses are the profits or losses that you incur when you sell or exchange a capital asset. Capital assets include such standard investments as stocks, bonds, and mutual fund shares. You may incur a capital gain or loss when you move assets from one mutual fund to another—even if both belong to the same "family"—and invest in closely related securities. The tax regulations governing capital gains and losses are complicated. They were changed drastically by the Tax Reform Act of 1986, and again in 1990.

To begin with, long-term gains (on investments held more than one year) are taxed at the same rates as ordinary income for married couples making under $82,150 and individuals making under

$49,300 in taxable income. For people who earn over those amounts, the top rate on capital gains is 28 percent as opposed to 31 percent on ordinary income.

Obviously, people who receive no benefit from long-term capital gains may want to realize any profits they make on investments promptly without consideration to holding them for more than a year.

Since 1986, both long-term and short-term capital losses are deductible, first against any capital gains and then, to a maximum amount of $3,000, against ordinary income as well. Losses that exceed this maximum can be carried over to the following year.

Toward the end of each year, experienced investors review their portfolios for the tax consequences and attempt to generate losses that will, to some extent, offset gains made earlier in the year. If you own a stock whose price has dropped since you bought it but that you want to retain, you can experience a loss by selling it and buying it back at its current price. But you should be careful to avoid a "wash" sale, which the IRS disallows on the grounds that it was executed for the sole purpose of tax reduction. If you buy the same or similar shares within 30 days before or after selling your original stock, you will have a "wash." One way to avoid it is to "double up"—that is, to buy the same or similar shares at least 31 days before you sell your original holdings. Unfortunately, you then tie up and put at risk that additional capital. Another way to avoid a wash sale is to wait at least 31 days after your sale to buy new shares. Check with your stockbroker or tax adviser if you are unclear about the timing.

If you own a stock that has appreciated, there are two ways of realizing a gain but deferring the tax on it to the following year. By buying a "put" option, you acquire the right to sell a stock within a specified time period in the following year at approximately its current price. This can protect you against loss because, in the event that the price drops, you can exercise your option and receive the higher price. (Your net gain, of course, is reduced by the cost of the put.) And since you need not deliver the stock until the next year, your gain will not be taxable until then. Should the price of the stock continue to rise, you are not obligated to sell at the option price; you merely let your option expire, lose what you paid for it, and take a deduction for the loss. Before starting this procedure, you should make sure that the price of the transaction is worth the savings from the tax deferral.

Another way to postpone capital-gains tax until the following year is to make what is called a "short sale against the box." Under this arrangement, you agree to sell shares at a certain price toward the end of the year but to deliver them at the beginning of the following year, at which time you receive payment and become liable for the tax. Of course, if in the interim the price has risen, you lose out on further profits. This is a complicated tactic suitable only for sophisticated investors.

Deductible Expenses

Certain direct expenses connected with investments, such as the interest charged on margin accounts, are deductible within certain limitations. Other expenses, however—safe deposit box rentals, the fees charged by custodians or investment counselors, subscriptions to advisory services or publications, and legal expenses related to producing income or managing investments—are deductible only to the extent that they (along with other miscellaneous deductions) exceed 2 percent of your adjusted gross income.

Travel expenses may be allowable, provided they survive IRS scrutiny of both their level and their direct connection with income-producing investments.

They, too, are subject to the 2 percent floor for itemized deductions. In addition, only 80 percent of the cost of any meals or entertainment expenses related to your investments are deductible. You must keep detailed records of expenses and of how your activities related directly to your investments. Even then, the IRS may disallow your deductions. For example, an art collector's deduction for travel expenses incurred in connection with a purchase was disallowed because the IRS held that the collection was not really an investment but merely a source of personal satisfaction. Travel to investment seminars—which are often held at attractive sites in the Bahamas or Switzerland—is no longer deductible except as a business expense by professionals in the investment field.

The deductions available to investors in income-producing real estate and limited partnerships are described in chapter 22.

DIVORCE

Although a divorce—even when it is amicable—often involves a complex division of the couple's property, this division usually has no immediate tax consequences for either party, though it may later affect capital-gains taxes when the property is sold. The components of a settlement that relate most immediately to income tax are alimony and child support, cash settlements, and the dependency exemption for children. Future tax problems can be avoided if these issues are negotiated prior to settlement so that all the details can be specified in the divorce decree.

Alimony and Child Support

Because alimony and child support have quite different tax consequences, the divorcing couple should attempt to choose the more advantageous form of the two. But because the choice must be incorporated in the divorce decree or written agreement and has long-term consequences, it must be made carefully and thoughtfully.

Child-support payments have no tax consequences because they are not deductible by the supporter or counted as income by the recipient. Alimony is tax-deductible for the payer and constitutes taxable income for the recipient, although the recipient has the right to shelter up to $2,000 of it by depositing it in an IRA (if the recipient qualifies for the IRA deduction otherwise). When the payer is in a higher tax bracket than the recipient, alimony has been used to disguise money that is actually intended for child support, because the payer receives a greater benefit from the deduction, while the recipient pays less tax on the income.

This strategy, however, is less valuable today than it was before 1987, because the current tax brackets are less likely to result in significant bracket differences between the two partners. In addition, changes mandated by the Tax Act of 1984 make the disguise of child support as alimony more difficult (though they apply only to decrees or agreements made after December 31, 1984. Likewise, changes made by the 1986 Tax Act apply only to agreements signed or decrees made after December 31, 1986, unless the parties amend the agreement or decree later). The rules discussed below reflect some of these difficulties and require great care and forethought in the preparation of the divorce decree. Always consult a lawyer or accountant before settling on any of these matters.

Dependency Exemption for Children

When a divorce involves the custody of children, a decision must be made as to which parent is to claim the dependency exemption for them. (This holds even if there is joint custody.) Generally, the parent who has custody for the longer time (more than six months each year) takes the exemption. But that parent can give up the exemption as part of the overall settlement. For agreements executed after December 31, 1984, or decrees entered after that date, the noncustodial parent must obtain a Form 8332 from the custodial parent. The noncustodial parent must file the form with his or her tax return. For agreements executed before that date, the parties' allocation of the exemption in their decree or agreement is still binding. If no allocation was made, Form 8332 may be used.

Other Deductions

Although only one parent can claim a dependency exemption, both can claim deductions for whatever share of the child's medical expenses they paid. These expenses are deductible, however, only if the taxpayer's total medical expenses, including those for children, exceed 7.5 percent of adjusted gross income.

Fees paid to attorneys, mediators, and others for arranging or contesting the divorce are not deductible, but you may claim as part of your miscellaneous deductions (to the extent that they exceed 2 percent of your adjusted gross income) the fees charged for the setting up of alimony payments or property settlements and for tax advice. It is important, therefore, that these professionals segregate their fees into each of these categories.

Timing the Divorce

The timing of the divorce can have significant consequences for the taxes of both parties. A divorced couple may not file a joint return for the year of their divorce, even if the divorce was effective on the last day of that year. If the divorce occurs in the first half of the year, the parent who provides the principal residence for the children for the balance of the year can claim "head of household" status. The noncustodial parent without other dependents must use the less advantageous "single" status.

BARTER

Toward the end of the 1970s, barter became a popular medium through which people tried to exchange products or services without paying income tax. Thus, for example, a writer might prepare a résumé for an electrical engineer in return for the assembly and installation of a stereo set, with no money changing hands. Neither one declared the value of the work on his or her tax return as income.

This kind of transaction undoubtedly persists on an informal basis today, but a decade ago its popularity prompted the development of formal barter clubs that issued transferable credits for work done. Thus, a painter could barter one of his or her works for a credit voucher that could be used to acquire services from another member of the club, not necessarily the person who acquired the painting.

When these clubs became conspicuous enough to attract public attention, they attracted the attention of the IRS as well. The IRS ruled that because barter transactions are taxable, the dollar value of an individual's credit vouchers must be declared as part of that person's income. As a consequence, the clubs have virtually disappeared.

If goods or services are sold for something other than money, each seller must declare as income the fair market value of whatever payment was received. If, for example, an artist pays monthly rent with a painting rather than cash, the landlord must declare as income the market value of the painting, and the painter must declare as income the market value of the monthly rent.

A form of barter can, in rare instances, be used by owners of business or investment real estate to defer tax on the sale of an appreciated property. If they can exchange one piece of property for another of like kind and equal value, no tax is due until either owner sells his or her newly acquired property. If some money changes hands to make the exchange equitable, only that sum is taxed as a sale.

Simple as it may seem, this kind of transaction is, in fact, rather complicated. There are so many rules governing this sort of transaction that it should not be attempted without the advice of a tax adviser experienced in real estate matters.

ALTERNATIVE MINIMUM TAX

Unless you have been trying to reduce your taxes through tax shelters, excessive deductions, or accelerated depreciations, you generally need not concern yourself with the alternative minimum tax. The AMT is aimed at taxpayers, usually wealthy ones, who attempt to reduce their tax bill—in some cases to nothing at all—through the use of what are called "preference items"—the exercising of incentive stock options, for example, or the donation of appreciated property to charities. The intent of the AMT is to collect a fair share from these taxpayers by requiring them to use a different method for calculating their taxes. Taxpayers who suspect that they may be subject to the AMT must calculate their tax liability by both the standard method and the AMT method, and pay the higher of the two results.

The AMT not only requires a different method of tax calculation, but also differs from the conventional return in its limitations on deductions and in other respects. Taxpayers whose income sources threaten to make them subject to this tax almost invariably enlist the help of experienced accountants or other tax preparers.

CLOSE-UP: HELP WITH YOUR RETURN

The levels of help available for preparation of your return range from the IRS and volunteer groups that charge nothing for their services to certified public accountants whose fees can run to more than $100 per hour. The level you choose should depend on the complexity of your return, but since many fees are calculated on an hourly basis, your actual cost may depend on your own efforts in assembling your records systematically and having in mind the specific issues on which you need consultation. Bear in mind that no matter who prepares your return, you remain personally responsible for its completeness and accuracy.

The IRS and Other Cost-Free Sources

The IRS publishes more than a hundred free bulletins targeted at specific areas and situations, such as a *Farmer's Tax Guide* and *Tax Information for Survivors, Executors, and Administrators.* These publications are listed, along with an order form, in the mailing containing your tax forms; the list, as well as some of the publications, is available in many public libraries. Information can be obtained and orders placed through the IRS national toll-free number (1-800-TAX-FORM) or your local IRS office. IRS Publication 910, *Guide to Free Tax Services,* lists all free IRS publications and other free IRS information sources. Publication 17, *Your Federal Income Tax,* is the most general guide to completing your return.

The IRS Tele-Tax (1-800-829-4477) offers, on a year-round, 24-hour basis, a selection of tape recordings on specific topics. Tele-Tax also has local toll-free numbers and can be used to find out the status of your refund if 10 weeks have elapsed since you filed your return.

The major limitation of the IRS publications and information tapes is that, unlike privately published materials, they offer little advice on reducing your tax liability. The IRS telephone assistance program, staffed by IRS personnel, suffers from the same limitation, but in addition, it cannot be relied on. Although the IRS points out that its accuracy rate has improved over the last several years, it still concedes that more than one of seven pieces of advice it gives is either inaccurate or incomplete. And, unfortunately, claiming you got advice from the IRS doesn't help you in case of an audit. A provision of the 1988 Tax Act gives some protection if you have used IRS advice that was supplied in writing. You'll no longer be assessed a penalty if the IRS gave you bad written advice, although you still will have to pay the right amount of tax. Keep the IRS's written advice, of course.

If you qualify in terms of your income or your age, you may be able to get free help with your tax form from volunteer tax preparers at a community center or a local library. These programs generally enlist college students and retired persons who have been trained to deal with basic, uncomplicated returns.

Professional Assistance

If your return is uncomplicated by investments or business income, you may be able to get adequate advice from a seasonal storefront or franchised operation. Your preparer is unlikely to be an accountant, but will have had several weeks or months of special training. Generally these services charge less than $100 for preparing a simple return. Beware, however, of the firm that bases its charges on the amount of the refund it can secure for you, or that boasts in its advertising that it can get you a larger refund than anyone else. The methods used by such firms may get you into trouble. Beware also of the firm that disappears entirely after April 15. Make sure you have a central business office number for your preparation firm that is valid after April 15. And find out what kind of support they will give you if you are audited.

If you have investments, your own business, or a substantial income, you should probably use a certified public accountant, who can not only spot deductions you may have overlooked, but also may provide you with general advice that can reduce your taxes in subsequent years.

Accountants on the staffs of large national or regional firms accustomed to dealing with corporate clients are likely to charge too much for taxpayers of moderate means—if, indeed, they don't reject such business outright. Unless your return involves substantial income from a number of sources, or unless you have a business tie to a larger firm, you should try to find—through the recommendations of friends, your banker, or some other financial professional—an individual practitioner or a small firm with a more personal approach. The person you choose should not be an auditor or a corporate accountant, but someone experienced in handling individual returns.

Tax attorneys are the most expensive source of help, and are usually unnecessary unless your return involves questions of interpretation of the tax code or unless you need legal advice about business or investment transactions. You may also need them in the event of an audit, but you should be aware that their fees can cost you far more than the amount at issue between you and the IRS.

No matter whom you choose, be sure to read the return before you sign it and ask for clarification of anything you don't understand. And, even though you are fully responsible for it, insist that the preparer sign the return. Because the IRS investigates preparers as well as taxpayers, having to sign may make the preparer more cautious.

CLOSE-UP: SCRUTINY BY THE IRS

Aside from sending you a refund, there are two reasons for which the IRS may contact you after you have filed a return. The audit—although widely known and feared—is actually rare. Much more frequently used is a letter from the IRS claiming that your tax liability is higher than your return indicated and instructing you to remit the difference.

These letters have become increasingly more common since the IRS has developed a computer matching program capable of comparing almost every taxpayer's return with other sources of information reported to it on interest, dividends, alimony, mortgage payments, real estate transactions, and state tax refunds.

This program makes it essential that you report precisely the income recorded on every Form 1099 and W-2 that you receive. Because the IRS charges interest on the delinquent amount from the day it was due, you may be facing a substantial cost, especially in view of the fact that the program is often two years behind in its processing. In addition, you will very likely be assessed a penalty.

The IRS claim for tax due may, of course, be baseless. Mistakes can occur because a bank changes its name or reports IRA interest incorrectly or simply makes a mistake in a Social Security number. Computers are likely to miss such discrepancies, but if you submit a letter of explanation, it will be read by a human being. If your bank or your employer is responsible for the error, an explanatory letter from them can help clear up the problem. In general, the IRS acknowledges errors of this kind and closes the file promptly. If you are in the wrong, however, no matter how innocent the error, delay will do nothing but add to your interest charges.

Two common errors involve stock dividends and state tax refunds. If your securities are in your broker's street account rather than in your own name, and the broker remits or credits the dividends to you, your return should list your broker, and not the individual corporations, as the income source. State taxes are tax-deductible, but refunds are counted as income for taxpayers who itemized (and thus took a deduction) in the year the state tax payment was made. For those taxpayers, the refund is income, even if it is applied to next year's estimated payment. This is often overlooked by the taxpayer, but not by the IRS.

An audit is a more serious but far less likely event, since only 1 to 2 percent of taxpayers have been audited in recent years. This percentage may increase because the IRS is expanding its audit staff. The IRS does not disclose its criteria for selection, but the taxpayers most likely to be audited are those with high incomes; those claiming disproportionately high deductions or deductions in such targeted areas as tax shelters, home offices, or personal computers; and those who receive much of their income in the form of cash. You may also be audited if your tax preparer is on the IRS list of suspect preparers.

If your deductions in any one area—medical expenses, for example, or charitable contributions—are high but legitimate, you may be able to avoid an audit by attaching an explanatory letter to your return.

Audits are of three types: the correspondence audit, the office audit, and the field audit. A correspondence audit uses the mails. For an office audit you are required to appear, with about six weeks' notice, at the IRS office by appointment and to bring with you pertinent records and documents. Such audits usually focus on one or two specific items rather than on your entire return.

In a field audit, the IRS auditor comes to your home or office, examines all your records pertaining to the year in question, and is allowed to question you about any aspect of your return.

In preparation for either of the latter two types of audit, you should discuss your strategy with your preparer or some other tax professional; you may, in fact, want him or her to represent you or accompany you at the audit. In fact, under 1988 legislation, the IRS is strongly encouraged to deal with your representative. You are entitled to have a representative with you and, in most cases, to have the representative go without you. An accountant or attorney is likely to charge you at least $100 an hour to appear on your behalf, but such professional representation may be worth its cost, particularly if you are likely to be emotional, angry, or overly talkative, or if you are not completely innocent.

You (or your representative) should, of course, bring to any audit all the receipts and documents on which your return was based. If these are not available, the IRS may accept secondary evidence, such as a written statement from a client or a calendar entry about a business meal. You are most likely to be vindicated in an audit, however, if you have retained solid documentation for all deductions, credits, and other tax matters. You should maintain such records for at least three years after filing your return—or longer if you think you may be questioned about your sources of income. Though generally the statute of limitations for audits is three years, the IRS has six years to question you if it believes that you have omitted an amount greater than 25 percent of the income you reported. There is no time limitation if you have not filed a return or if you file one that is fraudulent.

If you are selected for an audit, there is no reason to panic. Despite the horror stories reported in the media, most auditors are reasonable people, most issues are negotiable, and a few taxpayers, according to the IRS, even emerge from audits with a refund.

The 1988 Tax Act gives you even more rights in an audit than you had before. The IRS must provide you with a clear description of your rights. You can receive their simplified explanation of the audit and appeal procedure, even if you are not being audited, by requesting Publication 1, *Your Rights as a Taxpayer*, through the publication request number, 1-800-TAX-FORM.

If you disagree with the auditor's assessment in an office audit, your first level of appeal is the auditor's supervisor, who can review your case on the spot. If you remain dissatisfied, you can, within 30 days of receipt of a "30-day letter," request an appeal. Your case will then be assigned to an appeals officer, but this may take several months, and the appeals officer may end up raising questions about your return that the auditor did not address.

If the dispute is not resolved at this level, the IRS will notify you by certified mail that you must pay the disputed tax within 90 days or demand a court hearing. The longer the delay, the higher the interest charges if the decision goes against you. The rate of interest, set periodically by the IRS, approximates market rates and is treated as consumer interest.

If you take your case to a U.S. tax court and the decision goes against you, you need not pay anything until the matter is decided. If you go to a U.S. district court or the U.S. Claims Court, you must pay the disputed amount in advance and collect a refund if you win. The U.S. Claims Court is in Washington, D.C.; tax courts and district courts are local, and the latter provide a jury trial.

Because taking your case to court involves legal expenses as well as further delay, only large amounts are worth disputing, and you must be reasonably confident about your position.

IV

INSURANCE

12

Medical Insurance

Janet Bamford

PROTECTING YOUR MOST VALUABLE ASSET

Health insurance protects you and your family from the dollar cost of illness. If you need medical attention, a health insurance policy will usually pay most—and sometimes all—of your doctor, hospital, medication, and medical equipment bills.* Obtaining health insurance is therefore one of the first recommendations of financial planning and budgeting experts, and for good reason; your good health and the means to maintain or repair it are a cornerstone in your financial house. Poor health can greatly damage your ability to generate income, and if you are without health insurance, medical expenses can quickly erode the asset base you have built or are attempting to build.

The cost of health care has risen rapidly in recent years, outpacing the overall rate of inflation. Medical costs have increased faster than the consumer price index in nine of the ten years from

---

*Health insurance does not, however, cover the other costs of poor health; it will not pay your rent or mortgage or put food on the table while you are out of work because of your infirmity. Disability income insurance, which is covered in chapter 16, takes care of that.

1978 through 1987, according to the Health Insurance Association of America (HIAA). By January 1990, the average cost of one day's stay in a semiprivate hospital room stood at $297—about what it costs to stay in some top-priced hotels in Miami, Los Angeles, Honolulu, or New York. And that figure does not include surgical, laboratory, and physicians' fees.

As health-care costs have risen sharply, so too has the cost of medical insurance. Consequently, there is a growing trend toward "going naked"—that is, going without health insurance. According to the Employee Benefits Research Institute, a Washington, DC–based study group, the ranks of Americans under 65 who lack public or private health insurance stood at 37 million in 1991. Some of those people are unemployed and some self-employed, but many are employees of companies that do not provide medical insurance as a fringe benefit. Increasingly, companies simply are not sponsoring health coverage for their staff: They find it too expensive.

Despite this trend, however, the vast majority of consumers do have insurance, their health-care costs most immediately paid for either by an insurance company or by the government through programs such as Medicare and Medicaid. Approximately 85 percent of the population under the age of 65 is covered by such insurance, according to the Employee Benefits Research Institute. Everyone over the age of 65 is eligible for Medicare. Unlike such major industrial nations as Great Britain, Canada, France, and West Germany, the United States does not have a national health insurance system.

For most people, health insurance means some form of comprehensive group health insurance, usually provided by an employer. Individuals not subsidized by an employer or eligible for a government insurance program must make their own arrangements with an insurer if they want coverage (see p. 228).

Because of alarm over rising medical costs and insurance premiums, insurers are testing alternative types of health insurance coverage. Consequently, being covered by health insurance today does not necessarily mean that an insurer simply pays the bills for a doctor of your choosing. If you are covered by a health service contractor of a health maintenance organization (HMO), for example, your insurer may pay the entire bill but also dictate who your doctors will be. That—added to the confusing array of more traditional coverage options—makes the job of shopping for or just assessing your coverage all the more difficult.

This chapter will explain how the various types of coverage work and what you should look for to find the best health insurance coverage for your needs. Other kinds of health-related insurance, such as dread-disease policies and disability insurance—which do not provide coverage in quite the same manner as the health insurance discussed in this chapter—are covered in chapter 16.

TRADITIONAL INDEMNITY INSURANCE

Basic Hospitalization

Good health insurance coverage starts with basic medical protection, covering hospital expenses. Blue Cross, which was born at Baylor University Hospital in Dallas, Texas, in 1929, is probably the best known such hospitalization plan. At its inception, Blue Cross covered a small group of schoolteachers for 21 days of hospital care for a monthly premium of 50 cents per teacher. Today, Blue Cross covers some 71 million Americans. Blue Shield, which is Blue Cross's sister organization, was founded in 1939 to cover the cost of physicians' services associated with a hospital stay, although it has since branched out to cover other benefits as well. Blue Cross coverage and Blue Shield coverage are frequently linked under one Blue Cross/Blue Shield policy.

Generally speaking, basic hospitalization policies cover doctors' fees incurred during hospitalization; surgical procedures performed both in and out of the hospital; daily room and board fees for a semiprivate room (or in an intensive care unit); normal nursing services while in the hospital; and certain hospital services and supplies, including X-rays, lab tests, blood transfusions, and drugs and medication. Basic protection may also pay for lab tests and diagnostic tests performed outside hospitals. Kidney dialysis, radiation, and chemotherapy may also be covered. Blue Cross makes payments for such services directly to the hospital, so you will not normally be involved in the payment process, although you should receive a copy of the itemized bill; when you do, scrutinize it to make sure there are no incorrect charges.

Basic hospitalization does not pay the cost of such things as a visit to the doctor's office. That can be covered (subject to certain limitations) by an associated major medical policy, as we will see shortly.

For all practical purposes, since your employer pays all or part of the premium for basic hospitalization, you do not often have the opportunity to "shop around" and buy the best coverage for your needs. Some employers, however, offer a range of options called cafeteria-style benefits, or flexible benefits, or a menu of benefits. Such benefit plans, which are currently in the developmental stage in the employee benefits field and are thus not yet widely available, allow the employee to choose from a menu that might include, for example, a medical plan, life insurance, extended vacation, and day-care services. The employer cuts the costs of fringe benefits by giving an employee a limited amount of voucher money to "spend" on benefits, and the employee may then apportion his or her allotment to those elements he or she deems most important. Varying levels of medical coverage would likely be part of this package, so you might have a choice of a "good," "better," or "best" medical plan.

If your employer does not offer cafeteria-style benefits (and few do as yet), you can still purchase a supplemental health insurance policy that will fill the holes in your employer-sponsored plan and improve your coverage. Of course, you have to pay extra for this, but if your employer-sponsored plan is inadequate for your possible medical needs, you should supplement it. The best place to start looking for supplemental coverage is at the insurance company that already provides your employer's basic coverage; by so doing, you will likely pay less, because you are only buying an extra increment of coverage that will piggyback on the main policy.

The best basic hospitalization policies begin paying the bills the first day you are in the hospital. But some are not obligated to start payments until after a few days have passed. Since the average hospital stay is only 6.6 days, according to the American Hospital Association, you should aim for a policy that begins coverage immediately. Coverage that doesn't begin on the first day may not pay out much at all.

Not surprisingly, the longer the hospitalization coverage, the more expensive the policy. Typical coverage periods may be as little as three or four weeks to as much as a year or more. Some policies will pay the full cost of a room for up to 21 days, and then 50

percent of the cost for an additional 180 days. If you have used up
your limit of days, you are typically not eligible again for benefits
until a specified time period has passed, perhaps 90 days.

Look at any basic protection policy carefully to learn what is
not covered as well as what is. Some basic policies set limits on
coverage for drugs, supplies, and the like—either a set dollar limit,
or perhaps a coinsurance agreement in which the insurer picks up
80 percent while the patient pays the remainder. Other policies
have predetermined limits on payment for specific types of medical
procedures.

Regardless of what your doctor or surgeon charges, still other
policies may cover only part of the cost; patients are obliged to pay
the remainder. And certain types of elective medical procedures,
such as cosmetic surgery, are often not covered, even though hospitalization may be required.

Be sure the hospital you are likely to use is approved by your
insurer. Often, insurers will pay for care at nonapproved hospitals
only if you have emergency treatment. All this information is
spelled out in the materials your employer or insurer provides on
your benefits, or is available from the benefits specialists in your
company. If it isn't, or if you are confused about your coverage,
contact your insurer for details.

Major Medical Coverage

Going hand in hand with basic hospitalization is major medical
coverage. A major medical policy is designed to pick up where your
basic coverage leaves off, for medical treatment both inside and
outside of a hospital. Thus, it is usually coordinated with a basic
policy so that the two dovetail but don't duplicate each other's
coverage.

Almost all major medical plans pay for doctors (including specialists), osteopaths, and chiropractors. They also pay hospital
expenses that aren't covered by basic protection, including the cost
of outpatient care, although there usually is a limit on the daily
rate paid. Drug and medical supply expenses are also covered—
when they have been prescribed by a doctor. Be aware that medical
supplies are not limited to bandages and blood, but include some
products you might not think of immediately: wheelchair rentals,
respirators, prosthetic devices, X-rays, and lab expenses. Many pol-

icies also pay for ambulance charges. Not surprisingly, a major medical policy does not cover some items that may wind up on a hospital bill, such as television or telephone rental fees.

Typically, major medical policies have a deductible of anywhere from $25 to $200, although some deductibles are as high as $1,000. (The deductible is the initial amount of the bill you must pay before you are eligible for benefits.) This threshold can be calculated in different ways: as a flat fee—say, $500—or as a percentage of the expenses up to a limit—10 percent of expenses up to $5,000, perhaps.

If your major medical plan is provided by your employer, chances are your deductible will be whatever that employer chooses. According to a 1989 HIAA survey of 2,000 employers, the average deductible for individuals was about $200, while for families it was about $400. Since a high deductible represents less money the insurance company ultimately has to pay out, policies with higher deductibles are cheaper. Such coverage is truly protection against major illness, rather than coverage for every minor ailment.

For group policies, insurance rates are usually set according to how that group has used benefits in the past. This is called "experience rating." A company full of employees who are heavy users of health coverage benefits will pay more than a company whose employees rarely use their medical insurance. Rates for individual policies are based on actuarial tables that estimate how much of their benefits the individuals will use.

Some insurance policies have upper limits on what will be paid either per illness or over the lifetime of the insured. Some policies have lifetime limits for each type of illness or accident, which may increase your total coverage if you are struck by more than one serious illness. As a rule of thumb, policies that limit the amount paid for each illness should pay at least up to $25,000 per hospitalization in each benefit period, and $10,000 for other medical bills over a year. Policies with a lifetime maximum should pay at least up to $250,000 during that span. In recent years, though, lifetime coverage of $1 million has rapidly become commonplace. In the HIAA survey mentioned earlier, about 66 percent of covered employees had $1 million or more of lifetime coverage.

Many major medical policies are structured so that once you have paid the deductible, you are still responsible for 20 or 25 percent of all covered expenses. This is called coinsurance or copayments. You usually continue the copayments until you have spent a certain amount—in most cases, $2,000 or less. If bills amount to more than that, the insurance company picks up 100 percent of the covered expenses. Such provisions are known colloquially as "stop loss provisions," because your financial exposure is limited.

Whenever it is time to file a claim involving basic hospitalization and/or major medical, remember that two-wage-earner couples may enjoy some extra insurance benefits—100 percent coverage of their medical costs. If both you and your spouse receive family medical coverage from your employers, a claim should first be submitted to the patient's employer, which we will call Company A. Assume that Insurance Company A pays 80 percent of the bill. You can then submit the remainder of the claim to Insurance Company B. It will likely pay the remaining 20 percent of the bill in full, meaning that you obtain 100 percent coverage. You cannot receive more than 100 percent coverage; to attempt to do so would be insurance fraud.

DENTAL COVERAGE

A valuable option attached to many health benefit packages, often for a small extra fee, is dental coverage. In the 1988 HIAA survey, 53 percent of employers offered some sort of dental coverage. Generally, routine dental expenses such as oral examinations, X-rays, cleaning, fillings, extractions, bridgework, and dentures are covered, as is oral surgery. The insurer typically pays 80 percent of such charges after a deductible is met. If the dental coverage is part of a basic and major medical plan, the deductible for dental treatment is normally separate from the deductible for medical and hospital care. Dental work done solely for cosmetic purposes, such as bonding, is seldom covered. However, there is a trend toward covering orthodontic services; the HIAA survey showed that more than 37 percent of employees in group plans were covered for orthodontic care, for both children and adults.

HMOs AND HEALTH SERVICE CONTRACTORS

Health maintenance organizations (HMOs) and health service contractors, such as preferred provider organizations (PPOs) and independent practice arrangements (IPAs), are relatively new institutions that have grown out of the attempts of insurers to battle rising medical costs. Some of the largest HMOs include the Kaiser Permanente, with plans in 16 states and the District of Columbia; Blue Cross/Blue Shield's HMO programs, which have about 4.4 million members; and Cigna Healthplan, Inc., which covers some 1.4 million people in 24 states and the District of Columbia.

As the category of health-care providers has grown in recent years, the distinctions between them have blurred. An HMO, a term that is used almost generically, is a health-care plan that offers both coverage and service. Most HMOs consist of an affiliated group of doctors who practice together and are paid a salary, rather than a fee for each service they perform. For subscribers, an HMO is basically a prepaid group medical service. In exchange for a monthly fee, paid either by an employer or by an individual (or jointly), a patient can use the services of doctors who will provide specified medical treatment. In some cases, a patient visits a clinic where a group of doctors practice together literally under the same roof; in other cases, an HMO is a loose confederation of physicians who operate out of their own individual offices. HMOs generally provide all the medical services you would normally need, often excluding dental care, psychiatric care, and certain other procedures, such as cosmetic surgery. Depending on where the HMO is located, it may be a small group of physicians who sometimes rely on outside specialists to provide services they are not qualified to give. In such a case, the HMO sends the patient to the specialist and picks up the cost itself. Or the HMO may be a huge organization that counts among its doctors practitioners in every known specialty.

In a preferred provider organization (PPO), an insurer or a business negotiates with a limited group of doctors and hospitals to provide health care at a certain (preferably reduced) price per service. The insurer then offers the employees who are covered a financial incentive to use those particular doctors and hospitals. For instance, the PPO might pay 100 percent of the doctor bills if you go to one of their approved physicians, but only 80 percent if you go to another doctor.

An independent practice arrangement (IPA) is one in which independent doctors agree to treat members for a set fee. Patients visit the doctors in their offices. Many of these doctors also treat other private patients as well as IPA members.

Nationally, some 34 million people were enrolled in HMOs (of all varieties) in mid-1990. The number of HMOs in the United States has grown from 41 in 1971 to 556 in 1990. In California, home to some of the largest HMOs, about 9 million people are enrolled.

Growth has been spurred by the idea that HMO coverage is cheaper than traditional health-care coverage. The HMO (or the independent doctor employed by the HMO) has negotiated with the insurer to be paid a specific fee per month or per service for each patient. The HMO and the doctor thus have an incentive to cut costs.

Some company medical plans may offer you the choice of traditional coverage or coverage at an HMO. In fact, some employers are required to offer their employees such a choice. This is true if the employer is subject to the federal Fair Labor Standards Act, has at least 25 full- or part-time employees eligible for benefits who reside in the HMO's service area, and offers a health benefits plan to eligible employees.

When presented with such a choice, obtain details about the costs and services each option provides, and carefully assess that information in relation to the services you expect to need. Query fellow workers about their experiences with the HMO your company offers. Then visit the HMO clinic or facility you will be using. Because the HMO has an incentive to reduce costs, you want to be sure those savings are not offset by long lines in the waiting room, discourteous or abrupt service, or inadequate staffing. Try to find out the track record and reputation of the health-care provider.

For many physicians, the attraction of joining an HMO is the security of a dependable salary, even though that salary tends to be smaller than the income of an independent practitioner. (Salaries, of course, tend to be higher in urban areas, lower in rural ones.) In some parts of the country, an oversupply of physicians makes it difficult for them to attract patients and build a practice. An HMO also takes care of all the details of running a practice, such as payment of medical malpractice premiums, billing, and finding nursing staffs. Doctors cite such disadvantages as a loss of autonomy and pressure to keep costs down and profits up. There may also be pressure on the doctors from the HMO organization to avoid doing additional lab tests, for example, or sending patients to outside specialists who aren't part of the HMO and so must be paid separately by the HMO. Users of an HMO should thus keep those things in mind when weighing this type of coverage against traditional health insurance.

The highly touted advantages of HMOs, however, cannot be ignored. There is usually no deductible charged to the patient, although some HMOs will charge a nominal fee or co-payment (perhaps $5 or $10) for office visits. There are usually no insurance forms to fill out, either—a relief to anyone who has struggled with such claim-filing requirements.

HMOs tend to market themselves through groups, most often through employee groups. However, some accept individual members. At Kaiser, about 10 percent of the members are individuals. Some are offered coverage after they leave a group that belongs; others apply as individuals from the outset. Those people who are not converting from group membership must undergo a medical review and may or may not be accepted. Rates vary slightly, depending on geographical location, but an individual membership at Kaiser only costs between $100 and $135 a month; an individual with two or more dependents would pay $300 to $400 a month. That is significantly lower, however, than traditional individual coverage.

Generally, if you join an HMO, your health care will be coordinated by a primary physician, who will decide when you should see specialists both inside and outside of the HMO. You should be able to choose your primary physician from among those in the practice; if you are assigned one, there is a chance you won't get along with the doctor, a factor that can inhibit good medical care. If you become ill while away from home, the HMO will pay for services performed by outside physicians, as well as for emergency care at nonaffiliated hospitals.

An increasingly common variation is the open-ended HMO, in which members are not obligated to consult their primary care physician for a referral to a specialist. What's more, they can go to physicians outside the plan altogether, in which case the HMO functions more like an insurance company, though the HMO is not likely to pay 100 percent of the fees in this case.

What should you look for in a health maintenance organization? For one thing, make sure the HMO has a variety of staff doctors and specialists. The specialists should be board-certified in their fields. The HMO's affiliated hospital is important, too. University teaching hospitals, for example, tend to handle more sophisticated medical procedures than do nonteaching hospitals.

As with any comparison shopping, talk with customers currently using the service. If your employer offers an HMO as an employee benefit, ask coworkers about the complaints they may have. One common gripe concerns the length of time patients must wait to see doctors for nonemergency appointments. A wait of six weeks or two months for a routine examination—a not uncommon lead time—may not be medically harmful, but can be plenty annoying.

HMOs are regulated by the federal government, specifically by an HMO office in the Department of Health and Human Services. By law, HMOs have a grievance procedure in place for patients who are dissatisfied with care they are getting. Find out how the procedure works officially (from the organization) and how well it works in practice (again, ask coworkers or other HMO members).

You should also consider other factors concerning HMOs. Detractors claim the medical care is impersonal and that doctors have an incentive to deny medical care. Proponents contradict those charges, arguing that doctors on salary are motivated to give good care, but not to perform unnecessary procedures. In addition, supporters say preventive health care is emphasized in an HMO to the advantage of both doctor and patient.

Criticism about cost-cutting incentives versus the quality of care will likely never go away. But two significant studies conducted in the early 1980s, one by the American Medical Association and one by the Johns Hopkins School of Hygiene and Public Health, concluded that the quality of care at HMOs was just as high as in traditional health insurance arrangements. However, it's important to remember that to some extent the jury is still out. Because much of the rapid growth of HMOs has been in the past few years, many HMOs have not yet proved they can provide quality care to large numbers of patients and still keep costs down.

MEDICARE

Medicare is a federal program for which nearly every American over the age of 65 is eligible—but you must apply for it. Generally, if you are eligible for Social Security benefits, you are eligible for Medicare.

There are also some special situations in which Medicare may provide you with medical benefits. You may receive some benefits if you are under 65 and have been eligible for Social Security disability benefits for at least 24 months, for instance. Individuals under 65 who have kidney impairments that appear "irreversible and permanent," will also receive help, specifically in the form of dialysis.

Even if you are still working at age 65, you are eligible for Medicare. Exceptions to eligibility include noncitizens and some federal employees. But even these people may participate by paying monthly premiums of $177 for Part A and $29.90 for Part B (as of 1991) for the coverage.

Medicare is a two-part program. Part A, which is automatically included for people entitled to Medicare, covers in-patient hospital charges. It covers the first 60 days of an illness, then days 61–90 with a co-payment. Under the law, patients pay a calendar-year deductible of $628 in 1991 for Part A coverage.

Part B of Medicare, which covers some out-of-hospital charges, is optional. The Part B monthly premium of $29.90 a month in 1991 is automatically deducted from your Social Security check. Unless you elect not to take Part B, you are enrolled automatically in the program. Most Medicare recipients are enrolled in Part B, and we strongly suggest you take it. The monthly premium is tied to the Social Security cost-of-living adjustment, so it goes up by the same percentage as your Social Security benefit.

If you decide not to take Part B, you can enroll during the first three months of subsequent years. But for each year you delay, your premium will increase by 10 percent.

To enroll in Medicare, you should visit your local Social Security office at least three months before you turn 65. You must take along your birth certificate or some other proof of age. You may also apply by mail. Call the nearest Social Security office for an application. If you delay in applying, the Part A coverage can be retroactive for up to 12 months prior to the date you do apply. Part B, however, is not retroactive.

Long-term custodial care (more than 150 days per stay) is only covered in three instances: care in a Medicare-certified skilled nursing facility, part-time or intermittent home health services or hospice care.

Nursing homes—perhaps the most common deliverer of long-term health care—are not covered and can quickly deplete someone's assets. Moreover, most Medicare supplement policies are of little help in paying for long-term care.

After a patient's income and assets have been sufficiently devoured by medical expenses, he or she can qualify for Medicaid, which does pay for such services.

As a result of this situation, long-term care insurance may appear sensible for those individuals who want to protect their life savings. But be very careful before purchasing one of these policies. They can be very expensive. More important, many have limited coverage.

If you are thinking of purchasing such a policy make sure it provides the following:

- a daily benefit of at least $80
- a maximum benefit per stay of at least four years
- an unlimited number of days for all stays
- full benefits for skilled, intermediate and custodial nursing care
- nursing home benefits without prior hospitalization
- home health benefits without prior hospitalization or restrictions on the number of days
- coverage for Alzheimer's disease
- guaranteed renewability for life
- some protection against rate increases
- premium waivers if you are confined to a nursing home
- an elimination period of not more than 20 days
- protection against inflation in the cost of care

There are two ways to prepare for the debilitating financial effects of a possible long-term nursing home stay. You can "spend down" to the allowable limits for Medicaid by spending on yourself or giving away property to relatives (which you may arrange through an irrevocable trust or outright), though you should seek the help of an attorney or financial planner specializing in these matters before doing so. If you dispose of or transfer assets to qualify for Medicaid, you must do so at least 30 months before applying for Medicaid.

Another method is to buy an insurance policy for long-term care. These are expensive (from around $750 to $3,000 a year, depending on your age and the policy) and have many exclusions. For most people under age 60, such policies are too costly to be recommended, unless the benefits go up with inflation. If you're over 60 and have a moderate-to-high income, you might consider a policy with at least an $80-a-day benefit and an unlimited number of days covered. If you're over 60 and of modest means, the costly policy isn't worth it because you'll probably qualify for Medicaid quickly, with at least some of your assets protected. If you buy such a plan, make sure it covers custodial as well as medical care, is "guaranteed renewable" (that is, will be renewed as long as you pay the premiums), and specifically covers Alzheimer's disease.

Doctors' fees are not covered under Part A (although they are partially covered by Part B). Nor are private-duty nurses, conveniences such as a telephone or TV in the room, the first three pints of blood for a transfusion, incidental expenses such as transportation, or domestic help at home.

There are also payment schedules and rules covering hospice services for the terminally ill, psychiatric care, and home health services. If you require skilled home health care, then you may have an unlimited number of visits, and Medicare pays all costs. However, the rules for qualifying are strict. You must be "homebound" and living in your own residence, and your doctor must specify that you need part-time skilled nursing care, or physical, occupational, or speech therapy. There is no requirement of a previous hospital stay.

It's more likely that you will need unskilled nursing or homemaker services—that is, someone to help you walk, eat, or bathe— rather than a skilled person who can administer drugs or diagnostic tests at home. Neither Medicare nor most supplemental services will pay for that.

Part B covers physicians' services, outpatient care, X-ray and other diagnostic tests, physical and speech therapy, and medical equipment for home use. In 1991, along with the $29.90 monthly premium, beneficiaries pay a $100 annual deductible and 20 percent of what Medicare deems to be reasonable charges for a doctor's services.

Note, however, that the doctor's actual charge is often far more than the amount Medicare decides is "reasonable." Medicare determines the "reasonable" charge for a service by weighing the physician's actual charge, the prevailing charge in the community, and an economic index that uses 1973 charges by physicians as a base and increases the base by a fixed amount each year. Unfortunately, both the index and the "prevailing" charges may be out of date or unrepresentative of actual fees, resulting in less than full reimbursement.

The Department of Health and Human Services estimates that some 85 percent of Part B claims are reduced or denied. There is an appeal procedure, however, but only 2 to 3 percent of elderly and formerly ill beneficiaries ever utilize it.

However, 50 percent of the appeals are successful, so we strongly recommend you appeal a reduction or denial of a Part B payment. After you receive an Explanation of Medicare Benefits, you have six months to file your appeal, for which you use Form HCFA-1964, available through your local Social Security office. If you are not satisfied with Medicare's decision, and your claim is for more than $100, you may appeal for a hearing within six months after you receive the review decision. The hearing is held before a hearing officer appointed by Medicare, and you may present and cross-examine witnesses.

You may also appeal decisions on Part A reimbursements. The first form, called HCFA-2649, must be filed within 60 days after you receive your initial response from Medicare. With Part A claims, you may then go through a hearing, an appeals council review by the Social Security Administration in Baltimore (if your claim is for more than $100), and a judicial review by a federal district court (if the disputed claim is for $1,000 or more). For this last step, you must have an attorney.

One way to avoid having to pay extra for physicians' services is to try to find one who will accept what is called "assignment." Such a doctor agrees to charge whatever Medicare decides is the allowable charge. The doctor sends his or her bills directly to Medicare, which pays 80 percent of the allowable charge. You are still responsible for the other 20 percent.

Such doctors may be hard to find, however. They may also change their minds midway through treatment. However, if you know or hear of such a physician (and he or she seems well qualified), by all means use that person. You can find out from your nearest Social Security office which doctors and suppliers in your area participate in Medicare. Their names and addresses are listed in a book entitled *Medicare—Participating Physician/Supplier Directory*, available for you to look at in all Social Security offices, as well as in many state and area offices of the Administration on Aging.

To a limited extent, Medicare covers outpatient treatment for mental illness, but the maximum amount that medical insurance can pay for these services is $1,100 per year. (The annual $100 deductible would apply to outpatient psychiatric care if it has not been paid for other medical care.) Medicare coverage for chiropractors and podiatrists is a bit confusing. Chiropractic care is not generally covered; however, if a licensed and Medicare-certified chiropractor performs manual manipulation of the spine to correct a subluxation that can be shown on an X-ray, Medicare will pay. Routine foot care by a podiatrist is not covered—removal of corns and calluses, for example—but removal of plantar warts is covered. Medical insurance can help pay for routine foot care if you have a medical condition affecting the lower limbs, such as severe diabetes. Most dental care, such as the treatment, filling, and removal or replacement of teeth, or root canal work, isn't covered, either, but Medicare will pay for dental care if it involves such procedures as jaw surgery, or setting fractures of the jaw or facial bones. If you are in doubt about whether or not a specific procedure is covered, call your local Social Security office.

As mentioned earlier, Medicare also covers two other kinds of care that we will examine more closely: home health care and hospice care.

Home Health Care

More and more people today are deciding that for health care, there's no place like home. Given a choice, many would prefer to recuperate from an illness or have a chronic illness treated at home, in familiar surroundings, rather than in a hospital or other institution. The fact that Medicare may foot the entire bill for home health care no doubt adds to the attractiveness.

Under home health care, professionals such as registered nurses or physical therapists visit and perform such services as administering medicine or oxygen, changing dressings, or helping with rehabilitation.

Part A of Medicare requires that you meet several conditions to qualify for home health care coverage, including the following: You must be confined to your home, a doctor must plan and certify your care, and that care has to include skilled nursing, physical therapy, or speech therapy.

If you qualify, Medicare will pay the full cost of an unlimited number of home health visits; there is no deductible or copayment. Medicare pays for such services as part-time skilled nursing care, physical or speech therapy, medical supplies, medical social services, 80 percent of the approved cost of durable medical equipment, and part-time home health aides. It will not pay for full-time nursing care at home, drugs and biologicals, meals delivered to your home, homemaker services, or blood transfusions.

Medicare coverage won't go on forever; it will only pay as long as you are suffering from an acute condition requiring the help of a home health aide, but not a full-time skilled nurse or other professional.

Hospice Care

Hospices are designed to provide pain relief, symptom management, and support services to dying patients and their families. In 1983, Medicare began covering hospice care for terminally ill patients. As always, certain requirements must be met for a patient to be eligible: Care must be provided in a Medicare-certified hospice, and a doctor must certify that the patient is terminally ill.

If a patient is eligible, Medicare will pay the full cost for covered expenses—without any deductible or copayment, except for a portion of the cost of outpatient drugs and inpatient respite care.

The patient is responsible for paying 5 percent or $5—whichever is less—for each prescription. Inpatient respite care, which is a short inpatient stay at a hospice (the maximum is five consecu-

tive days), is sometimes necessary to relieve a person who is helping with home care. In this case, the patient pays 5 percent of the
cost during a benefit period. A benefit period starts when a hospice
plan is chosen and ends 14 days after hospice care is canceled.

Among the services that are covered in full by Medicare in a
hospice are doctors' and nursing services, drugs, physical therapy,
medical supplies and appliances, and counseling. Medicare does not
pay for treatment other than pain relief and symptom management of your terminal illness.

Supplemental Medicare Insurance

A whole category of private insurance, designed to provide coverage where Medicare doesn't has flourished. Commonly called
"medigap insurance," it covers such costs as hospital bills incurred
after patients had exhausted the number of days they were allowed
for a hospital stay, as well as the cost of such items as prescription
drugs.

Until recently, there have been thousands of these policies
available on the marketplace, leading to widespread confusion on
the part of the 20 million elderly Americans who purchased them.
However, a new federal law as of 1992 mandates that all such policies fit into one of ten standardized plans categories, which range
from high-grade coverage that pays for virtually all services not
covered by Medicare to a bare bones plan.

Each of these allowed alternatives has certain aspects in common, including payment of a patient's 20 percent share of bills for
doctors' services and payment of a patient's copayment during the
61st through 90th day of hospitalization.

Beyond that, the plans vary in terms of what is covered. Most
pay the annual deductible for hospital care, for instance. A few
cover the deductible for doctor's bills. A couple cover preventive
health services, such as flu shots.

By standardizing medigap insurance, consumers will now be
able to efficiently compare pricing policies offered by different
companies.

The Department of Health and Human Services has set up a
free telephone line to help people get more information about the
new policies: 1-800-638-6833.

What's Covered and What's Not*

Under Medicare Part A, most services you would need in a hospital or skilled nursing facility are covered. These include:

- Semiprivate room (two to four beds)
- Meals, including special diets
- Regular nursing services
- Special care units, such as intensive care or coronary care unit
- Operating and recovery room costs, including hospital costs for anesthesia
- Drugs given during your stay
- Blood transfusions covered by the hospital
- Lab tests
- X-rays and other radiology services, including radiation therapy
- Medical supplies, such as casts, surgical dressings, and splints
- Use of medical equipment, such as a wheelchair
- Rehabilitation services, such as physical therapy, occupational therapy, and speech pathology services

The following services are not covered:

- Personal convenience items such as a TV, radio, or telephone in your room
- Private-duty nurses
- Any extra charges for a private room, unless it is deemed medically necessary

Medicare Part B covers physicians' fees, outpatient hospital care, outpatient physical and speech therapy, home health care, and many other services and supplies that are not provided for under Part A, among them:

- Medical and surgical services, including anesthesia
- Diagnostic tests and procedures that are part of your treatment

*Source: *Your Medicare Handbook,* published by the U.S. Department of Health and Human Services.

- Mammography
- Radiology and pathology services by doctors while you are in the hospital
- Other services normally furnished in the doctor's office and included in his or her bill, such as X-rays, services of the doctor's office nurse, drugs and biologicals that cannot be self-administered, blood transfusions, medical supplies, and physical and speech pathology services

Medicare Part B also covers the following outpatient hospital services:

- Services in an emergency room or outpatient clinic
- Laboratory tests billed by the hospital
- X-rays and other radiology services billed by the hospital
- Medical supplies such as splints and casts
- Drugs and biologicals that cannot be self-administered
- Blood transfusions furnished to you as an outpatient

The following services are not covered:

- Routine physical examinations, and tests directly related to such examinations
- Routine foot care
- Eye or hearing examinations
- Immunizations (except pneumococcal vaccinations or immunizations required because of an injury or immediate risk of infection)
- Cosmetic surgery, unless needed because of an accidental injury or to improve the functioning of a malformed part of the body

Some Special Services

There are some areas of medical treatment in which Medicare covers some, but not all, items. Some of the more common of these are:

Chiropractic Care Medicare doesn't cover most chiropractic care, but it will cover physical manipulation of the spine to correct a dislocation, misalignment, off-centering, fixation, or abnormal spacing of the spine that can be demonstrated by an X-ray.

Foot Care Although Medicare won't ordinarily pay for routine foot care, including flat feet or corn removal, it may cover them if the treatment is necessary to the treatment of a separate medical condition. For instance, corns can cause serious medical problems for people with diabetes; in that instance, corn treatment would be covered.

Eye Care No routine eye exams or eyeglasses are covered. Corrective lenses which replace the natural lens of the eye are covered, however.

Dental Care Medicare will pay for dental care that involves surgery of the jaw or related structures; setting fractures of the jaw of facial bones and services that would be covered if performed by a doctor.

Durable Medical Equipment Medicare will pay for the cost of buying or renting equipment like wheelchairs and oxygen equipment. Be sure it is prescribed by your physician, however.

MEDICAID

Medicaid was started in 1965 to provide assistance for low-income individuals and families. Many people over age 65 are also eligible for Medicaid. For eligible senior citizens, all state Medicaid programs pay Medicare premiums, deductibles, and copayments.

Although there are broad federal guidelines, the plans are run by each individual state. Currently all states except Arizona have Medicaid. Washington, DC, Puerto Rico, and the Virgin Islands also have Medicaid. In 1991, 24.5 million people received benefits under Medicaid, at a total cost of $69 billion.

Eligibility rules vary from state to state, but Medicaid generally covers medical assistance to people who receive money under such cash assistance programs as Aid to Families with Dependent Children (AFDC) or Supplemental Security Income (SSI). States may also provide Medicaid to people considered "medically needy"—that is, those who can afford to pay for their own living expenses, but not for their medical care. Again, applicants must have a low income to qualify. In New York, for example, an individual may earn no more than $500 a month and have no more than $3,000 in assets (with some exemptions allowed, including home, car, and $1,500 for a burial fund); a couple may earn no more than $717 a month and have no more than $4,300 in assets (with the same exemptions allowed). If your income is higher than allowed, but your assets are not, you may qualify for a Medicaid Spenddown Program, which is for people whose medical expenses, when included in the income formula, reduce their income below the cut-off levels allowed by Medicaid.

Usually, Medicaid examiners look back 30 months into your financial history to see whether you have given away assets. For this reason it is a good idea to start giving away assets early, through a trust or directly, if you believe that you will need nursing-home or other extended care, and will eventually require Medicaid. This, of course, is a very sensitive subject, because many people are not comfortable giving away their resources. Aside from wanting to retain independence, they may not trust their children to care for them once they receive their inheritances. If you have substantial assets that you don't want eaten away in the event of a medical disaster, you should consult with an attorney to discuss the most reasonable strategy. Trusts and other estate-planning devices are discussed in chapter 26.

CLOSE-UP:
TIPS FOR BUYING INSURANCE

If your medical insurance is not provided or subsidized by an employer and you must obtain your own insurance, it is almost always preferable to do so as a member of a group rather than as an individual. For one thing, group insurance is less expensive than individual insurance. In any given policy, the insurance premium for covering each individual in a group is estimated to be about 15 percent lower than the cost of covering that person individually. A group can negotiate a better discount from an insurer; an individual doesn't have the same bargaining leverage. Group insurance also cuts down on administrative expenses for insurance companies. Instead of processing a thousand premium bills, the insurer processes one, and instead of selling policies to several individuals, it only has to sell to one group representative.

Another advantage of group insurance is that people who have a serious chronic illness usually aren't excluded; an individual policy, once you have a chronic illness, is difficult to get, and costly.

If you think you don't belong to any group that offers insurance, broaden your search to less-than-obvious groups of which you may be a member. Many colleges have special insurance programs for alumni. A professional organization, such as a society of engineers or a local bar association, may offer some type of insurance, as may religious groups. Be sure to compare the rates to those otherwise available, however. Generally, the larger the organization, the better. Companies are wary of insuring small groups they think may have been formed just for the purpose of obtaining insurance. Exception: Small companies, even as small as three to five employees, can qualify for group coverage.

When buying your own, rather than a group, insurance policy, renewability is of paramount importance. If a policy is guaranteed renewable, the company must continue insuring you as long as you pay the premiums on time. The company can raise the premium, but not unless it does so for an entire class (such as all the policies in your geographic area). Without guaranteed renewability, your coverage could be dropped by a company if you began having serious health problems. At that point you could have trouble getting insurance from another company.

Look for policies with an automatic escalation of benefits so that your coverage can keep up with inflation and rising health-care costs. If your policy doesn't have cost-of-living increase provisions, you must check your policy regularly to see that it can cover you.

Determine the maximum you can afford to assume in an illness and buy a policy with the highest deductible possible. The higher the deductible, the less expensive the policy. Be sure the deductible is for a calendar year or a 12-month period, not for each illness or injury. That way, you can better plan for and cope with the deductible expenses.

Don't lie about preexisting health conditions; if you do, you probably won't be covered when you file a claim for the condition. Sometimes policies will cover charges for your condition after a few years have passed without treatment for that condition. However, your policy should cover preexisting conditions you did not know about but discovered after you became insured.

At specific times in your life, you need to make sure your health insurance is covering you and your family. If you are expecting a child, for example, check that your policy will cover that child right from birth. If you have a dependent who becomes an adult, see if your policy still covers him or her. Policies vary. Some will cover children up to age 19, but that age rises to 23 if the child is in college. When you turn 65, whether or not you retire, check your coverage. Some policies automatically become Medicare supplemental policies at that point. If you are retiring, you will need to ensure that your spouse and any dependent children still have adequate coverage. If you are divorced or widowed, especially if you were covered under your spouse's policy, consult the policy handbook. Any major life changes could bring with them lapses in your coverage.

Ask your doctor specific questions about fees. If you merely assume he or she will accept only what the insurance company is willing to pay, you may get stuck with a surprise bill.

It is also useful for your policies to have a waiver-of-premium clause: If you are disabled and unable to make payments, the premiums are suspended but your coverage continues.

If you are considered a high-risk case because of chronic illness—such as cancer, heart disease, or alcoholism—and you cannot get group coverage, try your local Blue Cross/Blue Shield plan. In many states, the plans have open-enrollment periods during which they cover anyone who applies. Almost half the states have programs specifically for people who can't get coverage elsewhere. In any such case, however, coverage is likely to be expensive and limited.

Be aware of the waiting period before new insurance coverage takes effect. Some policies cover you immediately, while others do not become effective until perhaps 90 days have passed.

Check to see whether your policy covers you if you are traveling outside the country.

CLOSE-UP: HEALTH INSURANCE FOR THE UNEMPLOYED

Under federal law, if you are laid off or retire, you can remain in your company's group health insurance plan for at least another 18 months. Employers may charge you up to 102 percent of what the coverage costs them (the extra 2 percent is to cover handling charges). That could well cost you $1,000 or $2,000 per year, but whatever the price, the group coverage is bound to cost less than a comparable individual policy.

Under another provision of the law, if you are a dependent who is in danger of losing health coverage because the covered employee has died or is divorcing or separating from you, or has become eligible for Medicare, you can buy coverage for yourself through the covered employee's company/group plan for three years.

Passed in 1986, the law, called the Consolidated Omnibus Budget Reconciliation Act (COBRA), is designed to help people who are making an employment transition. Many people are forced to go without insurance if they lose their jobs.

COBRA has a painful sting for companies that do not comply. The company loses its entire tax deduction for the cost of medical insurance covering its employees. And the company's top executives face a special bite. If a company doesn't comply, it must add the value of company-paid health insurance policies to the income of the 25 percent highest-paid employees in the company. Thus, the executives must pay personal income tax on their corporate-provided health insurance.

There are restrictions: If you are eligible for other medical coverage, or if the company terminates the entire plan, you can't buy into the group under COBRA. The federal government, small firms (fewer than 20 employees), and church groups are exempt from the law.

13

Life Insurance

Janet Bamford

WHO NEEDS LIFE INSURANCE?

There is an old saying about life insurance: It is sold, not bought. You usually don't call an insurance agent and place an order for a life insurance policy. In most cases, an agent contacts you, sets up an appointment, and then tries to sell you a policy. Unfortunately, many of us are not familiar with different types of life insurance policies and their advantages and disadvantages, so we can sometimes be persuaded to buy a policy we don't need or pay too much for what we do buy.

The purpose of life insurance is to protect your survivors from financial disaster when you die. Adequate insurance should enable your family to maintain its standard of living, your spouse to keep the family home, and your children to get the college education you had planned for.

Not everyone needs life insurance. The question to ask when deciding whether or not to buy life insurance is: Who would suffer financially if you died? If you are the principal breadwinner in the family, but your spouse's income would be enough to support himself or herself without you, insurance on your life may not be necessary.

If you are a wage earner supporting several dependents, you almost certainly do need life insurance.

If you are single and have no dependents, your life insurance needs are minimal. Many single people choose to buy enough life insurance to pay what are euphemistically called their "final" expenses: funeral and burial costs and any debts outstanding at the time of their death.

The contributions of homemakers are sometimes overlooked in assessing life insurance needs. If you are a full-time homemaker caring for children, you may need life insurance. Your death could force your spouse to hire someone to do all the work you now do— an expense that could be considerable. Even so, properly insuring a breadwinner should take precedence over insuring an at-home spouse.

Life insurance for children is not a good idea, since few people are dependent on children for financial support. Agents also sometimes argue that a child, once insured, will not lose coverage even if he or she becomes ill later. That is true, but statistics show that few adults are refused coverage because of ill health. The risk that a future health condition will make a child uninsurable is so remote that, for all practical purposes, parents can ignore it. (It is also true that insurance companies usually refuse to cover people suffering from AIDS and other chronic illnesses; but unless you have some reason to suspect that your child may develop a life-threatening illness, the money you would spend insuring your child's life would be better spent elsewhere.)

If you have dependents, life insurance requirements tend to be higher when you are young and slowly decrease as you get older. As children finish school and become self-supporting, and your own financial assets increase, your need for life insurance coverage usually diminishes; the assets you own are often sufficient to meet financial needs. Some people, however, want and need life insurance even after they have retired—to provide some sort of pension for a spouse, for example, or to leave a legacy when they die.

HOW MUCH LIFE INSURANCE DO YOU NEED?

In deciding how much life insurance you need, your first priority must be to provide for the needs of your dependents if you die before they do.

Calculating how much life insurance you need to buy is a matter of taking a good look at your family's financial situation and estimating your dependents' expenses, income, and assets.

The most reliable method for calculating your insurance needs involves three steps: First, figure what your family's expenses would be if you suddenly passed away. The major expenses fit into two broad categories: *immediate expenses*, such as funeral costs, probate expenses, and estate taxes; and *future expenses*, such as daily living expenses and your children's education costs. Second, analyze your assets and all the sources of income that can be used to cover your immediate and future expenses. Third, once you have calculated your expenses and assets, subtract the assets from the expenses; the resulting figure represents the amount of insurance you will need to purchase.

Calculating Your Expenses

The model worksheet in table 13-1 should help you account for most of your expenses and needs. Not every item in the worksheet, of course, will apply to you.

Immediate Expenses The first part of the worksheet has entries for the immediate expenses your family would face if you died. These include federal and state estate taxes, probate costs, funeral expenses, and uninsured medical expenses.

Estate taxes. Generally, everything you own—your house, bank accounts, stocks, jewelry, and so on—becomes part of your estate. Property you bequeath to a spouse, however, is not subject to federal estate tax (see chapter 26).

Most people don't have to worry about federal estate taxes, because the value of an estate must exceed $600,000 before it is taxed. Some states allow a person to pass his or her entire estate to a spouse tax-free. It's best to check with a tax specialist for information on the rules in your state.

If your assets are so large that you want to exclude your life insurance policies from your estate in order to reduce estate taxes, you may do so if you give up the right to change the beneficiary of the policy, to borrow on it, or to use it as collateral for a loan.

Probate costs. Probate is the legal process by which the state validates your will after you die, makes sure your debts are paid,

TABLE 13-1   How Much Life Insurance Do You Need?

What You Need	Your Needs	Totals
Immediate Expenses		
Federal estate taxes	_____	
State inheritance taxes	_____	
Probate costs	_____	
Funeral costs	_____	
Uninsured medical costs	_____	
Total final expenses		_____
Future Expenses		
Family expense fund	_____	
Emergency fund	_____	
Child-care expenses	_____	
Education fund	_____	
Repayment of debts	_____	
Total future expenses		_____
Total needs		_____

What You Have Now	Your Assets	
Cash and savings	_____	
Equity in real estate	_____	
Securities	_____	
IRA and Keogh plans	_____	
Employer savings plans	_____	
Lump-sum employer pension benefits	_____	
Current life insurance	_____	
Other assets	_____	
Total assets		_____

Extra Insurance Needed

Total needs minus total assets		
Total needs		_____
Total assets		= _____
Additional insurance needed		_____

and guarantees that your wishes are carried out. Your will may have to go through probate, especially if you have property in your own name, make special bequests, give property to children, or set up trusts. The probate procedure can involve lawyers' fees, filing and administrative fees, and fees to your executor.

Attorneys' fees vary from state to state and from lawyer to lawyer. Some states set a maximum charge based on a percentage of the estate's value. Others require lawyers to charge "reasonable fees" based on the actual work they do. If your estate is complicated or relatives fight for portions of it, probate costs may be high.

If you do not have a will, there are still costs. The state will distribute your property and charge your estate a sum of money for its efforts.

Check probate costs with the lawyer who drew up your will or with a tax specialist.

Funeral costs. If you want to be buried in grand style, funeral costs can be stratospheric, but with intelligent cost-saving measures, you can keep them low.

The National Funeral Directors Association says that the national average for funeral charges and casket costs was about $4,085 in 1989. But that figure does not include cemetery expenses, monuments, or such items as flowers, clergy fees, and transportation, which can double the cost.

Uninsured medical costs. If you don't have good medical insurance coverage, a final illness can be costly. If you are not covered, you will need to budget several thousand dollars for uninsured medical costs. But a better idea is to get more complete medical coverage (see chapter 12).

Future Expenses   Future expenses represent the bulk of your life insurance needs. They include funds for family expenses, emergencies, child care, education, and the repayment of debts.

Family expense fund. This represents the amount of money your family would need to meet daily expenses. To calculate it, follow these steps:

1. Figure your monthly take-home pay by multiplying your weekly take-home pay by 4.33 (the average number of weeks in a month). If your spouse has income, make the same calculation with his or her take-home pay. Add the two numbers to arrive at the family's monthly take-home pay.
2. Determine how much of that amount your family would need to cover its expenses if you were gone. Most people feel that about 75 percent of their current take-home pay is adequate. It costs two people more to live than it does one, but not twice as much.
3. Decide whether or not you want the family expense fund to cover mortgage payments. If you do, your survivors would

keep on making monthly mortgage payments just as you do now. You may decide, though, that your insurance proceeds should pay off the mortgage entirely. In that case, include the outstanding amount under repayment of debts.

4. Determine the amount of monthly income your family will have after your death. Include your spouse's take-home pay, Social Security benefits, and any survivors' benefits from a company pension plan. (For most workers under age 55, company pension benefits will be small.)

5. Figure out the monthly shortfall—the amount by which your family's monthly income falls short of the amount it needs after you die—by subtracting the total in step 4 from the total in step 2.

6. Multiply the monthly shortfall by 12 to arrive at an annual figure.

7. Determine how many years your survivors will need the yearly income that you calculated in step 6. You might assume, for example, that your spouse will be self-supporting after the youngest child goes to college or leaves home. If your spouse has a good company pension plan and will have substantial private savings (such as IRAs and Keoghs), then you may not need insurance proceeds for your spouse's retirement income. But if your spouse does not want to work or has slim prospects for a good retirement income, you'll want this fund to last longer.

   Keep in mind that Social Security benefits to children end when they become 18, or 19 if they are in school full-time, and Social Security benefits to a nonworking surviving spouse stop when the youngest child reaches 16. A nonworking spouse will resume receiving Social Security survivors' benefits again at age 60.

8. Multiply the number of years by the amount of annual income you need, which was determined in step 6. Assume that the fund would be invested following the death of the primary breadwinner and would earn interest at a rate that equals the rate of inflation. This assumption is conservative, but it is wise to think conservatively in this case; if you overestimate your needs slightly, it might balance an underestimate in another area, such as medical expenses or major house repairs.

Emergency fund. Every family should have an emergency fund. Its size is a personal matter. Some financial experts recommend $10,000 to $15,000. Others suggest at least three months' after-tax income.

Child-care fund. For many couples, child-care expenses will already be factored into the family expense fund. But if one spouse is currently staying home with the children, then both parents should think about how the death of one parent would change that situation.

Let's say you're a homemaker and your husband is earning wages. If your husband dies, you might have to take a paying job and incur added day-care expenses. If you die, your husband may suddenly have to pay for baby-sitters or day care. That's a reason to consider life insurance coverage for a nonworking spouse.

Most parents now pay about $3,000 a year per child for care outside the home. In some cities, that cost can run as high as $13,000. Figure how much the yearly costs are likely to be in your area, and multiply that number by the number of years that remain until your children can take care of themselves.

Education fund. You may want to provide a sum for your children's private-school or college education. It is not easy to predict the expenses of college several years from now. While college costs have risen sharply over the years, they haven't always risen in step with inflation.

The College Board, an organization that monitors college costs, says that for the 1990–91 school year, the average annual cost of a four-year private college was $15,318. That figure includes room and board, books, tuition, personal expenses, and some transportation costs. A comparable figure for a four-year public college or university was $6,891. At some of the country's most prestigious private colleges, annual costs can exceed $20,000.

Bear in mind that part of the college bill may be defrayed through financial aid or loans.

Repayment of debts. A mortgage loan will probably be your survivor's biggest debt. If you have a mortgage insurance policy that will pay off your mortgage on your death, or if you want your spouse to keep making monthly payments, don't list your mortgage as a debt.

Do include other debts, such as car loans and credit card purchases, unless they are already covered by separate "credit life" insurance policies. Credit-life insurance is usually not a good buy. It is generally better to buy a single large insurance policy than several smaller ones. Buying individual credit-life policies is like buying nails individually; it's needlessly expensive.

Your Total Needs In order to determine your total needs, add together the amounts that you have calculated from all the categories of both immediate and future expenses.

Analyzing Your Assets

The next step is to add up all the assets that would be converted to cash upon your death. These may include cash and savings, equity in real estate, securities, IRA and Keogh plans, employer savings plans, employer lump-sum pension benefits, current life insurance, and miscellaneous assets such as an art collection or assets from a business.

Do not add in assets you don't expect your survivors to convert to cash. For example, if you want your survivors to continue living in your house, don't count the equity that has been built up. *Do* include IRA and Keogh accounts and employer-sponsored programs such as 401(k) plans. Money you have saved through these plans is payable without penalties to your survivors.

If you are covered by a pension plan at work, check with your pension administrator to see if there will be a lump-sum survivor's benefit payable upon your death. If there is, include it among your assets. If you have already listed a monthly pension benefit in step 4 of your worksheet, you probably will not have a lump-sum benefit. Normally, you get one or the other, but not both.

List any insurance policies on your life that you already own (many people have more than one policy). Include employer-provided group insurance and any policies that you may have bought through the mail. Do not include any credit-life or mortgage policies; they will simply pay your debts or mortgages.

Social Security Survivors' Benefits

For many families, Social Security survivors' benefits are a major source of income when the primary breadwinner dies, and they should be considered as part of a family's income and assets when estimating life insurance needs.

The monthly payments your survivors receive are based on a percentage of a certain "magic number" that the Social Security Administration (SSA) calculates for you, based on your earnings record. The actual amount that your survivors receive depends on several factors: the amount of your previous earnings, the age at which you die, the surviving family members' ages, and your spouse's monthly income.

A surviving spouse who is under 60 years old receives benefits only if he or she is taking care of small children and does not have substantial earnings. These benefits stop when the youngest child turns 16. They may resume when the spouse reaches his or her sixtieth birthday. If a spouse is disabled, however, benefits can begin at age 50.

If the surviving spouse earns less than a specified amount ($7,080 a year in 1991, or $9,720 for people age 65 or older), Social Security pays the full benefit. If the spouse earns more than $7,080 and is under 65, the benefit is reduced by $1 for every $2 of earnings above that. Between ages 65 and 69, you lose $1 for every $3 of earnings over the limit. In most cases, a spouse earning about $20,000 or more would receive no survivors' benefits. But note that the earnings test involves only employment earnings. Investment income, insurance proceeds, and pension benefits are not included in the earnings test.

If the spouse is caring for a child who was disabled before age 22, he or she receives a benefit for as long as the child remains disabled. A divorced spouse who was married for at least 10 years and is not currently remarried is also eligible for survivors' benefits.

Social Security also pays benefits to surviving children until they are 18, regardless of whether their mother or father receives a benefit. Children can continue receiving benefits until their nineteenth birthday if they are still in high school. Children who were disabled before age 22 receive survivors' benefits for as long as they remain disabled and are not married. Social Security used to provide benefits for college students but has phased them out.

If you have three or more family members who are eligible for benefits, Social Security will not pay full benefits to each. Instead, the family receives a predetermined maximum benefit.

The formula for determining the Social Security benefits you would receive is complex. Most people could not, or would not want to, wrestle with the math involved. The SSA has begun a service to help you estimate what your survivors' benefits would be. It is called "Personal Earnings and Benefits Estimate Statement" and is available through your local Social Security office. To obtain your estimate, you must fill out Form SSA-7004. You can also request the form by calling a toll-free telephone number: 800-937-2000. You should receive the information within four weeks.

Calculating Your Additional Insurance Needs

Once you have determined your total expenses and your total assets, subtract the assets from the expenses to arrive at the amount of insurance you should have. If your total expenses came to $400,000, for example, and your disposable assets added up to $150,000, then you would need to buy $250,000 worth of life insurance.

For most people, the result is a surprisingly large number. A large life insurance deficit is common.

Be flexible when it comes to your life insurance needs. The birth of a child may increase the amount of insurance you need; the departure of a child to become self-sufficient may decrease your requirements. You should review your needs at least every five years, and more often if your financial situation changes.

According to the American Council of Life Insurance, 81 percent of American families own some sort of life insurance. Employers often supply the bulk of an employee's life insurance coverage. In fact, group life insurance coverage is almost universally offered as an employee benefit in the United States. Typically, the benefit ranges from one to three times an employee's annual salary. That amount would usually be woefully inadequate if it were a survivor's sole source of income.

HOW INSURANCE COMPANIES MEASURE YOU AS RISK

When you apply for life insurance, the company asks you a series of questions about your medical history and health habits. The answers you give on the application and the results of a medical examination if one is required, determine the premium you'll pay—that is, the amount you pay for coverage.

Life insurance companies use actuaries to calculate certain risk factors associated with you and your living habits. Actuaries consult mortality tables in order to predict your chances of dying at a given age. By scrutinizing the characteristics shared by groups of people, such as smokers and nonsmokers, actuaries greatly improve the accuracy of their predictions about the death benefits insurance companies might have to pay.

Most applications ask for such information as your age, sex, and occupation; your family medical history; your smoking and drinking habits; and your history of treatment for heart disease, strokes, cancer, or high blood pressure. Some companies require certain applicants to undergo a physical examination. This is more common if you are buying a large amount of insurance or if your answers on the medical-history portion of the application indicate that you have health problems.

The company's underwriters tally the information you provide, adding points for unfavorable findings and subtracting them for favorable findings. The lower your score, the better your rating. Your final tally determines whether you will be rated *standard*, *substandard*, or *preferred*. If your scores are low enough—for instance, if you are a nonsmoker, not overweight, and with no history of heart disease—you may be able to buy the insurance at the preferred rate, if the company has such a category (not all do); if your score is high, the company thinks you have a greater than average chance of dying in the next few years and will classify you as substandard. Over the past few years, about 90 percent of life insurance policies have been issued at standard rates.

Rates vary from company to company, and one insurer's standard rate may be lower than another's preferred rate. In general, the older and the more unhealthy you are, the more your life insurance will cost. For instance, one company charges a first-year premium of $326 for $250,000 worth of term life coverage for a 35-year-old male who meets the preferred-risk classification, and $536 a year for the 35-year-old male rated as standard. A 45-year-old customer buying the same amount of insurance pays $619 if he is a preferred risk, and $1,051 if he is a standard risk.

You have an obligation to tell the truth when you apply for life insurance. If you lie or deliberately omit important information, and you die within two years of buying the policy, the insurance company can deny all or part of the claim.

TYPES OF POLICIES

After you have decided how much life insurance is best for you and your beneficiaries, you should consider what type of coverage to buy. You can find an enormous variety of policies among the 2,350 companies selling life insurance in the United States. But whatever the specific type of policy, it will offer either insurance protection only, or both protection and a savings program.

Policies that provide you with insurance protection only are called *term insurance;* those that also have a savings component are known as *cash-value insurance.* We'll examine the provisions of various kinds of term and cash-value policies, then discuss the issue of converting from one category to the other.

Term Policies

Term life is a straightforward and easy-to-understand type of insurance. You pay premiums, and in exchange, the policy pays a sum of money to your beneficiaries if you die while you are covered. There is no savings or investment component. The policy is in effect for a period of time—usually one year or five years, but sometimes as long as 10, 15, or 20 years. When the specific time period (or term) ends, your coverage ends unless you renew it.

For example, you might buy a five-year term policy for $250,000 worth of coverage at an annual premium of $400. If you should die within that five-year period and your premiums are paid up, your beneficiary will receive $250,000. Usually beneficiaries are given a choice of how they are to be paid—in a lump sum, in a series of payments, or as an annuity, for instance. Sometimes a policyholder can recommend or specify in advance how a settlement is to be paid.

Most term policies are renewable; that is, as long as you have paid your premiums, the insurance company must renew your coverage if you so choose, even if your health or occupational status has changed. This option to renew continues until you reach an age that is spelled out in your policy—usually 65 or 70, the customary retirement age. Under a renewable term policy, your premium rises when each new term begins, because as you get older, the statistical probability of death increases.

A few underwriters allow renewable policies into old age, but at virtually prohibitive rates. One firm, for instance, charges 80-year-olds $5,700 for a $50,000 policy.

The price of term insurance varies with the type and amount of coverage you want, and with your age and health.

Level Renewable Term Insurance With level renewable term insurance, during each term of coverage, there is a fixed annual premium and a fixed face amount of the policy. Each time you renew, the annual premium is increased, reflecting your age at that time. Under most insurance contracts, when you renew you have the option of reducing the amount of coverage, thereby decreasing your premium payments. But if you want to increase the coverage, you may have to undergo a medical examination.

Re-entry Term Insurance Insurance companies guarantee to renew these policies, even if the policyholder can no longer demonstrate that he or she can pass the firm's insurability standards. However, a premium must be paid over the ordinary rates if the individual would not be insurable otherwise. If the policyholder can demonstrate evidence of insurability, then the policyholder's coverage will be renewed at a lower rate.

Level Nonrenewable Term Insurance With level nonrenewable term insurance, there is a fixed face amount and a fixed annual premium throughout the term of the policy. The term of the policy may be 5, 10, or 20 years, but in almost all cases, this type of insurance is not offered after you reach your sixty-fifth or seventieth birthday. You are not allowed to renew the policy, but usually, during a limited time period, you can convert it to a cash-value policy despite changes in health or occupation (see p. 252).

Decreasing Term Insurance Decreasing term, which is also known as declining term, is a policy whose face amount gradually decreases but whose annual premium remains fixed. These policies are usually purchased for 10 to 25 or more years, often for the purpose of covering an outstanding balance on a major debt, such as a mortgage.

Mortgage life insurance is a decreasing term policy that will pay the balance of your mortgage upon your death. Many savings-and-loans institutions or banks that offer mortgages will also offer this type of insurance. As you make mortgage payments, and your outstanding balance decreases, the amount of cash that would be paid upon your death also decreases.

A major disadvantage of this type of insurance is that if you die, your beneficiaries may have no choice in using the proceeds of the policy. The funds may need to be used to pay off the mortgage. This could be a disadvantage if you have a low interest rate on your mortgage and would be better off continuing to pay off the mortgage and investing the insurance proceeds. A far better deal is a term insurance policy that is large enough to cover your family's mortgage and housing costs and other housing needs.

Credit-life insurance, another kind of decreasing term insurance, is designed to pay back a loan if you die while covered. Again, this type of insurance is not advisable. Instead, buy a single policy that is large enough to cover all your debts.

Cash Value Policies

Cash-value insurance, more complicated than term insurance, combines life insurance coverage with a savings plan. The policy is in effect for most or all of your life, rather than for a specific term. You pay periodic premiums, and the insurer agrees to pay a certain death benefit when you die. However, even if you don't die, the policy slowly becomes worth something to you: Like a savings account, it gradually builds up a cash value that you can borrow against or cash in. Over a long period, the accumulation can be appreciable.

Buying cash-value insurance is essentially a way of forcing yourself to save. But that forced savings plan usually comes at a price: Cash-value insurance is more costly than term.

With most cash-value policies, you pay a level annual premium throughout the course of the coverage. You actually pay more than is necessary in the early years to cover the statistical risk of death, but less than is needed to cover that risk in later years. A cash-value policy therefore affords a way for people to be covered by insurance into old age without having to pay the rising premiums that accompany renewable term insurance.

As time goes by, a greater portion of the death benefit consists of your cash value. As a result, the amount of money that the insurance company risks decreases, despite the fact that the policy's face amount never changes. Suppose, for example, you take out a whole life policy for $100,000. The death benefit will remain constant, but after you have paid premiums for several years, the cash value of your policy will gradually rise. Let's say the cash value of your policy has risen to $60,000. You can cash in that policy and take the money. If you cash in your policy, you are canceling your life insurance coverage.

As the cash value of your policy increases, the insurance company is risking less. If the cash value of your policy when you die is $60,000, they only have to add $40,000 to it to equal the death benefit.

The savings component of a cash-value policy exists for the benefit of you, the policyholder, not for your beneficiary. When the policyholder dies, the beneficiary receives only the face amount of the policy. You can, however, borrow against the cash value. If you die before the loan is repaid, the outstanding amount plus interest is subtracted from the face amount of the policy before any payment is made to the beneficiary. If you decide to cancel your policy, its accumulated cash value at the time of cancellation, less any outstanding loans plus interest, is payable to you.

A cash-value policy may be either *participating* (dividend-paying) or *nonparticipating* (nondividend paying). With a "par" policy, you receive annual dividends representing a refund of that portion of your premium payment, if any, that the insurance company did not use to pay death benefits to beneficiaries, to supplement the company's reserves, or to pay administrative expenses. (Par policies are possible but rare in term insurance as well.)

Why can companies afford to make these payments? First, the premiums paid for a participating policy are usually higher than those paid for a nonparticipating policy, and frequently the premiums are higher than the company needs to cover death benefits. In any year, the company may realize a greater return than it anticipated on the investments it made with the policyholders' money, or the mortality rate may be lower than expected.

Companies that offer participating policies are mostly mutual insurance companies, in which policyholders are also shareholders of the company.

Participating policyholders usually are not eligible to start receiving dividends until they have held the insurance with the company for a period of time—one to three years is customary.

If you own a participating policy, you have several dividend options. You can accept your dividend payments in cash; allow them to remain with the company in order to reduce your future premium payments; let them accumulate interest through reinvestment with the company; or use them to buy additional insurance with no further expense charges.

The dividends paid on participating policies are not taxable, since the Internal Revenue Service considers them to be refunds of premiums rather than interest or dividends. However, if you choose to allow your dividends to remain with the company and accumulate interest, that interest may well be taxable.

The insurers decide how much of their excess funds should be shared as dividends with policyholders, and the company makes no guarantees about the return in future years. The company's decision, of course, is based on many factors, including the percentage of excess funds, if any, that it wishes to reinvest. However, if you choose a participating policy, you can be reasonably sure that dividends will be paid in the future if the firm has a long and uninterrupted history of paying out dividends regularly.

Nonparticipating policies are generally sold by insurance firms owned by stockholders, though in recent years most such firms have switched to universal life. With a nonparticipating policy, premium payments are fixed at specific amounts derived from the company's estimates of what it will cost for them to insure the policyholder. No dividends are paid to policyholders. In most cases, insurance premiums on nonparticipating policies tend to be lower. Even so, participating policies tend to be the better buy in the long run.

Whole Life Insurance Whole life insurance is the best known and most widely sold type of insurance in the United States. As the name implies, whole life covers you until death. As with all policies, whole life policies require that you keep up your premium payments, and they specify the amount of money that your beneficiaries will be paid upon your death. The accumulating cash value—the amount of money you would receive if you decided to redeem or cash in your policy—is also spelled out. Many policies contain provisions for paying dividends. As long as you continue paying your premiums on time, there is no need for you to renew your policy periodically; that is done automatically.

With term insurance, your premiums cost more as you get older; under whole life, your premiums and the face amount stay constant as long as the policy remains in effect. The level-payment aspect of whole life insurance is one of its most appealing selling points. (A few companies have devised policies in which premiums, instead of remaining level, gradually increase for the first few years of coverage. Such policies are designed for young families who may have limited means during the early years of the policy. However, the vast majority of whole life policies have level premiums.)

Whole life premiums are very expensive—considerably more so than the initial premiums for term insurance. For example, a 35-year-old non-smoking man would pay approximately $2,000 to $3,000 annually for a $200,000 whole life policy. For a comparable term insurance policy, he would pay approximately $250 to $300. The term premium would increase with each renewal, while the whole life premiums would remain level. Only after many years—at a time when most people's insurance needs have decreased—would the annual term premiums be larger than premiums for whole life.

Although the cash value that you accumulate in a whole life policy can be seen as a type of savings account, there are differences between the cash value of an insurance policy and the cash in a bank account.

First, the only way in which you can take your money out is to cancel your policy, thereby relinquishing your insurance protection. This applies to both total and partial withdrawals. An outright withdrawal, then, is an all-or-nothing proposition.

However, you are allowed to borrow against the cash value at an interest rate that is spelled out in your policy. With policies that have been in force for many years, the interest rate tends to be low—perhaps 5 or 6 percent. With newer policies, rates are often variable and reflect current long-term bond rates.

The cash value of a whole life policy also differs from a savings account in the way it is treated for tax purposes. Since 1913, whole life policies, as well as other types of cash-value insurance, have enjoyed certain tax advantages. Currently, the interest on the savings portion of your whole life policy is tax-deferred and partially sheltered. Even when the cash value increases, you do not have to pay taxes annually on the appreciation in value. Consequently, whole life is a tax-deferred investment up to the time that you withdraw it. And when you do withdraw it, only part of the cash value is taxed: the amount by which the cash value exceeds the sum of premiums that you have paid, less any dividends that you received.

Death benefits are not normally subject to federal income taxes. However, the insurance proceeds may be considered part of your estate for estate tax purposes.

One very important shortcoming of whole life insurance is that insurance companies are not required to inform you about the effective rate of interest that you are being paid on your policy.

As with any kind of life insurance, shop very carefully if you're considering buying a whole life policy. It is not a good buy if you plan to keep your policy only for a short time. If you were to terminate your policy during the first few years, you would probably find that you had built up little or no cash value. During these early years, the sales commissions and administrative costs absorb much of your payments, which would otherwise accumulate cash value. It takes about a decade for cash values to build up significantly.

Unfortunately, people often let their policies lapse after a relatively short time. More than 18 percent of whole life policyholders terminate their insurance within two years. And more than half keep this type of policy for less than 10 years.

If you drop a whole life policy after three or five years, you will have overpaid drastically for your life insurance during that time. A term policy with the same face value would have cost perhaps one-fifth the price.

Universal Life Insurance With the introduction of universal life in 1979, the insurance industry increased interest rates paid on cash-value accumulations. By emphasizing the investment advantages of universal life rather than the death protection, insurance agents increased sales.

Universal life is similar to whole life in that it allows you to build up a cash value for your policy. But while whole life keeps you in the dark about what you get for your money, universal allows you to see what portion of your premiums goes toward covering company expenses, how much is used for the cost of protecting you, and how much makes up the savings component. You are also advised of the interest rate that your savings are earning.

The insurance company credits your annual premium to your cash-value account, and each month it deducts the cost of your insurance protection from that account. The company may also deduct its expense charges. What remains is your cash value, which then accumulates interest. As with other forms of life insurance, the cost of protection rises as you grow older. You are notified of all these transactions in your annual statement.

You have access to your money in the cash-value account after deducting any surrender charges, which accompany virtually all universal life policies. You are allowed to borrow against it, withdraw the entire amount (thereby losing your coverage), or withdraw only a portion of it (thereby reducing your death benefit). The ability to make partial withdrawals seems to be a significant attraction to most buyers of universal life.

With certain universal life policies, beneficiaries receive only the face amount of the policy, just as they do with term or whole life policies. These are called "Option A" policies. "Option B" policies allow your survivors to collect the face amount *and* the accumulated cash value. Not surprisingly, Option B is more expensive.

A universal life policy also offers a tax shelter, as does a whole life policy. The cash value is taxed only when you withdraw it, not as it accumulates. And when you do withdraw it, you pay taxes only on the portion of the cash value that exceeds the sum of the premiums you have paid. As with whole life, any taxable gain is valued at death.

Many (but not all) universal life policies allow you considerable flexibility in paying your premiums. A company will set a "target" premium, which keeps the policy in force and allows you to build up a cash value, but after you have made initial payments and a cash value has accumulated, you may be able to vary the amount you pay. If you pay less than usual, the premium is credited toward insurance protection and expenses, and your cash value grows more slowly or not at all. You must pay enough of a premium to keep up the insurance protection in your policy or it will lapse.

When actuaries determine the premiums for a universal life policy, they consider three factors: (1) the interest rate credited to the cash value; (2) the cost of the death benefit, which is often called the mortality charge; and (3) the expenses of the company. The interest rate increases your cash value, while company expenses and the mortality charge decrease it.

Companies guarantee that they will credit a certain minimum interest rate to your cash value. In recent years, the actual rate paid has been higher than the stated minimum. Minimums of 4 to 4½ percent are common, but in mid-1991 actual interest rates in the 8 to 8½ percent range were widespread. The rate fluctuates with prevailing interest rates. Sometimes the interest rate you earn depends on the size of your cash value.

Your mortality charge pays for your insurance. A company uses this charge to cover death claims. Each policy contains a table that shows the maximum amount the company might charge you for mortality costs, though no large companies use those maximum charges.

Expense charges or "loads" assessed against your policy usually do not change over the life of the policy. A policy may have either frontloads or backloads.

With a frontload policy, the company typically deducts from 5 to 9 percent of your premium for its expenses before it credits the premium to your cash value. With a backload policy, the entire premium is credited to your account, but when you want to surrender your policy—or, when you make a partial withdrawal—a penalty will be assessed. A 1986 *Consumer Reports* survey found that the penalty can be as high as 150 percent of the first-year premium. Because expenses for the company are highest in the early years, when agents' commissions and selling costs are also high, surrender charges gradually diminish in most backload policies, usually disappearing sometime between the tenth and twentieth years.

Some companies may lure you with a high interest rate at the time of purchase, switching to a more modest one later, or promise interest rates in future years that cannot be sustained. Be wary of such practices.

Variable Life Insurance   Variable life insurance is much like universal, with one big exception. With a regular universal policy, the money in your cash-value account is invested by the insurance company. The company determines what interest rate it will pay on cash values.

Under a variable policy, the buyer chooses his or her investment vehicle and the money earns whatever the investments earn. Usually you may invest in stocks, bonds, money market funds, or a combination. In other words, you choose the risk level you are comfortable with.

Each month the insurance company deducts the cost of insurance protection and expense fees from your cash value. Consequently, if your cash values fall too low, because you have not kept up premium payments, you may have to invest more money in order to keep your insurance in effect.

Converting from Term to Cash-Value Insurance

A convertibility clause in your term policy allows you to convert it to a cash-value policy, such as whole life or universal life. The conversion privilege is important in case you need life insurance after age 65 or so, since some term policies cannot be renewed after that age. If you think you'll need insurance in your later years—say, for estate-tax reasons, or because you have married a person much younger than you and expect to have dependents when you are past retirement age—you may want to convert to a cash-value form of insurance some day.

Although very few people have good reason to convert (despite insurance companies' yearly campaigns urging conversion to cash-value policies), you don't necessarily know in advance whether you will be one of those people. Hence, any term policy you buy should be convertible at least until you reach age 60.

You can usually convert your term policy to a cash-value one without a medical examination and regardless of changes in your health or occupational status.

When you decide to convert a term policy to a cash-value policy, the rates for the new policy are commonly based on your "attained age" rather than your "original age." This means that the new annual premium rates are based on your age when you convert rather than on your age when you first bought the term policy. If you convert on the basis of original age, your premiums will probably be lower, but you may well have to pay the insurance company a lump sum. The cost is meant to put you in the same financial position as if you had had the new policy from the original date. Premiums will be higher under an attained-age arrangement, but you will not have to pay a lump sum to the company.

Insurance companies encourage convertible policies because they stand to make more profit from whole or universal policies than from term policies. Some companies even give you an initial price break if you convert your policy.

Your insurance agent can tell you whether a policy he or she is pitching is convertible, and it will be spelled out in the policy itself. Be sure to check whether there is a deadline beyond which you may no longer convert. Many companies require you to decide by your sixtieth birthday; for others, the deadline may be even earlier. Ascertain the types of policy to which the term insurance is convertible. The more options you have, the better.

Group Life Insurance

About 75 million Americans are covered by some form of group life insurance—most commonly through their employers, but also through such other groups as unions, professional organizations, alumni associations, and credit card issuers. Group life insurance often costs less than individual insurance, and often you do not have to undergo a medical examination to be eligible. Once you give up membership in the sponsoring group, your eligibility for group coverage usually ends also. However, beware insurance sold as "group," by alumni associations, credit cards or professional groups. This can be more expensive than insurance you can purchase on your own.

HOW TO BUY LIFE INSURANCE

Deciding on a Type of Policy

Once you determine how much life insurance coverage you need, you must decide what type of policy—term or cash value—best suits your needs.

For most people, term insurance is the best buy. It is simple, understandable, and affordable. Other forms of insurance cost much more for the same amount of coverage, so people with limited amounts to spend often find themselves underinsured if they purchase cash-value insurance. A 1986 *Consumer Reports* study showed, for example, that a 35-year-old woman buying a top-rated term policy would pay about $200 for the first year for $200,000 of protection. For the same amount of coverage from one of the top-rated whole life policies in the study, she would pay more than $2,000. While term insurance premiums increase as you get older, the annual premium for the lowest-cost term policy in the study doesn't exceed $2,000 until the twenty-first year. Long before then, the typical family may find its insurance needs have substantially declined.

Comparing Costs

When buying life insurance, it's fairly easy to compare first-year premiums of different policies, and companies readily supply those figures. But a far more telling figure to compare—and one more difficult to obtain—is a number called the *interest-adjusted net cost index*. That index is an industry-sponsored method for determining the true cost of insurance to the consumer over the long run. It figures in not only the premium, but interest, dividends (if any), and timing of your payments and receipts.

The calculation of the interest-adjusted net cost index is more complicated than most people can easily do with a calculator or personal computer. Ask your insurance agent to give you the cost index of a policy under consideration. In most states, companies are required to furnish the number if the customer requests it, but many agents are reluctant to provide it or unfamiliar with its importance. You may also consult cost surveys of life insurance published periodically by *Consumer Reports*.

The index is usually expressed as a cost per $1,000 of insurance. A policy with a ten-year, interest-adjusted net cost index of 4.50, for example, is estimated to cost an average of $4.50 per $1,000 of coverage per year, or about $450 annually for a $100,000 policy. The lower the index number, the better the buy usually.

One possible alternative for comparing life insurance policies is to turn to one of several insurance quote services. You call these organizations on toll-free lines and provide them with some personal information like your birth date. They will then mail you a ranking of companies which appear to be least expensive for you. There is no charge for the service—these firms make commissions from selling insurance if you choose to buy from them.

Three of the biggest such services are LifeQuote (800-274-1144), SelectQuote (800-343-1985) and TermQuote (800-444-8376).

There may be some shortcomings to the quotes you receive, however. For one thing, these firms do not use an enormous number of companies for comparison; they only search through the companies they represent. What's more, the rates they send you might not actually be available—they may be for preferred risks, a category for which you may not qualify.

Table 13-2 shows the lowest, median, and highest cost indexes for $50,000 term policies that *Consumer Reports* compared in its June 1986 issue. The policyholder is a nonsmoker, and the figures are based on a 10-year holding period for the policy and a prevailing interest rate of 5 percent. The index indicates the cost per $1,000 of coverage; so for a 35-year-old woman buying a nonparticipating policy, the index of 2.97 means she would pay $148 a year for $50,000 worth of coverage.

Bear in mind that some term policies are at first inexpensive and have very low cost indexes for the 10-year period but then escalate in cost very quickly if kept for 20 years or longer. Of course, the opposite can also be true: A policy may have a high initial premium but still be a good deal if you keep it for 10 or 20 years.

TABLE 13-2   Cost Indexes for $50,000 Term Policies

Age	Lowest Cost	Median Cost	Highest Cost
Male rates, participating policies			
25	1.47	2.28	4.16
35	1.96	2.92	5.49
45	3.32	5.58	9.99
Male rates, nonparticipating policies			
25	1.49	2.59	3.62
35	2.11	3.45	4.93
45	4.45	6.57	10.40
Female rates, participating policies			
25	1.29	2.13	3.85
35	1.80	2.59	5.01
45	3.32	4.67	9.11
Female rates, nonparticipating policies			
25	1.45	2.34	3.34
35	1.66	2.97	4.52
45	3.37	5.66	7.90

Dealing with Agents

As in all professions, the degree to which you can depend on life insurance agents' advice varies. Many are honorable and trustworthy. In fact, those with the title Certified Life Underwriter are educated professionals who are supposed to abide by a code of ethics that puts a client's interests first.

However, some individuals in the business of selling life insurance are just out for the money. Insurers make more money from cash-value life insurance, for example, than term; consequently, some life insurance agents receive higher commissions for selling cash-value policies. Some agents are paid a commission of up to 100 percent of the first-year premium when they sell a whole life policy, but only 70 percent of a much smaller premium when they sell term insurance. Even agents who receive smaller commissions almost always earn more for selling cash-value insurance than they do for selling term.

As a result, some agents discourage customers from buying term insurance by referring to it disparagingly: Term insurance is called "temporary," while cash-value insurance is labeled "permanent."

In addition, life insurance agents may try to sell riders, or optional policy add-ons, when you buy a policy. Two common add-ons are accidental death benefits and cost-of-living riders. The former are redundant; when you die, your beneficiaries will need the same amount of money whether you die accidentally or otherwise. The latter, too, are superfluous, provided you review your life insurance needs every few years as recommended.

Recommendations

For most buyers, we recommend term as a simple, economical way to meet life insurance needs. In addition, we advise you to keep in mind the following points:

- Ask your agent to furnish the interest-adjusted net cost index for the term policies you are considering. Use the index to compare one term policy with another.
- Look for a policy that offers you good value whether you hold it for 5, 10, or 20 years; policies that are low priced only for the first year or two are not necessarily a bargain.

- Check the financial stability of any life insurance company before you buy its policy. Look up the company's rating in *Best's Insurance Reports,* which can be found in most public libraries. Do business with companies rated A+.
- Unless you are positive that you need coverage only for the short term, select a term policy that you can renew at least until you are 65.
- If you can, pay your premium annually. If you pay in installments, your total cost will be higher.
- Do not be swayed by disparaging remarks an agent may make about term insurance.
- If you want a cash-value policy, the National Insurance Consumers Organization will evaluate it for you for $35. (It can also evaluate a policy you already own.) For details, send a stamped, self-addressed, business-size envelope to Rate of Return Service, NICO, 121 North Payne Street, Alexandria, Virginia 22314.

14

Homeowner's Insurance

Janet Bamford

HOMEOWNER'S INSURANCE: PEACE OF MIND AND PROTECTION FROM LOSSES

Homeowner's insurance has come a long way since Ben Franklin organized the first fire insurance company in the country in Philadelphia in 1752. (The company he founded, the Philadelphia Contributionship for the Insurance of Houses from Loss by Fire—also known as the Hand in Hand—is still in existence.) Until the mid-1950s, homeowners had to buy individual insurance policies to cover each separate peril: one insurance policy against fire, another against windstorm damage, and additional policies to insure against such dangers as theft and liability claims. The property and casualty insurance industry eliminated this cumbersome system when it packaged together the most commonly needed protections into "multiple-peril" insurance. Single policies that protect against individual dangers are still available, but multiple-peril insurance is by far the most common way to buy homeowner's insurance today.

The property and casualty insurance business, of which homeowner's insurance is one major component (auto insurance is another), is somewhat fragmented; there are about 3,800 companies selling property and casualty insurance. However, about 40 percent of the homeowner's insurance market belongs to the top five companies in the field. It is a huge business, too. In 1989, homeowners paid more than $17.6 billion in premiums for multiple-peril insurance.

This big business thrives because expensive losses can and do occur, and because homeowners fear the unknown. For the individual, the purchase of insurance represents a modest expenditure for big protection against possible loss. Since no one can know what the future holds, the buyer of insurance is placing a bet that a loss will occur. (Anyone who does not buy insurance is wagering—and hoping—that a loss will not occur.) If a loss is in fact incurred, the insured is protected by the coverage; if a loss never occurs, all the years of premium payments have bought peace of mind for the insured. In either case, the insured person wins. The uninsured person, however, remains forever exposed to the risk of loss; even if his or her house does not burn to the ground after 30 uninsured years, there is always tomorrow and the risk that it could happen then.

The need for home insurance is clear enough. Choosing the best coverage for your needs, however, can be a difficult task. This chapter will explain what kinds of home insurance are available, how to find the best coverage for your needs, and how to avoid gaps in coverage that could expose you to the risk of significant uninsured loss.

INSURANCE FOR THE HOME

Most homeowner's and renter's insurance policies fall into one of six fairly standard categories, numbered HO-1, HO-2, HO-3, HO-4, HO-6, and HO-8. There are separate policies for homeowners, renters, and people who own condominiums or mobile homes. Although most policies include liability coverage, you can also purchase separate policies exclusively for this purpose.

The policies differ in what perils they cover, as explained below. For example, the basic homeowner's insurance policy (HO-1) covers most of the normal calamities that can befall a house: fire and lightning; explosions; damage caused by a car or airplane crashing into the house; burglars and vandals; or that beautiful old oak tree falling onto, or through, the roof. Broader policies cover more specialized damages, such as water pipes bursting and flooding your house; a blizzard dropping four feet of snow on your roof, causing it to collapse; or a volcano covering your home with lava and ash. (Protection against volcanic eruptions, which is fairly new to the list of standard perils, was added after the 1980 Mount St. Helens eruption in the state of Washington. Since many policies did not specifically address volcanic eruptions at that time, there was a great deal of confusion. Many homeowners argued that the general-purpose protection against explosions covered volcanic eruptions as well, and in most cases the insurer duly paid. However, the industry later decided to specify which policies insure against damage from volcanoes and which do not.)

An insurance trade group, the Insurance Service Office, promulgates the six policies, and revises the standards periodically.

- HO-1: The basic policy, which covers 11 standard perils.
- HO-2: The broad form, which covers 18 perils. A type of HO-2 is available for most mobile-home owners when modified by a special endorsement.
- HO-3: A special form that provides maximum protection for the dwelling, but less than maximum coverage for personal belongings. Mobile homes can be insured under HO-3 as under HO-2 when modified by a special endorsement (that is, an addition to a policy that changes its provisions or terms). This category encompasses what used to be HO-5. The additional protection for personal belongings that was provided by HO-5 is now available by endorsement to the HO-3 special policy.
- HO-4: The renter's policy, designed for tenants in a house, apartment, or cooperative apartment. This provides personal property and liability coverage, but not coverage for the structure itself. That's the landlord's (or the cooperative association's) headache.
- HO-6: The basic condominium policy, which covers only the space you live in, including structural parts owned by you such as kitchen, bathroom and light fixtures. The building itself and the common areas you share with other owners should be covered by the condominium corporation. A co-op can also be covered under HO-6 instead of HO-4. The more structural

parts of the apartments you own, the more likely you need to use HO-6.

· HO-8: A policy for older homes. Sometimes it may be impractical to rebuild an older home as it was originally built because its condition has worsened or it has lost value because the area has deteriorated. In such cases, HO-8 insures a home for its actual cash value, derived by a complicated formula that often takes depreciation into account or, in some states, true market value (the price the home would actually sell for).

Aside from volcanic eruptions, there are some other very real perils that standard homeowner's policies do not cover. The most important of these are damage from floods and damage from earthquakes. If you live in areas that are prone to either of these occurrences, it makes sense to buy separate coverage for flood and earthquake damage (see p. 267). Homeowner's policies also don't insure you against the perils of war or nuclear accidents, although damage from riots or civil commotion generally is covered.

Pay particular attention to normally covered losses that occur under certain unusual conditions and are thus not covered. For example, under some policies, vandalism and malicious mischief are not covered if the house was left vacant for 30 or more consecutive days before the damage was done. Damages that result from wear and tear, rust and mold, air pollution, settling of the structure, dry rot, insects, vermin, birds, or domestic animals are not normally covered, either.

However, some damages that you might think are excluded from the policy may actually be covered under certain circumstances. For example, though water damage from a flood is not covered, if a flood somehow causes a fire, explosion, or theft in your home, the direct losses from those may be covered. Similarly, though damage from nuclear accidents is not covered, if a nuclear reaction, discharge, radiation, or radioactive contamination causes a fire that in turn damages your home, you may be covered. And, while you would not be covered if local officials condemned your home to demolition, you could be covered if the fire department felt it was necessary to knock down your house to cut off and prevent the spread of fire through the neighborhood. Such exclusions and limits should be outlined in your policy.

Besides paying to rebuild or replace all or part of your damaged home, homeowner's insurance will pay other types of expenses that result from covered damages. If you had a devastating fire that destroyed your home and your belongings, for instance, you would need many kinds of help.

Homeowner's policies labeled HO-1, HO-2 and HO-3 cover not only your dwelling but also any outbuildings or structures on your property, such as a detached garage or tool shed. In that event, your home would be insured up to the full dollar limit, while outbuildings on the property are often covered for 10 percent of the amount of coverage on the main house. Thus, if your home were covered for $100,000, the maximum you would receive for additional structures on your property that are not attached to your house would be $10,000.

The policies will also pay for "loss of use." If there were serious fire damage to your home, for example, the policy would pay your living expenses while the damage was being repaired. This is extremely important; even if you couldn't live in your house, you would still be required to keep up mortgage payments, and this, coupled with the additional expenses of a hotel or other temporary quarters, could prove devastating. If you rent out part of your home and it becomes uninhabitable, the insurance company will pay you the rent you were unable to collect. Naturally, there is a limit to how much the company will pay for living expenses and for reimbursement of lost rent. Some policies specify that they will pay for the shortest amount of time required to repair or replace your home, while others limit their payout to 20 percent of the total amount of coverage.

If you can't use your home (or rent it) because civil authorities have prohibited you from being there, as occurred in one upstate New York town in the 1970s, after dangerous levels of toxic wastes were found leaking from a World War II dump site called Love Canal, the insurer will cover additional living expenses and fair rental value for a week, once the premises have been uninhabitable for at least 48 hours.

A home that is struck by fire or other disaster is usually full of debris that has to be removed. Your insurer will pay the reasonable cost of doing that.

Your house may be damaged and then collapse. Policies usually cover the complete or partial collapse of the building that has resulted from one of the perils listed in your policy.

If there is damage to your landscaping from insured perils (not including windstorms), the insurance company will pay as much as $500 for each tree, shrub, or other plant (including your lawn), up to an overall limit of 5 percent of the total insurance on the home. So, if your home was insured for $100,000, you would receive up to $5,000.

If temporary repairs need to be made to your home to protect it from even further damage, insurers will pay that additional expense.

In some areas, homeowners are required to pay for fire department services. Where this is so, insurers will reimburse insured homeowners up to $500. In most cases, your deductible does not apply to this coverage.

In the aftermath of a fire, you would probably move out of your home any personal possessions that were not damaged. These possessions would then be covered for up to 30 days against direct loss from any cause.

The cost of purchasing new clothing, dishes, linens, and other personal property destroyed in a fire would be covered under homeowner's insurance (see p. 270).

If you own more than one home, perhaps a vacation getaway in the mountains or at the beach, you will need separate coverage for that property. Your homeowner's policy provides some limited protection for your personal belongings while they are at the other house, but it's best to insure both properties fully.

There is often another area of coverage that you may not have expected to find in a homeowner's, renter's, condominium, or mobile-home policy: insurance in case charge cards or bank debit cards are lost or stolen. With most credit cards, by federal law you are generally liable for only up to $50 of unauthorized purchases per card. (See chapter 4.) Your homeowner's insurance company will pay up to $500 should you lose a credit or debit card. This coverage is also in effect if someone forges your signature on checks or if you unknowingly accept counterfeit money.

Your homeowner's insurance is designed to protect a home, not a business. Although most policies will provide coverage up to $2,500 for business property in your home, and $250 for property off the premises, you probably need separate coverage if you are operating a business out of your home. Coverage varies, of course, from company to company, so check with your agent.

How Much Coverage Do You Need?

Determining the amount of insurance you need to protect your home is no simple task. If you insure it for the amount for which you think you could sell the home, or the fair market value, you could be paying for too much insurance. If you insure the home for the sum for which you bought it, that may be too little. The key to insuring a home is figuring out how much it would cost to replace the house. The term for this, logically enough, is *replacement cost.*

In determining replacement cost, of course, you don't take the value of the land into consideration, since even a devastating fire that destroyed your home would leave the land intact.

Usually the insurance agent can help you figure out the replacement value of your home; frequently the insurer uses established formulas and tables to calculate and project building costs. You can take the square footage of your home and multiply it by the per-square-foot construction cost for similar construction locally. (That figure should be available from a local builders' association.)

Although you might be tempted to reduce premium costs by insuring your home for less than the replacement value, it is important that your insurance cover at least 80 percent of the replacement cost. Many insurers require that you insure at least 80 percent of replacement cost, or they will not fully cover a partial loss.

The formulas that insurers use to figure how much they will pay you for a partial loss are a bit confusing, but important to understand. Say a fire in your family room causes $10,000 in damages, and replacement value of your home is $100,000. If you are insured for at least 80 percent of that, or $80,000, you'll collect the entire $10,000 needed to repair the family room. But if you have only insured the home for $60,000, your payment for the partial loss will be $7,500 ($\frac{3}{4} \times 10,000$); or the insurer will pay you the actual cash value of the loss, which amounts to the replacement cost minus depreciation. This effectively means that if the stereo and video equipment in the family room cost you $5,000 originally but are now a few years old and have therefore depreciated, you will get only a fraction of what it would cost to replace them. Your insurance company will pay you the larger of the two calculations, but either way you will be reimbursed for less than actual replacement cost.

Don't make the mistake of insuring only up to the value of your mortgage. That protects your mortgage holder very nicely, but your down payment on the house and any appreciation the home might have enjoyed would be lost if your home were destroyed. Experts recommend insuring your home for a minimum of 80 percent of its replacement value, but preferably 100 percent.

Inflation is the other factor to consider when determining the dollar amount of your coverage. Many homeowners choose their coverage when they buy their homes and never increase the amount of coverage as the years roll by. Thanks to inflation, it will cost more to rebuild a home in 1995 than it did in 1990.

Some insurance companies automatically increase the coverage each year to bring the protection into line with current costs, unless the homeowner asks them not to do so. There are also endorsements commonly available that can be purchased by homeowners as an addition to their policy. One typical inflation-guard endorsement automatically increases the amount of protection given by the policy every three months, at the rate of 1 percent of the original coverage (for a total of 4 percent annually). During high-inflation periods, however, that still might leave you underinsured.

In any event, whether or not your insurance company automatically increases your coverage, it is wise periodically to update the market and replacement values of your home and assess whether your insurance coverage is adequate to protect your investment fully. Such updates should be done annually. However, in areas where home prices are rising rapidly—as was the case in the Northeast in the early to mid-1980s, when prices rose 25 percent and more each year—more frequent updates may be necessary.

The amount you'll pay for homeowner's insurance hinges on a variety of factors—many of them out of your immediate control. The closer you are to a fire hydrant or your local fire department, the less you'll pay. Brick or masonry homes are less expensive to insure than wood-frame houses. If you live in an area where construction costs are particularly high, your premium will reflect that fact, or if you live in a high-crime area, your insurance will be more expensive.

However, the matter of cost isn't completely out of your hands. All homeowner's policies offer several choices of deductible, which is the initial expenditure you must make to pay for losses before the insurance company begins paying. Deductibles usually range from $250 to $1,000; the higher the deductible, the less expensive your policy will be, and the savings from taking a high deductible can be dramatic. For this reason, it may be wise to take a high deductible and deposit the amount of money you save in the bank as a form of self-insurance.

Most insurance companies will also reduce your premiums if you install certain safeguards in your home, such as smoke detectors to limit the damage from fire, and deadbolt locks or burglar alarms to discourage would-be intruders.

Table 14-1 shows the price of a standard homeowner's policy in various parts of the country. In each case, the home is insured for $100,000, and the policyholder is insured for $100,000 in personal

TABLE 14-1 Regional Price Variations in a Standard Homeowner's Policy

Location	Annual Premium Guaranteed Replacement Cost Policy
Urban	
Tempe, AZ (Phoenix area)	$322
Jacksonville, FL	352
Suburban	
Des Plaines, IL	233
Malibu–Santa Monica, CA (L.A.)	391
Van Nuys–Englewood, CA (L.A.)	433
Rural*	
Warren County, TN	495
Blackhawk County, IA	386

*Although rural areas typically have a lower crime rate than urban areas, premiums tend to be higher because of the fire insurance component of multiple-peril coverage; rural policyholders usually live farther from fire hydrants or fire departments.
Note: These rates are for frame buildings, which are slightly more expensive than brick to insure.

liability coverage and has $1,000 in medical payment coverage. The policy has guaranteed replacement cost on contents. The rates quoted are from State Farm Insurance, based in Bloomington, Illinois, one of the largest homeowner's insurance companies in the country. These prices are for illustration only; they reflect the company's prices in early 1989 and may well have changed by the time this book is published.

Flood and Earthquake Insurance

If you live in an area prone to frequent earthquakes or floods, you should already be aware that a standard homeowner's policy does not cover either of these calamities. Residents of areas that do not commonly experience earthquakes or floods but are nonetheless prone to them may want to extend their policy to cover such events. A sizable earthquake rumbled along parts of the Mississippi River back in 1811; New York and New Jersey are known to experience earth tremors from time to time; and people living along some Great Lakes shorelines have been surprised to see water levels rising unabated in recent years.

Most earthquake coverage is available, through private insurers, as an addition to your standard homeowner's policy. Not surprisingly, more than half the policies in effect have been bought in California.

Until 1968, when Congress created the National Flood Insurance Program (NFIP), protection against floods was rarely available to homeowners. Today, flood insurance is available not only through the federal government's program, but also through about 200 private insurers. Some 18,010 communities participate in the NFIP, providing 2.5 million people with coverage.

To qualify for either one, you must live in a community that has adopted measures for controlling and reducing flood damage. Such measures include land-use control programs. A community joining the program must first enter the initial so-called emergency phase of qualification, during which citizens are allowed to apply for flood insurance at federally subsidized rates. The average premium is $280 a year for $85,000 worth of coverage on the home's structure.

After the community undertakes additional flood-control measures, and the Federal Emergency Management Agency (FEMA) conducts a flood study, the community can enter the regular phase,

TABLE 14-2   Flood Insurance

Insured Property	Emergency Program	Regular Program
Building		
Single Family	$35,000	$185,000
All other residential	100,000	250,000
Contents		
Residential	10,000	60,000

Source: National Flood Insurance Program
[Note: Higher limits of basic coverage are available under the emergency program in Hawaii, Alaska, U.S. Virgin Islands, and Guam.]

during which time local consumers are eligible for greater coverage.

Table 14-2 shows the maximum amounts of insurance available through the National Flood Insurance Program (NFIP). What is available depends on whether the community you live in is under the emergency program or the regular program. Your local insurance agent can tell you what phase your town is in. If your community is not a participant in either stage, you cannot buy insurance. There is a standard $500 deductible on buildings, and an additional $500 deductible on contents of buildings.

Often, if a policyholder takes measures to protect personal belongings (e.g., removing personal property from a home that has been declared in danger of flooding), he or she will be reimbursed for the cost of moving the property. The cost of temporary storage is also reimbursable. One warning: There is a five-day waiting period between the purchase of a flood insurance policy and the date when it becomes effective. So don't wait until there is a flood alert to buy.

Crime Insurance

Just as the federal government stepped in to insure homeowners in flood-prone areas in the late 1960s, so did it for residents of high-crime areas who found it impossible to buy private insurance against crime. Like flood insurance, crime insurance is administered by the Federal Emergency Management Agency (FEMA) and is available to anyone who lives in an area where it has been determined that crime insurance is difficult to obtain. Crime insurance is currently available in some areas of the following states: Alabama, California, Connecticut, Delaware, Florida, Georgia, Illinois, Kansas, Maryland, New Jersey, New York, Pennsylvania, and Rhode Island. It is also available in parts of the District of Columbia, Puerto Rico, and the Virgin Islands. Federal crime insurance covers burglary, robbery, and damages to a house or apartment during a burglary or robbery. Insured homes must meet certain crime-prevention requirements; for instance, doors must have deadbolt locks.

The cost of insurance in high-crime areas varies according to how much coverage is purchased, and there is a 5 percent premium discount if the home is protected by a residential burglary alarm system (see table 14-3). The deductible for this coverage is $100 per incident, or 5 percent of the gross amount of the loss, whichever is greater. There is also a limit of $1,500 total or $500 per item for jewelry; articles of gold, silver, or platinum (including flatware); furs; fine arts; antiques; and coin or stamp collections.

To apply for coverage in a high-crime area, write Federal Crime Insurance Program, P.O. Box 6301, Rockville, Maryland 20850, or call 1-800-638-8780.

TABLE 14-3   The Cost of Federal Crime Insurance Coverage

Amount of Coverage	Annual Premium Without Credit Program	Annual Premium With Alarm Credit
$ 1,000	$ 32	$ 30
$ 2,000	$ 42	$ 40
$ 3,000	$ 52	$ 50
$ 4,000	$ 62	$ 58
$ 5,000	$ 74	$ 70
$ 6,000	$ 84	$ 80
$ 7,000	$ 94	$ 90
$ 8,000	$104	$ 98
$ 9,000	$116	$110
$10,000	$126	$120

INSURANCE FOR YOUR PERSONAL PROPERTY

In a fire, your material possessions will likely be damaged or destroyed; in a burglary, they might be stolen. Homeowner's insurance also covers personal property: appliances, furniture, clothing, and other belongings. It even covers your personal property when you are away on a trip if, for example, your luggage or camera equipment is stolen. Of course, homeowner's insurance doesn't cover all your personal property; your automobile and any audio equipment used in it, for example, would be covered by an auto policy. Pets aren't covered by most policies.

It is important to note that there are strict ceilings on how much you will be reimbursed for the loss of certain types of valuable possessions, such as jewelry, antiques, artwork, and furs. If you own such valuables, you should investigate buying a "floater policy," which provides additional protection. (It's called a floater policy because it covers the insured article or articles wherever they are at the time of the loss.)

Property that you rent is considered yours while it is in your possession, so it would also be covered under your homeowner's insurance. Therefore, if you have rented a videocassette recorder for the weekend and you're robbed, it's covered. By the same logic, when you rent your personal property to someone else, that person takes responsibility for it, and it is not covered under your policy.

Most homeowner's policies provide for personal property coverage that is equal to 50 percent of the coverage on the dwelling, although some go higher. So, if you have $100,000 of insurance on a home, your personal property is covered up to about $50,000. That doesn't mean that if your home is destroyed, the insurer will blithely hand you a check for $50,000. You must prove what personal belongings you had and what they are worth. That's why it's important to compile a household inventory, along with receipts, and store the documents in a safe place away from your home, such as a safe deposit box.

There are limits to what an insurer will pay for certain special items. Typical ceilings are listed below, but you should check your own policy to determine what limits apply to you.

- $200 on money, gold, silver, and platinum (other than jewelry or flatware), coins, bank notes, and medals

- $1,000 on securities, deeds, manuscripts, tickets, stamps, and valuable financial papers, such as letters of credit and evidences of debt
- $1,000 on some watercraft, including trailers, furnishings, equipment, and outboard motors
- $1,000 on trailers not used with watercraft
- $1,000 on grave markers
- $2,000 for loss by theft of jewelry, watches, furs, and precious and semiprecious stones
- $2,500 for loss by theft of silverware, silver-plated ware, goldware, gold-plated ware, and pewterware
- $2,500 for loss by theft of guns and firearms

These limits apply to each category, not to each item within a category. So if you lose a diamond ring worth $1,000 and a fur coat worth $1,000 in a burglary, you can only collect the $1,000 maximum for the category that includes jewelry and furs.

If you own personal property worth more than the total allowed for each category, it's smart to buy a floater policy, either as an endorsement to your homeowner's policy or as a separate policy. Floaters generally insure against all types of perils, not just the ones listed in your homeowner's policy, so if your diamond ring is ruined in the garbage disposal, it's covered under the floater policy. To get a floater, you need to give your insurer a detailed description of each insured item and its worth, including information on style, manufacturer, and the like. Often you will need to prove the estimated worth of the item or items by having a professional appraiser look at them. Floaters vary in cost depending on the insured item and where you live. Obviously, insurance in high-crime areas costs more. Typically, floaters are priced per $100 of coverage. One insurer in a suburban New York City location has quoted a $50 annual premium for a $1,400 diamond ring.

Some insurance policies will pay your replacement cost for the contents of your home, since—as with the home itself—it can cost far more to replace lost possessions. Check with your insurance agent; often the replacement coverage on the contents of your home isn't particularly expensive, perhaps an additional 10 percent of a homeowner's premium and 20 to 40 percent for renters and condominium owners. There may be a limit to what the replacement-value policy will pay; a common ceiling is four times the cash value.

LIABILITY INSURANCE

Your homeowner's or renter's policy doesn't just protect the roof over your head; it also protects you in case you are sued. Imagine these scenarios:

- A neighbor slips and falls on your front steps and injures himself permanently.
- Your dog bites a visitor, or tears up someone else's furniture.
- Your child injures someone while mowing a neighbor's lawn.

Any of these incidents could result in a claim or lawsuit, and you could be financially liable. As anyone who keeps up with the news knows, court judgments of several hundred thousand dollars (at least initially, before appeal or post-trial settlement) against a defendant are not unusual, and the cost of defending lawsuits has never been higher. Also, the scope of a homeowner's liability has increased in recent years. The so-called host lawsuits that have gone to court in recent years are a good example of this. When a homeowner is entertaining guests and serving liquor, the host can be held responsible for some of the actions of guests. Thus, homeowners have been sued successfully by the victims of a drunk driver who had an accident after leaving a homeowner's party where he or she was served liquor.

Your homeowner's liability coverage protects not only you, but all family members who reside in your home. And liability coverage isn't limited to accidents that happen on the premises of your home. If you're on a trip and your dog bites someone, you're covered.

For the insurance company to pay a claim, all parties involved must agree, or a judge or jury must decide, that the policyholder is liable. Your insurance company will pay up to whatever limit your policy specifies. The insurance company will also pay for legal costs in a lawsuit, although it reserves the right to decide whether to fight the lawsuit or settle.

Liability policies do not cover problems arising from business or contractual matters—or, for that matter, anything even related to a business in which you are involved. You can often get coverage for business use at a nominal fee. A doctor who practiced medicine out of an office in his home would not be covered for medical malpractice under his standard homeowner's policy. Someone who provided regular child care at home would also probably not be covered if one of the children was hurt; that would require additional insurance. However, the occasional or part-time business activities of an insured member of your family who is under age 21—such things as mowing lawns, shoveling snow, walking dogs, or running a Kool-Aid stand—may be covered by your policy. Consult with your insurance agent to determine whether circumstances warrant additional coverage.

Most policies will provide for $2,000 of medical payments as coverage for injuries that occur to guests in your home or on your property. This feature is designed to take care of relatively minor injuries quickly. When an accident has happened on your property, the insurance company will generally pay even if it hasn't been established that you were at fault. If both parties had to fight in court to decide who was liable, the insurance company would find it more trouble and more expensive than for the injury itself.

Similarly, homeowner's policies provide for a specific amount of supplementary coverage for unintentional minor damage that you might do to someone else's property, no matter who is at fault. If you have a child under age 13 who had inadvertently damaged a neighbor's home, that damage is covered, whether or not it was intentional. (Simply because the child is under a certain age, it's considered accidental.) The limit that a company will pay ranges from $250 to $500 per incident.

How much liability coverage should you have? The standards keep rising. Homeowners used to feel secure with $25,000 in coverage. Now $100,000 is standard; however, the additional premium cost for increasing coverage to $300,000—generally no more than an additional $20 per year—is relatively small, and, in our opinion, well worth it.

Umbrella Policies

If you think you need even more liability insurance than the standard homeowner's policies provide, you can buy an umbrella policy, which will cover you for liability of $1 million or more. Such a policy would probably cost $125 to $200 a year—there is a great deal of variation in the rates. In addition to providing the extra cash coverage, an umbrella policy, as its name implies, provides broader coverage for you. Along with insuring against injury, umbrella policies protect you in case you're found liable for things such as libel, slander, defamation of character, and invasion of privacy. Such coverage would generally not apply in a professional situation. Journalists, for example, would need additional coverage. Umbrella insurance is not a replacement for your regular liability coverage; it is meant to be supplementary. In fact, most insurers will want you already to have $250,000 in liability coverage under your homeowner's policy, and $300,000 in liability coverage under your automobile policy, before they will provide you with umbrella protection.

Insurance for Workers in Your Home

Worker's compensation is necessary to protect homeowners or renters who employ domestic help either full or part-time in the event they are injured while working for you. A few states—New Hampshire, New York, and New Jersey—require that every comprehensive personal liability policy issued to individuals also include worker's compensation coverage for employees. California requires any homeowner who employs domestic workers—even part-time—to have worker's compensation. The yearly cost for this is minimal, usually under $5. Coverage is available in other states as well, but it is not required.

INSURANCE FOR RENTERS

Most people who rent rather than own their residences have neither insurance against loss of their personal possessions nor personal liability insurance. Considering the availability and modest cost of such coverage, the reasons for these lapses defy logic.

Even if you don't own a home, you still need insurance. Your landlord has insurance on the dwelling itself, but that protects his or her investment. If you are robbed, the landlord's policy won't cover you. If there's a fire in your apartment, or a pipe bursts and your belongings are damaged, your landlord is not responsible unless you can prove he or she was negligent.

Liability coverage is an even more crucial component of renter's insurance. If you were to cause a fire in the apartment or home that you rent, the landlord's insurance company would probably pay damages, but could then turn to you for reimbursement if you were proven liable. And, as with homeowner's liability insurance, renter's insurance covers you and your family members even if you're away from home (see p. 274).

Renter's policies generally start at $10,000 of personal property coverage with a $250 deductible. They cover additions and alterations you may have made to the apartment or home in an amount equal to 10 percent of the personal property coverage; and the cost-of-living expenses, should your quarters become uninhabitable, in an amount equal to 20 percent of the personal property coverage. The cost of tenant's insurance isn't terribly high: perhaps $100 to $110 a year for $10,000 worth of coverage.

Condominium policies also cover belongings for $10,000 and up, but they allow 40 percent of the total coverage amount for additional living expenses if the condominium becomes uninhabitable.

CLOSE-UP: YOUR HOUSEHOLD INVENTORY

A fire, burglary, or other disturbance in your home is a traumatic experience. Unfortunately, this is exactly the time when people are called on to perform a remarkable feat of memory: recalling all the personal belongings they have accumulated over the years so that the insurance company can reimburse them. To see just how difficult such a task would be, try simply listing the contents of one room, or even of a closet. Chances are that you will forget many valuable items.

Insurance companies and financial experts urge people to compile a detailed inventory of what is in their homes. Such a list can identify exactly what you have lost, not only to help settle insurance claims, but also to help report the incident to the police and prove a loss to the Internal Revenue Service, so that you can deduct unreimbursed losses from your income for tax purposes.

A good inventory lists the items in each room; gives a detailed description of each; and lists the serial numbers of items (especially appliances or electronic equipment), the date when you bought an item, how much it cost, and what it would cost to replace. Any available sales receipts should be included.

Go through each room carefully. Don't forget to include curtains, draperies, carpets, rugs, lamps, and wall decorations. When listing items of furniture, describe everything in as much detail as possible, including dimensions and the materials they are made of. (Example: "42″ × 60″ oval solid cherry Queen Anne dining table, with four matching cherry side chairs upholstered in velvet.")

In the dining room, describe china and silverware as well as furniture. In the kitchen, don't forget to describe appliances in detail. (Simply listing a GE refrigerator isn't good enough. How many cubic feet? What style? Does it have extras, such as an ice-maker?) Include such items as dishes, pots and pans, utensils, and small appliances. Individual items may seem insignificant, but if you had to replace them all, costs would mount. In bedrooms and baths, include linens, electrical appliances, mattresses, and clothing. Don't forget to list items in your closets. You will be surprised how it all adds up.

In taking inventory of your clothes closets, be sure to include anything especially expensive, such as coats, suits, and perhaps evening gowns. If you don't want to describe every shirt and sweater you own, at least count them: 10 pairs of shoes, 12 dresses, and so forth.

Don't overlook items stored in your attic, basement, or garage: sports equipment such as golf clubs, skis, or bicycles; lawn mowers; wheelbarrows; luggage; furniture; lawn furniture; barbecue grills; and washer and dryer.

Once you have listed your belongings, it's a good idea to take a photograph of every wall in your home, with all closet or cabinet doors open to show what is in them. Note the date, the location of each photo, and the major items shown. For unique or valuable items, such as an antique clock or a set of silverware, take a separate photograph. This will help to prove that you owned the items if you have to make a claim.

Once you have completed an inventory and have taken pictures, store the documents somewhere away from your home, preferably in a safe deposit box. If your house burns down, your list and photos could burn too. If your home is robbed, such a detailed list can amount to a thief's guide to your valuables. Your inventory will need periodic updating as you increase your belongings.

A pamphlet entitled *Taking Inventory* is available from the Insurance Information Institute, and it gives consumers a head start on developing such an inventory. Single copies are free and can be obtained by calling 1-800-942-4242, or by writing to Publications Department, 110 William Street, New York, NY 10038.

CLOSE-UP: TIPS FOR BUYING HOMEOWNER'S INSURANCE

Here are some tips for buying homeowner's insurance:

- When choosing an insurer, don't forget to consider the firm's financial stability. For maximum security, you should buy insurance only from firms that have an A+ or A rating from *Best's Insurance Reports,* a publication of the Best Company independent rating organization.
- To save money on your insurance, investigate whether you can consolidate several of your insurance policies—your homeowner's, auto, and a separate umbrella liability policy, perhaps. If you do this, some firms will give you the equivalent of a quantity discount.
- Shop around. The insurance for the same home can vary greatly. Remember also that high deductibles can save you a lot of money.

If your home is damaged or destroyed, you may be approached by a public claims adjuster who will try to sell you his services as the negotiator of your claim with your insurance company. Adjusters take on a case in return for a percentage of the money you receive from the insurer, perhaps 10 to 15 percent of the settlement.

Public claims adjusters have been hailed as heroes by many people who otherwise would have missed reporting some damage to their home if it hadn't been noticed by the adjuster. And for some people, merely having someone to act as a negotiator with the insurance company, and cope with the hassles involved in claims, is worth the fee.

On the other hand, detractors tell stories of unethical and incompetent public claims adjusters who charge 60 or 80 percent of the settlement as a fee, or even fail to file the papers on a timely basis. Critics also claim that an adjuster merely duplicates the work of the insurer's own investigator.

If you think you do need help, a lawyer may be a better choice than an adjuster, according to the National Insurance Consumer Organization. If you do hire an adjuster, don't just choose the first one to call you—and an adjuster will probably call you first, if you suffer a major loss. Adjusters can usually be found in the Yellow Pages under that heading. If you hire a public claims adjuster, make sure he or she is a member of the National Association of Public Adjusters. Ask for references from several previous clients.

15

Automobile Insurance

Janet Bamford

PROTECTION FOR YOU AND YOUR CAR

Automobile insurance protects you from the cost of damage to your automobile. More important, it also protects you from the cost of damage your automobile may do to others.

In 1989 alone, there were some 34.4 million auto accidents—one for every five licensed drivers. The cost of those accidents was substantial, too: 46,900 deaths, nearly 5.6 million injuries, and, according to the Insurance Information Institute, an economic cost (a figure that includes property damage, medical costs, lost productivity, the costs of emergency services, legal and court costs, public assistance programs, and insurance administration expenses) estimated at an astounding $93.9 billion.

To protect people from that burden, insurance is not merely a good idea—it's also the law. All states have financial responsibility laws that require drivers to prove they can pay specific amounts if they are involved in an accident and cause bodily injury or property damage. In 41 states and the District of Columbia, registered car owners are required to have certain minimum levels of liability insurance. In states without compulsory automobile insurance

279

laws, drivers who don't have insurance must post a bond if they are involved in an accident.

Unfortunately, auto insurance can be expensive. Although the A.M. Best Company calculated the average U.S. automobile insurance premium in 1988 at $517.71 per year—and more in high-premium states such as New Jersey, Massachusetts, Nevada, Maryland, and California—an individual's rate can easily range up to $3,000 a year and higher. In some cities, it's possible to pay more over time to insure a car than to buy one. For a couple with a 17-year-old son and two cars, premiums of more than $8,000 a year are possible in urban centers such as New York and San Francisco. Small wonder, then, that many motorists are driving "bare"—without insurance—even though that is illegal in most states.

You can save money by shopping wisely and knowing what kind of coverage you need. The goal is to buy no more insurance than you need—but no less.

An auto insurance policy is a package of several types of coverage, each with its own premium. The sum of those premiums is the total you pay for your policy. You can raise or lower the price tag by taking higher or lower amounts of these coverages.

Not everyone needs the same coverage. The two most important types of coverage are bodily injury liability insurance and property damage liability insurance. Other types of coverage—medical payments insurance, uninsured motorist protection, collision insurance, comprehensive insurance, rental reimbursement insurance, and towing and labor insurance—may or may not be important to you.

BASIC AUTOMOBILE INSURANCE PROTECTION

Bodily Injury Liability

In most states, the only type of coverage you must carry is liability—insurance that protects others against damage you may cause by driving negligently. It is also the most expensive coverage and, unfortunately, the most necessary.

Bodily injury liability pays for losses resulting from death or injury in an accident that's your fault. People you injure can collect against this coverage to pay their medical bills and lost wages and to compensate for pain and suffering. Awards for pain and suffering can be high enough to bankrupt you if you are underinsured.

Depending on the company, you can buy liability coverage with a multiple (or "split") limit or with a single limit. Split-limit policies pay a certain amount to each person injured in an accident. The total amount paid out, however, is subject to a maximum for each accident. If the policy pays a maximum of $100,000 per person and $300,000 per accident, and one person suffered damages of $200,000, the policy would pay only $100,000 to that person. If four people suffered injury in a single accident, the policy would pay up to $300,000 for damages.

A single-limit policy pays one amount per accident, regardless of how many individuals are involved. This form is slightly more expensive than the equivalent amount of split-limit coverage because it provides more benefits per person. If the driver carried $300,000 of single-limit coverage, one injured person could collect up to $300,000.

States that mandate automobile insurance specify minimum levels of liability coverage. These minimums are typically expressed in a form of industry shorthand: 25/50/10 would indicate that an insurer will pay a maximum of $25,000 to each person injured in an accident, a maximum of $50,000 for everyone injured, and $10,000 to cover property damage caused by the accident.

For most people, the required minimum levels of liability insurance are not enough. If a judgment is entered against you that exceeds the limit of what your insurance company will pay, you must pay the remainder out of your own assets, which may mean digging into your savings, liquidating investments, or even selling property to pay the damage award. These days, automobile damage awards can be large, although the much-publicized million-dollar awards are frequently reduced on appeal or in posttrial settlements.

Extra liability coverage doesn't cost that much more. For what is often only an additional 25 percent of your liability premium, you can boost liability coverage from 25/50 to 100/300 (split liability limit). Most experts recommend carrying 100/300/50 liability limits or a $300,000 single liability limit.

If you have substantial property to protect from liability limits, you might want to consider adding an umbrella insurance policy, which begins where other liability policies end. Umbrella policies generally provide $1 million of liability coverage and require that you have basic liability coverage first, so they are an addition to, not a replacement for, coverage such as bodily injury liability insurance. (This type of policy was discussed in chapter 14.)

In states with no-fault laws, your bodily injury insurance generally covers you for medical treatment when you're driving your own car, and it usually covers any family members or others driving your car.

Property Damage Liability

Just as you are responsible for paying expenses when your driving causes bodily injuries or death, you probably will be liable if you cause property damage.

The most common type of property damage in an auto accident is damage to another party's automobile, but damage to buildings, telephone poles, and fences isn't unusual.

As with bodily injury coverage, states require that you carry a certain level of property damage insurance, ranging anywhere from $5,000 to $25,000. The most common minimum—which about 30 states require—is $10,000 of coverage. But again, experts advise that you carry far more than the minimum; $25,000 to $50,000 of coverage is recommended. Considering all the expensive cars on the road, an accident that damages several cars, or even one, could easily cost more than $10,000.

Generally, increasing your property damage liability to a more adequate level doesn't add much to your premium and may be worth the additional expense. For instance, an adult suburban driver who pays $90 a year for $10,000 of property damage coverage from State Farm Insurance could increase coverage to $25,000 by adding less than $10 to the premium.

Medical Payments Insurance

Medical payments insurance will pay medical expenses resulting from an automobile accident without regard to who was at fault. In states with no-fault laws, a comprehensive form of medical payments coverage called PIP (for personal-injury protection) is required (see below). In states without no-fault laws, medical payments insurance usually is not required.

Medical payments insurance covers family members and guests who happen to be riding in the policyholder's car. You and your family are also covered if you're hit by a car while walking (but not riding a bicycle), or if you're injured while riding in someone else's car (typically, that driver's coverage will reimburse you up to the limits of his or her policy; after that, your own coverage takes over). In addition, the insurance often pays for funeral expenses if there has been a death. The insurance amount covers each person injured; if you have bought $10,000 worth of medical payments coverage, it will pay $10,000 for each person injured.

Many people with good health insurance policies forgo automobile medical payments insurance, since injuries sustained in an accident may well be covered under medical and hospital insurance. But a small amount of additional coverage can make sense. For one thing, health insurance usually doesn't pay a funeral benefit. For another, additional coverage through auto insurance will cover nonfamily members who may be injured while riding in your car. Their medical bills will then be paid immediately by your carrier. Without that coverage, injured passengers would have to sue to collect against your liability coverage.

Some auto insurers won't pay for medical expenses that have been paid by your health insurance coverage. However, you can apply your automobile medical payments coverage toward the deductible on your health insurance.

In states with no-fault laws, you are required to buy personal-injury protection (PIP), which covers not only medical bills but often lost wages while an injured person is unable to work; replacement services while a person is unable to perform routine tasks such as child care; and some funeral expenses. Drivers in no-fault states generally can buy as much as $50,000 of PIP coverage, but most buy only $10,000.

If your state's no-fault rules allow policyholders to "coordinate benefits" with their health insurance policies, you may save on PIP premiums. By electing to make your health insurance "primary"— that is, to seek reimbursements for medical expenses from your health insurer before applying to your auto insurer—you could reduce your premium for personal-injury protection by as much as 40 percent.

Uninsured Motorist Protection

An alarming number of people drive around without automobile insurance. If you are hit by one of them and you are not sufficiently insured, you are in trouble. You can, of course, recover damages from the driver's personal assets, but chances are that if the driver doesn't have insurance, he or she probably doesn't have much else in the way of assets either.

To guard against such a situation, you can buy uninsured motorist coverage. With this insurance, you look to your own policy for coverage rather than to the other motorist's policy. Most policies cover only bodily injuries; others pay for damage to your car. This protection also covers you if you are in an accident with a hit-and-run driver. The minimum coverage that companies offer usually matches the minimums required by state laws. But many people carry coverage comparable to the amounts carried for bodily injury liability.

Uninsured motorist coverage won't pay you if you or a member of your family owns the car that hits you and it is not insured, or if the car is a government-owned vehicle. Nor will it cover you if you are hit by a vehicle designed for use off public roads (such as a tractor, snowmobile, or all-terrain vehicle) while that vehicle is off public roads.

In most states, uninsured motorist coverage is part of every insurance policy, although you may elect in writing to reject the coverage. If you live in a state without good no-fault laws, it's wise to keep the coverage. As premiums rise, more and more drivers neglect to carry insurance, or fail to renew a policy purchased solely to satisfy registration requirements.

Similarly, rising rates have increased the need for a related coverage—underinsured motorist coverage. If you are injured by a person who carries minimum liability coverage and your damages exceed the limits of the driver's policy, your underinsured motorist coverage will begin where the other party's coverage leaves off.

A typical premium for both uninsured and underinsured motorist coverages may range anywhere from under $10 to over $50.

Collision Insurance

Collision insurance pays for damage to your car if it is in a collision or if it turns over, regardless of who was responsible for the accident. If you are not at fault, your insurer may pay you and then try to get the amount they paid you from the other driver (or his or her insurance company).

Collision coverage is always limited by the deductible, the amount you pay before the coverage kicks in. Deductibles between $100 and $250 are the most common, but the deductible can be as high as $1,000.

When considering collision insurance coverage, you need to consider whether or not you need it, and, if so, what amount of deductible you should choose.

If you have a new or expensive car, you probably should have collision insurance. Car repair costs are extremely high. In 1990, according to a study by the Alliance of American Insurers, the cost of the parts and paint to rebuild a totally demolished 1990 Ford Escort LX was almost four times the car's factory sticker price—and that didn't include the labor involved in assembly. Average labor rates nationally range from $20 to $60 an hour.

If you have an automobile loan, the lender probably will insist that you carry collision insurance until the loan is repaid, to protect the lender's investment. (Remember, though, that if the insurance doesn't cover the entire loan amount outstanding, you are still liable for the remainder owed the bank.)

It makes sense to drop collision coverage entirely on an older car with a low resale value, since the resale, or "book," value of a car also represents the maximum insurance settlement possible.

Most U.S.-made cars depreciate rapidly; five years after purchase, a domestic car is typically worth only about 30 percent of what it cost originally. So the amount you are reimbursed by your automobile insurance company could be quite small, especially when compared to the premiums you may have to pay for the insurance. It usually pays to carry collision coverage for cars less than three years old; for those older than seven years, it usually doesn't. And if the car is between three and seven years old, the decision depends on how much risk you are willing to assume. As with any insurance coverage, you shouldn't take risks that you can't afford. Some foreign cars depreciate less rapidly, or even appreciate.

If you do decide that collision coverage is warranted, one way to save on insurance is to take the highest deductible you can afford. The price of collision coverage with a $500 deductible is 15 to 30 percent less than the price for coverage with a $250 deductible.

The savings can be significant where insurance rates are high. In New York City, for example, State Farm would have charged you $632 per year for collision coverage on a new Toyota Camry in 1991 if you took a $200 deductible, but only $354 with a $500 deductible—a savings of $278.

Comprehensive Insurance

Comprehensive insurance is the companion to collision coverage. While collision covers damage to your car if it is in an accident, comprehensive covers just about everything else that might befall an automobile. If the car is stolen or vandalized, comprehensive coverage takes care of your loss. If your car is hit by falling objects, if it catches fire, if there is glass breakage, or if it is damaged in a flood, you turn to comprehensive coverage for reimbursement. If you hit a deer on a stormy autumn night, comprehensive insurance, not collision, covers the damage to your car. Comprehensive does not cover mechanical breakdown of the car, however, or normal wear and tear; if your fan belt breaks or there's a leak in the radiator, it's up to you to pay for repairs. Comprehensive insurance also doesn't usually cover losses related to accessories such as tape decks, radios, CB radios, or car telephones unless they are installed permanently in the car.

Some insurance policies will cover personal property you may be carrying in the car if the loss is from fire or lightning, or sometimes from theft. However, comprehensive is primarily designed to cover your car, not what's in it. If you do lose belongings from inside your car, your homeowner's or renter's insurance policy will likely cover such losses. If your car is stolen, comprehensive coverage may well cover the cost of a rental car (within certain monetary limits and for a limited period of time).

As with collision insurance, if you have an older car, you might think twice about how much, if any, comprehensive coverage you should carry. The most an insurer will pay you for your car is the current retail value.

The price of comprehensive insurance varies with what kind of car you have and where you live. Not surprisingly, luxury and sports cars are among the most frequently stolen cars; station wagons are among the least frequent targets of thieves. And because of higher theft incidence, comprehensive coverage costs more in urban areas than in suburban or rural areas.

As with collision insurance, each comprehensive policy is sold with a deductible, which ranges from $50 to $500. Of course, the higher the deductible, the lower the insurance bill, so consumers should choose the highest deductible with which they feel comfortable.

Rental Reimbursement Insurance

If you have collision and comprehensive insurance, and you have an accident or loss for which you're covered under those policies, rental reimbursement insurance will pay you for car rental expenses while you don't have your own car. Policies and costs vary, but there are usually fairly strict limits to this coverage. One basic policy, for example, pays up to $14 a day for 28 days for car rental, and pays for commercial transportation or extra meals and lodging up to $400. The cost of this coverage is $17 to $30 a year.

Towing and Labor Insurance

Towing and labor coverage will pay perhaps $25 for the cost of towing your car. Only labor actually performed at the scene of the breakdown is covered. This coverage is inexpensive, usually $5 to $10 a year, but you may be able to do without it. The AAA (American Automobile Association) offers its emergency road service as one of the benefits of membership. A year's membership costs about $40.

NO-FAULT INSURANCE

No-fault automobile insurance got its start in the mid-1960s in response to widespread dissatisfaction with high premiums, long and costly lawsuits, slow payments, and inadequate or capricious awards by judges and juries. No-fault was intended to eliminate the need to sue the other driver to gain compensation for the economic cost of injuries. Instead, a policyholder's own insurance company would pay him or her for injuries and lost income regardless of who was at fault in an accident. It would not pay for nonquantifiable costs such as "pain and suffering." Hence, victims would no longer have to wait years for a court to decide how much they should be paid for their injuries, or whether they should be paid at all. Premium dollars going toward attorneys' fees would be redirected instead to accident victims. Since many lawsuits, especially those for minor injuries, would be eliminated, the resulting savings could be passed through to policyholders as lower premiums.

The prospect of speeding compensation to accident victims and holding down the cost of premiums was appealing, and several states adopted mandatory no-fault systems in the early 1970s. But in state after state, trial lawyers, who had the most to lose from this consumer-oriented initiative, succeeded either in defeating no-fault laws or in weakening them to the point where lawsuits continued as before, making no-fault provisions useless in controlling premiums.

To date, 26 states, the District of Columbia, and Puerto Rico have adopted some form of no-fault system. Typically, no-fault provides coverage for you and your family, for passengers in your car, and for pedestrians who are hit by your car. In other matters, coverage varies widely from state to state, most notably in restrictions on the right to sue, benefits paid for medical or funeral expenses, and benefits paid for wage loss and replacement services.

Restrictions on lawsuits vary. In some states, liability lawsuits are forbidden except for injuries explicitly outlined in state law. Typically, such injuries include disfigurement or permanent impairment. Other states don't allow you to sue for damages until your expenses reach a certain threshold, or until you have been disabled for a certain length of time. When someone has died in an accident, all states allow liability lawsuits to be brought against a negligent driver.

Lawsuit restrictions apply to the state where an accident takes place. If you're from a state that allows liability suits to be brought only in the most extreme cases—such as death or permanent impairment—and you have an accident in a state with no restrictions, you can still find yourself sued for a relatively minor matter. Thus, the need to maintain adequate liability insurance is clear.

Thirteen states require that car owners carry both personal-injury protection (PIP) and liability insurance: Colorado, Connecticut, Hawaii, Kansas, Kentucky, Massachusetts, Michigan, Minnesota, New Jersey, New York, North Dakota, Pennsylvania, and Utah. In all of those states, there are restrictions on when you can bring a lawsuit in an auto accident.

Florida and Puerto Rico require drivers to buy PIP but make liability insurance optional. They also place certain restrictions on when accident victims or their families can sue.

Delaware, Maryland, and Oregon, all compel car owners to buy no-fault and liability insurance, but they place no limits on lawsuits. Arkansas, the District of Columbia, South Carolina, and Texas have optional no-fault insurance, compulsory liability insurance, and no restrictions on lawsuits.

Five states—New Hampshire, South Dakota, Virginia, Washington, and Wisconsin—don't require drivers to purchase auto insurance and impose no restrictions on lawsuits. They do require insurance companies to offer no-fault insurance on an optional basis.

Michigan has the most comprehensive and what are generally acknowledged as the best no-fault laws in the country. The no-fault law in Michigan requires that insurance policies provide unlimited medical and rehabilitation benefits, up to three years' worth of wage-loss benefits (an injured person receives 85 percent of gross income up to a maximum, currently $2,939 a month), survivors' benefits, and a $20 daily benefit for replacement services. Michigan is also the only state where no-fault insurance extends to property damage. Policyholders can buy collision coverage to pay for damage to their own cars and only enough property damage liability coverage to protect them when driving outside the state. Suits for damage to vehicles are severely restricted.

The generous benefits in Michigan have been balanced by tough restrictions on the right to sue. Suits can be brought only if a victim dies, suffers permanent and serious disfigurement, or suffers serious impairment of bodily function. A 1986 analysis by The Auto Club Insurance Association revealed that in Michigan, 73 cents out of every premium dollar compensated accident victims, while only 4 cents was spent on court costs and attorney fees. In contrast, in states with watered-down no-fault insurance, only 48 cents of every premium dollar went to injured parties, while 32 cents was spent on court costs and legal fees. According to the A.M. Best Company, the average premium in Michigan is 30 percent lower than that in New Jersey, where the right to sue is not similarly restricted.

HOW PREMIUMS ARE ESTABLISHED

The premium you pay depends on how the insurance company sizes you up as a risk. A lot of variables go into the calculation, and there's not much you can do about many of them. Companies have different rate-setting procedures, and every state has its own regulations with regard to rates. Typically, the basic premium is determined by where you live, your record of accidents and traffic violations, and the make and model of your car. Initially, a company underwriter will place you in one of three risk tiers—preferred, standard, or nonstandard. (Some companies have only two tiers, while others have more than three.)

Once your base rate is determined, it is fine-tuned by the addition or subtraction of certain amounts reflecting such factors as your age, your marital status, how often you drive, and how many insurance claims you have had.

Auto insurance is one of the most expensive types of insurance—far more expensive than, say, homeowner's insurance. That's because the types of expenses that auto insurance pays for—health care, auto parts and labor costs, liability awards, and legal fees—have been subject to very high inflation over the last several years.

Where you live has a great influence on your insurance bill. It's no surprise that premiums tend to be higher in densely populated urban areas, where there is more theft and vandalism. Insurers divide states into rating territories and set insurance premiums according to how many claims are made in each area. The cost of automobile repairs in your rating territory also affects your premiums.

As any parent with children of driving age can tell you, it costs a lot to insure young drivers because they statistically have more accidents. One insurance company charges a young male who is an occasional driver of a car 2.2 times what it charges an adult male driver. According to the National Safety Council, drivers under age 25 made up 16.5 percent of the driver population in the United States in 1989, and accounted for 30.7 percent of all drivers involved in accidents. Typically, you are no longer considered a "young" driver once you reach the age of 25, and if you are a driver with a clean record, your insurance premium will drop after that birthday. Some states (Hawaii, Massachusetts, and North Carolina) prohibit insurers from taking age into account when figuring premiums.

Statistically speaking, male drivers are more dangerous than female drivers, so insurance is more costly for them. (The difference is due in large part to the fact that males do more driving than females.) In 1989, there were a little more than three times as many fatal accidents involving male drivers as there were involving female drivers, according to the National Safety Council. Again, some states—Hawaii, Massachusetts, Michigan, Montana, and North Carolina—don't allow insurance companies to take gender into account when setting insurance rates.

Marital status is another variable in rate-setting. Among young drivers, married people tend to have fewer accidents than single persons. So if you're a young married man, you are not considered a youthful driver after age 24, while a young woman is no longer considered youthful (for auto insurance purposes, that is) whenever she gets married.

If you drive an expensive car, collision and comprehensive insurance will generally cost more. But the sticker price of your car isn't the only consideration. What it costs to repair your car and how much damage it's likely to sustain in an accident are extremely important in setting rates. Compact cars and cars without bumpers designed to withstand a 5 mph crash typically sustain more damage in a collision than larger cars. In descending order, sports and specialty cars have the highest collision losses, followed by two-door cars, four-door models, and station wagon/passenger vans.

Companies take personal injury statistics into consideration, too. Passengers in an accident involving a larger car tend to suffer fewer injuries than do passengers in smaller cars. So if you are about to buy a new car, it is worthwhile to ask your insurance agent how the insurance premiums vary for your different choices.

How much driving you do has an impact on your insurance bill as well. A car that you drive 30 to 100 miles a week to work will cost 10 to 15 percent more to insure than one you drive less than 30 miles a week.

The number of your loss and damage claims also affects your premium. Insurers generally care more about the number of claims than about the sizes of those claims.

Insurers typically offer several discounts on auto insurance. Ask your agent; you may qualify for one that you don't know about. For example, many insurance companies have a discount for drivers above the age of 50 who have no unmarried young drivers in the household. The discount is about 5 to 20 percent off your total premium. If you insure more than one car with the same company, most firms will give you a discount of anywhere from 10 to 25 percent on the whole package.

Most insurers will also give you a discount if you have had driver training courses; typically, the savings amounts to 5 to 10 percent. Some will give you a discount for driver refresher courses. If you have a young driver in your household and he or she is a good student, there's credit to be earned. For example, several insurers will discount the young driver's rate 5 to 30 percent (depending on age) if he or she maintains a B average. If you have a youngster who is away at school and only drives the car occasionally, most companies will discount his or her rate.

If you install antitheft devices in your car (such as an alarm), you can often get a discount on the comprehensive portion of your coverage ranging anywhere from 5 to 20 percent. Be sure to take into account the cost of the antitheft device when trying to decide whether the insurance discount justifies buying it.

Some companies also give a discount on the no-fault and medical payments portions of your auto insurance if you have passive restraint devices in your car, such as seat belts that close automatically, or air bags. (Cars that simply sound a buzzer for a few seconds if the seat belt isn't fastened aren't eligible for this discount.) Discounts are typically 10 to 35 percent, though a few companies go as high as 60 percent with full front air bags.

INSURANCE FOR HIGH-RISK DRIVERS

Most companies reject the worst drivers of all ages, such as those with drunk-driving convictions. Those people must buy insurance either from companies specializing in substandard drivers or from state-operated insurance pools or facilities. In either case, the premiums are likely to be considerably higher.

In the voluntary insurance market, many major insurers have subsidiaries that offer coverage to high-risk drivers. Indeed, if you find yourself labeled a high risk, your carrier might try to shunt you to a subsidiary rather than write you a policy itself. Such a subsidiary often has a name similar to that of the parent company: State Farm Mutual Auto, for instance, has the State Farm Fire and Casualty subsidiary, and Allstate is parent company to Allstate Indemnity.

High-risk subsidiaries may still refuse to insure you if they consider you too poor a risk—say, because you've had one too many tickets or accidents, or you have an unusually expensive and fancy car, or you're an unmarried male under 25 years old. You can't go without automobile insurance, since, practically speaking, a form of it is required in all 50 states.

Drivers who can't find an insurer to cover them voluntarily end up in the shared insurance market, also commonly called the "assigned-risk pool," where coverage is guaranteed—for a price. Approximately 8 percent of all insured motorists in this country are covered in the shared market. There are four main systems at work in the various states:

The Assigned-Risk System

This is the most common plan, used by most states. Uninsured drivers are distributed among different companies in proportion to the amount of business each company does in the state. So the state's largest insurer has the largest number of high-risk drivers, the second largest insurer has the second largest number of unattractive risks, and so forth.

Joint Underwriting Associations

These are plans in which a few insurance companies service the risky customers and all automobile insurers doing business in the state share in the expenses.

Reinsurance Facilities

In this plan, every company is required to accept any insurance applicant but can then reinsure those drivers with a state reinsurance facility, allowing them to transfer the risk to that facility. Any profits or losses incurred by the reinsurance facility are shared by all companies in the state.

State Fund

Only one state, Maryland, uses this mechanism, in which the state sets up its own insurance company, which accepts applicants if they've been rejected by at least two insurers. Insurance companies operating in the state subsidize the losses incurred by the state fund.

If you are insured through the shared market, don't give up trying to get voluntary coverage. Keep applying to companies. If you are considered a bad risk because of factors such as your youth, companies might be persuaded if they see that you are a good risk at your age. If you've been turned down because of accidents or traffic violations, companies likewise might reconsider insuring you after you accumulate a few years of incident-free driving.

SHOPPING FOR INSURANCE

You can save a significant amount by comparison shopping for auto insurance. It is not uncommon to encounter differences of hundreds of dollars a year in the annual premium for identical coverage from different insurers. Consider, for example, a couple with a 17-year-old son, a 1987 Buick LeSabre used to commute to work and a 1985 Chevrolet Cavalier, and a clean record. In San Francisco, such a couple might pay as much as $4,258 a year to insure their cars—or as little as $2,022 for identical coverage. In Manhattan, their premiums might be as high as $4,806 or as low as $2,553. In Chicago, they could pay as much as $2,976 or as little as $1,516.

Or consider a retired couple with no record of accidents or violations and a 1979 Oldsmobile Delta '88 that they drive some 4,000 miles a year. In suburban Florida, their premiums could range from $574 to $1,077; in suburban New York, from $499 to $765; in suburban Ohio, from $326 to $1,206. (For more figures on the range of premiums charged in the 10 most populous states, see *Consumer Reports*, October 1988.)

Not only do some insurance companies offer lower premiums than others, but any two companies can come to far different conclusions about the degree of risk presented by the same applicants.

Clearly, it makes sense to shop around for automobile insurance. We recommend that you follow this procedure:

1. Use the worksheet (table 15-1) to determine the amount of coverage you need.
2. Ask for a premium quote from each of several companies in your state. You may want to consult surveys of customer satisfaction with insurance companies, published periodically in *Consumer Reports*.
3. Select the company that offers the best combination of price and service.

CLOSE-UP: WATCH OUT FOR PACKAGED POLICIES

Increasingly, insurance companies are refusing to issue or continue an auto policy unless the person seeking insurance agrees to buy additional policies.

Homeowner's and renter's policies are generally profitable; auto policies may not be. If a company captures both policies, there's a good chance the entire account will be profitable, and the policyholder will remain with the company longer.

Are such practices legal?

In some states, these tie-in sales are plainly illegal. In 1988, in Pennsylvania, for instance, the insurance department accused a major broker and two major companies of illegally requiring customers to purchase homeowner's insurance in order to obtain an

TABLE 15-1   Auto Insurance Buyer's Worksheet

	Write amount of coverage here	Write premium quotes here	
		Company name 1: _____	2: _____
Minimum coverage your state requires for:			
Bodily injury liability	_____	_____	_____
Property damage liability	_____	_____	_____
Personal-injury protection (no-fault states)	_____	_____	_____
Uninsured motorist	_____	_____	_____
Level of coverage you desire for:			
Bodily injury liability	_____	_____	_____
Property damage liability	_____	_____	_____
Medical payments	_____	_____	_____
Personal-injury protection (no-fault states)	_____	_____	_____
Collision:			
a. $100 deductible	_____	_____	_____
b. $250 deductible	_____	_____	_____
c. $500 deductible	_____	_____	_____
SUBTOTAL A:		_____	_____

Comprehensive with no deductible:
  a. $100 deductible _____
  b. $250 deductible _____
  c. $500 deductible _____
  Uninsured motorist _____

SUBTOTAL B: _____

Other coverages you might consider:
  Towing and labor _____
  Rental-car reimbursement _____

SUBTOTAL C: _____

Do any other charges apply?
  Membership fee _____
  Surcharges _____

SUBTOTAL D: _____

What's your choice? (Subtotal A or
  B, plus C and D) _____
Does company have accident-
  forgiveness program?   Yes ___ No ___
After how many years does it
  apply? _____

TOTAL PREMIUM: _____

auto policy. New York prohibits tie-in sales if such arrangements are not clearly spelled out in the policy forms approved and on file with the state insurance department. On the federal level, the McCarran-Ferguson reform recently has been reintroduced in Congress, and is designed to prevent tie-ins.

Tie-ins should not be confused with "cross-sell" discounts, which companies must file with state insurance departments. These discounts are legal and have the same effect as tie-in sales— they get policyholders to put all their eggs in one basket. Under cross selling, a company encourages a policyholder to buy both policies by offering a discount on one or both of the coverages.

Be aware that both tie-ins and cross-selling discounts appear to save money. But you may save more and enjoy better service if you comparison shop for insurance.

CLOSE-UP: IF YOU ARE INVOLVED IN AN ACCIDENT

What do you do if you have an automobile accident? Many people panic even after a minor fender-bender. In those first frantic moments and hours after you've had an accident, the Insurance Information Institute recommends several steps you should take to expedite your claims:

1. Get help for anyone who is injured. It can be a felony to leave the scene if you're involved in an accident. Contact the police and tell them briefly what happened, how many people are injured, and how badly they are hurt. The police can contact the ambulance or rescue squad more quickly than you can.
2. Don't try to move any injured persons; cover them with a blanket to keep them from getting cold and going into shock.
3. If your car is in the middle of the road and in danger of further damage, or if it will endanger someone else, put up flares or try to move it.
4. Cooperate fully with the police, and give them whatever information they require. To the institute's advice we add that you should avoid jumping to admit guilt in having caused an accident. Even if you believe, in your upset state, that you did cause an accident, you may *not* have, in fact,

done so. Be certain you tell police only what you *know* are the facts. Do not report your assumptions, guesses, or beliefs as fact.

5. Find out from the police where you can obtain a copy of the police report. If you are unfamiliar with the area, it can be confusing to try to figure out what municipality you were in when the accident occurred.

6. Make sure you obtain the following information: the names and addresses of all drivers and passengers in the accident; the license plate numbers, makes, and models of all cars involved; and the drivers' license identification numbers and insurance identification numbers. If there are witnesses, make a note of their names and addresses, as well as the names of the responding police officers or other officials. Make a habit of carrying a pen and paper in your car at all times so they are handy if there's an accident.

7. If you have a camera, photograph the accident scene, including skid marks. If you don't have a camera, make a rough sketch of the scene.

8. If you run into an unattended car or object and you can't find the owner, leave your name, address, and telephone number.

9. Call your insurance agent or local representative as soon as possible. Carry the company's phone number with you so that you can contact your insurer promptly if you're away from home. Ask what forms or documents you will need to prove your claim. This will probably include the police report and auto repair and medical bills. An insurance company will probably want to have an insurance adjuster inspect your car and appraise the damage before you have the car repaired.

10. Cooperate with your insurer in its investigation, settlement, or defense of any claim, and turn over to the company any legal papers you receive. If there is a lawsuit, your insurer will defend you.

11. Keep careful records of all your expenses, including lost wages, rental-car expenses, or the amounts you might have to pay a temporary housekeeper.

12. Keep copies of all paperwork. You may need to refer later to such papers.

To represent you properly in the event of any legal action, your insurer needs to be notified of any accidents as soon as possible. You may think that if you take care of the damages yourself and don't report an accident you can prevent your insurance bill from going up. This may be true, but it is risky, since a claim or lawsuit could be filed against you at some later date. But if you simply hit a tree and there is no injury to yourself or damage to the car or tree, it may make sense not to report it.

16

Other Insurance

Janet Bamford

It is possible to insure almost anything, if you can find someone willing to take the risk. You can buy aviation insurance, marine insurance, space flight insurance, kidnap and ransom insurance. Whether you need additional insurance beyond the basics—medical, life, home, and automobile—depends on your circumstances. Before considering a specialized policy, ask yourself the following questions:

- Am I covered by existing policies? If not, should I be?
- Is the risk significant, or are my worries based on atypical horror stories?
- Can I afford to self-insure—that is, to run a risk without insurance coverage and pay for the loss, if it should occur, out of my own pocket?

The key question to address is whether you are insured against loss by other types of policies than the one you are considering. You should not buy a specialized policy to cover a risk that is—or should be—covered by a broader policy, such as a medical or life insurance policy.

Although you may be well aware that the odds of a particular loss are improbable, you may want to buy coverage because the potential costs are far too great for you to bear personally, no matter how unlikely they may be. On the other hand, some kinds of coverage are unnecessary either because you are not exposed to the risks they cover or because the premiums are disproportionately high.

This chapter deals with several common types of "optional" coverage: disability insurance, dread-disease insurance, travel insurance, title insurance, and legal insurance. Obviously, some of these policies are needed only on special occasions or in special circumstances. Keep the foregoing questions in mind when considering any such policy; their answers can protect you against the blandishments of insurance salesmen and help you determine whether the protection the policy offers is worth its cost.

DISABILITY INSURANCE

If you are younger than 65, you are much more likely to suffer a disability of longer than three months than you are to die. Yet while most people carry life insurance, few carry an individual disability insurance policy. A disability such as a heart attack, cancer, or arthritis can interrupt your flow of income long enough to be financially disastrous.

About 40 percent of people under 65 have some kind of disability income protection, often through their employers. But for too many, the duration of the coverage is too short or the benefits are too skimpy.

A disability income policy is designed to cushion you against loss of income resulting from sickness or accident. Policies vary, depending on how much they pay; how soon after a disability occurs they start paying benefits; how long the benefits last; and how they define disability.

How Much Do You Need?

To calculate how much disability coverage you would need if you were no longer earning an income, figure your monthly take-home pay after taxes and subtract the monthly disability benefits you currently have, as follows:

1. Social Security pays disability benefits after you have been disabled for at least five months if your disability is expected to last at least a year and if you are unable to do any job whatever. The amount paid is a percentage of your previous monthly earnings. The local Social Security office or your insurance agent should be able to tell you how much Social Security would pay if you were disabled.
2. Ask your company benefits manager to help you calculate the company benefits. Find out what sick pay or wage-continuation plans are in effect, and whether they are taxable. Find out whether your company has a group disability insurance plan.
3. Add up the monthly disability benefits to which you are already entitled through Social Security and employment.
4. Subtract the monthly total of your existing benefits from your current monthly take-home pay. The result will show the monthly disability benefits you'll need in order to maintain your current after-tax income.

As with most types of insurance, the premium you pay depends on the amount of the benefit you receive. Premium scales are affected by your sex, age, and occupation; women (who are disabled more often than men partly because pregnancy and maternity-related absences are considered disability leaves), older people, and workers in higher-risk occupations pay higher premiums.

When Do Benefits Begin?

Most insurance companies give you a choice about how long a waiting period you have before a policy begins paying benefits. Benefits can begin 30 days, 60 days, 90 days, 6 months, or 12 months after you are disabled. The longer you are willing to wait, the lower the premium. We recommend you select the longest period your financial situation permits. Most people can hold out for 90 days by using employer benefits, seeking temporary help from relatives, or dipping into savings.

How Long Should Benefits Last?

The "benefit period" in your policy determines how long benefits continue. We recommend that most buyers select benefits payable to age 65. A shorter benefit period could leave you open to the devastation of a long-term loss of income, while having benefits go beyond age 65 usually makes a policy prohibitively expensive.

How Is Disability Defined?

What constitutes a disability is a more complex issue than might appear at first glance. Each policy contains its own definition of disability, depending on the following criteria: Is the person able to do any work at all? Is he or she able to work at his or her old job? Has he or she suffered a loss of income? If so, how much?

Since income loss resulting from ill health is what you're insuring against, a pure income-loss test of whether you're disabled makes the most sense, in our judgment.

Insist on seeing a sample policy before purchase. It is the policy's written definition, not any phrasing of it by a salesperson, that determines what benefits will or will not be paid.

Buying a Policy

Disability coverage is widely available but tends to be expensive. Moreover, comparison shopping is not easy; policies sold by different companies vary considerably. Once you've determined the four basic questions discussed above—how much coverage to obtain, how soon a policy should kick in, how long it should last, and what circumstances it should cover—consider the following additional points:

- Check to see that a policy is guaranteed renewable. If it is "class cancelable," the company can cancel the policy if it does so for all policies in a certain group—such as policies issued in a particular state, or policies issued before a certain date. Try to obtain a policy that is "noncancelable."
- As with any personal insurance, you must tell an insurer if you have preexisting health conditions. Some companies will

cover disabilities that arise from that condition; others will not for a certain period, which varies from insurer to insurer.

- Along with your basic coverage, you can choose any of several riders, or optional provisions, usually at extra cost. A useful option is a social insurance benefit, which pays the benefits you would receive under Social Security if you don't qualify as disabled under the agency's definition. Another rider deserving consideration is the "option to purchase," which gives you the right to buy more insurance in the future regardless of changes in your health. Cost-of-living riders, which adjust your benefits according to some measure of inflation (often the Consumer Price Index), can also be useful.

- Look for a policy that has favorable terms in three crucial areas: estimated cost, renewability, and definition of disability. A good policy is guaranteed renewable and noncancelable; it measures disability by loss of income rather than loss of ability to perform all the duties of your regular job; and it qualifies you for partial disability benefits regardless of whether or not your partial disability was preceded by a period of total disability. Buy insurance only from a company with an A+ or A rating from *Best's Insurance Reports.*

DREAD-DISEASE INSURANCE

Many insurance companies offer so-called dread-disease policies— insurance policies limited to specific diseases such as cancer. These policies usually provide specified benefit amounts for a number of separate categories of expenses, such as hospital bills, doctor bills, radiation treatment, and surgery, subject to strict limitations. Because the cost of treating cancer and other dreaded diseases can be fearfully high, insurance companies have found a responsive market to ominous advertisements that emphasize the prevalence of cancer and the expense of its treatment.

Some states have banned or severely restricted the sale of dread-disease policies on various grounds. First, dread-disease policies usually do not offer much value for the dollar; second, cancer insurance often excludes coverage of the complications of cancer; third, misleading promotional fear tactics are often used in selling these policies; fourth, sales and administrative expenses for such policies tend to be unduly high.

Consumers Union agrees with the reasoning of those states that have banned dread-disease policies. Most such policies offer only fragmentary protection against the cost of cancer treatment, and no coverage at all for numerous other diseases that can also be expensive to treat. On balance, it is generally wiser to spend money on improving your broad health insurance coverage rather than on cancer insurance.

TRAVEL INSURANCE

Because travel, especially travel abroad, places you in an unfamiliar environment, some of the risks of everyday life increase and new ones are likely to arise. To begin with, there is the possibility (though it is infinitesimally small) that you could be killed or injured in a plane crash. Slightly more probable is an illness that requires medical attention or that forces you to abandon a series of noncancelable flights, cruises, train trips, and hotel reservations. There is the risk that the operator of your tour or your charter flight will go out of business suddenly and leave you stranded in a foreign country with a useless ticket in your hand. And there is always the possibility that your baggage, your camera, or some other essential or expensive part of your equipment will be lost or stolen.

You are first likely to be offered insurance coverage against such risks by your travel agent (who earns a commission of about 30 percent for selling the policy), but you can also buy one from tour and cruise operators or direct from some insurance companies. Most such policies allow you to choose both the amount and the types of coverage you prefer, but because both the coverage and the premiums are sometimes confusingly combined, it's important to determine how much protection you need against each of the possible contingencies specified in the policy.

Flight Insurance

The typical policy sold at airports pays a specified amount if you are killed or injured in a plane crash during your trip. Although the premiums are temptingly low (for example, $300,000 of coverage for $10), the probability of your dying in a crash is very much lower, and such policies are far more expensive than an ordinary life policy, which provides full-time protection against a wider range of risks.

Moreover, a number of credit card issuers provide "free" coverage. American Express offers $100,000 of coverage and Visa Gold offers a minimum of $150,000, depending on the issuer, to passengers who charge their tickets on their credit cards. The terms of these coverages are explained in their literature or on the backs of their monthly statements.

We don't recommend flight insurance policies. If you have the amount of life insurance you need, the manner and likelihood of death are irrelevant. If you don't have enough life insurance, you should buy more life insurance, not flight insurance (see chapter 13).

Accident and Medical Policies

Accident and medical policies provide coverage in case of death or dismemberment and pay medical expenses incurred through injury or illness in the course of your travels. Such policies may seem attractive to travelers aware that most people are at greater risk of injury and illness when traveling than they are at home. But if your health and medical insurance covers you regardless of the cause of the illness or the location where you become sick, then there is no reason to duplicate it with other coverage.

Before buying any such policy, review your existing health insurance; it may very well be that it covers you during travel. Only if existing coverage doesn't stretch are accident and medical policies worth buying.

If you are eligible for Medicare, however, it is important to note that Medicare provides only limited benefits in Canada and Mexico, and none at all in other countries. Consequently, you should check on the coverage provided by your medigap policy, or buy such a policy if it offers you protection in foreign countries.

Premiums for these policies vary, but coverage that provides $50,000 for death or dismemberment, up to $5,000 in medical expenses resulting from accidents, and sickness benefits of $50 per day, ranges from $25 to $60 for a 14-day trip. The policy covers you only for incidents that occur within the 14 days, but medical benefits can continue for 52 weeks from the date of the accident, and sickness benefits continue for as long as 60 days if you are hospitalized and 10 days if you are not.

Unlike certain conventional health insurance plans, these policies do not make payment directly to hospitals or physicians. Instead, you must pay your bills and wait for reimbursement from the insurer.

Baggage Insurance

Baggage insurance reimburses you for loss or theft of your baggage during your travels. But, as is true of other short-term policies, the premiums are high. For $500 of coverage for a two-week trip, the premium runs to $20 or $25—a high cost even if your itinerary involves airports, taxicabs, and hotels in high crime areas.

Moreover, baggage insurance specifies a number of exclusions. Some insurers set a maximum reimbursement of $1,000 for the loss or theft of jewelry, furs, or photographic equipment. Other items often excluded are contact lenses, cash, credit cards, securities, dentures and other prostheses, and items officially seized by government authorities or lost or damaged as a result of war. And all such policies require that you report any loss or theft promptly to the local authorities.

Before considering baggage insurance, check the coverage on your homeowner's or renter's policy. Many of them cover possessions that accompany you away from home, such as luggage, cameras, and the like. (As discussed on p. 270, there is a limit to the amount you may be reimbursed for these items if you have not purchased a separate "floater" policy on them.) Under any coverage of this kind, it is important to leave at home a detailed inventory of what you are taking with you, including documentation on the age and cost of especially valuable items.

Trip Cancellation/Interruption Insurance

Policies are available to reimburse you in the event that circumstances prevent you from starting or finishing a trip for which you have made nonrefundable reservations, or in the event that the operators of a charter flight or cruise are unable to fulfill their commitments and leave you stranded at the point of origin or at some point on the itinerary.

There are, of course, certain restrictions with respect to cancellation. You won't be reimbursed, for example, if you simply change your mind. But the policy issued by Travelers illustrates the typical benefits. You will be reimbursed if you are forced to cancel or interrupt your plans because you, a family member, a business partner, or a traveling companion dies, is injured, falls ill, is called to jury duty, or is subpoenaed as a witness in court proceedings. Coverage also applies if you miss a flight because of an accident on the way to the airport, or if you are unable to begin or continue a trip because of bankruptcy of the airline, tour operator, or cruise line.

You will also receive some payment if your trip is interrupted by an unannounced strike, a hijacking, or natural disaster. If your trip is interrupted by your own injury or by an illness not due to a preexisting condition, you will be paid for emergency transportation to the nearest hospital or medical facility. The premium for this policy is $5.50 per $100 of coverage.

Automobile Insurance

If you are traveling abroad in your own automobile, it's important to check the insurance requirements for the country in which you intend to travel. In Canada your American policy is recognized, but you must carry the Canada Nonresident Interprovince Motor Liability Insurance Card, which your regular insurer will issue on request. Mexico does not honor American coverage and requires you to buy a Mexican policy.

If you rent a car in Europe, damage to it is usually covered by the automobile liability insurance for your car in the United States. But check with your insurer to make certain you are covered. If you do not own a car, the car rental rates in Europe include coverage for third-party, fire, and theft claims. They also include collision coverage, but check with the rental agency before you sign the rental agreement.

If you are buying a car in a European country, the seller can usually arrange short-term coverage for the duration of your visit, and the shipping line or customs broker will issue you a marine policy to insure the car for its journey across the ocean if you are bringing the car home.

Insuring Rented Automobiles

The typical car rental agreement usually includes liability coverage in case you are responsible for someone's death or injury or for property damage, but the maximum amount of coverage varies by state. You would be wise to make specific inquiries before signing the rental agreement.

If you check with your own insurance agent, you are likely to find that your personal automobile policy covers your use of rented cars at a liability level that you have chosen as adequate. In addition, some companies carry liability policies to cover employees who rent cars in the course of their work (although not necessarily for recreational use). If neither of these possibilities applies to you, you might ask about a limited insurance supplement policy, which is offered by a number of insurers.

Personal accident insurance, offered at an extra charge of $1 to $5 per day by some car rental firms, covers drivers and passengers in case of accidental death or injury. The current Hertz policy, at $3.95 per day, provides $175,000 in death benefits for the renter and $17,500 for each passenger. Medical expenses up to $2,500 and ambulance charges up to $250 are covered for each occupant, but the total benefits available for any one accident are limited to $225,000.

Whether such a policy is worth its premium depends in large part on your other insurance coverage. If your own life, automobile, and health insurance policies provide an equivalent amount of coverage, there is no point in duplicating it.

As to the car, you can be held liable for the full value of the rented vehicle, even if the accident was not your fault. Be aware that rental agents often will pressure you to protect yourself from this liability through the so-called collision damage waiver or CDW. This is available at $9 to $13 per day—a staggering annual premium seemingly without justification based on loss experience.

For most people, this is unnecessary. About 60 percent of all automobile insurance covers rental cars. Even for those who are not covered through their own policies, protection may be available through an employer, or the credit card that they pay with. Check carefully on your coverage, however, because it's not all alike—some credit card protection, for example, only provides reimbursement after you pay, or does not cover in case of theft. Some employers may not protect you if you rent a car for pleasure.

A number of associations also have arranged with car rental companies to cap the renters liability—at $3000, for instance. Usually, this is only available if you rent through your association membership. It may be necessary at time of rental to show an association membership card.

If you decide to turn down the CDW, make sure to inspect the car minutely before you drive away, and insist that the rental clerk make a written record of every existing nick, dent, and rust spot.

Insurance on truck rentals—generally for local or long-distance moving—is more of a problem. To begin with, your automobile policy will not cover you. In addition, if you are a once-in-a-while renter unfamiliar with a truck's handling characteristics and maneuverability, your risk of an accident is likely to be much higher than when you're at the wheel of your own subcompact. And this risk may be significantly increased by the tension and stress that almost inevitably accompany a move.

Three kinds of coverage are available: for medical and life insurance, for the collision deductible, and for the cargo, should it be damaged or destroyed. Although your basic coverage for life and health care may be adequate, you may find the premiums for the other coverage a relatively low price to pay for increasing your peace of mind for the short duration of the rental.

TITLE INSURANCE

When you buy a house or other piece of real estate, you must be certain that you have "clear title" to it—that is, that the seller actually owned it, that it was clear of any liens or other debts that might give someone else a claim on it, and that any easements, mineral leases, and other encumbrances have been clearly disclosed. Otherwise you might find yourself having paid for a property that you don't legally own or that has less value than you assumed.

Title insurance is usually issued by a title company, which makes a search of local records to trace ownership and sale of the property back to the original owner—in some cases a state or territory. This search is undertaken to discover any problems or irregularities that might present problems. When the title search is completed, an insurance policy is issued that protects you from unpleasant surprises.

If a claim arises against your property, the insurer will provide for your legal defense and, if necessary, settle the claim. If, for example, an earlier owner had pledged the property as collateral for a loan, the insurer will pay off his creditor. Or if an electric utility company that has an easement on the property that the search did not disclose builds a transmission line across your land, the insurance policy will compensate you for the loss in the value of the property.

Title insurance is available in two forms: lender's insurance and owner's insurance. Lender's insurance is usually required by the institution that provides the mortgage—although the buyer is almost invariably required to pay the premium. Because it protects only the lender and not the buyer, this insurance is usually written to cover only the amount of the mortgage. Owner's insurance protects the total value of the property.

Unlike most insurance policies, which require periodic premium payments, title insurance is a one-time cost. Typical charges are $2.50 per $1,000 of coverage for lender's insurance and $3.50 per $1,000 for an owner's policy. If both are bought simultaneously, you may get a discount, depending on state practice, and only one title search is necessary.

Although there is little likelihood that some kind of problem will arise from a title irregularity, the typical investment in a home is so large that owner's title insurance is probably a sensible coverage for most homeowners. In fact, in almost every situation a lender will insist on title insurance to protect its interest.

LEGAL INSURANCE

Prepaid legal services plans, also called legal or litigation insurance, originated in 1971 as an employee benefit but have since become increasingly popular. A number of large unions—the AFL-

CIO and the National Education Association, for example—provide this benefit to their members. Increasingly, eligibility has extended beyond union members and corporate employees. Several credit card issuers offer such plans to individual subscribers. The American Prepaid Legal Services Institute estimates that today some 12 million people in the United States are eligible for some sort of prepaid legal assistance.

These plans differ widely from one another in both their benefits and their restrictions. Some plans offer no free services but provide discounts when members consult an attorney. The typical "access" plan available to individuals might offer unlimited advice and consultation by telephone or correspondence and a document-review service for wills, leases, and other contracts. Some plans will prepare a will for members. More complex legal matters—including court appearances—are handled on an hourly basis, and members may be referred to an attorney outside the plan—in some cases at a discount from the attorney's regular hourly fee. The monthly premium for this kind of plan ranges between $7 and $14.

Group legal insurance plans tend to be more comprehensive. In addition to providing the services described above, some will represent their members in court and handle fairly routine matters such as real estate closings, uncontested divorces, and bankruptcies.

Advocates of these plans point out that they can be of help in resolving minor disputes—between customer and retailer over defective merchandise, for example—in which the amounts involved do not justify the trouble and expense of finding and hiring a lawyer; a lawyer's letter often resolves such disputes promptly. And they note that these plans also provide helpful advice to the individual who is uncertain about whether a case is worth pursuing.

But the restrictions and limitations need to be considered carefully. Not all plans, for example, entitle you to court appearances by a lawyer. And, like most health insurance plans, most won't cover you for a "preexisting condition"—that is, in this case, an ongoing lawsuit or divorce. Many will deal only with personal affairs, not business problems. Some may employ young lawyers who have little experience and unimpressive credentials.

Above all, it is important to realize that these plans in no way

eliminate the need for liability insurance. They usually will not pay
for extensive legal defense costs if you are sued, nor will they pay
any damages or fines that might be assessed against you. For this
kind of protection, you still need the broad liability coverages discussed in the chapters on homeowner's and automobile insurance
(chapters 14 and 15).

V

INVESTING

17

Principles of Investing

Aileen Jacobson

During your lifetime, you are almost certain to encounter some large expenditures—for a new or vacation home, a college education for your children, a business of your own—that you won't be able to meet from current income. And during your retirement years, you will need additional money to supplement your pension or Social Security in order to maintain your standard of living and enable you to do the things you've postponed during your working years. You can achieve these plans only if you discipline yourself to set aside a fixed portion of your current income for investment in ways that ensure its steady growth, or, at the very least, protect it against loss.

Whether you label this do-it-yourself payroll deduction plan "savings" or "investment" is immaterial, because all savings are, in fact, investments, and all investments constitute savings. Whatever you call it, your fundamental purpose is to prevent yourself from spending 100 percent of your current income shortly after (or even before) you receive it, and to make your investments grow until you need them.

LIQUIDITY, SAFETY, AND TOTAL RETURN

Once you have resolved to set aside a portion of every paycheck, you will have many possible investments to consider: savings accounts, certificates of deposit, mutual funds, stocks and bonds, and real estate, to name a few. But before making any kind of investment decision, you need to recognize that every investment offers you three potential advantages—liquidity, safety, and total return on your investment (in terms of interest or dividends and growth of your original capital). You should also be aware of their relationships to one another. Liquidity and safety usually go hand-in-hand, but for a higher return you generally have to sacrifice some liquidity or safety, or both.

Liquidity

Liquidity defines the ease with which you can convert your investment immediately into cash. Thus, money in a bank account or a money market fund is highly liquid because you can, at a moment's notice, write a withdrawal slip or a check for whatever amount you have on deposit. Mutual funds, stocks, and bonds are less liquid, not only because you may have to wait a week for your redemption check but also because you may suffer a loss if you need the money when the stock or bond market is at a low. Real estate, artworks, and coin collections have, of course, very low liquidity, because you may have to wait months for a minimally acceptable offer from a buyer.

The price for high liquidity is usually a reduction in total return. In general, the higher the liquidity of any investment, the lower its return is likely to be. This is one reason why money market mutual funds usually offer a lower rate of return than, say, corporate bonds, and why passbook savings accounts yield less than long-term CDs.

Many investors overestimate their need for liquidity and thus sacrifice return unnecessarily. Before deciding on how much liquidity you need, you should consider carefully not only the kinds of emergencies you are likely to encounter but also the various insurance coverages you have that may diminish your need for liquidity (see chapter 6). Bear in mind that health insurance, automobile insurance, and unemployment insurance, although they may not protect you completely, can make your need for liquidity lower than you might anticipate. And, of course, money that you set aside for your retirement while you are still young may be put into investments of very low liquidity because you will have ample time to liquidate them in the years before or after you retire.

If you are in the market for a new home or if you think you may encounter an irresistible investment opportunity, you may want to keep your liquidity high. No matter what your personal situation, a careful assessment of your need for liquidity can do much to maximize the overall return on your investments.

Safety

Investors who concentrate on achieving the highest available yield from an investment often fail to consider the possibility that they may lose it entirely or see its value drop dramatically. Total loss is likely to occur if, in the hope of making a killing, an investor buys stock in an unknown company, only to see it go bankrupt within a few months. But even investments in century-old companies can drop in value by 50 percent or more—if, for example, an established electric power company encounters rate problems with the state utility commission or construction problems with the nuclear regulatory authorities. Investments in small business ventures, precious metals, art, antiques, or collectibles can be just as hazardous for the novice investor.

You usually pay for protecting your investment in the form of lower return. This is why bank CDs, most of which are insured by the federal government, pay a lower rate of interest than corporate bonds, why corporate bonds of established blue-chip companies pay a lower rate of interest than junk bonds issued by corporations whose future performance is uncertain, and why the common stock of a major corporation is less likely to rise sharply in price than the stock of some smaller, aggressive, and innovative newcomers. Similarly, short-term bonds offer a lower return than long-term bonds, because locking your money in for the long term makes both the principal and the interest more vulnerable to erosion through inflation.

There are two levels of risk to consider in long-term investments. One is the investment risk: Can you get back your money and expected gains when the investment matures? The other is market risk: Will inflation reduce the value of your investment, or will you suffer a loss if you must pull out early and interest rates are not in your favor at the time? For example, if you buy a long-term government bond, your investment risk is extremely low if you hold it to maturity. But if you must sell it early, while prevailing interest rates are higher than those of your bond, you will be forced to sell at a lower price. Even if you hold it to maturity, inflation may erode its value. Thus, your market risk may be high, even when your investment is secure in terms of getting back capital and promised earnings at maturity.

Just as they exaggerate their need for liquidity, however, many investors exaggerate the importance of safety. Although few of them store cash in their mattresses for safekeeping, many maintain large passbook savings accounts, which usually earn them a lower yield than they would enjoy from a money market mutual fund, despite the fact that such accounts, although not insured, have an almost perfect record of safety. Moreover, as your net worth increases, you may feel that you can set aside a portion of it for investments involving higher risk, as long as its loss will not seriously affect your standard of living or your general financial health.

Total Return

The return on your investment can take several forms: interest (on bank accounts, certificates of deposit, money market accounts, and bonds); dividends (on stock mutual funds and common and preferred stock); and price appreciation (on stock or bond mutual fund shares, stocks, real estate, and works of art, for example).

Investors seeking a steady return, perhaps because they seek safety, often prefer a predictable interest or dividend rate. Thus, they may lock into a five-year certificate of deposit with a guaranteed interest rate, or they may buy preferred or common stock in a company that has paid dividends uninterruptedly for more than 30 years. But investors who put *all* their money into such long-term income-producing investments fail to anticipate the possibility of inflation or a change in interest rates. The interest rate on the CD or the dividend rate on the preferred stock may look very attractive, but if interest rates rise or the inflation rate soars, not only will the rate of return prove inadequate but the buying power of their CD investment will diminish and the market price of their preferred stock may drop.

Another problem with a high dividend rate is that the investor may be tempted to regard the dividends as mad money and spend them, even though the purpose of the investment was to accumulate capital. This can be avoided, of course, if the investment offers an automatic dividend reinvestment plan—as most mutual funds and some corporations do—but the temptation may nevertheless be strong.

Other investors prefer to forgo an immediate return in favor of an investment that promises to increase in value. Although the dividend rate that a corporation pays on its common stock is not directly related to its stability or its future growth, many of the strongest companies pay what appears to be a penurious dividend in order to use their earnings for further expansion, which could eventually increase the value of each share. Some investors prefer a low dividend rate and good prospects of appreciation because dividends are taxed as they are received, whereas the profit on an appreciated investment is taxed only when it is sold. And some investors (in undeveloped land, for example) are willing to receive temporary negative dividends—that is, they not only tie up their capital but also pay taxes and insurance each year while awaiting the increase in value that prompted them to make the investment.

Generally, investments that promise price appreciation should be more attractive to younger investors who have other sources of income and may be able to forgo a high yield. Older investors, especially if they are retired, are likely to prefer a high yield to supplement their retirement incomes.

The choice you make between a high-yielding investment and a low-yielding one is not easy, because neither of these terms can be described in specific numbers. Thus, there is no way of describing a rate of, say, 6 percent as low, average, or dangerously high. Aside from comparing it to other yields, one way to make such an assessment is to subtract from the 6 percent the current rate of inflation. Thus, if the inflation rate is currently 7 percent, a 6 percent yield is clearly negative, because your total investment, including your interest, will have less buying power at the end of the year than it had initially, especially after you have paid taxes on the interest or dividends. On the other hand, if the inflation rate is at 4 percent, your 6 percent yield is satisfactory, although an 8 percent rate would, of course, be preferable. Because the inflation rate is not predictable, you need to monitor your investments continuously.

AN INVESTMENT STRATEGY

Every person's combination of income, obligations, and net worth is unique, so no formula for investing is universally applicable. The following pattern, however, can be used selectively by most people; it assumes that as time passes, income and net worth are likely to increase and the obligations of child rearing and mortgage payments are likely to place less of a burden on income.

If you are determined to save and invest, the first step is to write yourself a check each month equal to a fixed percentage of your gross salary (10 percent is good if you can afford it), deduct it from your budget, and label it as savings or investment. If you can discipline yourself to do this, you will have a realistic notion of what you have left to spend. If you find that the deduction forces you to modify your standard of living, bear in mind that it also provides you with a degree of security for the future. (For advice on budgeting, see chapter 6.)

If you are starting out with consumer debt, particularly at high interest rates, you should first pay off those debts. Then start writing yourself a check each month with the same sense of obligation you had when paying off those bills.

This voluntary payroll deduction should be deposited in a highly liquid account—either a savings account or a money market fund—until you have accumulated an emergency fund adequate to meet such possibilities as loss of your job, unexpected financial losses, and chronic family illness. Many experts advise that this fund should equal at least three months of your take-home pay, but much depends on your personal situation: the security of your job, for example, the self-sufficiency of your elderly parents, the imminence of college tuition payments.

Once you have accumulated this amount in liquid form, you should deposit your subsequent checks in an IRA account (to the maximum of $2,000 a year) in which earnings accumulate tax-free until you withdraw them, or in a salary-reduction plan, such as a 401(k) plan, if one is available. If you are not eligible for a tax deduction for IRA deposits, you may want to consider other tax-advantaged retirement savings (see chapter 24). Salary reduction plans also offer significant tax advantages. Bear in mind that IRA accounts, although more vigorously promoted by banks, are also available from mutual funds and stock brokers. Your IRA account is nothing more than a basket. Its yield depends on what you put into it. If you are self-employed, you should consider a Keogh plan or a Simplified Employee Pension (SEP) plan. And, of course, there's nothing to stop you from considering tax-free bonds as part of your retirement savings.

Despite the enormous tax advantages of retirement accounts, they do not generally allow easy access to the funds before you reach age 59½. Thus, for interim goals—such as saving for a home or a child's education—you must make investments outside these accounts. The range of investments is, of course, virtually the same as for investments within a retirement account. However, you must pay attention to the tax consequences and the timing of these investments from the outset, since the earnings are not tax-sheltered and you are likely to need the money at specific times much sooner than retirement funds.

Although the stock market may tempt you at this point, it is important to recognize that small investments are expensive because brokerage commissions are relatively high, and that investing in a single company is less desirable than diversifying your investments among several.

Until the surplus beyond your emergency and retirement funds accumulates to $10,000 to $20,000, you might consider short-term (six months to one year) certificates of deposit, Treasury bills, or a stock or bond mutual fund that does not require a high initial investment.

At this stage, you will begin to appreciate the importance of timing your investments. Because interest rates are unpredictable, putting $5,000 into a five-year CD or a U.S. Treasury bill at 7 percent may be a very good move if interest rates fall, or a very bad move if they rise. A better plan, therefore, might be to keep your $5,000 in a money market account at a bank or in a money market mutual fund (either of which is immediately responsive to changes in interest rates) and to buy a one-year CD for $1,000 once every six months or so at the current rate. In this way, your money rotates and becomes available for reinvestment at whatever rate is prevalent at the time. (This is not to say that after you have accumulated more funds, you may not wish to put some of them in long-term investments, which also have their place in a diversified portfolio.)

By the time you have accumulated a significant fund for investment, you have undoubtedly realized that investments require continuous supervision. You have become aware that competition among banks and mutual funds works to your advantage in the form of higher interest rates and a wide variety of account options, and that fluctuations in general interest rates and the rate of inflation may cause you to shift from one type of investment to another within the course of a year or less. In short, you are on the way to becoming a moderately informed and sophisticated investor. Nevertheless, if you contemplate investing in the dozens of products available through financial institutions, you may feel the need for professional advice on investments that satisfy your particular needs for liquidity, safety, and total return.

IS SOUND ADVICE AVAILABLE?

Unfortunately, although many people—estate planners, financial counselors, accountants, insurance salesmen, stockbrokers, and others—label themselves as *investment experts*, the performance records of many of them over the long term calls that label into question. And this skeptical evaluation applies not only to the experts available to the small investor but also to the money managers who handle billion-dollar portfolios for pension funds and other large-scale investors. Although some of them legitimately boast of beating the market averages over the course of a year or two, few have produced consistently superior results over as long a period as you may want your investments to run.

The individual investor, whether he or she studies the market very carefully or operates purely by hunch, may not fare any better. You are likely to hear and sometimes read about the success stories of individuals who have gotten rich by playing the stock market. But people who have lost most of their investment on Wall Street are probably more numerous, though understandably less motivated to talk about it.

Professional Sources

Many states have laws prohibiting physicians from operating pharmacies on the side. Their purpose, of course, is to discourage the physician from prescribing unnecessary but profitable drugs for patients. Unfortunately, very few states prohibit anyone—insurance salespeople, mutual fund salespeople, or stockbrokers—from recommending stocks or other investment instruments to a client and then earning a commission or some other reward for selling them.

Thus, your local banker is likely to sing the praises of bank instruments—certificates of deposit, for example, or money market accounts—but to tell you little or nothing about stocks and bonds. Your insurance agent will almost certainly try to sell you the kind of policy that provides investment opportunities as well as life insurance, even though most experts are quite skeptical about such policies. Similarly, an account executive at a brokerage firm is likely to tout the products he or she sells—stocks, bonds, options, mutual funds with sales charges, and futures—and perhaps to recommend with special enthusiasm a stock that the firm has underwritten. But mutual funds that you can buy without any sales charge whatever may not be mentioned. Moreover, an account executive may "churn" your account—that is, buy and sell shares frequently—at considerable profit to him- or herself but little or none to you.

All of this would be of no consequence if you were able to find an adviser whose recommendations turned out to be consistently profitable. But, as we have noted, this is altogether unlikely—especially if you are a small investor. Profitable stock trading depends far less on intelligence, insight, or a mastery of economics than it does on current information—information about takeovers, unanticipated profits or losses, and other facts that are perishable and not widely publicized. (This, of course, is why insider trading, although illegal, has been extremely profitable to those who have engaged in it.) By the time potentially valuable information trickles down to the junior account executives assigned to small investors, the prices of the stock have already responded to it and you are likely to be too late to realize a quick profit from your investment.

It is true, of course, that some account executives (and some of their enriched customers) boast that stocks they have recommended have, in fact, gone up. They may be giving good recommendations, but there are other possible explanations as well. First, when the research department of a large brokerage firm issues a "buy" recommendation on a stock, so many of its customers flock to buy it that their demand raises the price of the stock—at least temporarily—and the recommendation becomes a self-fulfilling prophecy. Second, the market as a whole may be on an upswing and most, though by no means all, boats rise with the tide. Last, it may be a matter of chance: Since stocks either go up or go down over time, even a totally uninformed prediction is likely to be right some of the time.

If you simply can't afford the time to choose and monitor your investments, you may want to visit several brokerage houses and interview account executives in the hope of finding one who has valid credentials in finance and demonstrates some understanding of your investment aims. But you can expect to pay a fairly high commission rate for a broker's advice. If you do decide to use a broker or some other adviser, always keep an eye on your account and never allow any transactions that you don't understand completely.

You can get advice that may be just as good and much less costly by investing in a mutual fund, which is likely to be managed by people with access to the same information as your account executive and which offers you far more diversification than you can manage with your own limited funds.

DO-IT-YOURSELF INVESTING

If suddenly you were to get a windfall of $50,000 or more through an inheritance or through some stroke of luck, you might well be uncertain about how and where to invest it and want to seek help—although the quality of this help might turn out to be no better than what we have just described. But if you follow our general strategy, your accumulation will probably be gradual, and any mistakes you make in the early stages are not likely to be serious. You may lose a percentage point or two in yield, but you are unlikely to lose your principal.

If, as your investment increases, you make a commitment to

learn more about the process and the alternatives, your sophistication may, in fact, grow more rapidly than your accumulation, and you are likely to become familiar with the possibilities open to you and the various ways of protecting your principal against serious losses.

Learning about investing does take time and persistent effort, but it is worthwhile for those who seek financial security.

Some Hazardous Shortcuts

There are, however, shortcuts that can be very dangerous to the do-it-yourself investor. The first is the temptation to follow hot tips that may come to you from associates at work or other sources. You have no way of knowing whether these tips are reliable.

A second danger is reliance on books that promise to help you make a fortune in the stock market, in precious metals, or in real estate. There are, in fact, a number of sensible books that explain investments instead of promoting a particular system or formula, and careful study of a number of them can make your investing rational and relatively safe.

A third danger stems from the temptation to equate trends with potential investment success. If you walk into a new fast-food operation and see it crowded with customers, or if you spot a new fad (such as tanning salons or physical fitness equipment), or if you drive past some attractive land that strikes you as having potential for development, you may be tempted to make an immediate investment. Beware, usually in such cases, sophisticated investors who have more information than you have already brought the cost of such an investment to its fair market value, and you are unlikely to get in at the bottom and get out at the top.

Reducing Your Transaction Costs

Most stocks and bonds can be bought and sold only through a broker. But the increasing number of do-it-yourself investors has led to a proliferation of discount brokerage firms. These no-frills brokers charge commissions as much as 70 percent below those of full-service brokers, because they confine their activities to the execution of customers' orders and need not maintain expensive research departments to provide customers with advice. Their account executives, being salaried order-takers, have no incentive to churn your account or to urge you to trade actively in order to increase their commissions, but in most other respects they provide the same services as full-service brokers. The savings they offer in commissions are especially important for the small investor, because commissions can eat up a significant chunk of your capital, especially in small transactions.

INVESTMENT ALTERNATIVES

Although the chapters that follow are devoted to a detailed discussion of each of several investment alternatives, the brief summary that follows is intended to outline the salient features of each and thus to provide you with a general orientation to the investment market as a whole. The sequence in which the alternatives are discussed reflects the order in which the typical small investor might consider them—that is, it begins with low-risk investments requiring a small outlay and moves on to investments in which both risk and outlay increase. Remember that bank products, such as CDs and bank money market accounts (discussed in chapter 2), are other low-risk alternatives. Once you have chosen a type of investment that tentatively interests you, read the appropriate chapter carefully before making a firm decision.

Money Market Funds

When large corporations and banks need substantial amounts of cash for the short term, they borrow it at interest rates higher than those available to the average investor, who simply hasn't enough cash to lend these huge borrowers. Money market funds make such loans to the corporations by using the cash deposits of thousands of their shareholders and distributing the interest to them after deducting a small percentage for operating expenses. They also buy government instruments that normally aren't available to the individual investor. Thus, the small investor may enjoy a higher yield than could be found as a single investor. The loans made by these funds are for the short term, and interest rates change regularly to reflect the prevailing rate.

Your investment in a money market fund is converted into

shares with a fixed value of $1; interest is calculated and earned daily. Thus, you can redeem your shares at any time at the same $1 value, although inflation can affect the buying power of the shares you redeem. These funds are completely liquid, and many of them offer free check-writing privileges in minimum amounts ranging from $250 to $5,000. Some investors, in fact, deposit their salary checks into a money market fund, write checks against their account to pay large bills, and transfer into their bank checking accounts only enough money to pay small bills and provide themselves with cash.

The great advantages of money market funds are instant liquidity, preservation of principal, and a yield usually higher than investors can obtain at local banks. Money market accounts offered by banks usually have slightly lower yields. Even very affluent investors use money market funds as a temporary parking place for dividends and transaction proceeds pending reinvestment. A disadvantage is that the share price does not appreciate, as it can with other kinds of mutual funds.

Not all money market funds perform equally well, but their performance is rated weekly and published in the financial sections of major newspapers.

Mutual Funds

Although there are mutual funds that specialize in every imaginable investment alternative, the principle on which they operate is essentially the same as that of the money market funds (which are also mutual funds)—that is, they pool the money of thousands of small investors to buy a larger variety and quantity of investments than the individual investor can afford. Dividends and capital gains are distributed to the investors after charges for expenses and management are deducted.

Of the hundreds of mutual funds currently operating, some specialize in producing income, some in capital growth, some in a combination of each. Some describe themselves as conservative, others as high risk. Some specialize in common stocks, some in bonds, some in tax-free investments, some in specific market sectors (such as utilities, energy, gold, or entertainment), and some in a mixture of all these alternatives.

Unlike the money market share, which maintains its $1 value, the value of the mutual fund share may fluctuate daily, since it reflects the net asset value, which is based on the total value of all investments made by the fund. Investors stand to gain or lose on their investment when they sell their shares, depending on the price they paid when they bought, and the returns they received while holding the investment.

This risk can be diminished by a technique known as dollar-cost averaging—that is, investing a fixed sum of money periodically (for example, $100 monthly), no matter how the stock market is doing or how high or low interest rates are. Although you may not want to follow a stringent schedule, you are far better off investing—and withdrawing—over time than trying to hit the "best" time to invest a set amount. Investing a fixed *amount* periodically rather than buying a fixed *number* of shares each time you invest can reduce your average cost per share, over time. That's because when prices are high, your $100 will buy fewer shares; when they are low, your $100 will buy more shares. If you buy 10 shares when the price is $10 a share, for example, and five shares when the price goes up to $20, your average price per share will be $13.33. In contrast, if you buy 10 shares at $10 and another 10 shares when the price is $20, your average cost is $15. (Of course, if you were lucky enough to buy all of your shares at $10, you would be better off— but few people are that fortunate or prescient.)

Dollar-cost averaging with mutual funds offers investors a way to diversify over time as well as over types of investments. If you do engage in dollar-cost averaging, experts advise, you should invest more frequently than semiannually or you may miss some of the benefits because the time span is too great.

Dollar-cost averaging is also possible for the direct purchase of stocks, especially if you are in a dividend reinvestment program in which you purchase stocks directly from corporations without paying commissions, or if you have larger sums to invest in individual stocks.

The advantages of mutual funds are that they offer more diversification than most individuals can afford, the fee is usually far lower than brokerage commissions, and investments can be made in small increments. In addition, the investor is relieved of the effort involved in evaluating each potential investment and carrying out the transaction. The investor must still decide in which mutual fund to invest, but because of the relatively small amounts needed to get in (as low as $100 to $250) it is far easier to diversify among different types of funds—long- or short-term bond funds, income-producing stock funds, growth-oriented stock funds, or aggressive stock funds, among others. The greater your level of diversification, the greater your protection against swings in the economy.

A major disadvantage of stock and bond mutual funds is relatively low liquidity. You can withdraw funds at any time, but withdrawals sometimes require a written request with signatures guaranteed, and your redemption check may take as long as 10 days to arrive. More important, the selling price of your shares will be their net asset value on the day they are sold—something you cannot control. You can alleviate this liquidity problem to some extent by investing in a family of funds that includes a money market fund with check-writing privileges and permits telephone transfers between different funds in the family. This permits you to transfer funds from your mutual fund to your money market fund and write a check immediately. But not all members of a fund family perform equally well, and you may be sacrificing some return for the sake of convenience. You should also be aware of the tax consequences (and possible fees) every time you switch money from one fund to another.

The performance of stock and bond mutual funds is far more erratic than that of money market mutual funds. Some have made spectacular gains, attracted thousands of investors, and then proceeded to lose money. Others have shown slower but consistent growth. The performance of mutual funds is not easy to evaluate, but *Consumer Reports* periodically publishes a scrupulously detailed rating of major stock funds. When a highly successful mutual fund attracts large numbers of new investors, however, its performance may deteriorate because it reaches a saturation point with the investments that made it successful and is forced to invest in other, perhaps less productive, securities. Faced with this possibility, some funds reject new investments; others accept them and risk diminished performance. Although good past performance doesn't guarantee future gains, it usually at least indicates a good management team behind the fund.

Stocks

When you buy the common stock of a corporation, you become a part-owner (albeit your part is infinitesimally small). As such, you are entitled to share in the profit or the loss that the company generates, although you cannot lose more than your total investment. Your profit can take one or both of two forms: dividends, which may be paid regularly or sporadically (or omitted), and a change in the price of the shares themselves, on which you will realize a profit or a loss when you sell them. As a part-owner, you are entitled to attend the annual stockholders' meeting and to vote on certain issues, but these privileges usually are meaningless unless you own a substantial proportion of the shares—a virtual impossibility for the small investor.

Over the long run, common stocks have proved to be a better investment—in terms of both their yield and their value correction for inflation—than any widely available alternative, but this statistical finding covers *all* stocks over a long period. It offers no comfort to investors who bought only one or two poorly performing stocks or who were forced to sell during one of the many stock market lows that recur inevitably over time. Buying stocks entails risk—a lower risk (but often a lower return) if you buy long-established companies, a higher risk (and the prospect of a much higher return) if you buy unknowns.

The advantage of common stocks is the potential for good return. In addition, common stocks, unlike mutual fund shares, can be bought and sold at the price you specify. You can, for example, give your broker a buy order for XYZ Corporation at 24 even though it is currently selling at 27, and your order will be executed only if the price drops to 24, which presumably you regard as a good buy. Similarly, having bought shares at 24, you can tell your broker to sell when the price reaches 30 if you are satisfied with a profit of 25 percent.

The disadvantages, however, are several. To begin with, buying just one stock can involve a considerable amount of money because, if you buy an odd lot of fewer than 100 shares, you will usually have to pay more per share and your commission will be quite high, even if you use a discount broker. Some corporations offer automatic reinvestment of dividends, which saves you the commission, but the number of companies that offer this program is limited.

Perhaps more important, if you spend $2,500 for 100 shares of XYZ Corporation, you may not have enough money to diversify to other stocks. In this situation, not only have you put all your eggs in one basket but also you may find yourself in a difficult position if you should need cash when XYZ is selling at 22½. This is why you should not consider the stock market until you have enough money to own a diversity of stocks and enough assets in more liquid form to solve any foreseeable cash flow problems and can thus afford to buy stocks for the long term.

In addition to issuing common stock, some companies issue preferred stock. The advantages of preferred stock are that the amount of the dividend is specified in advance, and if profits fall, the preferred stockholders must receive their dividends before the common stockholders do. Since the dividend is fixed, the price of the preferred stock of a well-established company is more likely to be influenced by a change in interest rates than by the fortunes of the company.

Bonds

A bond is essentially a loan that the borrower will repay you, the lender, on a specified date, usually paying you periodic interest at a specified rate in the interim. The borrower may be a corporation, the U.S. government, or a local government, and the term of the bond may vary from a few months to as long as 30 years.

Many investors prefer bonds because they are safer: If the issuer runs into difficulties, the bondholders must be paid before the stockholders are paid. In addition, bond interest payments, unlike stock dividends, are specified in advance and can be counted on. When the bond matures, the buyer gets back every cent of his or her original principal even though the price of the bond may fluctuate until it reaches maturity. However, if a corporation files for bankruptcy, it may default on some or all of its debt—even if it continues to do business. In this instance, bondholders will get their money before stockholders do, but they may still never receive all, or even most, of their money.

There are two disadvantages of which some bond buyers seem unaware. First, some bonds are *callable*—the issuer has the right to call in and redeem the bond when its interest rate is higher than the issuer needs to pay to borrow the money elsewhere. Thus, if you bought a bond with an 11 percent interest rate several years ago, but the current interest rate is 7 percent, you can continue to enjoy your investment only if the bond you bought was not callable—a matter of reading the fine print or asking your broker when you purchase the bond.

Whether or not a bond is callable, its market price will be strongly influenced by the prevailing rate of interest. If interest rates rise, the resale value of your bond will drop accordingly, and when interest rates fall, its value will rise. The right time to buy bonds, then, is during a period of high interest rates. Unfortunately, interest rates, like stock prices, are unpredictable.

Yet another disadvantage of bonds is that they are subject to erosion by inflation. If, for example, you buy a $10,000 30-year bond (which is likely to pay a higher rate than a 10-year bond), you may find that its earnings do not keep up with interest rates and inflation. Of course, you can always sell the bond before it matures, but if interest rates have risen since you bought it, you can be certain you will not recoup your original purchase price.

As with stocks, bonds come in a variety of forms. Some, known as convertible debentures, can be converted into common stock at a specified price and time. The interest on certain bonds issued by governmental units is free from federal income tax and, in some cases, from state tax as well. Tax-free bonds may strike you as appealing, but their yield is usually significantly lower than that of taxable corporate bonds. It is easy enough to apply your tax bracket to the yield on a taxable bond and a tax-exempt one and calculate whether the tax exemption offers you an advantage.

Real Estate

For most people, the home they live in is the single largest investment they will ever make. Although many personal considerations go into the purchase of a home, it's important to keep in mind the appreciation potential when selecting a property.

People who can afford a second home, whether they are seeking appreciation or extra income from rental, often find it a lucrative—if time-consuming—venture. Those who become landlords must pay special attention to complicated tax rules (see chapter 22). Real estate is an illiquid investment, however, since you can never be sure that you'll be able to sell at a reasonable price when you want to.

Many types of pooled real estate investments are available, from limited partnerships to mutual funds. With these, you do not own land or a house directly but join with other investors to purchase a shopping center or a group of mortgages. Some of these investments offer high returns but can be very risky. Others are only moderately risky. Be sure you thoroughly understand the nature and risk level of any such venture before investing.

High-Risk Investments

The risk involved in the investments described above ranges from low to moderate, although the level of risk in the purchase of stocks and bonds can be fairly high for the investor who makes choices that seem to promise a very high rate of return—junk bonds, for example, or low-priced shares in a fledgling company. There are a number of investments, however—precious metals, commodity options and futures, some real estate investments, oil exploration ventures, artworks, and collectibles—that carry very high risk and should be avoided by small investors unless, like Las Vegas tourists, they deliberately set aside a sum of money that they are fully prepared to lose.

A Business of Your Own

One rather common investment that usually involves far more risk than the investor anticipates is the start-up of a business of one's own. Vast numbers of people—either because they don't like working for a boss or because they are confident that they can derive income from a particular skill or enthusiasm—risk most of their assets (and those of trusting relatives) to start a business without recognizing the full costs of financing it or the management skills needed to operate it profitably. Although success stories about small entrepreneurs abound, the overwhelming majority of small businesses fail before they can celebrate their first birthday.

TIMING AND DIVERSIFICATION

As you may have inferred from the preceding pages, the two keys to successful investing are the timing of each investment and diversification of your total holdings. In some respects, they are related to each other.

Because both interest rates and stock prices fluctuate continually—the latter often with dramatic suddenness—it would seem very sensible to take advantage of these fluctuations. Thus, it would be advantageous to buy stocks when the market is low and to buy bonds when interest rates are high, since the value of the bond would rise as interest rates fell and the price of the stock would rise as the market improved. Unfortunately, this kind of market timing requires a prescience not available to human beings, and large numbers of investors have lost money because they made confident but faulty assumptions about the future of interest rates or stock prices.

The far safer strategy is not to invest a large sum of money at one time on the basis of your forecasts but to invest small amounts regularly without regard to interest rates or market prices in the hope that over time your investments will average out the fluctuations. This can be done most effectively through dollar-cost averaging (see p. 330), a strategy that you can apply to almost any investment (except large-ticket items such as real estate).

Diversification of your portfolio is equally important, and it should be applied at three levels. To begin with, you should diversify among types of investments—cash (money market funds, savings accounts, or CDs, for example), bonds, stocks (whether through direct investments or mutual funds), real estate, and other types of investments that may appeal to you. This diversification can offer you some hedge against sharp changes in interest rates, the inflation rate, or the stock market.

At a second level, you should diversify within each of your types of investments. A given sum of money is likely to produce better results divided among three mutual funds than invested in one. Buying a dozen common stocks is a far better investment than buying one or two. Buying stocks in various soundly managed companies is far more sensible than putting all your money into an electric utility simply because it pays higher dividends.

Buying one stock can be a gratifying experience if it takes off shortly after you bought it. But this happens rarely, and diversification is a far more certain route to safety and to steady, if sometimes unspectacular, growth.

At the third level, you should diversify among whatever levels of risk you can tolerate, keeping some funds very safe, others at moderate risk for the sake of higher yield, and, if you can afford it emotionally as well as financially, some at very high risk.

18

Stocks

John R. Dorfman

STOCKS: A PIECE OF THE ACTION—AND THE RISK

When you buy common stock, you're buying part-ownership in a business enterprise. The enterprise may be old or new, small or large, an obscure chain of restaurants or a well-known colossus such as General Motors. As a stockholder, you are entitled to vote for members of the board of directors, who make basic policy decisions and who elect the officers of the company. You are also entitled to a share in the profits of the enterprise.

For large stockholders, the voice in corporate governance is very real indeed. In 1986, for example, Loew's Corporation had acquired approximately 23 percent of the stock of CBS, the communications company. Dissatisfied with the way CBS was being managed, Laurence Tisch, the chairman of Loew's, sparked a boardroom upheaval, ousted CBS's president, and had himself installed as president.

For most of us, however, the vote that comes with being a shareholder verges on being a mere formality. And for most of us, that's fine: Small purchasers of stock are usually more interested in buying a stock that may increase in value than in being boardroom kingmakers. That is because, historically, investment in the stock market has provided a better return—on average—than many other investments. Over the 25-year period ending in 1990, stocks provided a 9.5 percent compound annual return to investors, according to the Chicago-based research firm Ibbotsen Associates. That compares very favorably to the average annual returns of about 6 to 7 percent that certificates of deposit, bonds, and Treasury bills yielded over the same time span. When the 6 percent average annual rate of inflation is taken into account, an investment in the stock market may actually be the best way for your money to grow over the long term—again, on average.

Even though most people are interested in the investment aspect of stocks rather than in running the company, it is still worthwhile to bear in mind that stock holdings are more than just paper certificates: They represent ownership of real financial assets.

Let's say, for example, that in mid-1988 you decided to buy 100 shares in the Coca-Cola Company. For $3,900 you would have gained ownership of about one-third of 1 percent of the company. Your part-ownership would entitle you to about $280 of Coca-Cola's $1 billion in annual profits. The fraction of the company you owned would also have a net worth (assets such as factories, trucks, cash, and receivables, minus the company's liabilities) of about $930. Over the course of a year, your small section of the company would sell some $2,410 worth of soft drinks, motion pictures, Coca-Cola–brand clothing, and other items. And you would be entitled to annual dividends of about $120.

Should you then invest in the stock market? That's not a simple question, because your 100 shares of Coca-Cola—or of any company—also entitle you to ownership of a certain share of the risk associated with the company and its businesses. The decision whether or not to invest in the stock market should be based in part on your tolerance for that risk, as well as on your age and your financial condition.

Individuals who want a riskless portfolio should forget about stocks. Any investment in common stocks entails risk that you will lose part or all of your money. Companies do, from time to time, go bankrupt, and in bankruptcy situations it's not unusual for all of the company's assets to go toward paying off debts, leaving nothing for the stockholders. You can lessen the chance of a big loss by selecting stocks of solid companies, but you can incur a loss even by investing in the bluest of blue-chip stocks if you buy when the share price is high and must sell when it is low.

You can lessen your risk of both bankruptcy losses and price declines by diversifying—choosing a portfolio of a dozen or more stocks in various industries—but that doesn't make the risk disappear completely. Indeed, the movement of the stock market as a whole probably accounts for at least half the price movement of any individual stock.

Your age enters into the decision of whether or not to invest in stocks, because you may wish to hold less risky investments as you approach or pass retirement age. Often, retired people choose to hold their assets in the form of bank certificates of deposit, which are not subject to market price fluctuation. Or they may choose investments, such as government bonds, in which there is some market price fluctuation but the asset can be redeemed at a specified time for a preset price.

Even if you are young and like the idea of taking some risk in the hope of a greater investment return, you shouldn't necessarily rush out and buy stocks. Good financial management calls for you to fulfill certain preconditions. Don't invest in stocks until your debts are under control. (One guideline is that monthly payments of principal and interest on all your debts, not counting a home mortgage, should not exceed 15 percent of your gross income.) Don't invest in stocks until you have adequate insurance (see part IV, Insurance). And don't invest in stocks until you have a cushion of savings to see you through hard times. We recommend a savings fund equal to at least three months' take-home pay (see chapter 6, Budgeting).

Diversifying your holdings is a sound principle to follow, too. For many individuals, the best way to invest in the stock market is through a mutual fund, an investment company that pools the money of many small investors and buys stocks (or other investments) with it. Instead of owning stocks directly, the individual investor owns shares in the fund. The main advantage is instant diversification: The investor owns a little piece of many companies, and therefore is likely to achieve results not too drastically different from those of the broad stock market averages. The investor hopes, of course, that the mutual fund's manager will outperform the averages. He or she can study the past history of the mutual fund to see how well the fund's portfolio manager has done over the years. (For more information on mutual funds, see chapter 20.)

Finally, don't enter the stock market unless you are in a position to ride out big short-term waves that can push prices down suddenly. Today's market is dominated by large institutions—banks, insurance companies, pension funds, and mutual funds—that trade huge amounts of stock at a time. These institutions sometimes become bullish or bearish simultaneously on a given stock (or on stocks in general). An individual investor running counter to the wave may be swamped. Therefore, individual investors shouldn't enter the market unless they can be flexible about when they buy and sell. (The savings cushion helps provide that flexibility.)

If you are ready to invest in stocks, you'll need to make a decision about how much of your net worth you want to keep in that form. Many of the considerations just discussed will enter in. A 26-year-old single person might choose to have most of his or her net worth in stocks. A 59-year-old married person might deem it prudent to have only 15 percent in the stock market. There are no fixed guidelines as to how much of your wealth to keep in stocks; it depends on your risk tolerance and your liking for stocks as opposed to other investment vehicles.

Finally, it cannot be stressed too often that there are no sure-fire formulas or shortcuts that lead to wealth in the stock market. At least, there are no legal ones. Ignore anyone who tries to sell you a newsletter, tip sheet, or book purporting to teach you the secrets of quick or enormous wealth through dabbling in the market.

In this chapter we'll tell you how investors determine the value of various stocks, and how experts believe you may be able at times to spot bargains. As a first step, though, let's look at the information contained in the stock pages of daily newspapers. Major newspapers throughout

STOCK MARKET BASICS

Stock Tables

Table 18-1 is excerpted from the New York Stock Exchange listings published in *The New York Times* of May 22, 1991, describing the trading activity of the previous day. Major newspapers throughout

TABLE 18-1   Excerpt from Stock Page, *The New York Times*,
May 22, 1991

52-Week High	52-Week Low	Stock	Div.	Yld. %	PE Ratio	Sales 100s	High	Low	Last	Chg.
70¼	19¾	AMR	—	—	—	3665	60½	59¾	60⅛	+¼
40	17½	Bnk Am	1.20	3.2	9	4235	38¾	37¾	38	—
17⅜	9⅛	Chryslr	0.60	4.8	—	3965	12⅝	12⅜	12½	−⅛
30½	25⅝	DetEd	1.88	6.5	9	788	28⅞	28⅝	28⅞	+⅛

the country use similar formats to report on stock trading. Smaller papers sometimes use more condensed formats. The four stocks shown are abbreviated as AMR (the holding company for American Airlines); BnkAm (BankAmerica, the parent of the West Coast's largest bank); Chryslr (Chrysler, the automaker); and DetEd (Detroit Edison, a large utility).

The first two columns show the highest and lowest prices for which each stock has been traded during the past year (52 weeks). The price, as is customary on Wall Street, is expressed in units as small as one-eighth of a dollar—that is, 12½ cents. For example, the low price shown for Chrysler is 9⅛, which is $9.125. The "high" and "low" figures define the bounds of the stock's trading range over the past year. If a stock is near the high end of its trading range, it often means that favorable recent developments have made investors hopeful about the prospects for the company.

On the day of our example, BankAmerica was trading fairly close to the top of its trading range. At the time, the bank was considered to be one of the strongest regional banks, many of which have been plagued by financial woes. Chrysler, on the other hand, was trading in the lower half of its range as many investors were dubious that the auto industry would recover soon from its slump.

To experienced investors, the current price of a stock compared to its previous price pattern is an intriguing bit of information— but only one piece in a complex mosaic. A price that has risen is a sign of favorable developments, but the astute investor will always ask whether most of the gains are now past or the stock has been bid up too far. A price that has fallen can indicate a company to be wary of—or one whose shares are now bargain priced and perhaps present a good opportunity to purchase. Furthermore, much of the movement in a stock's price is due not to factors affecting a particular corporation, but to broader movements in the entire stock market or in a particular industry. When the entire stock market is euphoric, many stocks touch new highs. When investor sentiment is particularly languid, many stocks fall to new lows. Astute investors, therefore, watch particularly for stocks whose movement goes beyond, or runs counter to, the general trend.

The first column to the right of the stock's name tells what dividend (if any) the stock is paying. Like the interest on a savings account, the dividend affords current income to the stockholder. But unlike the interest on a savings account, the dividend a company pays its stockholders is not guaranteed. The company's board of directors can change its mind anytime it wishes and adjust the dividend rate for the next quarter (three-month period). Though dividends are normally paid quarterly, the figure shown is the anticipated sum of the dividends for an entire year.

The dividend is paid at a specified date (for example, November 15) to people who owned shares as of a previous specified date (for example, October 31). During the time between the two dates, the stock is sold *ex-dividend,* which means "without dividend." If you buy the stock during that time, the dividend for the quarter goes to the seller, not to you. During the ex-dividend period, the price of the stock normally falls by roughly the amount of the dividend. Newspaper stock tables footnote any stock that is ex-dividend, often with an X.

In our sample table, three of the four stocks were paying a dividend. Most stocks—or at least most stocks of large companies, such as those listed on the New York Stock Exchange—do pay them. We'll have more to say about dividends in the section beginning on page 350.

To the right of the dividend column is the yield column. This expresses the dividend as a percentage of the price of the stock. It thus allows you at a glance to compare the current dividend income you receive from a stock with the flow of income you could receive from an alternative investment, such as a bond, money market bank account, or savings account. In most cases, the yield from a stock will be less than the yield from fixed-return investments that provide income only. That's because investors in stock have hopes of a return beyond the current income; they hope to achieve a capital gain by selling the stock for a higher price than they paid for it. The less likelihood of a capital gain, the higher the yield that investors will demand. When a company—or a whole industry—is not expected to show much growth, the yields on its stock probably have to be competitive with bond yields in order to attract investors. During the 1980s, utility stocks generally fit into this category. That's why, in the accompanying table, Detroit Edison shares were yielding a return of nearly 13 percent.

The next figure in table 18-1 is the p/e ratio; p/e stands for "price/earnings." It equals the price of the stock divided by the company's earnings (profits) per share over the most recent 12-month period for which figures are available. If a company has profits of $3 per share, and each share sells for $30, then the p/e ratio is 10.

The p/e ratio can be calculated only when a company is making a profit; if there's no profit, there's no number to plug into the denominator of the ratio. That's why, in our sample table, three companies have p/e ratios (4 for Chrysler, 10 for Detroit Edison, and 12 for AMR), but one does not. At the time, BankAmerica had been experiencing losses, so no ratio could be calculated for it.

The p/e ratio is a figure widely used on Wall Street, and it has several analytical uses. By way of introduction, though, think of it as a popularity index, or a measure of confidence. When the p/e ratio (often simply called the p/e) is high, it means that investors believe the company can sustain its current profits and probably increase them, perhaps rapidly. A low p/e ratio indicates a lack of confidence that earnings can be sustained or increased. This does not mean that a high p/e indicates a well-run company and a low p/e a poorly run company. In addition to investors' opinions of management, many other factors may be considered. A company, for example, may have experienced some special event recently that caused earnings to be abnormally high or low. Sale of a division, for example, might make earnings rise; a strike might make them fall temporarily but sharply. Also, the p/e reflects investors' opinions about the outlook for an entire industry, not just a particular company.

It's revealing, therefore, to compare the p/e's of companies within a given industry. If Universal Widget carries a p/e of 12, while Amalgamated Widget carries a p/e of 8, it suggests that most investors think Universal is stronger financially, better managed, or otherwise has a comparative advantage over Amalgamated.

It's also instructive to compare a company's p/e against the p/e of the average stock. But what's "average"? The answer changes from time to time. When investors are quite pessimistic about the outlook for stocks and for the economy, as they were in 1979 and early 1980, the typical stock will have a p/e of about 6 to 9. A more customary "normal" range, historically speaking, would be about 10 to 14 for the typical stock. In times of market euphoria, such as early and mid-1987, p/e's may go even higher; the typical stock might carry a p/e ratio of 15 or more, and stocks that are investor's darlings can shoot up to 30, 40, or even 60 times earnings. In early 1988, after the crash of October 1987 interrupted the bull market, p/e ratios fell back to roughly the normal range. The p/e ratio, then, measures investor enthusiasm not only for a particular stock, but also for the prospects of the stock market and the outlook for the national economy.

To the right of the p/e ratio in the stock tables is the column for sales, measured in hundreds of shares. In table 18-1, the figure of 3,665 for AMR means that 366,500 shares of AMR changed hands on the preceding day. While the figure for a particular day may not be revealing in and of itself, changes over a period can be. An increase in volume can indicate a takeover attempt in the works, or buying or selling by large institutions; or it could simply mean that a stock has been in the news and grown popular (or unpopular).

After the trading-volume column appear three columns that describe the price pattern of the stock on the preceding day. The "high" and "low" columns show the highest and lowest prices reached during the day's trading. The "last" column shows the closing price—that is, the price at the end of the day's trading.

The column labeled "change" is the last column in the table but the first column most investors read. It shows how much the price of a stock rose or fell compared to the final price on the previous day. On the day our sample table was compiled, holders of AMR shares were 25 cents a share richer than they were the day before. But Chrysler stockholders went home 12.5 cents poorer.

Where Stocks Are Traded

If you own some shares of Exxon, and you decide you want to sell them, nothing prevents you from standing on the street corner and buttonholing passersby until you find a buyer. Likewise, if you're looking to buy stock in, say, General Motors, you could ask all your friends and relatives if they happen to have any GM stock they wish to sell.

But common sense suggested long ago that such arrangements were unwieldy. In the late eighteenth century, a group of traders used to meet in New York under a buttonwood tree. In 1792 they founded the New York Stock Exchange as a place where buyers and sellers of stock could come together conveniently. Today, most trading in stocks of the nation's largest corporations occurs on the New York Stock Exchange (also called NYSE, or the Big Board). The common stock of more than some 1,800 companies is traded on the NYSE, and trading volume typically is well over 100 million shares per day.

Traders meet face-to-face on the floor of the exchange and conduct an abbreviated and formalized auction process. For each stock, the exchange designates a specialist—an exchange member who keeps tabs on trading activity in the stock and that also acts as a buyer or seller when no other buyer or seller steps forward.

The American Stock Exchange, a competitor to the NYSE (also located in New York City), operates in a similar fashion. As a general rule, the largest corporations have their stock traded on the NYSE, while the American Exchange (sometimes called AMEX) is home to medium-sized corporations. Some 900 stocks are traded on the American Exchange. A few hundred stocks are traded on other, regional stock exchanges, such as the Midwest Stock Exchange (in Chicago) and the Pacific Stock Exchange (in Los Angeles). All told, about 3,000 stocks are traded on the various exchanges.

A larger number of stocks—perhaps 20,000—are traded in the *over-the-counter market*. Such stocks are called over-the-counter stocks—OTC for short. For the most part, but with some notable exceptions, OTC stocks are issued by smaller companies than those of the NYSE and the AMEX.

While the stock exchanges feature face-to-face contact between traders, the over-the-counter market is geographically diffuse. The traders, often hundreds or thousands of miles apart, communicate with one another through automated quotation systems or computer networks. Trades can often be executed instantly, but with some rarely traded stocks, a transaction may take hours or, in unusual instances, days to arrange.

Because there are so many OTC stocks, because they are not traded in one central location, and because most OTC stocks are issued by relatively small companies, it is sometimes more difficult for investors to get detailed information about OTC stocks than about stocks that are traded on the major exchanges.

Stockbrokers

No law requires investors to buy or sell stocks through a broker, but in practice it's cumbersome and impractical to do otherwise.

A stockbroker (also known as a registered representative or an account executive) is a person licensed to buy and sell stocks for other people, and to hold people's stocks and other assets in a brokerage account. Some of the attributes investors look for in a broker are excellence in investment advice, availability, prompt and clear responses to questions, a desire to sell clients the financial products that best suit their particular needs (rather than whatever will generate the highest commission), and restraint in trading so that excessive commission costs can be avoided. Judging by the brisk pace of arbitration and litigation between customers and brokers, this ideal is not always attained.

By custom, once an account is established, most brokers will execute orders you place by telephone. For that reason, you should check your account statement promptly when it arrives each month to be sure there's no mistaken or unauthorized trading. For similar reasons, you should formally close an account if you don't intend to use a particular broker in the future.

With investment information widely available, many investors see little need to pay the relatively high commissions charged by so-called full-service brokers—those who give investment advice as well as execute trades. Instead, an increasing number of investors prefer discount brokers, who generally offer lower commission rates and don't give investment advice.

Brokerage houses pay hundreds of thousands of dollars for seats on the major stock exchanges. A seat gives the holder the right to be present on the exchange floor to make stock purchases and sales. The price of a seat varies, depending on the state of the securities business. In 1929, a New York Stock Exchange seat sold for $500,000, a record that endured for 57 years. In 1942, a seat sold for a mere $17,000, the record low in this century. During the bull market of 1987, a seat fetched $1.15 million, the current record high. In early 1991, the price was about $410,000. Brokers also have computer hookups that tie them into the National Association of Securities Dealers Automated Quotation (NASDAQ) system for trading over-the-counter stocks.

A key question is how much discretion you should give your broker. In our view, it's unwise for investors to give their brokers complete discretion to buy and sell securities at will. When a broker has an investment idea for you, it's better to talk it over and determine how it fits your investment philosophy, risk tolerance, and overall investment plan. Many of the lawsuits and other problems that arise between investors and brokers occur when the broker is free to trade on the client's behalf, and indulges either in excessive trading (called "churning") aimed at increasing commissions, or in trading that is riskier than the client meant to authorize.

Another question is how much you should pay your broker. Brokers' commission schedules are complicated, and sometimes confidential. In general, the commission you'll pay is determined by the number of transactions your broker executes, the number of shares involved, and the price of each share.

Beyond their complex commission formulas, many brokerage houses also have a minimum commission for each trade. (You pay either the formula commission or the minimum commission, whichever is higher.) Generally in 1991, the minimum was as small as $25 at some brokerage houses, as large as $50 at others. If you're buying or selling only a few shares at a time, the minimum may loom large as a percentage of the transaction. On medium-sized transactions involving $2,000 to $5,000, you're likely to pay roughly 2 percent. On larger transactions, you may get away with 1 percent or less. Big institutions, such as banks and pension funds, routinely pay 0.5 percent or less to trade, because they deal in block trades of 10,000 shares and more. On a small transaction—such as buying $1,000 of stock in January and selling it in July—the commission can easily take 5 to 10 percent of the investor's capital.

From those facts flow two conclusions. First, most individual investors should not leap into and out of the market. Trading a great deal only runs up heavy commission costs. Thus, most individuals should buy and hold for the long term. (That should not be too disappointing, since some studies show that buy-and-hold strategies do at least as well as frequent-trading strategies.) Second, individuals should seriously consider using a discount broker. The commission at a discounter can be half or less than that of a full-service broker's commissions.

Stock Market Indexes

If you want to know "how the market is doing," there's no single index that will tell you, because "the market" means different things to different people. If someone says, "The market was up 10 points today," chances are he or she means the Dow Jones Industrial Average was up 10 points. But that is only one of many indexes, and a narrow one at that. It reflects the price of 30 industrial companies, commonly known as "blue chips" because they are very large and well established in their industries.

To calculate the Dow Jones Industrial Average, Dow Jones & Company adds together the prices of the 30 component stocks and divides by a constant. Originally, the constant was 30, but it has been changed many times over a period of decades to adjust for corporate mergers, additions to or deletions from the list, stock splits, and other technical factors.

The Dow Jones Industrial Average cannot, by itself, statistically represent the entire stock market. It underweights the service sector of the economy and does not include transportation companies or utilities. Most important, it does not include the stocks of smaller companies. Dow Jones & Company does promulgate three other indexes: one for transportation stocks, one for utility stocks, and one—a 65-stock average—that is a blend of its three more specialized indexes. But by force of custom, it is the Dow Jones Industrial Average that remains the most quoted index in newspapers and on TV and radio.

Stock market professionals who wish to compare their investment performance (or the performance of someone they've hired) against "the market" usually choose a broader index, often the Standard & Poor's 500. As its name implies, this index includes 500 stocks. Like the Dow industrial stocks, these stocks are issued by large, well-established companies.

Each of the three major arenas of stock trading—the New York Stock Exchange, the American Stock Exchange, and the over-the-counter market—also has its own index. (The over-the-counter index is called the NASDAQ composite index.) These three indexes are of analytical interest because of the connection between a company's size and where its stock trades.

There are also some broad-scale stock market indexes that include a selection of stocks from all of the major exchanges, plus the over-the-counter market. Probably the best known of these is the Wilshire 5000 index, which traces the price movement of 5,000 stocks.

Most of the time, and roughly speaking, the various indexes move in concert. That's one reason why people are often content to let the Dow Jones industrials serve as a surrogate for a broader measure. But there are differences. For example, during a 12-month period ending in the spring of 1991, the broad market, as measured by the Wilshire 5000 index, was up 9 percent, but the American Stock Exchange index was down 1 percent. Meanwhile, the Dow Jones Industrial Average had risen 8 percent. It's not too unusual to have a stretch of several months during which one index shows losses while another shows gains. The NASDAQ and Wilshire indexes do well when investors are excited about the growth potential in small companies; the Dow Jones and the S&P 500 often do better when investors are concerned about possible adverse economic developments and want the security of larger, well-established companies.

Dividends

Most companies listed on the major stock exchanges, and a significant number of smaller, younger companies as well, pay dividends on their common stock. The company's board of directors sets the rate to be paid on dividends each quarter. The approved dividend per share is then paid to shareholders of record on the company's books as of a specified date.

For you as a shareholder, dividends serve a number of functions. First and foremost, they allow you to receive in cash a portion of the company's profits as those profits are earned. To be sure, if your company does well, you may eventually be able to sell your shares for a nice profit. But for any of a large number of reasons, you may not want to sell your shares. And just possibly, by the time you do want to sell, the company will have fallen on hard times. Dividends are a reward that's here and now—a check in the hand rather than a promise of a future capital gain.

The second benefit of dividends is that they lend some stability to the price of a stock. The value of stocks that don't pay dividends often swings more widely, depending on the company's current prospects, than the value of stocks that do. That's because a stock that pays a dividend can be valued based on its yield, and that yield can be compared to fixed-income investments such as bonds or bank certificates. Suppose that a bank certificate of deposit yields 7 percent, or $70 a year on a $1,000 certificate. In that case, stock that pays $70 a year in dividends arguably is worth about $1,000 too. The stock's price, of course, will fluctuate. But the dividend provides an anchor that will keep the price from dropping much below $1,000—unless the overall level of interest rates rise or investors are convinced that the company will soon need to cut its dividend.

A third positive aspect of dividends, which a fixed-return vehicle such as a bond or a certificate of deposit does not offer, is that the dividends may grow over time. As a matter of policy, companies usually make an effort to keep corporate dividends stable or growing. To be sure, a company that steadily loses money will eventually have no choice but to cut or even eliminate its dividend. However, companies that lose money for a few quarters often try to maintain shareholder loyalty (and the corporate reputation) by maintaining the payout. Companies that are making a profit will usually attempt to keep the dividend at or above the amount paid the previous year, or the previous quarter. When a company's profits are growing, dividends usually grow too.

In talking about dividends, financial analysts commonly refer to two numbers, the *dividend yield* and the *payout ratio*. The dividend yield, which is listed in daily newspaper stock pages, is the percentage obtained by dividing the amount of the dividend (per share per year) by the price of the stock. You can compare the yield on a stock to the yield obtainable from fixed-return investments such as bonds or certificates of deposit. In recent decades, dividend yields have commonly been lower than the yields on fixed-return investments, because investors are willing to accept smaller current return in the hope of generous capital gains in the future. The smaller the dividend yield, compared to yields on other investments, the greater the risk that the investor is assuming in hope of capital gains.

The payout ratio, which you can compute by dividing the dividend per share by the earnings per share, is an indication of how easily (or with how much difficulty) a company is paying its current dividend. A payout ratio of 75 percent signifies that a company is spending three-quarters of its profits to distribute the current dividend to stockholders. That would be an unusually high ratio. Typical, in the 1980s, was a ratio of around 50 percent. If a company is struggling to cover its dividend, that is often a sign that the company will soon have to cut its dividend, or else weaken itself financially by depleting its assets.

In recent years, a number of Wall Street followers have regarded dividends as stodgy and old-fashioned. Some have even argued that paying high dividends (or, in the extreme form of the argument, paying any dividends at all) is a waste of corporate resources. To a large extent, the basis for this attitude lay in the tax code. Dividends were taxed as ordinary income, which could mean an effective tax rate as high as 50 percent before the Tax Reform Act of 1986 went into effect. By contrast, capital gains (profits from selling a stock that had risen in price) were taxed at lower rates, with an effective maximum of 20 percent. Under those circumstances, it was argued, companies were silly to pass profits on to shareholders in the form of dividends. Doing so was merely exposing the shareholders to heavy taxation. Better, the argument ran, to reinvest the money in the company, building up the possibility of future profits and thus helping to raise the stock price.

The 1986 tax-reform legislation significantly altered the rules of the investment game. The marginal tax rate (the rate paid on the last dollar of income) is now 28 percent for many investors. There are, in essence, three tax brackets—15 percent, 28 percent, and 31 percent. (For details on the tax law and how it affects investors, see chapter 10.) You now pay the same rate on ordinary income (including dividends) as on capital gains up to a maximum of 28 percent on the latter. Therefore, a corporation's decision about how much of its profits to distribute to shareholders in the form of dividends has become less driven by tax factors than it used to be. Analysts predicted that the change in the tax law would lead investors to demand higher dividends from their companies. And indeed, as of this writing, there were signs that some companies were responding by paying out a higher share of their profits in the form of dividends.

Another technique used in lieu of paying dividends was the stock buyback, first popularized by John Singleton, the chairman of Teledyne, and later used by a large number of corporations. In a buyback, a company purchases some of its own shares on the open market. In shrinking the pool of publicly held shares, the company provokes an increase in the price of the stock. The supply of stock goes down, while the demand for the stock presumably remains constant; hence the price rises. Assuming that profits stay constant, each share of stock now is backed by a larger sum in profits. Therefore, if investors are willing to pay the same p/e ratio as before, the value of each share is greater.

Some people—especially academic students of the market—say that investors theoretically *shouldn't* pay the same p/e ratio as before, so buybacks shouldn't lead to higher stock prices. They argue that the corporation could have done something else—perhaps something better—with its money instead of buying back shares. But in practice, share buybacks have often worked to produce a higher stock price. Therefore, they've been popular in recent years.

Some corporations will always pay a higher percentage of profits in the form of dividends than others. There are several considerations that affect the dividend payout ratio. Here are some of the major ones:

· Companies that are young, small, and growing rapidly often need to plow back all available profits into the growth and development of the enterprise. Therefore, they often pay skimpy dividends or none at all.
· Companies that are old and well established, but no longer growing rapidly, do not need to plow back such a high percentage of profits to finance growth. Furthermore, investors, knowing that the company's growth prospects are undramatic, will demand other compensations as an inducement to

commit their investment capital. Thus, a mature company can afford to pay higher dividends—and often needs to, in order to keep investors interested in buying its stock.

· Companies vary in their philosophies concerning how much should be paid out in dividends and how much should be reinvested in the business. To some extent, the payout ratio reflects the business philosophy of a company's board of directors.

· The nature of stock market activity exerts certain pressures on the dividend yield (and indirectly on the payout ratio). If a company is regarded as a hot prospect in a growing field, investors will bid up the price of its stock. Assuming the dividend remains constant, the dividend yield will decrease. However, if prospects seem poor, the stock price shrinks, making the dividend yield rise. During the first half of the 1980s, for example, investors generally were negative about the outlook for utility companies. With depressed stock prices and substantial dividends, many utility shares offered a yield comparable to that obtainable on bonds.

In general, whenever a stock or group of stocks is out of favor (because growth prospects are believed to be poor), it will tend to trade on the basis of yield alone. The trading pattern in such a stock (or group) will resemble the pattern normally seen in bond trading, where the yield is the single most important determinant of the security's value.

Table 18-2 shows the dividend yield and payout ratio for 10 sample stocks as of mid-1991.

INVESTING IN THE STOCK MARKET

All investors secretly share the investment philosophy of humorist Will Rogers, who proclaimed that the stocks to buy are the ones that are going to go up. "If they don't go up, don't buy 'em," said Rogers.

The crystal ball brigade excluded, most of us judge the future from some hint or indicator in the present. What are the signs that a company or its stock is bound for greater things?

TABLE 18-2   Dividend Yields and Payout Ratios
(Sample data as of mid-1991)

Company	Stock Price	Dividend	Yield[1]	Payout Ratio[2]
American Express	$23	$0.92	3.9%	37%
Boeing	47	1.00	2.1%	21%
Chase Manhattan	19	1.20	6.4%	59%
Delta Airlines	70	1.20	1.7%	NMF
E-Systems	41	0.75	1.8%	22%
Federal Express	38	0.00	0.0%	0%
General Motors	38	1.60	4.2%	NMF
Hershey Foods	43	0.90	2.1%	36%
Idaho Power	26	1.86	7.2%	93%
Johnson & Johnson	94	1.60	1.7%	37%

Source: The Value Line Investment Survey. Some figures are estimates; stock prices are rounded to nearest dollar.

NMF = Not meaningful figure (earnings nonexistent or negative)
[1] Dividend per share as percentage of stock price
[2] Dividend per share as percentage of earnings per share

There are many stock-picking theories, some supported by a good deal of evidence, others by mere hunch. No single theory is sure-fire; a sound approach can improve your odds but will not guarantee success. Many theories work well during certain periods or economic climates, and then lose their magic.

Naturally, there are myriad theories on how to pick stocks. We can't discuss them all here, but we can discuss some of the major ones you're likely to encounter. To stay current on theories of portfolio management, and also to learn about companies in which you might want to invest, there are a number of well-regarded business publications you can read. Among the best known are *The Wall Street Journal* and *Forbes, Barron's, Fortune,* and *Business Week* magazines.

Low-Priced Stocks

Some people try to concentrate on stocks that sell for less than a specified absolute price per share—less than $10, for example. Underlying this approach is the assumption that it's easier for a $10 stock to jump to $20 than for a $100 stock to jump to $200.

In a purely theoretical sense, there's no reason why that should be so. As we've seen, the price of a stock reflects a company's earning power and the number of shares that have been issued. The choice of how many shares to issue is totally at the company's discretion. In a sense, a company can pick any price it wants for its stock, simply by making an arbitrary decision about how many shares to issue.

In actual practice, low-priced stocks do tend (with many exceptions) to be the stocks of smaller companies. Small companies are more volatile than large ones. It's easier for a small company to double its size than for an IBM or a Ford to do so. But, by the same token, it is easier for a small company to go bankrupt.

When people opt for low-priced shares, then, what they are really doing is overweighting their portfolios with small-company stocks. The result is likely to be a collection of holdings that outperforms the market averages during a bull market (that is, a time of rapidly rising stock prices) and underperforms the market averages during a bear market (a time of falling prices).

The extreme case in the world of low-priced stocks is the so-called penny stock, meaning a stock whose shares trade for less than $1. Most penny stocks are traded over the counter; some, especially of small mining companies, are traded on regional stock exchanges. Dealers in penny stocks like to recall the cases in which a small stake could earn an investor a fortune. People who bought 100 shares of Tandy Corporation (which operates Radio Shack stores) in the early 1960s, for example, would have laid out about $60 for shares that subsequently rose in value to more than $75,000. What the penny stock enthusiasts don't like to discuss is the number of investors who have lost their entire investments in little companies that have gone bankrupt—companies whose names have long since been forgotten.

On the plus side, low-priced stocks are not usually owned by the big institutions (banks, insurance companies, and pension funds) that count so heavily in most of the stock market. Many institutions have a rule against buying a stock that costs less than $10. Accordingly, if you buy the inexpensive stock of a good company, you may profit if institutions "discover" the stock in a year or two.

On the negative side, the commissions for buying and selling a low-priced stock (especially a penny stock) may loom larger as a percentage of your investment than they do when you buy higher-priced shares. Also, securities fraud seems to be more common with penny stocks than with stocks listed on major exchanges. All in all, the evidence in favor of buying stocks based simply and solely on price isn't compelling.

Small-Company Stocks

A related but essentially different approach is to seek out the stocks of small companies, whether they sell at $1 a share or $100 a share. Again, the underlying idea is that small companies have a potential for more dramatic growth than do large companies. Also, the market in small-company stocks may be less efficient than the market for large-company stocks, since each stock is scrutinized by fewer analysts and investors. By concentrating on small companies, so the theory goes, the investor has an increased chance of ferreting out a previously unspotted bargain.

Size, in this connection, may be measured by a company's sales or in other ways, but is most often measured by a stock's market capitalization, or cap, as it's known for short. This figure is the stock price times the number of shares outstanding. It arguably represents what investors collectively, at a given moment, think a company is worth.

Some of the interest in "small-cap" stocks stems from studies done in the early 1980s by Rolf Banz, a professor at Northwestern University. Looking at periods covering several decades, Banz found that the stocks with market capitalizations in the lowest one-fifth outperformed other groups. Some other studies have made similar findings. But critics quarrel with both the method and the conclusion of these studies. The critics say that Banz and others didn't satisfactorily account for those small-capitalization stocks that went broke or were delisted from the New York Stock Exchange. They also argue that the results of the Banz study are heavily dependent on a couple of periods, particularly the period from 1941 to 1945, which (because of the wartime economy and regulations) was an exceptional time. The subject deserves, and is receiving, further study. In the meantime, it may well be that small-company stocks—like low-priced stocks—provide a portfolio with more volatility than most, doing well in good times and poorly in bad ones.

Volatile Stocks

A volatile stock is one that rises more than most when stocks in general are rising, but sinks more than most in a declining market. Some advisers suggest that investors who can tolerate the risk should deliberately seek out volatile stocks (regardless of price or company size). The underpinning for this theory is twofold. First, the marketplace generally gives greater rewards to investors who assume greater risk. Second, the stock market has shown an overall tendency to rise over the long term. Despite short-term bull and bear markets, the prices of stocks over the long haul have kept up with the growth in the economy, and have more than kept up with inflation. Smooth out the violent zigzags on a stock price chart that covers a few decades, and you'll see an underlying upward trend. Since volatile stocks tend to move with the overall market, only more so, a long-term investor should do well with stocks that are above average in volatility, the argument goes.

Stock market analysts who subscribe to the school of thought called *modern portfolio theory* have developed a statistical measure of volatility, called Beta. A stock with a Beta of 1.00 rises and falls, on the average, in keeping with the overall rise and fall of the market. A stock with a Beta of 1.20 tends to rise 20 percent extra in good times and fall 20 percent extra in bad times. A stock with a Beta of 0.80 rises and falls less than the market as a whole, and is therefore considered a good "defensive" holding. A food company, for example, might well have a low Beta, because people must continue to eat even in bad times but aren't likely to increase their food consumption dramatically in good ones. The same might be said of a shoe manufacturer—as long as we're not talking about high-fashion shoes. By contrast, electronics companies and insurance companies have been perceived as having high Betas, in part because their industries go through boom-and-bust cycles. Typically, a little swing in the overall stock market would mean a big swing in these stocks, according to the theory.

Some studies show that high-Beta portfolios, in general, have produced higher returns historically than portfolios with low or average Betas. The studies disagree about the strength of Beta's effect. But from the standpoint of the individual investor, there are more serious problems with Beta as an investment tool.

The biggest problem is that Betas will not hold still. A stock that was volatile in the past may settle down and become stable. A stock that was predictable may suddenly become volatile. Times change; corporations change.

In the fourth edition of his highly regarded book, *A Random Walk Down Wall Street,* Burton Malkiel, dean of the Yale School of Organization and Management, provides an interesting example of how a stock may have a low Beta in one period but not in another. The example was Mead Johnson & Company (since merged into Bristol-Myers Company), the maker of a diet product called Metrecal. Malkiel points out that Mead Johnson was measured during certain periods of the 1960s as having a Beta of less than 1.00— that is, the stock price moved less than the general market. This was because Metrecal was successfully introduced while the stock market was down, tailed off as the market rose, and was replaced with another successful product during another market decline. Thus, Mead Johnson stock went against the general market trend and appeared more stable than the typical stock. There was no reason, Malkiel points out, for the low Beta to last. And a number of studies have shown that Betas in general do not stay constant over time.

Thus, while the Beta may have some analytical value for portfolio managers who deal with dozens or hundreds of stocks at a time, it has less value for individual investors whose portfolios may consist of only a handful of stocks, or a couple of dozen.

Finally, the strategy of deliberately picking volatile stocks presupposes that the investor will be able to hang in through any bad times and sell when the market is doing well. But unexpected cash needs can occur at any time. If that time happens to be when the market is down, the high-volatility investor may have to sell at a loss.

Growth Stocks

As we've seen, the value of a company's stock is closely tied to the size of the company's profits. If you knew that a company's profits were going to increase rapidly, you could almost be sure that the stock price also would advance nicely.

Almost, but not quite. Here's where that handicapping device, the price/earnings (p/e) ratio, comes in. If investors as a group anticipate rapidly rising earnings, they bid up the price of the stock relative to its current earnings. For the stock price to climb further, the company not only must show good profits, it must show profits that exceed people's expectations.

International Business Machines (IBM) provides a case in point. During the 1970s the company showed unquestionably impressive growth in sales and earnings. Sales rose from $13.10 a share in 1970 to $44.90 a share in 1980, while earnings went from $1.78 a share to $6.10. Who could complain? Only the shareholders. The value of an IBM share in 1980 was generally $70 a share or less, compared to a 1970 high of $73. The company did fine, the stock poorly. Why? Because investors' high expectations were built into the p/e ratio, which was consistently about 30 during the early 1970s.

The moral of the story is to not overpay for anticipated growth. And keep in mind that growth, like other variables, is difficult to predict. A straight-line extrapolation of past trends rarely will be accurate. Or, to use an adage popular on Wall Street, "Even trees don't grow to the sky."

Almost any investment principle works less well when everyone is trying to use it. If there were a vogue for companies whose names began with Q, the stocks of those companies probably would be bid up to unrealistic levels, and latecomers would be hard pressed to make a profit. In the case of growth stocks, the great fad came in the 1960s and early 1970s. It was popular then to pick stocks for perceived earnings-growth potential, with little regard for other considerations (such as a company's balance sheet), or for the price paid. Little wonder, then, that many of the people who invested at the height of the growth-stock boom experienced disillusioning losses.

During the late 1970s and early 1980s, the growth-stock boom had run its course, and stock prices (and price/earnings ratios) were lowered. It became possible to buy the stock of a company with a good earnings growth record without paying an exorbitant amount of money. A case in point, again, is IBM. People who bought its shares in 1980, undiscouraged by a full decade in which the stock had shown no progress, could have bought the shares for less than $70 and more than doubled their money by 1985.

High-Dividend Stocks

Some investors pick the stocks with the highest dividend yields (that is, dividends that are large in relation to the stock price). In recent years this approach has created a portfolio heavily weighted with utility stocks and the stocks of mature companies in manufacturing industries. As noted in our earlier discussion of dividends, the companies that offer the highest dividend yields do not always offer the best chance for capital appreciation.

However, companies that pay good dividends are often steady, relatively secure outfits. Their shares therefore may be well suited for the portfolios of people at or near retirement age. Such people often couple high-dividend stocks with bonds and other fixed-income investments.

In mid-1991, the median payout of the 100 highest-yielding stocks (out of 1,700 stocks followed by *The Value Line Investment Survey*) was 8 percent. That compared favorably with typical rates at the time on one-year bank certificates of deposit (about 6 percent) and was slightly less than the rate on 30-year Treasury bonds. In a sense, the investor who bought stocks for yield got prevailing market rates of interest, the potential for rising dividend rates over time, plus a chance for capital gains as a bonus—if he or she was in the top bracket. But, of course, the investor in high-yield stocks was taking a greater market risk, since the value of the stocks could drop.

Even though a dividend lends some stability to a stock's price, it's certainly no guarantee of stability. Sometimes the dividend yield is high because the stock price has been falling. (In such cases, it may be a danger sign or an opportunity for an investor who seeks "turnaround" situations, in which a company that has been facing difficulties overcomes them.) Sometimes the dividend yield is high because the company, despite rough times in its business, has been hanging on, resisting chopping the dividend. In such cases, the payout ratio (the percentage of the company's profits paid out in dividends) will have been rising. Before buying a stock because it has good current dividend yield, it's wise to read up on the stock to find out whether experts think the dividend will soon be cut.

Low-p/e Stocks

As the IBM example previously mentioned demonstrates, a company's record alone is not enough to predict whether its stock is a good buy. You must also consider how dearly you are paying for the stock, or how inexpensively you can obtain it. In that connection, the price/earnings ratio is a better indication than the simple price of the stock as to whether a stock is "cheap." People lost money by buying IBM at 33 times earnings in 1970. Some made money by buying it at 10 times earnings in 1980. The difference was not in the business performance of the company, which was admirable in both the 1970s and the 1980s. The trick was to buy the stock at a bargain price rather than at a premium price.

Viewed over several decades, a p/e ratio of less than 10 can be considered low, 10 to 15 a normal range, and more than 15 high. At any given moment, however, the p/e of the average stock may be more than 15 or less than 10. As we noted, p/e ratios in general rise when investors are enthusiastic about stocks, and they fall when investors are pessimistic. (In early 1991, p/e ratios were around 17 on average. But in the pre-Crash euphoria of 1987, many stocks sold for more than 20 times earnings.) Buying a stock with a low p/e doesn't guarantee a profit by any means. Often the p/e is low because a company's managers have shown themselves inept, or because the whole industry is in trouble. A company wedded to making adding machines when electronic calculators were coming into vogue was probably a bad investment, even if it had a low p/e. But several well-constructed studies do show that portfolios of low-p/e stocks generally outperform portfolios with high or average price/earnings ratios.

The reason, in large part, lies in unpredictability. Just as investors are prone to believe that today's hot company will stay hot forever, they tend to overreact to the woes of a troubled company. Over time, conditions in troubled industries improve; new managers take over poorly run companies; front-runners stumble and laggards gain. It doesn't always happen, but it happens with sufficient frequency to make a strategy of purchasing low-p/e stocks worth considering. A high-p/e stock must exceed people's high expectations for investors to profit. With a low-p/e stock, the company only needs to exceed people's low expectations.

Low-p/e investing has had many exponents, beginning with Benjamin Graham, the famous securities analyst of the 1930s. These days, the leading exponent of the theory is probably David Dreman, an investment manager, *Forbes* magazine columnist, and author of several books, including *The New Contrarian Investment Strategy*. The word *contrarian*—implying that one should do the opposite of what the crowd is doing—lies at the heart of the low-p/e strategy. The theory is that the mass of investors overreact to temporary conditions and put too much faith in predictions, which are necessarily unreliable. Therefore, money is made by going against conventional wisdom.

Dreman cites a number of studies done over the years showing that investment returns increase as p/e ratios decline. Among these are studies by William Breen, professor of finance at Northwestern University; by Francis Nicholson of Provident National Bank; and by Benjamin Graham. But perhaps the most interesting study was Dreman's own, summarized in table 18-3.

Dreman's study of more than 1,200 stocks over a nine-year period shows a strong inverse correlation between p/e ratios and investment returns. With few exceptions, the higher the p/e, the lower the return. A portfolio of low-p/e stocks held over the entire period provided a total return (capital gains plus dividends) of 7.89 percent a year, compared with 0.33 percent for the high-p/e stocks.

When the portfolio was adjusted periodically to regroup stocks into the appropriate p/e band, the results were even more dramatic. With yearly switching, low-p/e stocks showed a return of 10.26 percent, while high-p/e stocks lost 1.13 percent of the investors' money per year. Quarterly switching produced a return of 14 percent for the low-p/e group.

As with any stock selection method, a low-p/e strategy will work better in some markets than others. And it certainly is not a panacea. But of all the popular methods of stock selection, it seems to have the strongest theoretical and empirical basis.

This table shows the compound annual rate of return for groups of stocks arranged according to p/e ratio. The study on which the table is based covered 1,251 stocks over the period from August 1968 to August 1977. It was directed by David Dreman and used a data base from Compustat, a subsidiary of Standard & Poor's, with technical assistance from Rauscher Pierce Refsnes Securities.

TABLE 18-3   Investment Returns and p/e Ratios

Group of stocks	Quarterly switching of holdings*	Yearly switching of holdings*	Original stocks held for nine years
10th decile (lowest p/e)	14.00%	10.26%	7.89%
9th decile	11.85	6.08	6.40
8th decile	8.83	8.56	6.35
7th decile	7.90	6.85	6.08
6th decile	4.84	6.70	4.52
5th decile	2.19	2.93	3.72
4th decile	3.06	3.31	5.36
3rd decile	0.51	1.63	3.30
2nd decile	0.92	0.56	1.27
1st decile (highest p/e)	−2.64	−1.13	0.33

Source: David Dreman, *The New Contrarian Investment Strategy* (New York: Random House, 1982), 144–45.

* No allowance is made for the commissions that would be required, in practice, for such switching.

Balance-Sheet Measures

Most of our discussion up to now—and most securities analysis— attempts to peg the value of a stock to the size of the profit a company can earn, or to the amount of dividends it can generate. However, there's another way to measure the value of a company (and its stock)—not by what it earns, but by what it owns. For this analysis, you turn to the balance sheet, where a company's assets and liabilities are calculated.

You can find balance-sheet information, along with other financial figures, in a company's annual report. (Almost any company that issues stock will send you an annual report on request.) Or you can look up the figures at your local library in such financial reference books as *Standard & Poor's Reports, The Value Line Investment Survey,* or *Moody's Handbook of Common Stocks.*

The sum of everything a company owns (its assets), minus the sum of everything it owes (its liabilities), equals the company's *net worth.* That figure is also called the company's *book value.* If the stock price is greater than the book value per share, the stock is said to sell at "a premium to book." If the stock price is less, it sells at "a discount to book." Benjamin Graham and his colleague David Dodd, in their classic book *Security Analysis* (first published in 1934, and since revised several times), suggested that investors purchase only stocks selling at or below book value.

That advice was fairly easy to follow during the Depression, when stock prices were scraping bottom. In more recent times, very few securities analysts follow Graham and Dodd's strict criteria. But a number of investors and analysts continue to think of themselves as disciples of Graham and Dodd and thus look for stocks selling at a discount to book value. If none of those stocks meet their other investment criteria, they try at least not to pay too high a premium above book value.

Book value is especially important in placing a value on privately owned companies, and in assessing takeover situations. The increase in mergers and acquisitions in recent years thus has had the effect of reviving this criterion and focusing investor attention on it. *The Value Line Investment Survey* publishes each week (along with a wealth of other valuable statistical information) a list of major companies selling at a discount to book value. It should be noted, however, that reported book value does not necessarily accurately reflect the current value of the assets.

When a company borrows money, the borrowing has no immediate effect on its net worth. Suppose General Motors borrows $150 million to build a factory. It has a $150 million asset, the factory, and it has a $150 million debt. The two cancel each other out, with no immediate effect on book.

The borrowing does, however, show up on the company's balance sheet. Many investors and analysts study that ledger to be sure debt levels are not excessive. Too heavy a debt load could drag a company into bankruptcy. Short of that, the interest payments on a heavy load of debt can have a negative impact on a company's earnings.

How much debt is too much? Obviously, that depends on the size of the company. Debt that would have no effect on General Motors could sink a small scrap-metal business. Accordingly, financial analysts usually discuss debt in terms of various ratios.

Perhaps the most important of these is the *debt-to-equity* ratio. Stockholders' equity is the amount of money a company has raised in any and all stock offerings, plus the amount of profit it has reinvested in the business over the years. Comparing the company's debt with stockholders' equity puts the debt figure into perspective. A prudent level depends on the industry in which a company operates. (Utilities, for example, can safely assume more debt than can most companies, since they traditionally operate as a monopoly and the demand for their product tends to be stable and predictable.) For most companies, a ratio of debt to equity of greater than one-to-one is considered risky.

Return on Capital

A final way of assessing whether or not to purchase a stock is to measure the rate of return the company is earning on its capital. That rate of return can be compared to other rates, such as those available on bonds or other fixed-return investments.

One common measure is *return on stockholders' equity*. This fairly forbidding phrase simply means the company's profits divided by the equity figure discussed above. Generally speaking, a return on equity of 15 percent or more is considered outstanding.

The other common measure is *return on total capital.* Total capital includes stockholders' equity plus any money the company has borrowed. The return on total capital is the company's profit divided by the total-capital figure. For a company that has no debt, return on equity and return on total capital will be the same. For a company that has at least some debt (which means most companies), the return on equity (positive or negative) is magnified by the use of borrowed funds. Generally speaking, a return on total capital of 10 percent or more is considered good. However, with this measure—as with most other measures—it's often most instructive to compare a company against others in its industry.

As we've said, no single method of selecting stocks is foolproof. In an unpredictable world, none can be. Besides, if a single method did deliver guaranteed results, everyone would copy the method before long—and then it would probably cease to work.

We believe common stocks merit serious consideration in individual investors' portfolios. The long-term rates of return from stocks compare favorably with those from bonds and other fixed-return investments. And, unlike precious metals, commodities, and most other tangible investments, stocks can provide current income in the form of dividends.

Investors should, however, be mindful of the risks inherent in stock investing. And we repeat what we said earlier: No one should invest in stocks until he or she has adequate insurance, debts in reasonable proportion to income, and a savings cushion. People living completely from paycheck to paycheck are not financially ready for the volatility and uncertainty of the stock market.

As mentioned earlier, the risks of investing can be lessened, although not eliminated, through diversification. For that reason, most small investors should consider entering the stock market through a mutual fund (see chapter 20) before buying the stocks of individual companies.

In assessing the various methods for choosing stocks, we cannot point to any one as definitively superior. We are impressed, however, by the amount and quality of evidence for the thesis that investors should pay careful attention to price/earnings ratios. The evidence seems clear that, on the average, buying unpopular stocks has provided investment returns superior to the returns on the most popular stocks.

Many investors develop a method of their own, perhaps containing several of the elements we've discussed here. A person might, for example, decide to seek out stocks selling for 10 times earnings or less, issued by companies with a sound balance sheet and stable or growing earnings. To the extent they can, investors should also take into account their own judgment of a company's products, managers, and perhaps social, environmental, or labor-relations practices.

CAN ANYONE BEAT THE STOCK MARKET?

Once you become familiar with stock-picking theories and know how the various stock market averages work, if you're like most investors, your natural instinct will be to try to beat the averages. "If the Dow Jones goes up 10 percent, my stocks should go up 15 or 20 percent." So thinks everyone—or at least everyone except some chastened, experienced, realistic investors. The truth is, beating the averages consistently and over the long run is extremely difficult. If you could do it, you could command a handsome six-figure income as an investment adviser. But few advisers who command such incomes can do it either.

In fact, some of the most compelling evidence for the theory that no one can, over the long haul, do much better than the market averages comes from studying the track records of professional investors. Certain professional investors, such as mutual fund managers, are required by government regulators to set forth their full investment records in a systematic way. A careful study of those records suggests that professional investors do not seem to do better than amateur, individual investors (although good statistics on the performance of individual investors naturally are hard to come by). As one example of this, consider the performance of mutual funds that invest in stocks. It's a rare year in which the average mutual fund performs better than the market averages (such as the Dow Jones Industrial Average or the Standard & Poor's 500). For the most part, mutual funds do a little bit worse than those averages—not too surprising, since mutual funds (like all buyers and sellers) must pay commissions when they buy and sell, while the market averages, being mere statistical creations, do not.

The bad news is the difficulty of beating the market. The good news is that, by merely doing as well as the market in general, investors in stocks have done well over the years. Averaged over decades, the compound annual return on stocks has been about 10 percent per year. (Of course, it varies greatly from year to year, with dramatic gains in some years and big losses in others.) That historical rate of return is better than a long-term investor would have achieved in fixed-return investments such as savings accounts or bonds, and is also handily above the rate of inflation over the long haul.

Academics who have studied the stock market have come up with a persuasive theoretical reason why it is difficult, if not impossible, for an investor to show consistently above-average results year after year. It is called the *efficient market hypothesis*. The gist of this theory is that buyers and sellers instantly reflect all known information about a stock in its price. If, for example, Supreme Manufacturing announces that it plans, two weeks hence, to offer $25 a share to gain control of Lowly Industries (whose shares have been selling for $16), the price of Lowly shares is likely to rise to about $25 quickly as speculators snap up the shares. In some cases, if speculators expect a better offer to come along, the price will actually rise to a bit more than $25. Conversely, if investors think that the acquiring company may have trouble lining up financing to make its bid, the price will rise above $16 but will fall short of $25. In any case, the price changes happen remarkably fast.

If a company is believed to have good earnings prospects, those favorable prospects will be reflected in the price of the stock. How? Through a higher price/earnings ratio. Investors will pay more for each dollar of current earnings because those earnings are expected to grow rapidly. If a company has poor earnings prospects, its stock will carry a low p/e ratio. The effect is rather like that of a horse race in which the fastest horses must carry the heaviest saddles. The handicapping effect evens out the odds, so that your chances of making money by betting on a fast horse may be no greater than your chances of making money by betting on a slow one. In a perfectly efficient market, picking stocks is a toss-up.

Proponents of the efficient market hypothesis suggest, therefore, that a portfolio of stocks chosen by throwing darts randomly at a page of stock tables should produce results as good as those achieved by professional investors. To the extent that this theory has been tested, it has held up rather well. Perhaps the best-known randomly selected portfolio was born in 1967, when the editors of *Forbes* magazine picked a collection of 28 stocks by literally throwing darts at the stock pages of *The New York Times*. The resulting "dart board fund" handily outperformed almost everything in sight (including the market averages and the average mutual fund). As of 1980, it was up 134 percent, compared to a 27 percent increase in the Standard & Poor's 500 index. The experiment made its point rather sharply.

Such an isolated example, of course, proves nothing. But other observers, mostly academics, have constructed randomly selected portfolios to test the efficient market hypothesis. Almost invariably, the experiments show that random choices do as well as professional picks.

Besides testifying to the speed with which all new information is reflected in stock prices, the random-portfolio experiments also show how difficult it is to predict the future. One of the chief determinants of a stock's price, as we've already noted, is the company's earnings. And the ability of anyone, including professional financial analysts, to predict earnings has been very poor. As *Barron's* magazine stated on June 4, 1984, "The sad truth is that, ... Wall Street research departments have consistently erred by wide margins in their earnings forecasts." How wide? Over a 10-year period (from 1974 through 1983), *Barron's* put the average annual error (the difference between the actual earnings and the figure predicted by a consensus forecast of analysts one year earlier) at 53.8 percent. Even earnings forecasts for the current year were off—by an average of 18 percent over 10 years, and by as much as 56 percent in one particularly bad year (1983). Another study by researchers at Harvard and MIT reached a similar conclusion. Between 1977 and 1981, they found, the consensus forecast for the current year's earnings was off by an average of more than 31 percent.

People familiar with the world of business—indeed, people familiar with the world—will understand why predictions are so difficult. Here are but a few of the factors that have affected stock prices in recent years: the Persian Gulf War in 1991, the stock crash of 1987, the strengthening (and subsequent weakening) of the OPEC oil cartel, the passage of a sweeping tax-revision law in 1986, the long rise in the value of the dollar during the early 1980s and the sudden fall of its value in 1985 and 1986, the space shuttle disaster of 1986, and the political turmoil in South Africa in the latter half of the 1980s. Predictable? Well, perhaps some people can predict some of the events some of the time.

Clearly, an investment strategy that will work over the long run must take into account the fact that the world is a fairly unpredictable place, that companies' fortunes (like all fortunes) can rise and fall, and that the companies with the best estimated prospects are already carrying the highest stock prices relative to earnings.

CLOSE-UP: A SHORT COURSE IN LIVING DANGEROUSLY

Two techniques that some stock investors use to try to enhance their returns are buying on margin and selling short. Both involve taking on some added risk in the hope of a higher return.

Buying stock on margin means buying it partly with borrowed money. Who lends the money? Your stockbroker, at a rate that is usually a bit above the prime rate. How much can you borrow? Under current rules, half the price of the stock.

Suppose you buy 100 shares of a $50 stock. Normally, that would cost you $5,000. Using margin, you can buy the stock by putting up only $2,500, plus the interest on your loan. This works marvelously when a stock is going up. Suppose, for example, that your $50 stock rises to $60. You have made a $1,000 profit (minus interest and commissions). Had you put up the full $5,000, that would have been roughly a 20 percent profit. But since you put up only $2,500, your profit works out to almost 40 percent.

But what if your stock should happen to fall? Suppose that $50 stock falls to $40. Then your $1,000 loss is a 40 percent loss, exacerbated by the interest you must pay on the loan. Furthermore, if the stock falls too far, your broker will require you to put up additional cash, in a procedure called a *margin call.* In the example above, a margin call usually would be triggered if the stock fell to $35 or so. (Exact rules vary from broker to broker.) At that point your stock would be worth only $3,500, and you would owe your broker $2,500 plus interest. If you can't come up with the additional collateral, your broker is allowed to sell your shares, whether you like it or not, to pay off the loan.

The brokerage house is always protected, because it has a margin of safety. It can require you to sell shares long before the share value is less than the amount you've borrowed.

You, on the other hand, are taking a good deal of risk, since it is possible for you to lose more than the amount of cash that you've put up. For example, if you buy 500 shares of a $5 stock in the conventional way, the most you can lose is $2,500—the amount of your investment. If you buy on margin, you can control 1,000 shares by putting up only about $2,500, but if the company goes bankrupt, you can lose $5,000 (plus interest), or more than twice the amount of money you put in.

During the stock market boom of the 1920s, margin was used as liberally as peanut butter on a 10-year-old's sandwich. A nickel of cash could buy a dollar's worth of stock. But when the market started to fall in 1929, a wave of selling triggered by margin calls helped to worsen and accelerate the crash. Margin calls were also common during the 1987 crash from a less leveraged basis, though, because of stricter margin requirements, investors were not as badly overextended.

Selling short is a technique for profiting from a decline in a stock's value. When you sell short, you sell shares of stock that you don't own. How is that possible? Again, through borrowing. You borrow shares through your broker and sell them. A few days or weeks later, you buy the shares—at, you hope, a lower price—to replace the borrowed ones.

Short selling requires the use of a margin account (in which you must put up half the value of the transaction as initial collateral), and a short sale has many of the characteristics of a purchase using margin. Short selling, however, is riskier. The added risk has several aspects, but the most obvious and biggest is this: Losses when you buy on margin are limited; losses when you sell short are not.

Suppose you sell short 500 shares of a stock that is trading at $10. Because of a takeover offer and a bidding war, the share price rises to $22. Now what? You had put up $2,500 in cash at the start, and received $5,000 from the short sale. You are legally required to buy back the stock so you can replace the shares you borrowed. To buy 500 shares at $22 will cost you $11,000. You have lost $6,000 on a $2,500 initial investment.

CLOSE-UP: TECHNICAL ANALYSIS

On Wall Street, there are basically two kinds of securities analysts: "fundamental" analysts and "technical" analysts. The fundamental analysts look at factors such as earnings growth, balance sheets, and price/earnings ratios in order to determine which stocks to recommend and what is an appropriate time to invest. As we've seen in discussing the efficient market hypothesis, the life of a fundamental analyst isn't easy; corporate earnings and the economy are hard to predict.

But if the fundamental analyst must push a heavy stone uphill, the technical analyst must make the stone levitate. For it is the job of the technical analyst to predict future prices (of individual stocks or of market indexes) primarily from the clues found in previous price movements.

Can it be done? Clearly, many people on Wall Street think so. Most brokerage houses have technical analysts on staff, and a fair number of investment newsletters are devoted entirely to technical analysis. Plenty of people among the investing public seem to believe in technical analysis, too. Someone is paying for those newsletters and listening to those technical opinions from brokerage research departments.

Some investors, and some fundamental analysts, believe that technical analysis verges on superstition. They are joined in this curmudgeonly view by the majority of academic economists who study the securities markets. Among academics, even those who do not subscribe completely to the efficient market theory generally believe that past price movements alone aren't enough to predict future price movements.

The tools of the technician's trade are many. Three of the best known are *resistance levels, support levels,* and *formations.* A resistance level is a price that seems to be a barrier to upward movement. If a stock approaches the $20 level three times and each time backs down, a technical analyst would say that the stock "encountered resistance" at $20, or that $20 is a resistance level. From this, two conclusions often follow: First, the stock will have great difficulty piercing $20, and second, if it somehow *does* manage to get past $20, that is a bullish sign for future upward movement.

Support levels are like resistance levels in reverse. If a stock repeatedly sinks toward $15 and then rebounds, it is said to have "support" at the $15 level. It probably won't fall any farther. But if it does, look out below.

Formations are visual patterns formed by graphing stock price movements. One of the most famous is a head-and-shoulders formation, which involves an initial upward movement and decline (the left shoulder), then a stronger (higher) upward move and decline (the head), and finally a weaker upward movement and decline (the right shoulder). As prices in the right-shoulder stage decline through the "neckline," technicians perceive an urgent reason to sell the stock.

In addition to price movements, some technicians (or chartists, as they also are called) use figures on trading volume and other statistical indicators, such as a comparison of odd-lot purchases and sales (i.e., transactions by small investors involving fewer than 100 shares) with overall purchases and sales.

The academics counter that technicians are seeking to super-impose patterns on events that are essentially random or unpredictable. Several studies, at the University of Chicago and elsewhere, have presented considerable evidence that such patterns can be—and have been—reproduced by a computer spitting out random variations, or by spoilsports tossing coins in sequence.

The argument will probably never be settled to everyone's satisfaction, but we are on the side of the skeptics. We have seen no evidence to convince us that future price movements can be predicted from past price movements and similar data.

CLOSE-UP: HOW TO HANDLE
PROBLEMS WITH YOUR BROKER

If problems arise with your stockbroker—if you believe he or she is churning your account, for instance, or engaging in riskier trading than you want—there are several ways to resolve them. First, complain to the broker directly. If that doesn't solve the problem, complain to the branch manager of the brokerage house. If that also fails, stronger steps can be taken. Many brokerage houses have a standing agreement to take disputes before a neutral arbitration panel. This is quicker and less expensive than going to court. (Investors, when opening an account, often sign an agreement to take any disputes to arbitration rather than to court.) Obviously, not everyone is ultimately satisfied with this process, however. In fact, there have been a number of legal challenges to this binding arbitration process in the last several years amid criticism that the arbitration panels are rigged against investors. The New York Stock Exchange, the American Stock Exchange, and the National Association of Securities Dealers also will try to handle broker-customer arguments. Finally, you can complain to the Securities and Exchange Commission (SEC), the branch of the U.S. government responsible for regulating the securities markets. The SEC received more than 50,000 investor inquiries and complaints in its fiscal year that ended in September 1990.

19

Bonds

Aileen Jacobson

BONDS: FIXED-INCOME SECURITIES

Bonds are IOUs. They are issued by a company, government, or government agency with a promise to repay the borrowed money—which may be used to buy equipment, expand a factory, build a sewage treatment plant, or run a government—at a specific time. When you buy bonds, you are actually lending money to the issuer, who pays you a set interest rate periodically, perhaps twice a year.

Once upon a time, buying bonds was simple. Investors would purchase a bond and hold it 10 to 30 years until it matured, in the meantime clipping the bond's coupons and turning them in at a bank for interest payments due. Today, trading in bonds has become vastly more complicated. Coupons have disappeared, replaced by computers; the variety of bonds available has multiplied to a dizzying number; and new packaging has increased the number of choices available to investors.

Nevertheless, bonds should be part of a balanced investment portfolio, for two reasons: First, they provide a high degree of safety—as long as they are highly rated and held to maturity. You are not likely to lose your capital or the promised interest, even though inflation may erode the buying power of your dollars. If your bonds are issued by the U.S. government, they are the safest investment around.

Second, bonds usually provide protection in times of falling interest rates. Most have a fixed rate of interest when you buy them. If interest rates fall, the value of the bond you purchased before the decline goes up, if you choose to sell it before maturity, because it pays a higher interest rate than a new bond issue would. Unfortunately, the reverse is true too. If you buy a 10 percent bond and interest rates rise to 15 percent, your bond is worth less in the resale market than you originally paid; an investor wouldn't pay face value for a bond paying 10 percent annually when he or she could buy a current bond paying more than that.

Because of their relative safety, and because they can be bought with a wide range of maturity dates that can be timed to come due at specific points in your life, bonds are often used to save toward a particular goal, such as college or retirement. Because they provide a steady income with a high level of safety, they are also frequently a good investment after you retire.

INVESTING IN BONDS

Bonds come in three forms: *bearer, registered,* and *book entry.* Bearer bonds, which carry coupons, have not been issued since 1982, when a change in the tax laws eliminated them. Nevertheless, many remain on the secondary market, where bonds are traded by brokers after their initial issue. Bearer bonds have no record of the owner's name on them; they belong to the person who has possession of the certificate. Consequently, they may not be as safe from theft as the other two types of bonds.

Registered bonds carry on the certificate the name of the owner or the owner's agent (a bank or broker), and they cannot be resold without an endorsement and change in the issuer's books.

Book entry issues are similar to registered bonds, but there is no certificate you can hold in your hands. Instead, the bonds exist as a printed or electronic notation on the issuer's books; buyers receive statements of periodic interest payments from their brokers. Even the U.S. Treasury is switching to book entries, which are a lot less cumbersome for the individual and the institution.

How to Purchase Bonds

You usually buy bonds through a brokerage firm or bank (although U.S. Treasury securities may be bought directly from the government). Except for U.S. savings bonds, they ordinarily come in denominations of $1,000, $5,000, or $10,000 each. But it isn't easy to buy them in lots of less than $250,000 for corporate bonds or $25,000 for municipal bonds, and the transaction costs for trading in smaller lots—if a broker even handles small lots—tend to be prohibitively high. At that price, achieving diversification—a must with municipal and corporate bonds, where default is always possible—is infeasible for all but the wealthiest investors.

For these reasons, the average investor with limited assets is better off buying bonds through mutual funds or through unit investment trusts, which are diversified portfolios of bonds that can be purchased for as little as $1,000 (see p. 380).

The only types of bonds the average investor may want to consider purchasing directly are U.S. Treasury issues—called bills, notes, or bonds, depending on how long they will take to mature—and U.S. savings bonds. Both of these are secure investments that do not require huge sums of money. Savings bonds can be bought for as little as $25 and are among the best investments available for the person with very limited investment funds, while Treasuries require as little as $1,000. In certain limited cases, which will be discussed later, individuals may also want to buy zero-coupon bonds when they are saving for a specific purpose, such as retirement or college.

To purchase individual bonds directly, investors should shop around, calling several brokers with their specifications—the amount of money they want to invest, the grade of bond they want, the maturity date they desire, and, if they want state and local tax breaks, the location of the municipality or agency issuing a bond—and then compare prices and yields. If a brokerage firm has large inventories of bonds at a particular time, it may offer them at a better price. Discount brokerage firms don't sell bonds at discounted prices, so their prices aren't necessarily lower.

Although you generally don't pay a commission if you buy a bond that your broker or investment banker has on hand, you do pay the difference between the "bid" and the "ask" price (i.e., the seller receives a different price from what the buyer pays). The difference, which goes to the broker, is called the *spread*. Effectively, the spread is the broker's commission and can range from .75 to 5 percent of the purchase. Commissions are usually much greater for small lots than for large ones.

Bond mutual funds are bought the same way you buy any other mutual funds, through a fund salesperson or broker or directly from the fund sponsor (see chapter 20). Unit trusts are generally sold through brokers or bond dealers, who advertise their offerings in the business sections of newspapers, in business magazines, and sometimes by mail. They generally charge around 4 percent as a sales fee.

Understanding How the Bond Market Works

Anyone considering investing in bonds, whether directly or through funds or trusts, should be aware of three important factors: price, interest rates, and yield.

Purchase Price and Interest   Bonds may be bought new or "used." If you purchase a bond when it is first issued, you pay "par" value for it—that is, the face value, which is the amount it will pay at maturity. You may also buy a bond on the "secondary market," after it is first issued. There, a bond's value or price fluctuates, depending on what it can command.

The value of a bond on the secondary market changes with prevailing interest rates. If interest rates go up, the value of a bond paying lower interest goes down. And if rates go down, the value of a bond paying relatively high interest goes up.

In addition, the longer the term remaining until maturity, the more the market price of your bond may fluctuate with changes in prevailing interest rates.

A bond you buy on the secondary market may sell either at a "discount" (less than face value) or a "premium" (more than face value). The price is based on the interest rate the bond pays, compared to the current interest rate, and takes into account such factors as supply and demand and the number of years till maturity, when the issuer will pay you the full face value of the bond.

Yield   The purchase price of a bond, or principal investment in it, is only half the story. The other half is the yield. There are three types of bond yields:

Coupon rate. Even though most bonds don't use coupons any-more, the term still applies to the bond's percentage yield at par value. For example, if your bond has a $1,000 face value and pays $130 a year in interest, the coupon rate is 13 percent.

Current yield. This is obtained by dividing the $1,000 bond's annual interest payout by its current price in the secondary mar-ket. For example, the 13 percent bond might be selling for only $950 (it would be quoted as 95 in the newspaper listings of actively traded bonds) if interest rates had gone up since it was issued. You would compute the current yield by dividing the $130 annual inter-est by the current market value of $950, to find that your current yield was now 13.7 percent.

Yield to maturity. This is the important number to watch if you are buying a bond in the secondary market, because it takes into account both the interest payments and the capital gain or loss that you will record when your bond is due. Mathematical tables, available in bookstores, can provide you the yield to matu-rity for many issues, but you can also do an approximate calcula-tion yourself, as follows:

1. Subtract the purchase price ($950) from par ($1,000) to get the discount, which is $50.
2. Divide the discount ($50) by the remaining years of the bond (let's say five years). You get an annual gain of $10.
3. Add the capital gain to the annual coupon ($130), and you get a yearly total of $140.
4. Take the annual return ($140) and divide it by the purchase price ($950). You get a yield of 14.7 percent.
5. Subtract the annual capital gain ($10) from par. You get $990. Then divide the annual return ($140) by $990. You come up with 14.1 percent.
6. Finally, take the average of the two yields (14.7 percent and 14.1 percent) and you get a yield to maturity of 14.4 percent.

Callable Bonds

You cannot always count on a bond's continuing to its date of maturity, because some have a "call" feature. A callable bond may be redeemed or paid off early by the issuer, often after a period of several years. If interest rates fall, the issuer may want to call in the old debt and issue new bonds at a lower interest rate, even though it has to pay the old bondholders a premium over par to do so. Ask your broker whether a bond you're considering is callable, and if it is, make sure that the timing of a possible call is acceptable to you. Be particularly careful about the call feature if you are buying a bond at a premium: It could be called the next week at a price lower than the one you paid for it.

Comparing Bonds to Other Investments

Before buying any government or corporate bond, check whether comparable investments—such as a long-term certificate of deposit issued by a bank—might not give you the same return or better, after you count in the transaction costs or sales commissions associated with the bond. Comparing the interest rate on a bank CD to a municipal bond, however, is impossible, because CDs don't offer the same tax savings as tax-free municipal bonds. So you must compare the after-tax return on each investment vehicle.

When bonds are used as a long-term savings device, keep in mind one drawback: the interest you earn can't always be reinvested at the same rate that the original bond pays, as is the case with a fixed-rate CD. If interest rates go up, that's not necessarily a disadvantage, because you will be able to reinvest at a higher rate. But it does make planning more difficult.

It is possible to avoid the complexity of reinvesting by using a bond mutual fund, a deep-discount bond (which pays little current interest but provides a capital gain when it matures), or a very deeply discounted bond known as a zero-coupon bond, which will be discussed later.

Mutual Funds and Unit Trusts

As previously noted, investing in bonds through a mutual fund or unit investment trust is usually more suitable for small investors. Among the advantages of funds and trusts are their relatively low expense, their liquidity, and their diversification.

Both funds and trusts pool money from many investors and buy a wide variety of bonds. With mutual funds, the bonds are "actively managed"—that is, for a fee, a professional money manager keeps an eye on the market, constantly buying and selling bonds for the portfolio. With a trust, the portfolio remains fixed, and the trust dissolves when most of the bonds in it have matured. The interest a mutual fund pays will fluctuate as bonds are bought and sold, while a trust will continue to pay the same amount of interest until the bonds in it mature.

According to Gabriele, Hueglin & Cashman, a brokerage firm specializing in bonds, an individual would have to invest at least $50,000 in individual corporate or municipal bonds to achieve the diversification of a trust. Moreover, trusts are more easily sold than bonds in lots of less than $20,000 face value. However, brokers usually charge a greater commission to sell a trust unit for you than they do to sell an individual bond.

Which is better for your needs, a mutual fund or a unit trust? The answer depends on your investment objectives. With bond funds, the price of a share and the interest rate paid fluctuate with the interest-rate market and with the management of the fund. That's because a large part of the fund's yield comes from trading bonds, rather than just collecting the interest payments. With a trust, the interest earned annually remains stable because there is no trading activity, though default and the calling of bonds in the trust's portfolio can affect the annual yield.

The two approaches can lead to very different results. If you invest in a unit trust paying 8 percent annually, your rate will be locked in whether interest rates in general rise to 12 percent or fall to 5 percent. If your investment is in a bond fund, your yield will tend to reflect changes in interest rates. In addition, with a fund you can have interest payments automatically reinvested.

Because there is no management fee with a trust (whereas a fund usually charges an annual management fee of around 1 percent), a trust often offers a slightly higher yield than a fund at the outset. But a trust nearly always carries a sales charge, while a no-load mutual fund does not (see chapter 20). So the trust is better suited to long-term investing, where the cost of the sales charge can be averaged out over several years. If you think you'll have to cash in early, you're better off with a fund, which is usually easier to sell. In either case, always read carefully the prospectus of any fund or trust you are considering.

TYPES OF BONDS

Fixed-income securities, as bonds are also called, fall into one of four major categories: corporate bonds, municipal bonds, U.S. Treasury issues, and government agency securities. In addition, two special groups of bonds, technically subsets of the above four categories, are becoming increasingly popular: zero-coupon bonds, which pay no interest until maturity, and convertibles (bonds that may be converted into stock).

Corporate Bonds

Corporate bonds, as the name indicates, are issued by corporations, and the interest they pay is fully taxable. When you buy a corporate bond, you aren't entering into part-ownership of a company, as you do when you buy stock. You won't participate in the company's growth, because the value of your bond won't increase even if the company does well. If it does very poorly—that is, if it goes bankrupt—your claim to repayment comes before the interests of the stockholders, because you are one of the company's creditors. Actually getting your money back, however, may prove cumbersome and costly, since it may involve going to court. That is one reason why an individual investor should stick with the bonds of established companies and with bonds that are highly rated. Besides being more readily salable, and having lower transaction fees than the bonds of small or obscure companies, high-rated bonds are also less likely to go into default.

Nothing is as certain in the bond market as it used to be. AT&T, once a favorite of conservative investors, has been broken up into many smaller firms, some with bonds that are highly rated, others with bonds that are not. Utilities also were once considered surefire investments. But those that have ventured into building costly nuclear power plants, sometimes with unforeseen problems or opposition, may be less of a sure investment.

Rating of Corporate Bonds   Two major companies rate corporate (and municipal) bonds. They are Moody's Investors Services and Standard & Poor's. Although they use slightly different designations, their evaluations of a bond's safety are usually the same. Whether you are evaluating a single bond issue or a bond held in a fund or trust, you should always use the ratings of at least one of these services as your guide. Here is what their designations mean:

- Standard & Poor's AAA/Moody's Investors Services Aaa: Best quality; issuer's capacity to pay interest and repay principal is extremely strong.
- AA/Aa: High quality; ability to pay is very strong.
- A/A: Upper medium; strong capacity to pay, but somewhat more susceptible to adverse changes in circumstances and economic conditions than bonds in higher-rated categories.
- BBB/Baa: Medium quality; adequate capacity to pay, but adverse economic conditions or changing circumstances are more likely to lead to a weakened capacity to pay interest and repay principal. These are considered investment quality by some experts (commercial banks, for example, are allowed to invest in them, although they are prohibited from owning anything of lower grade). However, many believe that these bonds are too risky for an individual. If you are investing in a bond fund or trust, you might be able to tolerate a few bonds of this category in the portfolio, but stay away from them if you are buying bonds directly. You should also steer clear of bond funds or trusts that concentrate on bonds in this category or lower—unless you are deliberately investing in a "junk" bond fund for its high income potential and are aware of the risks. In no case should more than 5 percent of your investment funds be in such speculative ventures.
- BB/Ba: Speculative.
- B/B: Low grade.
- CCC/Caa: Poor, risky.
- CC/Ca: Highly speculative, major risk.
- C/C: Lowest grade; income bonds on which no interest is being paid.
- D/D: In default; payment of interest and/or repayment of principal are in arrears.

Some of these ratings may be modified by a plus or a minus sign to show relative standing within a major rating category.

As you might expect, there is a direct relationship between the rating and the interest rate paid. The higher the rating, the lower the interest payment is likely to be; you give up some return for safety. But a good rating is no guarantee against default. Occasionally, though not often, ratings for bonds are changed either upward or downward. A change in the rating doesn't affect the coupon rate, but it can affect the bond's price in the secondary market, since people might be willing to pay more for a more highly rated, and thus safer, bond. When people invest in junk bonds, it's sometimes because they think that something will improve in the company that could lead to a higher rating, and thus a higher return for the bond.

Bonds with a rating of BB/Ba or below are often referred to as junk bonds. They have become more popular as an investment in recent years, but we advise against them unless you are already well diversified, have a high risk tolerance, and are going to commit no more than 5 percent, at most, of your total investment funds.

We generally recommend avoiding this fad because corporate bonds with such low grades—which are often issued by corporations borrowing heavily to finance the takeover of another company, or by companies in financial distress—are the most likely of all bonds to default. Sixty-eight percent of corporate bonds that defaulted in the period 1970–1988 were originally rated BB+ or lower. Concurrent with the rising popularity of junk bonds has been an increase in total bond defaults. Defaults in junk bonds reached an estimated $15 billion in 1991, and Standard and Poor's expects failures to remain high through 1993. That's a big jump from 1986, when total corporate bond defaults were only $3.28 billion. (There are also junk municipal bonds, but they're just as risky as low-grade corporate issues funds.)

The attraction of junk bonds is their higher yield, which is supposed to compensate the investor for the higher risk he or she takes. Such was the case during the twelve months ending in May 1991, according to A. Michael Lipper of Lipper Analytical Services, which tracks mutual funds. During that year, junk bond funds returned an average 19.27 percent compared to 4.63 percent for high-grade corporate bond funds (with bonds rated A and above) and 3.31 percent for U.S. government bond funds. The extremely high yield reflected in large part the fact that junk bond prices had been badly beaten down in the previous year. Moreover, investors are understandably skeptical of how safe returns on such bonds are—so they demand a high rate of return.

If you insist on taking a gamble to gain higher yields, the safest way is through a junk bond mutual fund. Investing directly in low-grade bonds is much too risky. But be choosy, even with a fund. The bulk of the fund's portfolio should be made up of bonds with ratings not lower than BBB/Baa.

Types of Corporate Bonds There are several types of corporate bonds, defined by how they are secured.

Debentures. Also known as unsecured bonds, these are the most common type of corporate bond. They are backed by the issuing company's general credit standing instead of by particular collateral assets. This doesn't necessarily make them less desirable than bonds secured by hard assets, because in any event it is difficult to collect on a bond's security when a company fails or becomes insolvent.

Equipment trust certificates. Usually issued by railroads, these are certificates of ownership interest in specific rolling stock, locomotives, freight cars, and other equipment. The trustee for the equipment trust leases the rolling stock to the railroad at a stipulated rental. These bonds are not suitable for the average individual investor.

First-mortgage bonds. A common type of bond, it is backed by a first lien on specified property belonging to the company, such as real estate or equipment. The arrangement is supposed to (but in reality often doesn't) give added protection to the bondholder, because the real estate or equipment can be sold to pay off the bonds.

Guaranteed bonds. These are backed by another corporation (or by the government or a government agency in the case of municipals), which guarantees that it will pick up the interest, principal, or both, should the issuer be unable to pay. The guarantor is usually an affiliated or parent company.

Collateral trust bonds. These are secured by such collateral as bonds, notes, or stocks.

Income bonds. These are usually issued to holders of defaulted bonds after a reorganization. Interest payments are contingent upon the company's earnings.

Convertible bonds. These may be exchanged by the holder for a specified number of shares of common stock. Generally, they pay slightly less interest than other comparable bonds but hold out the possibility of capital growth, should the holder wish to convert them to stocks. They provide a great deal of flexibility. (See p. 398.)

Municipal Bonds

Historically, municipal (or "muni") bonds have had the highest appeal for taxpayers in the highest income tax brackets. In exchange for yields that were somewhat lower than those available on taxable corporate bonds, investors in muni bonds received income free of taxation.

When buying tax-exempt bonds, consider not only your current tax bracket but what you expect it to be in future years. If you think you'll be moving into a lower tax bracket, perhaps because of retirement, you may not want to invest in tax-free bonds. Of course, if you are in a fund, you can get out easily—but not necessarily at a profit, because the value of your shares could be low at the time you want to sell. Social Security recipients should also be aware that municipal bond interest, even though it is not taxed, is counted along with other kinds of income in the formula that determines whether or not Social Security income is partly taxed.

Types of Municipal Bonds There are nine types of municipal bonds.

General-obligation bonds. These are the most common and generally the safest, since they are backed by the "full faith and credit" (that is, the taxing power) of the governmental body issuing the bonds. They generally have the highest ratings and pay the lowest interest.

Limited tax bonds. Though backed by the full faith of the issuer, these are not backed by full taxing power. Usually they are based on a particular tax.

Revenue bonds. Repayment of these bonds is based on revenues produced by projects such as sewers, airports, dormitories, toll roads, bridges, tunnels, rapid transit systems, and resource-recovery plants. Their quality is therefore dependent upon the success of the underlying project. The major ones are rated by Standard & Poor's or Moody's. For smaller issues, scrutinize available documents, such as annual reports; or, better yet, have some personal knowledge of the project or the officials running it, which is certainly possible if the project is local.

Industrial development bonds. These are actually corporate bonds issued by development agencies, which are set up by a state or city but are not backed by the governmental entity. Until 1987, these bonds were exempt from federal income taxes. Now if more than 10 percent of the bond issue proceeds are used for nongovernmental purposes, the bonds are considered private activity bonds and the interest earned on them is taxable. Municipalities still issue the bonds, but they are now referred to as taxable municipal bonds. Tax reform also exempted from these restrictions bonds for certain types of private/governmental projects. However, bonds that are used to finance such projects as airports, certain multi-family residential rental projects, and solid waste disposal facilities remain tax-exempt.

Anticipation notes. These are not generally feasible for an individual investor, but they do show up in mutual funds. They are short-term obligations, intended to raise cash while the issuer is waiting for funds from a bond issue or from taxes. They offer high yields and short maturities.

Authority debt. Short or long term, these are issued by governmental agencies such as housing authorities or publicly owned utilities. Also known as revenue bonds, they are considered safe (although not as safe as general-obligation bonds of the same rating) and usually offer liquidity (i.e., you can sell them if you need to).

Option tender bonds. These permit the investor to turn in the bonds at face value for cash before maturity, after a five-year waiting period and subject to six months' written notice. This option protects them from the secondary-market price variations due to fluctuating interest rates; they usually sell close to par, no matter what their interest rate in relation to current rates.

Floaters. The principal remains static with these bonds while the interest rate fluctuates in relation to a particular index, such as a set percentage of current Treasury bill or bond rates.

Insured tax-exempts. These are issues that might not get a very high credit rating otherwise—perhaps because they're issued by a small community—but are guaranteed by consortiums of private insurers. With that insurance, they get a AAA rating from Standard & Poor's, but they must sacrifice a little in yield because of the insurance and reduce the yield for the added safety. The insurance provides protection only in the case of default—timely payments of principal and interest are guaranteed—and does not protect against fluctuations in the price of a bond in the secondary market.

Investment Advice Generally, municipal bonds are considered safer than corporate bonds, but you have to look at the specific issue. There is always a possibility of default or a chance that the bond ratings might be lowered (as happened with the state of Massachusetts in the early 1990s), which would make the issue harder to sell, or would lower its secondary-market price.

Municipal bonds may be callable, just as corporate bonds are. Thus, it is not a good idea to buy high-coupon bonds (which pay a high interest rate) at a premium without first checking the call provisions. If the bond is called early, it will reduce your overall return and could result in a net loss.

You should shop around for bonds, because both the cost of similar bonds and the yields on bonds with similar maturities and ratings may vary from one broker to another. Before investing in tax-free bonds, be sure to compare the after-tax return of alternative investments. Some bargain prices can often be found in December, when many investors swap bonds to set up tax losses.

To time your investment, you can buy an old or a new bond that is simply due on a specific date. Many municipals are issued as serial bonds. That is, instead of all the bonds coming due at once, the maturity dates are staggered, usually at intervals of six months or a year.

Most unit trusts for bonds are built around tax-free issues. Look for good quality, of course, and if you live in a state that taxes municipal bond interest earned on out-of-state muni issues, look into a trust—or a fund or individual bond—with issues from your state, because they will be free of state and local taxes, too. As with corporate bonds, check the ratings of the bonds in a trust or fund, and stick with the A (or higher) ratings, or at least a high proportion of them, if you are looking for safety.

U.S. Treasury Bonds

T-Bills, Notes, and Bonds Issues of the U.S. Treasury are considered the safest of any investment because they are backed by the "full faith and credit" of the U.S. government. Treasury issues are known by three names (though technically, all are bonds). Treasury bills, also known as T-bills, have maturities of 91 days (sometimes officially referred to as 13 weeks or three months); six months (or 26 weeks); or a year (52 weeks). The first two are issued weekly, the third once a month. They have a minimum face value of $10,000, but are sold at a discount. Instead of receiving interest payments, you pay less than the face value for them and get the full face amount back when they're due. The difference represents their yield.

Treasury notes mature in from one to five years, pay interest semiannually, and sell in minimum denominations of $5,000 for those with terms of less than four years and $1,000 for four to five years.

Treasury bonds come in medium-term (5- to 10-year) and long-term (10- to 40-year) maturities. Interest payments are semiannual, and denominations are a minimum of $1,000.

With Treasury securities, you don't have to worry about two items that must be considered when buying other bonds. First, they will never slip in their ratings. In fact, they aren't rated, because they are considered to be above even the AAA rating. Second, they never have a call feature, so you know exactly what you will get if you keep them to maturity.

The yields of short- and medium-term Treasury securities can be compared to bank CDs. The CD yield might be higher once you count in transaction costs or sales commissions on the Treasury bill or note when you buy through a bank or broker. (You can also buy Treasury securities for no additional commission by buying directly—in person or through the mail—from the 12 Federal Reserve Banks around the country.) Treasury securities, on the other hand, offer a benefit that many bank CDs don't: Like other bonds, they can be sold anytime before maturity if you need the money, because there is a ready secondary market for them. But they are, of course, subject to the same fluctuations in price, due to changing interest rates, as any other bond.

At the longer maturities, Treasury securities can be compared to other bonds. They don't offer the exemption from federal taxes that municipal bonds do, although their earnings are exempt from state and local taxes. And, because they offer greater safety, they generally pay slightly lower interest rates than AAA corporate bonds of comparable maturities.

As with most bonds, Treasuries usually offer higher rates at longer maturities, though when interest rates are unusually high this isn't necessarily so. In January 1981, for example, short-term Treasury yields were nearly 17 percent while 30-year bonds offered a little over 12 percent. By October of that year, Treasuries with maturities of two to three years offered the highest yields.

When deciding on the appropriate maturity date, do not use the highest rate of the moment as your only guide. If you believe rates will go down considerably in the not-too-distant future, then locking in a fairly high yield might be preferable to getting a great yield for six months and then having to reinvest the money at much lower rates. Conversely, if you think rates will rise during the next 12 months or so, it might be wise to buy short-term Treasury securities so that you can keep pace with the rising rates when your bills mature in perhaps three months, so that you will be able to reinvest at what may then be a higher rate.

You should also, of course, weigh your own time goals. But the longer time until the maturity date, the greater your interest-rate risk, since long-term bonds will fluctuate more in price in the secondary market (although this would affect you only if you sell before maturity).

As mentioned, you can buy Treasury bills, notes, and bonds directly from the government through your local Federal Reserve Bank (or, for those living in the Washington, D.C., area, through the Bureau of the Public Debt). For convenience, you might prefer to work through your bank or broker, both of whom will charge a service fee. They will also make it easy to sell on the secondary market, if you need to sell your security earlier than planned. But if you are interested strictly in yield, try to buy directly.

You may buy directly either through the mail or by using Treasury Direct (see below). To buy through the mail, you find out from a Federal Reserve Bank when the bond, note, or bill you want to purchase is sold (every Monday for bills with 13- and 26-week maturities, less frequently for securities of longer maturity) and mail the bank a check for the value of the security so that it arrives by the specified date. The exact interest rate will be determined by an "auction" held on that date, in which only large institutional investors bid. With T-bills, which are sold at a discount, the Federal Reserve Bank will credit your bank account a few days after the auction with a check for the interest you have earned, determined by taking the average of all the competitive bids made at the auction. You get your principal back when the security matures.

For details on auction dates and other information, contact your local Federal Reserve Bank or write to the Bureau of the Public Debt, 1300 C Street SW, Washington, D.C. 20239-1000, or call 202-287-4113 for recorded information.

Until mid-1986, the Treasury still used the mail for checks, and sent engraved certificates to those who bought bonds and notes directly. Under a new system, called Treasury Direct, you don't have to wait for the mail, because your Fed Bank can credit your interest and principal electronically to your account at any institution you choose. The new system also allows you to reinvest T-bills automatically for up to two years without having to complete a reinvestment request each time.

To sell your issue on the secondary market, you must transfer your securities to a bank's or broker's account. Buying directly works best for those who intend to keep their Treasury issues until maturity.

To learn more about Treasury Direct and about buying Treasury securities directly, contact the government securities department of your local Federal Reserve Bank or the Bureau of the Public Debt.

A positive feature of T-bills is that, even though you receive your interest right up front, you are required to pay taxes on it only in the year in which the bill matures or is sold. That tax deferral can be a great advantage unless you expect to be in a higher tax bracket the following year.

There are two ways to figure the interest on a T-bill. One is the discount yield, which is the interest divided by the face value (i.e., if you receive the $1,000 in interest in a one-year, $10,000 T-bill, the discount rate is 10 percent). This is the number usually used in newspaper reports of T-bill rates. The other method, which is the one that should be used when comparing the yield to other investments, is called the coupon equivalent yield. That is the interest rate divided by the amount you paid for the bill (i.e., since you paid only $9,000 for the bill, your yield is 11.11 percent).

U.S. Savings Bonds Once considered a convenient birthday or graduation gift but not a very wise investment, the reliable old

U.S. savings bond has become a pretty good deal. It still isn't normally the bond of choice for the serious investor, but it offers several advantages:

- It's easy to purchase at any bank, without a transaction charge.
- Sometimes it's linked to a payroll-deduction savings plan, a good vehicle for those who otherwise find saving impossible.
- The interest is exempt from state and local taxes.
- It comes in small denominations. The smallest bond, with a $50 face value, can be bought for $25.
- It can be cashed in at any time with no loss of principal, although perhaps with a reduced yield.
- The interest can fluctuate with market rates, but it has a floor below which it cannot dip.
- Taxes on the interest on Series EE bonds can be deferred until the bond is redeemed—or even further, if the bond is exchanged for another.
- It is as safe as the U.S. government.

The yield on Series EE savings bonds, compounded semiannually, is equal to 85 percent of the average return of U.S. Treasury notes with five years to maturity. The Secretary of the Treasury is allowed to change that minimum at any time, but the new minimum rate applies only to bonds issued after the change. In 1991, the minimum yield was 6 percent (a rate in effect since November 1986).

The bonds issued now are called Series EE or Series HH. Series EE bonds (which replaced Series E bonds in 1980) sell for one-half their face value, which ranges from $50 to $10,000. If the bond is cashed in during the first six months, no interest is paid, and it takes five years before the full yield is paid. In essence, they are like zero-coupon bonds, because you don't get the interest until maturity.

Series HH bonds (which replaced Series H bonds in 1980) are issued in denominations from $500 to $10,000. Those issued after October 31, 1986, pay a fixed rate of 6 percent over a 10-year period to maturity. The interest is paid out twice yearly via Treasury check, and the bond is redeemed at face value.

Series HH bonds may be acquired only through an exchange for

E or EE bonds (but you must have a minimum of $500 worth), and there is no penalty for early withdrawal.

You can defer taxes on the interest from E or EE bonds for as long as 20 years by exchanging them for an HH bond. But you do have to start paying current taxes on the new semiannual interest from the HH.

Before redeeming a bond, you should find out when the interest is credited. Older bonds are credited only once every six months, and if you cash one in a day early, you lose six months' interest. New bonds are credited at the first of every month, so you should buy them at the end of the month to get maximum interest payments.

During the life of an E or EE bond, you may either report the interest annually or wait until the bond is redeemed. Most people prefer to defer the taxes, but that is not always the wisest choice, especially for those with minimal income, as was pointed out by a tax court case decided in 1986.

The case involved a mother who had purchased 49 Series E savings bonds over a period of years, and had them issued jointly in her name and her son's. During the time she was a joint owner, she did not need to file annual federal income tax returns because of her low income. Thus, she never reported the savings bond interest annually.

Two years after she died, her son redeemed the bonds, which had by then matured, and collected all the interest—which he did not report. The IRS, however, believed he should have reported all of it as income. He argued that he owed taxes only on the amount of interest income that had accrued since his mother's death, because, even had his mother reported the interest every year, she didn't have enough income to owe any taxes on it.

The tax court agreed with the IRS ruling that the mother was required to file tax returns each year, even though she owed no taxes, for her son to avoid the tax levy later. Hence, children or anyone with minimal income should file a return and declare the interest on savings bonds annually, even if no taxes are due, so that a larger tax can be avoided later.

Interest on U.S. savings bonds issued after December 31, 1989, can be free of federal tax if, during the year you cash in the bonds, you spend an amount equivalent to their proceeds on tuition and fees for college or graduate education for yourself, your spouse, or your children. This exclusion is available only if your adjusted gross income (modified for certain income, deductions, and credits) is no more than $62,000 for married taxpayers filing jointly, or $41,950 for those filing as single or head of household in 1991. The benefits are phased out for joint filers whose income is between $60,000 and $94,350 ($40,000 and $57,700 for single filers, with both sets of figures to be adjusted for inflation annually). The purchaser must be at least 24 years old and own the bonds solely or jointly with a spouse.

Government Agency Securities

Government agencies may also issue securities. By far the most popular of these are GNMAs (issues of the Government National Mortgage Association), commonly known as Ginnie Maes.

Ginnie Maes are mortgage-backed securities, which are basically pools of mortgage loans. After you obtain a mortgage from a bank, for example, the bank will likely put your mortgage into a bundle with several others. A certificate representing this bundle is issued in denominations of at least $1 million. This certificate— a mortgage-backed security—is then sold to a broker, who will in turn slice it up and sell shares of the whole (minimum denomination $25,000) to individual investors, mutual funds, or unit trusts.

The bank that issues a mortgage-backed security collects the monthly loan payments from the homeowners and passes them on to the ultimate buyers of the security. Such certificates are always backed by some federal or state agency, which guarantees timely monthly payments to the ultimate investor. Thus, even if the homeowner defaults, the bank must still make its monthly payment to the security holder.

Various state agencies provide these guarantees. Quasi-federal agencies (such as the Federal Home Loan Mortgage Corporation, popularly known as Freddie Mac) and private corporations (such as the Federal National Mortgage Association, popularly known as Fannie Mae) also guarantee mortgage-backed securities (see chapter 3). But by far the most popular backer is the federal government, through the GNMA. The GNMA guarantee is backed by the "full faith and credit of the United States," just as Treasury securities are.

Ginnie Maes combine the safety of government guarantees with high yields. Historically, Ginnie Mae yields have surpassed the yields of AAA-rated long-term industrial bonds and of 10-year Treasury notes.

Ginnie Maes pay higher yields than other government-backed securities because they must make up for a few drawbacks. The biggest risk with Ginnie Maes is that the underlying mortgages can be prepaid. When interest rates fall, people tend to pay off their mortgages and refinance with lower-rate loans. When that happens, the Ginnie Mae investors receive their principal and interest sooner than expected. They are then faced with the task of reinvesting the money at the then-prevailing lower rates. Thus, Ginnie Maes are not a sure-fire way of locking in high yields.

It is even possible to lose money on a Ginnie Mae if an investor has paid a premium for an older certificate with a higher yield. If most of the mortgages underlying that certificate are suddenly prepaid at par immediately or soon after the purchase date, the investor loses the premium above par that he or she paid, without enjoying the benefit of the higher yield. The risk is similar to the call provision on corporate and municipal bonds.

Buying a Ginnie Mae at a discount, on the other hand, may be an advantage. Its yield is lower than the prevailing rate, so there is little chance of prepayment of the underlying mortgages because of refinancing, although a certain percent of the underlying mortgages do get prepaid simply because people sell their homes and pay off the mortgage so they can purchase a better home or move to another community. Buying an older certificate also requires a smaller initial investment. There's no liability if the certificate is paid off early, because the investor makes a profit on the difference between the purchase price and the par value he or she receives when mortgages are prepaid.

Ginnie Mae investors sometimes become confused about what their monthly check represents, because principal and interest payments are issued as one lump sum. Just as mortgage holders pay off both interest and principal—more interest toward the beginning of a mortgage, more principal toward the end—so Ginnie Mae investors receive both principal (which is not taxable) and interest (which is) each month, in changing proportions. Though the checks explain the differences, people sometimes fail to realize what they are receiving and spend the principal when they hadn't intended to or report the amount of interest incorrecly on their tax returns. One way to avoid spending principal is to have your monthly check sent directly to a bank or money market account. With a mutual fund, you can usually have the principal, or principal and interest, reinvested automatically.

Getting back principal presents another problem for investors, because the money must be reinvested at current rates, which may be lower than the Ginnie Mae's rate. Moreover, the rates of short-term investments, such as money market funds, are generally lower than those on longer-term bonds.

Another problem is the minimum investment required. The minimum amount for a GNMA certificate is $25,000 (though old ones can be bought for less). The high price puts them out of the reach of most small investors, which is why Ginnie Mae mutual funds and unit trusts, with their $1,000-and-less minimum investments, are popular.

Unit trusts pool individual investors' money and buy a set portfolio of Ginnie Maes. The trust lasts until all the Ginnie Maes in the portfolio are paid off. The advantage of a trust is that the yield remains relatively fixed for the life of the trust, although prepayments do affect the overall yield of the total investment.

A Ginnie Mae mutual fund works in a significantly different fashion. You buy shares of the fund, and the fund buys and sells Ginnie Maes the way any bond fund would trade in bonds. Because of that, your yield is not fixed. It rises or falls in relation to interest rate trends and the trading savvy of the fund's portfolio managers. The share price may also rise and fall, as with any mutual fund other than a money market fund.

Some bond funds, including those that invest in Ginnie Maes, enhance their yields by trading in futures and options on futures. These are hedging devices, which work the same way as futures in the stock market do, but they are too risky for the average individual investor to use. Some investment advisers also believe that they are too risky for use in a fund that people seek out for safety and security.

Because of the different ways Ginnie Mae trusts and mutual funds work, each has its place in the universe of investment objectives. A trust can be used to lock in rates (subject to the limitations mentioned earlier of Ginnie Maes and the borrowers' urges to refinance the underlying mortgages) if you believe interest rates in general will fall. A fund, on the other hand, will tend to be related to and keep pace with changes in interest rates, and thus can be a better investment if you believe rates will rise.

Private issuers, such as mortgage banks and financial firms, may issue mortgage-backed securities or collateralized mortgage obligations, which are privately insured and which may be based on conventional mortgages instead of those issued (and insured or guaranteed) by the FHA or the VA. Naturally, they are riskier.

Zero-Coupon Bonds

Zero-coupon bonds (or "zeros," for short) pay no interest until they mature. You buy them at one price and know exactly what you will get when the bonds mature. Because the bonds are discounted like savings bonds, you can invest for the very long term with a minimal amount of money. For example, in May 1991, you could have paid $1,294.90 for zeros that in November 2016 would be worth $10,000 (an 8.19 percent yield). And you don't have to worry about how to reinvest the interest, which is usually at least as high as, or higher than, comparable regular bonds that pay interest regularly.

The major drawback of zeros is that, even though you don't receive the interest, the IRS insists upon taxing you annually as though you did. Thus, zero-coupon bonds are usually practical only in tax-deferred retirement accounts and in custodial accounts for children under 14 whose annual unearned income does not exceed $1,000, or those 14 or older who pay no or little taxes. Tax-free zero-coupon bonds, issued by municipalities, also exist, but they are much in demand and difficult to come by. Zeros are particularly useful as a means of saving toward retirement or college, because their maturities of up to 30 years can be timed precisely. They are not good for investors who think they have to cash in early, because, even though there is a ready market for zeros, their market prices tend to be more volatile than those of regular bonds, and brokers' fees tend to be high.

The most popular types of zero coupons are Treasuries, which brokerage firms package and refer to under such commonly used brand names as CATS (Certificates of Accrual on Treasury Securities) and TIGRs (Treasury Investment Growth Receipts). The U.S. Treasury issues them directly as STRIPS (Separate Trading

of Registered Interest and Principal of Securities). They are sold
through banks and brokers and usually carry a face value (the
value at maturity) of $1,000. Because the packaging costs and bro-
kers' fees are already wrapped into the price of the bonds, rather
than being stated separately, yields can differ considerably. It can
be worthwhile to shop around for prices of comparable maturities.
Buying zeros with maturities staggered over a period of time, then
rolling them over as they come due, is a good way to dollar-cost-
average their price.

CATS, TIGRs, STRIPS, and their cohorts are not really bonds.
They are the coupons that have been stripped from long-term
Treasury bonds. You are buying receipts representing claims on
future interest payments. The original securities are held in trust
by a custodial bank. Although there have been some difficulties
about misrepresentation, they are generally considered safe and
secure, since they are based on Treasury securities.

Problems may occur when people have to sell zeros early,
because their price is often more volatile than regular bonds.

Convertible Bonds

Convertible bonds, which may be exchanged for stocks in the same
company that issued the bonds, are always corporate bonds. But
they are a special variety and bear a little more scrutiny on their
own. There are mutual funds that trade in convertibles, so you
can rely on professionals to evaluate the particular issues if you
wish.

Convertible bonds are similar to convertible preferred stocks,
which can be exchanged upon demand by the holder for a specified
amount of common stock. In the case of the bond, the year of maturity and the twice-yearly interest payments are fixed. Because of
the exchange feature, the interest rate is lower than that of a
straight bond of the same maturity offered by the same company.
(For preferred stock, the dividend rate is fixed but there is no
maturity date.)

Convertibles are riskier than similar straight bonds, because
they may fall in value if the company's stock falls in value, or if
interest rates go up. On the other hand, they are generally conservative investments compared to stocks, because you always have
the cushion of the fixed yield until you convert. If the company's

stock goes up, you can switch to the stock and make a profit because your bond entitles you to a fixed number of shares.

When investing in convertibles, it's important to evaluate the attractiveness of the stock, since you are giving up bond yield in order to have the opportunity to cash in on a rise in the value of stock. The more attractive the stock is perceived to be, the greater the spread, usually, between the interest paid on a straight bond and a convertible. That is, investors are willing to give up interest in some proportion to the amount they believe the stock will rise. Investors in convertibles are generally hoping for higher overall yields than they could get by investing in either stocks or bonds.

Nearly all convertibles allow the issuer a call privilege. For example, if a $1,000 bond was initially offered to investors when the price of a share of common stock was $10, each bond might be convertible to 100 shares. After one year, if the stock moved up to $15 a share, the bond would be worth $1,500 (100 times $15). In bond language, that's known as 150. If the call feature allows the issuing company to call in the bond at 107, then the company can effectively force conversion by announcing its call; then bondholders will choose to take the 150 they can get by converting rather than the 107 they'd receive by cashing in the bond. After converting, the holders can sell the stock or hold on to it.

If, before conversion, the price of the stock falls, then the price of the bond falls too, if it is sold before maturity. It is also important to remember that issuing corporations treat convertible bonds as future stock rather than as debt, so their quality rating is usually at least one notch lower than that of the firm's straight bonds. On the other hand, the interest obligation comes ahead of dividend payments on common or preferred stocks.

There are several ways to evaluate convertibles. The "conversion value," expressed in dollars, is the number of shares into which a bond can be converted, multiplied by the market price of a share (for example, 25 shares × $32 = $800).

Because the convertible pays a yield higher than the value of the common stock, it usually carries a higher market price, known as the premium—the percentage paid for the convertible in excess of the "conversion value" of the common stock. Thus, if the convertible with the $800 conversion value has a market price of $1,000, the premium is 25 percent.

Another comparison to examine is between conversion and

investment values. If long-term interest rates are at 7 percent, a company may issue a 5 percent, 20-year-maturity bond convertible to 40 shares of common stock at $25 per share for each $1,000 bond ($1,000 = 40 × $25). The convertible's investment value may be computed by looking in the yield book (which brokers have) to find the price at which a 5 percent with 20 years to maturity would have to sell in order to have a 7 percent yield to maturity. This turns out to be $785 per $1,000 bond. That's the price at which the convertible issue would probably sell, if it were not convertible.

Companies issue convertibles partly because this allows them to borrow at a lower interest rate. The interest an investor receives should be compared not only to the rate paid on straight bonds but to the dividend paid by the common stock. If the stock pays a higher dividend, then the investor should probably convert.

20

Mutual Funds

Aileen Jacobson

Mutual funds offer three main advantages: a larger pool of investment funds, reduced risk, and professional management of your
investment.

When you invest in a mutual fund, you are pooling your money
with other investors' capital. The added buying power of a larger
aggregate of invested funds in turn makes greater diversification
possible, thus spreading your risks. In addition, you are hiring a
professional money manager to relieve you of the mechanics of
investing—choosing stocks or bonds, deciding when to buy and sell,
and keeping track of prices.

The mutual fund managers invest the pool of money in a wide
variety of companies, and each individual investor owns a proportionate share of the fund's entire portfolio. (The type of investments the fund makes, and its investment goals, are detailed in a
prospectus the fund issues to potential investors.) Thus, when you
own shares in a mutual fund, you are not affected as directly or
seriously by the vicissitudes of a single company as you would be
if you bought stock exclusively in that company. This ability to
diversify is a major reason for the great surge in popularity of

stock funds, bond funds, and money market funds that occurred in
the 1980s.

Moreover, investors with only small amounts of money can
readily enter the mutual fund market. There are funds that allow
you to invest as little as $100, or that have no minimum. And even
if a fund requires a relatively large initial investment, it often calls
for small amounts in subsequent investments.

When you invest in a mutual fund, you have quick and automatic liquidity. A mutual fund is always willing to buy back its
shares from you whenever you want to sell.* All mutual funds will
either wire a transfer to your bank account or write you a check
for the amount you want to redeem. Moreover, funds will, if you
like, automatically reinvest your earned dividends and any capital
gains that you have realized.

Buying into a mutual fund puts your investment in the hands
of a professional manager who analyzes and tracks the different
components in the portfolios he or she handles as a full-time job.
Professional management means overseeing such daily details of
investing as picking the stocks or bonds to buy, executing the buy
and sell orders, and following the market.

Professional management does not necessarily mean, however,
that the fund's portfolio manager is endowed with extraordinary
investment prowess. Investment profits depend on many factors,
among them strategy, timing, and luck. No professional manager,
however savvy in terms of strategy and timing, can claim to be
infallible.

A study published by *Consumer Reports* in 1990 concluded that
in recent years, a minority of mutual funds managed to "beat" the
average market performance as expressed by the Standard &
Poor's index of 500 large-company stocks. Only one in seven stock
funds in the survey produced a total return on investment higher
than a similar theoretical investment in the S&P 500 would have
produced over the last five years. Thus, it is important to choose a
fund with a good long-term performance record and, since there
are no guarantees of future performance, to avoid putting all of
your money in only one fund.

---

*We are discussing here the characteristics of open-end mutual funds, not the
far less common closed-end funds, which issue a fixed number of shares that
are bought and sold on the stock market just as stocks are.

TYPES OF MUTUAL FUNDS

Since 1980, the number of mutual funds has more than quintupled. Of the more than 3,200 mutual funds operating in 1991, most invest in stocks, bonds, or short-term securities. Some aim for growth while others emphasize income; the majority diversify holdings while a few concentrate investments in one industry. We'll take a look at various kinds of mutual funds, starting with stock funds—which in recent years have included funds with many different investment objectives and specialties—and continuing with bond and money market funds.

Stock Funds

One of the most popular and common types of mutual funds is the stock mutual fund, in which an investment company pools money from many investors to buy a variety of securities—usually shares of common stock. The company raises money by selling shares in its mutual fund to investors. When you cash in your shares, the fund redeems them for the net asset value per share: the value of the stocks and other assets that the fund owns (minus the fund's liabilities) divided by the total number of shares outstanding.

The mutual fund pays lower commissions on stock transactions than you would as an individual investor trading in stocks. Mutual funds, pension funds, banks, and other big institutional investors typically pay a lower percentage in commission because they deal in large-volume purchases and sales. Those savings are passed on to the mutual fund investor.

Described below are the major types of stock funds, along with three that contain primarily stocks but a few bonds as well.

Long-Term Growth Funds Long-term growth funds seek capital gains from companies that have realized steady growth in earnings. Their growth rates generally have surpassed the inflation rate, and the fund managers usually maintain that these issues have certain special characteristics that will enable them to continue to perform well over the long run.

Generally these are relatively stable funds suitable as conservative, long-term investments.

Balanced Funds Balanced funds try to find a good mixture of common and preferred stocks and bonds while minimizing risk.

Each fund lists the ratio (which may fluctuate within certain bounds) of these types of investments in its prospectus.

As with long-term growth funds, these are generally stable, with the added advantage of even greater diversification than a pure stock fund.

Growth-and-Income Funds As the name implies, growth-and-income funds seek a balance in their stock investments, trying to provide current income from dividends with capital appreciation. They are considered safer than stock funds concerned with growth alone, because they invest partly in established companies to get high dividends and because those dividends may help to offset any dips in stock prices.

Aggressive Growth Funds These are funds that attempt to achieve high returns by investing in small companies with a potential for large growth and other speculative stocks. Some of these funds choose to take additional chances by investing in volatile securities. Some take risks by trading with borrowed money or engaging in short selling. Also known as capital appreciation funds, they maximize capital gains income at the expense of income from dividends, as do the firms in which they invest. Instead of distributing a portion of corporate profits to the stockholders as dividends, they reinvest the profits into the company in order to fund expansion. Usually, these companies pay very little or no dividends.

Aggressive growth funds may invest in anything that they feel is poised to experience impressive growth at the time; the potential for rapid and significant growth is the most important criterion for investment. Such investment techniques as option writing, short-term trading, leveraging (borrowing to invest), and buying unregistered securities are often used in order to increase yields. The fund's prospectus must tell you which of these devices it uses.

As you would expect, these funds are risky. In times of economic boom and a rising stock market, they can significantly outperform other types of stock funds. But in a down market, they tend to fall more precipitously.

Precious Metals Funds Precious metals funds invest in the stocks of gold-mining and other firms engaged in the precious metals business. Because they lack diversification, and because the fortunes of the precious metals business are highly volatile, these funds are extremely risky forms of investment.

During the 1970s, when gold prices were high, precious metals funds for the most part did very well. But gold prices began to fall dramatically and remained depressed for a decade. Precious metals funds do offer some hedge against inflation, but not as much as you may get by investing directly in precious metals, which are protective during periods of high inflation. Gold funds also tend to invest in South African mining companies, which many investors find objectionable.

International Funds International funds invest in stocks traded on foreign stock exchanges, including the Tokyo, London, and Paris exchanges. These funds performed very well in 1985 and 1986. Although they suffered in the 1987 stock crash, they rebounded in 1988. Many financial advisers believe that they provide an extra degree of diversification in a stock fund portfolio.

Some international funds also invest in foreign bonds, and some invest in American and foreign securities. A few are limited to one country or area of the world—Japan or the Pacific Basin, for instance—but these tend to be riskier because they are less diversified. Their returns also depend partly on the strength of the U.S. dollar against other currencies. In early 1991, for instance, a strong dollar meant these funds seriously underperformed those with domestic stock.

Sector Funds Whereas the most important advantage of a stock fund is the diversification of its portfolio, the sector fund seeks to reap greater profits by investing only in specialized portions of the economy. Most sector funds invest only in the stocks of a single industry, such as oil, technology, financial services, or utilities.

Sector funds, which have received a great deal of publicity over the past few years, contrast with the traditional diversified funds. These sector funds try to capitalize on the rapid price appreciation that sometimes occurs in a single sector of the market. Because they eschew diversification, they are far riskier than other types of mutual funds, offering both greater gains and greater losses.

In sector investing, the goal is to anticipate which industries will do well in the near future and to buy shares of the sector fund that invests in that industry. When the industry peaks, you sell out of the fund and put your money in the next sector that you think is going to boom. Consequently, those who push sector funds invite investors to do exactly what investors in mutual funds try hard to avoid—time the market.

Perhaps some people can successfully "time" the market on occasion; certainly many investors lose a great deal trying. In general, although you can make a killing relatively quickly by investing in sector funds, you can also lose your money just as fast. Unless you are nimble and knowledgeable, you could end up doing as poorly as your sector. For most people, a better investment strategy is to pick a diversified mutual fund with a history of consistent gains, buy it, and hold it for the long term.

One general exception to these warnings is utility funds, which invest in an array of the stocks and bonds of utility companies. These have the advantage of a portfolio in a generally stable industry. Although they yield somewhat less than direct investment in utility stocks, professional management can avoid the pitfalls of investing in utilities that face regulatory problems you cannot foresee.

Index Funds   A relatively recent type of fund, the index fund takes a different tack from those of the others described. They collect investors' money and then put together a portfolio of stocks that reflects the makeup of the leading market indexes, such as the S&P 500. The performance of the fund should therefore be a carbon copy of the index on which it is based. Sometimes the timing of buying and selling stock—because new investors enter the fund or current investors redeem their shares—throws off the index fund's return a little. Also, of course, a management fee is deducted, and there are transaction and other costs that will affect the total return.

The index fund is the opposite of a sector fund, and quite different from an ordinary mutual fund, both of which try to beat the market. Instead, an index fund starts with the assumption that few mutual funds are likely to perform better than the market as a whole over a long period of time. So why try to beat the market? Simply buy the market as a whole.

Bond Funds

Municipal Bond Funds   Municipal bond funds offer tax-free income. They invest in long- or intermediate-term municipal bonds, which are generally used to fund such revenue-producing projects as highways, bridges, waterworks, and waste disposal facilities.

Some municipal funds invest in bonds issued by the municipalities of a single state to take advantage of the favorable tax laws in some states. While most states do not tax the income from bonds issued by its municipalities, some states do tax the income of bonds issued by out-of-state governments. (The federal government genrally does not tax municipal bonds, although under the Tax Reform Act of 1986, municipal bonds issued to finance certain nongovernment projects are no longer federally exempt from federal income taxes. These bonds are generally referred to as industrial revenue bonds.)

While one-state funds are designed to keep the income you get from that fund tax-free, they carry a slightly higher risk because the fund's investments are not geographically diversified. One state may begin to experience a recession while other major areas of the country enjoy stable or growing economies.

Corporate Bond Funds   Corporate bond funds, as their name implies, invest in the bond issues of public corporations. Consequently, the income from these bond funds is taxable, both by the federal government and by some state jurisdictions. Sometimes, part of the portfolio of these funds may be invested in United States Treasury and other government securities.

United States Government Income Funds   For the conservative investor, U.S. government bond funds offer a good level of security, because they invest in U.S. Treasury bonds, federally guaranteed mortgage-backed securities, and other government notes. If the majority of the portfolio is invested in mortgage-backed securities issued by the Government National Mortgage Association (GNMA), they are called GNMA or Ginnie Mae funds.

When interest rates fall, there is a big disadvantage to GNMA funds, becuse homeowners tend to pay off mortgages underlying the GNMAs and refinance at lower rates. Although GNMA investors get their principal back, they must reinvest it at reduced rates. Therefore, the funds may pay lower yields than shareholders had been led to expect. (For more information about investing in GNMAs and GNMA funds, see chapter 19.)

By comparison, U.S. Treasury bonds are not "callable"; that is, the government cannot call them in and issue new ones at lower rates. Also, the yield of funds investing in them would not drop as quickly as would that of GNMA funds when interest rates drop. However, when issued at about the same time and with the same maturity, GNMA bonds tend to offer a higher yield than do Treasury bonds. Consequently, during times when interest rates remain stable, GNMA funds usually pay more.

Money Market Funds

Taxable Money Market Funds Money market funds, which are also referred to as money funds, are mutual funds that invest in a variety of short-term (usually less than 30 days) debt instruments or securities, such as Treasury bills and government agency notes; jumbo certificates of deposit (which are CDs in amounts greater than $100,000) offered by large U.S. banks; commercial paper debt obligations of corporations; and overnight loans to banks and brokers, which are called repurchase agreements.

In order to join a money market fund, an investor opens an account by buying shares of the fund. Each share costs $1, and there is normally a minimum amount required to open an account, usually $500 to $2,000. A few funds will allow you to open an account with any amount.

Money market funds offer several attractions for investors. The short-term interest rates keep pace with general interest rates and are typically higher than those offered by regular savings accounts and imitative money market accounts offered by banks. Usually, interest is credited to your account each day, and most of these funds permit you to write checks in minimum amounts ($250 or $500) on the balance of your fund. In contrast to other mutual funds, money market shares always remain at the same price ($1), while the return fluctuates. There is no danger of losing part of your principal, as there is with a stock or bond fund (barring the unlikely event of default of a great portion of a money fund's investments)—but also no opportunity for capital appreciation.

In one important sense, your money is more liquid in a money market fund than in other types of mutual funds. Not only can you sell at any time, but you can be certain that whenever you sell you will receive at least what you paid for your shares, since the share price always remains constant at $1. Some investors use money markets as a place to put money on an interim basis, until conditions become more propitious for making long-term commitments. Others use them as long-term vehicles for the liquid part of their savings, as an alternative to bank accounts (see also chapter 5).

Tax-Exempt Money Market Funds Tax-exempt money market funds are actually short-term municipal bond funds set up to function the way money market funds do. That is, the cost of shares stays constant, while the rate of return fluctuates daily, depending on the rates offered by the bonds held by the fund.

Because they offer tax-free income, these funds are popular with investors in the 28 percent and 31 percent tax brackets, as long as the tax-free returns are higher than the after-tax returns of regular money market funds.

However, these funds are also slightly more risky because they rarely invest in any instrument backed by the United States guarantee, since most such instruments, like Treasury bills, are taxable.

Moreover, some of the short-term investments—such as tax anticipation notes, project notes, and floating-rate demand notes—were created by municipalities or financial institutions solely to meet the short-term needs of tax-exempt money funds. Cities use such instruments to meet current operating costs rather than to fund revenue-producing projects, for which long-term bonds are issued. Some advisers consider this short-term debt a slightly riskier proposition than long-term bonds.

Asset Allocation Funds A relatively new type of mutual fund, it attempts to time the market by switching all or part of your investment among different types of investments. When, for example, the fund managers anticipate a drop in interest rates, they may move the fund assets into fixed-income securities, on the grounds that these may appreciate in value faster than common stocks. On the other hand, if they anticipate a rise in interest rates, they may shift fund assets out of bonds and into money-market funds.

Most who invest in such funds do so because they offer broad diversification. However, much of the success of these funds depends on the ability of their managers to time the market, and, as we have pointed out, even professional managers cannot count on doing this.

FEES CHARGED BY MUTUAL FUNDS

All mutual funds charge some kind of fee; some are expensive, others are modest. Typically, a management fee of 1 percent of the amount invested will be assessed in both load and no-load funds, and in many cases you will encounter other fees as well. In the past, many funds tried to hide their fees from prospective shareholders. New government rules now require that the fees be set forth at the beginning of each fund's prospectus and that they be taken into account when figuring a fund's performance in a way that is consistent with that of every other fund. This way you can compare fees in your selection of a fund.

The new rules require a prospectus to include a table that shows how the expenses and fees would affect a hypothetical $1,000 investment, growing at 5 percent annually, after one, three, five, and ten years. (Over many years, heavy annual expenses could make more of a dent than a one-time up-front load coupled with lower annual fees.) The new rules, which took effect in 1988, also require that if a fund advertises its performance, it must include its average annual total return, after expenses, for the most recent one-, five-, and ten-year periods. It must also state any sales load. Income funds that advertise yields must use a uniformly calculated 30-day figure.

Below are the five major categories you should be aware of.

Loads

A "load" is a sales commission usually paid up front when you invest in a fund. The money usually goes to a stockbroker or someone else on the fund's sales force. More than three-quarters of all funds are now sold through brokers or sales agents. By law, funds may charge up to 8.5 percent of the amount invested as a load when you first invest and make subsequent investments in your account, although most charge less. Funds that have a systematic savings plan may charge higher loads. Investors making fixed monthly payments as low as $25 in these special types of funds are charged up to half the first year's payments as a "sales and creation charge." Some funds charge no load at all.

Whether or not a fund charges a load has no effect whatsoever on its investment performance. However, the load significantly reduces the amount of your investment put to work for you. When that is factored into the fund's total return, load funds tend to fall below no-load funds. Avoid load funds, and you will not only save your money but also improve your total return. Unless you want or need the services and advice of a brokerage firm, don't purchase funds through a stockbroker or other sales agent, who is always paid somehow, through a load or 12b-1 fee (described below). You can contact funds that sell directly to the public, with no load or a low load, by phone or mail. The Investment Company Institute, a trade group, publishes a guide listing over 3,000 funds, with phone numbers, minimum investments, and other information (but no performance records). To order one, send a check for $5 payable to The Directory of Mutual Funds, Investment Company Institute, P.O. Box 66140, Washington D.C. 20035-6140. The Mutual Fund Education Alliance, the Association of No-Load Funds, has a guide to mutual fund investing and a list of about 500 funds (some of which charge low loads, up to 3.5 percent, or 12b-1 fees), available for $5 by writing to the Mutual Fund Education Alliance, 1900 Erie, Suite 120, Kansas City, MO 64116.

Management and Expense Fees

Mutual funds have always charged annual fees for management and expenses, typically in the range of .25 to 1.5 percent. These fees pay the cost of running the computers, mailing periodic account statements, and paying staff salaries. Ordinarily, they should not concern you unless they are unusually high—anything over 1.5 to 2 percent a year. High charges may indicate poor management of the fund's costs.

12b-1 Fees, Exit Fees, and Deferred Sales Charges

Rule 12b-1 in the Investment Company Act of 1940 permitted funds to charge fees to cover marketing and advertising costs. Advertisements and marketing are supposed to bring the fund additional customers and its managers more money. However, they do nothing to improve the fund's performance. In fact, since every investor pays for these costs, they erode your yield. About half of the nearly 2,800 funds in 1989 charged 12b-1 fees, ranging from .25 percent to about 1.25 percent of assets.

Increasingly, 12b-1 fees have been used to pay sales commissions, which in fact makes them load charges. If a no-load fund charges a hefty 12b-1 fee in order to pay its sales force, the fund is not really a no-load fund; instead, it is a hidden-load fund. A 12b-1 fee can be more onerous than a load, since it is charged every year, whereas a load is charged only when you put new money into your account (or, sometimes, when you reinvest dividends). Annual charges such as the 12b-1 fee and management fees reduce a fund's net asset value. Although some funds have done well with these fees, as a general rule you should try to avoid 12b-1 charges. Remember also that, as the fund grows, the fee increases, since it is based on a percentage of the fund's assets each year.

Exit or redemption fees are levied by some funds when you sell your shares. They range from a flat $5 to 2 percent of the amount that is withdrawn. Sector funds are more likely to charge these fees.

Like an exit fee, a deferred sales charge is a "back-end load" charged when you take money out of the fund. Intended to discourage frequent trading in the fund, it may range as high as 6 percent of assets. It is usually scaled back each year after your initial investment, until it disappears after the sixth year. Try to avoid funds with these fees.

THE PERFORMANCE OF MUTUAL FUNDS

Stock Funds

The performance of various types of stock funds varies widely, depending on the astuteness of the fund's management and performance of the types of stocks in which the fund may concentrate.

Stock mutual funds offer both advantages and potential pitfalls. When they are riding the wave of a strongly rising market, as they did in some recent years, stock funds seem to be most attractive and their performance appears to be virtually effortless. During the periods ending in March 1983 and March 1986, when the S&P 500 increased 44 and 38 percent, respectively, most funds gained. However, during the down period from March 1984 to March 1985, many funds lost money. And during the crash of October 1987, the question wasn't whether they lost, but how much.

More recently many funds have done well—reporting over a 20 percent gain through the first six months of 1991.

Stock prices crest and then fall—individually, in groups, or virtually across the board. How well you do in a stock mutual fund depends in large part on when you buy and sell your shares. If you bought just before the October 1987 crash and sold a month later, you almost certainly lost money. The best strategy with funds is to stagger your buying by dollar-cost averaging (see chapter 17) and to hold on to your funds as long-term investments. Over most 10- and 20-year periods, the stock market has generally outperformed other kinds of investments.

A fund's performance during a down or bear market is as crucial as its performance during extremely good times. Many funds have done better than the S&P average in a down market, a few even appreciating in value as the market falls. Perhaps luck plays an important part. But astute portfolio management probably also plays a role. A fund can take assets out of the stock market during a storm and deploy them into short-term investments, such as Treasury bills and jumbo certificates of deposit. That kind of strategic flexibility allows some mutual funds to perform well during hard times.

Performance under adverse market conditions should be an important element in your selection process. The October 1987 crash showed many investors just how volatile the market can be.

Bond Funds

Bond funds are generally considered more conservative than stock funds, because bonds usually don't fluctuate in value nearly as much as stocks do, and they usually provide an income no matter what their share price may be.

Bond funds that invest in U.S. Treasury issues are the safest, because there's no chance the bonds will default, nor may they be called early.

You're likely to get a higher interest rate, however, on funds that invest in GNMAs (Ginnie Maes) and other mortgage-backed securities because the bonds themselves usually pay higher rates, since they're based on banks' mortgage lending rates, which are higher than interest paid by any institution.

Corporate bond funds also can pay higher interest rates than money market funds or bank savings accounts. But the value of the fund shares may fluctuate. Usually, the longer the term, or average maturity, of the bonds (more than 10 years is considered long), the more the fluctuation. The fund's prospectus must tell you whether the fund holds long-, medium-, or short-term bonds. Although long-term bond funds pay higher rates to compensate for their greater volatility, medium- and short-term funds provide greater stability.

If you're in the highest tax bracket, you should consider municipal bond funds. Almost consistently, higher returns are paid by bonds with low ratings. The risk of default, of course, is greater with low-rated bonds, but buying them through diversified bond funds rather than directly lessens that risk somewhat. If you're risk-averse, stick with higher-rated bond funds.

Money Market Funds

Money market funds offer lower interest rates than bond funds, but the value of their shares never varies, so they are much less risky. They're very similar, in fact, to the money market accounts offered by banks—except that they usually pay higher rates and they don't have federal insurance (a very minor risk).

The rates money funds pay vary, but not much. According to *Donoghue's Money Fund Report*, the average 12-month yield on 486 taxable general-purpose money funds (as of April 30, 1991) was 7.34 percent, while the top-rated fund for that period paid 8.19 percent.

SELECTING A FUND

The securities market is risky. Unless you are comfortable assuming that risk, invest only in things that are inherently safer than stocks or even bond mutual funds, such as CDs or Treasury bills. You may miss out on a big gain, but you will also miss out on a lot of worry.

Before investing in a mutual fund, do your homework. Look at the recent performance of the fund and records of its performance over the past 5 and 10 years. Such records are available periodically from *Consumer Reports* and regularly from various magazines covering different types of funds.

Look for the funds that have demonstrated not only good long-term performance but also relative freedom from risk during downturns in the market. Give special consideration to those without sales charges, 12b-1 fees, or redemption fees. When you have come up with a list, telephone for the prospectus of each. Read each carefully to unearth any fees that may have been established recently. (Fees change constantly.) Also make sure that the same management that made you choose the fund is still running it. And read through the section on risk factors to be certain you are comfortable with the level of risk involved.

A regular, periodic investment program is preferable to a large lump-sum investment. Using a strategy called dollar-cost averaging (see p. 330), you invest a fixed amount of money each month. You will buy more shares of the fund when the price is low and fewer as the price rises. That averages the price at which you buy shares and allows you to avoid the losses that could occur from unlucky timing. Most funds permit you to make additional investments for much less than the amount required to open an account.

21

Your Home

Aileen Jacobson

Buying a home is the single largest purchase most people ever make. For that reason alone, it is imperative that you learn as much as possible about the subject before beginning house hunting. But the importance of choosing a home goes beyond financial considerations. A home is where you and your family will spend the largest portion of your time. It reflects your tastes and expresses your identity. And to some extent it influences your choices for the future. It is no wonder that buying a home is a complicated, multifaceted, and daunting process. Even so, careful and well-directed groundwork can go far toward making the task manageable and ensuring that it proceeds to a satisfactory conclusion.

The first question you must resolve, even before beginning the process of buying a home, is whether rental or purchase is better for you. Renting has advantages that home ownership lacks, and vice versa.

One of the benefits renters cite is that they have more mobility than homeowners. Renters are not bound to a long-term financial investment. Some renters are not even bound by a lease. Most do not have to worry excessively about property values declining in their area.

But to millions of Americans, these advantages of long-term renting pale when compared to those of owning their homes. In addition to the obvious emotional benefits—such as the realization of a dream, and the greater security of ownership—there are many pragmatic financial benefits to ownership.

For one thing, over the long haul, the median price of existing, single-family homes in the United States has tended to rise each year. Throughout the 1970s, the annual increase hovered around 10%—running higher some years. In the 1980s, home prices increased at between 2 percent and 6 percent each year nation-wide and far more than that in some regions. The median price of an existing single-family home in the northeast more than doubled between 1982, when it was $63,500, and 1990, when it was $141,200.

However, the housing market is not without risks—especially short-term. An average home in the northeast actually declined in value by about 2 percent between 1989 and 1990 to $141,200. In some parts of the northeast, including New Jersey and Connecticut, buyers could simply not be found during that period for any reasonable price.

A very significant benefit of buying is that if you buy a home with a mortgage (see chapter 3), you are building assets for retirement. In effect, the principal payments on the mortgage are a form of compulsory savings—and you get the additional benefit of living inside your "savings account." Moreover, your property taxes and the interest on your mortgage payments are deductible.

There are other advantages to owning a home. If you realize a capital gain when you sell your principal residence, you may defer taxes on it, provided you invest in a new residence within two years. And after you reach the age of 55, you may be exempt from taxes on up to $125,000 in capital gains realized from selling your principal residence, even if you do not reinvest the proceeds (see p. 170).

Once you resolve the question of whether to buy or rent, purchasing a home involves six steps: (1) determining how much you can afford; (2) deciding what type of housing to buy (single-family home, condominium, or cooperative); (3) finding the right location and structure; (4) making an offer; (5) arranging the best way to pay for it; and (6) settling or closing the purchase. We'll look at each of these steps in turn, and then examine issues that arise once you own a home—protecting your investment, refinancing, and selling your home.

DETERMINING HOW MUCH YOU CAN AFFORD

For most families, monthly home costs should not exceed one to one-and-a-half week's take-home pay. High-income families tend to spend a smaller percentage of their income on housing than do lower-income families.

Many real estate experts suggest that a middle-income family can safely afford to pay 35 percent of its gross annual income for housing. This figure includes utilities, heating, insurance, taxes, maintenance, repairs, and mortgage payments. (The figure cited used to be 22 percent, but inflation and the increasing cost of housing have pushed it up over recent years.)

Banks use two formulas to determine the limit of the mortgage that they will grant, based on guidelines established by the Federal National Mortgage Association, FNMA (see chapter 3). First, your monthly debt obligation on the house—principal and interest payments, real estate taxes, maintenance charges (for condominiums and cooperatives), and insurance—may not exceed 28 percent of your total gross monthly income. Second, if you have other outstanding debts, including installment loans and revolving credit cards, those debts plus the housing obligations may not add up to more than 36 percent of your gross monthly income.

Most banks will allow you to use a greater portion of your monthly income if you make a larger down payment. The 28 percent rule is based on a down payment of 10 percent. If you put down 20 percent, many banks will raise the 28 percent figure to 32 percent, according to the National Association of Realtors. If you put less than 20 percent down, the 28 percent/36 percent guideline will still apply, but most banks will insist that you have "private mortgage insurance" at an additional cost of about .25 percent interest. Usually, you have to pay the extra quarter percent only until you have paid off enough principal so that your equity in the house reaches 20 percent. (It is not uncommon for the bank to "forget" that you have crossed the 20 percent threshold, so you should keep track of your equity percentage.)

If your loan is guaranteed or insured through a government agency, then you do not need private insurance. Veterans who qualify for Veterans Administration loans, for example, may buy a home with no down payment, but there usually are maximum limits on the amount of the mortgage.

It is a good idea to calculate the size of loan you can carry long before you start looking for a home so that you can set savings and income goals and get an idea of how much time it will take before you can own your first home or move to a more expensive one.

Calculate your monthly gross income by dividing your annual gross income by 12. Multiply that number by .36 to arrive at 36 percent of gross monthly income. That is the amount you can spend on your monthly mortgage payments, property taxes, homeowner's insurance, and repayment of outstanding credit debts or installment loans. Subtract your estimated monthly property taxes and homeowner's insurance and your monthly debt payments. What remains is the maximum monthly mortgage payment you can afford.

To determine how sizable a loan you can take out at current interest rates, given the amount you are capable of paying each month, you will need to consult a loan payment handbook, available at most bookstores. It will provide you with monthly mortgage payment amounts for different loan terms, amounts, and interest rates. Changes in interest rates affect affordability. If interest rates climb, the loan you can afford will be smaller if you're paying the same amount each month.

In addition to the down payment, you must also pay closing costs on the loan. Usually these amount to between 3.5 percent and 5 percent of the mortgage (but check with a few local banks to see what their charges are). You should also set aside some money to cover moving expenses, essential household items, and other potential costs, particularly if the house you buy has not been well maintained.

The amount that people spend on their home is based on many factors, including their assets, their savings, and their anticipated income over the ensuing several years. If you are certain that your income will rise, it is possible to incur higher housing costs, provided the lender allows it.

DECIDING WHAT KIND OF HOME TO BUY

Whether you buy a house or a condominium or cooperative will depend partly on what is available in your area and what fits in with your lifestyle.

Single-Family Houses

Most home buyers choose single-family houses, mainly because there are more houses available and houses usually offer more space, freedom, and flexibility than co-ops or condos. Moreover, although co-ops and condos often appreciate in value, houses generally have more potential for capital appreciation, especially if the owner makes improvements.

Cooperatives and Condominiums

Most condos and co-ops are apartment buildings, garden apartments, or attached townhouses. They require much less maintenance, since someone else takes care of such matters as overall building repairs and mowing the lawn, if there is one. Many offer swimming pools or other amenities. On the other hand, they also tend to carry more restrictions, commonly not allowing pets, children, or certain kinds of structural changes to your own apartment.

A condominium is a residence in which you are the sole owner of the specific living space that you occupy—and joint owner, along with other owners in the building, of the land and "common areas." You hold title to the unit or apartment that you paid for and own, and you share proportional interest or ownership in such common areas as the lobby, corridors, parking lots, swimming pools, and elevators of the building or townhouse. Each owner contributes a proportionate monthly maintenance fee, which may cover heating and air-conditioning, groundskeeping, mortgage payments, taxes, building improvements, and insurance.

When a condominium is built, the developer eventually passes ownership to an owners' association, usually after a specific number of units in the building have been sold or after a specified amount of time has passed. From then on, the owners' association, through an elected board of directors, operates and controls the condominium. Condominium owners realize virtually the same tax benefits as do single-family homeowners.

The financial structure of a cooperative is considerably different from that of a condominium or single-family dwelling. Each co-op participant owns shares of stock in the cooperative, which is a corporation. And the corporation holds title to the co-op's land, buildings, and other facilities. When you "buy" a specific apartment, you are actually buying shares in the co-op, and you become a shareholder of stock in proportion to the dollar value of that particular space. The value is usually assessed according to the size and location of the apartment in proportion to the value of the entire co-op. You receive a proprietary lease that gives you certain rights to use the common areas as well as your own apartment.

Instead of taking out a mortgage loan, as you would to purchase a house or condominium, you would obtain special co-op financing, which consists of a secured loan that uses the co-op shares as collateral.

Where cooperatives are common, such as in New York and Miami and throughout the Northeast, it is not difficult to find financing, although there may be fewer options than with conventional mortgage financing. Some New York banks, for example, offer co-op owners only adjustable-rate mortgages.

The initial down payment for a cooperative may be far less than the down payment for a condominium. However, the monthly co-op maintenance fee could be twice that for a comparable condominium, because the co-op payment covers the mortgage payments, taxes, and insurance on the entire co-op, not just the common areas.

If you own a co-op apartment, you are allowed to deduct from your income taxes the proportionate share of the monthly payment that covers mortgage interest payments and property taxes. If another owner is delinquent on his or her payment, or if all the units are not sold, the remaining owners are responsible for the added expense.

One of the attractions of co-ops and condos is that they frequently provide amenities that would be prohibitively expensive to install in a single-family home. Swimming pools, tennis courts, game rooms, and appealing landscaping are not uncommon. If something goes wrong with any of these facilities, it is not a single owner's sole responsibility to fix it.

On the other hand, co-op and condo owners find that monthly maintenance fees often exceed what they thought they would be. When money is due for upkeep of the building, it must be paid; there is no putting off repairs till the finances allow. Nor can a co-op or condo owner enlarge a unit at a later date, as a homeowner can.

Co-op owners can also run into difficulties when it comes time to sell their shares. The co-op board, which is composed of current owners, may reject a potential buyer for any reason other than racial or sex discrimination. The ease with which would-be buyers may be rejected could make reselling a co-op difficult. Sometimes co-op owners encounter inordinately long delays when it comes time to sell.

A condo usually gives you a wider range of choices than a co-op does. As the owner, you usually have sole discretion over buying, selling, and subleasing. Often, if you decide to sell, the cooperative association has the right of first refusal.

When deciding to buy a condominium or cooperative, you must assess your current financial situation and future status, just as you would when purchasing a single-family home. Some guidelines and pitfalls include the following:

- Before signing a contract, ascertain with as much accuracy as possible what the scale of monthly maintenance fees will be one, five, and ten years in the future. Find out whether there are any repairs to be made or whether the co-op or condo board is considering any additions. Be skeptical of initial fees that seem too low; they probably are—as an inducement for you to sign up.
- To avoid costly and unpleasant surprises in the future, scrutinize the rules before you buy.
- If a building is being converted from a rental property to a condominium or cooperative, find out if the conversion seller has provided a sufficiently large reserve for repairs; if not, chances are that your future costs will rise appreciably. If you are a renting tenant confronted with a conversion, you may want to hire an experienced lawyer to advise you concerning your options. The legal fees may save you money in the long run.

- When considering buying a co-op or condominium, hire an attorney to decipher the papers if necessary. Make sure you understand the lease arrangement on recreation facilities. If the developer were to retain ownership of the swimming pool, for instance, and lease it to the owners' association for up to 100 years, such an arrangement could entitle the developer to raise monthly charges for use of the pool at his or her discretion.
- When buying a co-op, ascertain whether or not you are allowed to sublet. If you encounter long delays in getting the co-op board's approval of a buyer when you later sell, you may need to sublet your co-op apartment while the resale terms are being finalized.
- When purchasing either a condominium or a cooperative, pay careful attention to current and projected costs. Are they likely to rise inordinately over the next several years? Examine the minutes of previous board meetings to determine what problems were emphasized. Interview other owners who already live in the complex. Ask the board to let you or an engineer of your choice review the engineer's report on the building, and try to arrange to have the apartment space you wish to purchase inspected by a qualified home inspector. Try to find out if the occupants have had a history of displeasure with the developer. If there has been turmoil in the past, how do things stand now and in the future? Have lawsuits been filed because tenants have had unsatisfactory and dilatory responses?

In short, you should approach this major purchase with care, trying to anticipate any problems that may crop up in the future rather than plunging in because you like the building's decor or its swimming pool. Insufficient investigation in the beginning can lead to unwelcome surprises later.

FINDING THE RIGHT LOCATION AND STRUCTURE

Once you have decided what type of housing to buy, your next step is to begin narrowing down the location and looking at specific buildings. At this point, you will have to decide whether to use a real estate agent or to pore over newspaper advertisements on your own.

If you are looking for a newly built home or plan to custom-build one, chances are you will not need an agent. (An agent may be necessary, however, if you are looking for land on which to build.) Although new houses tend to be more expensive than older ones and usually come with higher property taxes, they are usually better insulated and more energy efficient, and they often carry warranty protection on construction and appliances. The builder can often arrange financing. Before choosing a builder, check his or her reputation with some previous clients. Consult the Better Business Bureau in your area to obtain information about the builder's reputation for performance.

Most people choose to use an agent, and for most it is a good idea. Although agents almost invariably represent the seller, they can be enormously helpful to buyers as well. They can offer expertise on different aspects of real estate, information about listings of properties for sale, and assessments of the neighborhoods in which you may wish to live.

An agent has a license to work for a real estate broker, who in turn has a license to operate a real estate company and to receive a fee for engaging in real estate negotiations. Realtors are brokers who belong to a large nationwide trade organization, the National Association of Realtors. Agents almost always work strictly on commission, which they receive from the seller.

Make sure that an agent you choose has wide experience in selling real estate in general, and, most important, expertise in the particular neighborhoods that you are considering. Do business only with a reputable real estate agency.

It is nearly impossible to overstate the importance of location. Simply put, buy a home in the best location that you can realistically afford. If you must choose between the best home and the best location, it is usually wiser to choose the latter. It is easier to improve a poorly built home in a good neighborhood than it is to improve a neighborhood where property values are depressed.

How do you find a good location? Real estate prices are usually fairly accurate indicators of the desirability of a neighborhood, since they reflect supply and demand. There are personal factors as well. Does the area have good access to your job? If it is on the periphery of a city, or farther out in the suburbs, is there public transportation leading to the city? Is the house served by a highly regarded public school system? Are there other nearby amenities, such as parks, libraries, and adequate shopping facilities?

After choosing the location of your new home and agent or agents to work with, determine the specific features you seek in a house. It is just as important to consider what will attract other people to whom you may eventually sell your home as it is to consider your own current preferences.

Before you start looking at houses, make a list of all the features that you want. Rank them in order of importance to you, in case you consider houses that lack some of these features. Pay attention also to features that you may not want—such as a busy street.

According to a 1988 survey, the most sought-after feature of home buyers was a quality kitchen. Next came an upgraded bathroom, followed by good lighting.

When considering a house, it is important not to look at the selling price alone. Property taxes, which almost always go up but never go down, will add to your carrying costs as years go by. The weather affects your expenses; winter heating bills in New England and summer air-conditioning bills in Houston can add appreciably to your costs. Some people overlook such obvious additional expenses as lawn care, yard maintenance, repairs, and periodic painting. A house in disrepair will require a relatively large outlay of money just to bring it up to minimum standards.

MAKING AN OFFER

When you have settled on a house you want to buy, you will want to make an offer.

Prices are open to negotiation, and you can offer an amount that is well under the asking price. There may be some bargaining involved—or the deal may fall through if you and the seller can't agree on a price. If you're working with a broker, the broker usually relays bids, rather than having you and the seller deal directly. Do not forget that the broker will be receiving a commission from the seller, not from you. The broker isn't working for you, so don't tell the broker how high you're really willing to bid.

Although local customs sometimes differ, the next step, after you've agreed verbally on a price, is to present a binder, or earnest money agreement. This is accompanied by a deposit that the potential buyer pays the seller when making an offer. The binder sets forth a selling price, closing date, and certain contingencies that may arise. One common contingency is that the sale be subject to a structural inspection of the property by a professional.

The binder secures the buyer's right to purchase the house, if the parties can agree to a contract within a specified number of days. The amount of money deposited with a binder agreement can range from a few hundred dollars to thousands. It is held in escrow by the seller's attorney and is returnable if the deal falls through or the offer is rejected. Ask the agent not to deposit the money, so that you can get your deposit back quickly if you decide not to buy the home.

If you are dealing directly with the seller, give the deposit to your attorney as your fiduciary representative. Make sure that the binding agreement states clearly and unequivocally that the purchase is subject to a mutually agreeable contract. This allows you sufficient time to negotiate the final details. Remember that a binder *is* a contract, and both parties are bound to its terms.

The exact terms of the binder vary. Sometimes the binder is not specified until the parties have agreed verbally on a final price. In other cases, after the binder is spelled out, negotiation continues. Some attorneys believe that binders are unnecessary, and that you should go directly to a formal, full contract. A binder can be considered a legal contract so do not present one idly.

Price is not the only important variable during final negotiations before signing a contract. If you are able to keep the closing date flexible, for example, the seller may lower the price if he or she is in a hurry to sell or, alternatively, hasn't found a new home yet and wants to delay. Also, if you are able to pay cash or already have a tentative attractive loan commitment from a financial institution, you are usually in a better bargaining position; the seller will not have to be concerned that the agreement will be delayed or will fall through because of your inability to arrange a satisfactory mortgage.

The Home Inspection

Always have your prospective home inspected by an expert before buying it. It is up to the buyer to select the inspector and pay for the inspection. Check carefully with friends or other people in the community for names of qualified inspectors, and do not forgo getting your independent evaluation even if the seller has already had the property inspected. Many inspectors charge a flat fee, but some calculate it as a percentage of the selling price.

Inspectors do not "pass" or "fail" a house, and they do not recommend whether or not you should buy it. Instead, they give you detailed information and a thorough explanation, both positive and negative, about what they have found. A good, complete inspection involves checking the house from top to bottom. The crucial systems of the house—electrical, heating, and plumbing, for example—are carefully scrutinized.

Make every effort to accompany the inspector on his or her rounds so that you may see firsthand what is being done and ask your own questions after hearing the inspector's comments. If the inspector refuses to allow this or balks, hire another one. Do not hire someone who is not a full-time, professional inspector, and steer clear of inspectors who also provide a service to repair whatever needs fixing—obviously, you want to avoid such a conflict of interest.

Your home inspector should be licensed in a building-related profession, such as architecture or engineering, and have several years of on-the-job experience. As always, check references. If you can't get a trustworthy recommendation, contact the American Society of Home Inspectors (ASHI), the major trade association for inspectors, at 1735 N. Lynn Street, Suite 950, Arlington, Virginia 22209-2022. Tel. 703-524-2000. Its members must meet stringent educational and experience requirements and subscribe to a code of ethics.

According to ASHI, the most common problem that home inspectors find is water penetration, which usually seeps into the basement through the walls or through the roof. Plumbing deficiencies are also common. Water damage can be disguised superficially by one or two coats of paint applied over the trouble spot, so be on the lookout for fresh paint that is sporadically placed. If you notice mildew, make sure you and your inspector are completely satisfied that it is not symptomatic of a more serious condition. Freshly painted floors and baseboards, too, should be examined with at least a modicum of suspicion.

If your inspector finds that certain aspects of the property are not up to par, you may demand that the seller remedy the situation before you make your final commitment to buy the house. Or you may buy the house in its current condition at a reduced price, and make the corrections yourself. Be prepared to refuse to buy the house if your inspector discovers major structural defects—unless, of course, you opt to live with the shortcomings for a while as a trade-off for a significant price reduction.

Going to Contract

Do not sign a sales contract until you have completed the inspection and are certain you want to buy a particular house (unless the contract has a contingency clause allowing for the inspection and your right to back out if it isn't up to par). The contract you sign will be binding. You will need a knowledgeable attorney to help you draw up a contract that contains clauses to protect you. A sales agent may tell you that all contracts are the same, and it is true that certain basic points are spelled out in almost all contracts, but yours should be tailored to your needs and desires.

At least five points usually should be included in contracts:

1. The seller must agree to provide title to the house free and clear of all liens and encumbrances, unless you agree to some in advance of the contract. You and the seller negotiate payment for the title search.
2. Your deposit must be refunded, and the sale canceled, if you are unable, within a clearly stated time period, to secure a mortgage of the type (amount, rate, and/or length of term) that is set forth in the agreement. From the buyer's point of view, this time period should be fairly long, from 90 to 120 days, in case there is a problem getting approval of the mortgage.
3. A certificate should be provided at settlement time, or at closing, stating unequivocally that the house is free of termites and termite damage. Usually the seller must hire the service guaranteeing that the house is termite free. Make sure that any pest-control service engaged by the seller is reputable. False statements are not uncommon. Check with the local Better Business Bureau.

4. State, in writing, how all charges—such as taxes, water and sewer costs, premiums of existing transferable insurance policies, utility bills, interest on mortgages, and rent (if there are tenants)—will be divided at settlement time.

5. All contracts should include the sale price, method of payment, and exact date on which the buyer is to take possession. List the specific items, such as appliances, fixtures, blinds, and other house contents, that are to be sold with the house.

These basic provisions should be augmented by any clauses that you and your attorney deem necessary. Do not hesitate to include items that may initially appear too specific or petty. Putting it in writing avoids misunderstandings in the future.

FINANCING THE PURCHASE

Down Payment and Mortgage

Arranging the financing is, of course, a sine qua non of buying a home. Whether you are buying a first home or already own one, you'll have to deal with two issues: down payment and mortgage. If you are buying your first home, you must have saved a sufficient amount to serve as a down payment and you'll need to shop around for the most favorable mortgage terms. If you already own a home and are buying a more expensive or larger one, you should make exact calculations concerning your equity (that is, the difference between the price you receive when selling your current residence and the amount remaining on your mortgage). When you sell your home, your equity (less the real estate commissions and other costs related to the sale) can be used toward covering the down payment and closing costs on your new house.

If you qualify for a Veterans Administration loan or for certain special loan programs available to low-income people, you may not have to produce a down payment. But examine your alternatives carefully; banks sometimes charge higher interest for such loans than they do on others. For further information, contact the Department of Veterans Affairs, 810 Vermont Avenue, NW, Washington, D.C. 20420, Attention: Robert Jones, Department of Veteran Benefits, or your local VA office, for its pamphlet, *VA-Guaranteed Home Loans for Veterans.*

When buying a home for the first time, many people turn to relatives for assistance with the down payment. One survey found that the first-time homeowner in America received an average of 20 percent of the down payment from a relative, friend, or close acquaintance. The danger here is the significant emotional burden that accepting relatively large amounts of money carries and the damage to family relations it often causes.

The other major part of the finance package associated with buying a home is the mortgage. (The details relating to mortgages are discussed in chapter 3.) Here, remember that it is very important to shop around for an institution that will offer you the best combination of rates and terms. If you think you have a good chance of getting what you want from more than one financial institution, apply at the one where you have received reliable and pleasant service in the past. If you conclude, based on the financial estimates and guidelines outlined earlier in this chapter, that your chances are borderline, you should not file more than one mortgage application at a time. All banks use the same credit information and each application is recorded on your credit report. A past rejection may prejudice a bank against you. In addition, applying for a mortgage is not cheap, with application fees ranging from $75 to $250; you can spend quite a sum of money and still be turned down.

Under the Truth in Lending Act, the mortgage lender is required to tell you such information as the annual percentage rate, or APR, of the loan you are seeking; the exact schedule of payments; and any late-payment charges. You are also entitled to know whether the loan is assumable and whether there is a prepayment penalty if you decide to pay off the balance of the loan early. Check with your lawyer or other expert adviser to make sure that you fully understand your rights as delineated in the Truth in Lending Act. Check all computations carefully. Computers and banks do make mistakes, especially if erroneous information is supplied initially.

As if buying a home were not stressful enough, banks can add to your anxiety by not revealing to you the exact interest rate that you will be paying on your loan until the closing or settlement date.

The rate will be based on prevailing interest rates at the time of closing—whatever they may be. The bank may offer a cap, but doesn't have to. Some lenders will allow you to lock in a rate at any time between their approval of your mortgage and the final closing. But that privilege usually costs you an extra point, or 1 percent of your loan. Over the life of the average loan, a one-point charge up front is equivalent to adding .25 percent to the overall price. It is therefore advisable for you to lock in a guaranteed rate only if you are reasonably sure that interest rates will rise by more than .25 percent between the time your loan is approved and your closing date. During a period of falling interest rates, it is not wise to enter into such a binding agreement.

Mortgage Sources

There are many possible sources for obtaining a mortgage. The principal choices are as follows:

Banks and Savings Institutions These are the most commonly used sources. They are also usually the most conservative, requiring you to meet stringent rules concerning down payments and overall financial solvency.

Mortgage Bankers They borrow money directly from a bank, lend it to consumers, and then resell the loan to an investor. Borrowers continue to make payments to the mortgage company, which turns over the money to the investor after deducting a service fee. While you may pay extra middleman fees, the loan you obtain through a mortgage bank may fit your needs better than any offered by banks; mortgage bankers are often more flexible, and their rates and fees may be competitive with, or even better than, those of banks.

However advantageous a mortgage from this source may seem, a word of caution is in order. In some states, mortgage bankers do not have as solid a reputation as do bankers. State banking departments have had complaints about mortgage bankers charging much higher rates at closing than a buyer anticipated, adding charges that were not fully disclosed, and excessively delaying final approval of a mortgage. State banking commissions can inform you of the reputation of a mortgage banker in your area. Also check with the state and local consumer affairs departments and the Better Business Bureau.

Mortgage Brokers As the term implies, mortgage brokers will try to find a loan for you from a less traditional source or from a lender in another community. Generally, you will not be required to pay them a fee until they find you a loan. However, you may be asked to pay an application fee in order to cover the costs of a credit check on you and a home appraisal. But that fee would also be charged by a bank or mortgage firm if you applied directly for a loan.

In some cases, the mortgage brokers' fees are paid by the lender, in exchange for the brokers' processing the loan. Mortgage brokers, given their numerous contacts, can sometimes arrange better terms for you than you could get by dealing directly with the lending institution.

Credit Unions If you belong to a credit union, it may offer a better arrangement for you than your local bank or other alternatives (see chapter 5).

Government Agencies If your state has a housing finance agency, it may raise money periodically through bond sales that offer below-market-rate financing for low- or moderate-income people. The U.S. Department of Housing and Urban Development (HUD) sometimes offers limited amounts of money through its Section 235 program for low-income people. The Farmers Home Administration also offers limited numbers of loans through its Section 502 program for low- and moderate-income families in rural areas.

THE CLOSING

You haven't really bought a house until you have finished a process known as the closing or settlement, when the title is transferred from the seller to the buyer. At the closing, you finally sign the mortgage and pay the settlement costs. Any other money due the seller or buyer is handed over at this time.

In most regions of the country, the closing is conducted at a meeting among buyers, sellers, their attorneys, the bank's agent, and a real estate agent. In a few areas, it is done instead by an escrow agent, who may be the lender, a real estate agent, or an attorney. In that case, you will have deposited the necessary documents and funds with the escrow agent in advance.

At the settlement, you will be expected to present a certified check or checks covering all the settlement costs and any remaining down payment. Personal checks are seldom accepted, because the amount of money is so large.

Federal regulations call for the lender to send you a "good faith estimate" within three days after you have applied for a loan. This estimate states what your settlement costs are likely to be. The law also requires that the lender send you a copy of the HUD guide *Settlement Costs*, but since lenders sometimes neglect to do so, you should obtain a copy from a real estate office or a HUD regional branch.

Settlement charges usually include the points that the lender plans to add to your loan; the cost of title insurance (which protects the lender if the title is not free and clear); the lender's attorney fees; and fees for termite inspection, a survey of property boundaries, and an escrow account to pay property and transfer taxes. You will also be required to cover document, filing, and notary fees, as well as homeowner's insurance premiums.

On the day before the closing, you are entitled to examine the Uniform Settlement Statement, which itemizes the services and fees that will be charged to you. Usually, the settlement agent— the bank or lender—has this form. Of course, you must know who the settlement agent is and where to contact him or her.

As in every vital economic and legal matter, you should be certain that you fully understand every document that you sign, and you should not hesitate to ask questions of your attorney or others involved in this process. It is possible to negotiate some items up to the last minute.

Avoid the temptation to leave everything to your representatives, as some people do. Such a course is not wise, especially in a transaction involving thousands, often hundreds of thousands, of dollars.

Common charges at settlement include the following:

Mortgage application fee. If this is charged, it is generally not refundable. It may range from $100 to several hundred dollars, depending on the lender and on what kinds of charges are included in the application fee.

Appraisal fee. This covers the cost of having a qualified person tell the bank what the house is worth. If the appraisal figure is less than the amount you have agreed to pay for the house, the bank may not give you the full mortgage you want. If that figure is correct, however, it is better to find out now that you are overpaying. Otherwise, you may end up selling later at a loss. The appraisal is supposed to contain information about how the price was reached, and about comparable home sales in the same neighborhood. If you are the buyer, ask to see a copy. Question it if you think it is wrong. Expect to pay $150 to $300 for an appraisal. Sometimes the seller may pay the fee. Sometimes it is included in the application fee.

Bank attorney fees. You are usually expected to pay the lender's attorney, although your contract may say that the seller will share this cost with the buyer. The fee can range from $75 to $600 or $700.

Credit report fee. The lender generally charges you for looking up your credit rating. This is a minimal fee, around $30 or $40 (although it costs the lender less). Sometimes it, too, is nonrefundable or is included in the application fee. You have a right to see your own credit report at no charge if you are turned down for a loan because of it, but you must obtain it from the agency that was used. (The lender must provide the name of the agency.)

Origination fee. This is an amount charged by the company handling the mortgage application for processing the loan. Generally expressed in terms of percentage points, it is usually 1 percent of the loan amount. Some lenders may use it to disguise points, the one-time charges that may be added on to boost the rate of return on the loan.

Points. These are one-time advance interest charges, percentages of the loan amount, paid to the lender at closing. You may pay, for example, one, two, or three points. A lender must disclose to you the annual percentage rate (APR) of the loan, with the points added onto the stated rate.

Broker's commission. The seller usually pays the real estate broker's commission at the closing or settlement. Typically, the commission is 5 to 7 percent of the selling price of the house.

Lender's inspection fee. This covers the charges for inspecting a home, usually a newly constructed one, by an employee of the lender or an outside agency.

Mortgage insurance application fee. This is a fee for processing the application for private mortgage insurance, often required if your down payment is less than 20 percent.

Private mortgage insurance. If such insurance is required, you will have to pay an initial premium at the closing. The amount will depend on the size of the mortgage, but could range from $800 to $2,500.

Assumption fee. This fee, charged only when the buyer assumes the mortgage held by the seller, is for processing the papers.

Interest. You will probably have to pay the interest on the loan that will accrue between the closing date and the beginning of the next interest period, usually the first day of the next month.

Hazard insurance premium. The first premium for this insurance—which protects you and the lender against loss due to fire or most other natural disasters and may be part of your homeowner's policy—is often due at closing. Even though the bank may require the insurance and act as the conduit for paying the premiums, you should shop around yourself for the best price.

Escrow accounts. These are reserves that the lender requires for paying such items as homeowner's insurance, hazard insurance, and property taxes.

Title charges. These include fees for a title search and for title insurance. A title search firm is paid to research the title and make sure it is free of liens, unpaid mortgages, judgments, or other impediments to clear ownership of the property. Title insurance places the burden of proof on the title insurance company, so that the lender or homeowner does not suffer if the company is in error. Usually, the bank requires that you pay for title insurance covering only the lender. (The cost depends on the size of the mortgage and could range from $500 to $1,000.) Owner's coverage, also known as fee title insurance, must be purchased separately. In some areas, the seller pays for the owner's coverage. It usually costs about half the lender's fee and provides added protection to the homeowner. We recommend that you buy it even if the seller does not pay for it.

Document preparation. If such a heading appears on an itemized statement, ask what it covers. It may cover services you've already paid for elsewhere, so you may be able to eliminate it.

Once you and the seller have signed all the documents and you've handed over the checks, the home is yours. When the closing is over, however, your life as a homeowner is just beginning.

PROTECTING YOUR INVESTMENT

When you buy a home, you are investing a substantial sum of money. As with any investment, it is important to protect your assets and to take reasonable measures to help them grow. With a home, this means paying close attention to maintenance and record-keeping, making improvements, and being aware of the potential advantages of refinancing.

Maintenance

A basic rule of home ownership is that it is better to do preventive maintenance than it is to correct a problem after it has become relatively severe.

Watch for potential problems before they occur. Check the basement, foundation walls, roof, and other areas periodically for signs of water damage. Make sure that your gutters stay clean, and cut back or cut down trees that pose a threat to your house. Check the caulking and weather stripping around your windows at least once a year. Make sure that your smoke alarms remain in working order and that electrical wiring, including lamp cords and extension cords, is in good condition. Plumbing must also be kept in good repair.

Know where all emergency equipment is located in your home: electrical panel boxes for circuit breakers or fuses, the main shutoff electrical breaker and main shutoff water valve, and the emergency switch for the heating and air-conditioning systems.

Know where and how you would leave the house swiftly in case of fire or other life-threatening situations. If you have children, make sure they know about safety exits and can get out without your help.

Make sure that you receive from the previous owner or the builder all warranties, guarantees, and instruction manuals that pertain to appliances and other mechanisms in your house. Keep them all in a place where you can readily find them, along with bills and a list of the names and telephone numbers of reliable repair people who have been to the house before or have been recommended.

ASHI offers a useful checklist for home maintenance called "Maintaining Your Home." (Write to ASHI at 1735 N. Lynn Street,

Suite 950, Arlington, Virginia 22209-2022, and enclose $1 and a self-addressed envelope. Ask for other relevant publications they might have.)

Remodeling

Before undertaking a remodeling project, consider what certain improvements will mean to you financially in the future. The National Association of Realtors maintains that, as a general rule, the amount you spend on remodeling added to the current market value of your home should not exceed the value of the highest-valued homes in your neighborhood by more than 20 percent. In other words, do not improve your home so much that when you decide to sell it, it will be overpriced for your neighborhood. On the other hand, there are many improvements you can make—both small and large—that will increase not only your pleasure and comfort but also the resale value of your home, sometimes out of proportion to their expense.

Relatively few homeowners have the ability or the time to undertake major remodeling projects themselves; most must rely on "professional" contractors. It's safe to say that no single endeavor concerning your home has more potential for turning into a horror story than does hiring a contractor. While there are, of course, many reputable contractors throughout the country, there are also thousands of fly-by-night operations that disappear immediately after receiving your first payment for their home-improvement services. The home-improvement field spawns many who call themselves contractors without the requisite skills, business acumen, or simple honesty.

When hiring a contractor, it is imperative that you talk to other people to find out not only how well a job will be done, but also—perhaps just as important—whether the contractor will show up regularly and see the project through to completion. Contractors, especially the smaller ones, often undertake many jobs simultaneously and see no problem with leaving yours uncompleted to begin another one (usually bigger), never to return. Unscrupulous contractors will cut corners—substituting inferior materials, skipping items that the plans call for, or simply doing a terrible overall job.

Make sure you have a clear and detailed idea of what you want to do in your remodeling project. In any sizable job—say, one that will cost more than $10,000—consider hiring an architect to draw the specific plans, and pay him or her extra money to come to the job site regularly for inspection.

By all means, solicit bids from at least three contractors. If you have hired an architect, he or she should know of trustworthy contractors in your area. If you do not know any architects, call or write the American Institute of Architects (1735 New York Avenue NW, Washington, D.C. 20006. Tel. 202-626-7300). At a minimum, the contractor must be licensed and bonded.

Whether or not you hire an architect, you must have a written contract with your contractor. The contract should be thorough and detailed, expressing what the architect (if you use one) has shown in his or her explicitly drawn plans. For larger jobs, your attorney should review the contract. The contract should include a detailed list of all materials to be used, with their exact measurements, the duration of the project, and precise figures on cost.

Build in a schedule for paying the contractor. Each pay period should be based explicitly on the contractor's having completed, to your satisfaction (and that of the architect, if you are using one), a specific portion of the job. Do not let the contractor substitute one portion of the job for another or sway you with plaintive pleas concerning advances of money because he or she will be unable to proceed to the next step without money to buy supplies.

Do not pay the contractor more than 15 percent of the total dollar amount of the project on signing the contract. And under no circumstances should less than 20 to 25 percent of the total payments remain due at the end of the project. Nothing "guarantees" that the contractor will return to finish the job more than holding back a significant portion of the money. If you keep only a small portion for final payment, many contractors, even more honest ones, will simply move on to the next job, forfeiting the relatively small percentage still owed to them. Finding someone else to finish the job is not an easy task.

Keep records on payments you made to remodel or expand your home, because they will help determine the tax you may owe when you sell your home (see chapter 10). The costs of all capital improvements (but not routine repairs or maintenance) can be added to the purchase price of your home to arrive at your "basis."

The basis is subtracted from the selling price to determine your capital gain.

Short of remodeling, there are many improvements you can make to enhance the value of your home before selling it. An interior face-lift is invaluable. Paint or wallpaper the walls, sand the floors if that has not been done recently, refinish surfaces, polish wood. Make sure the kitchen and bathroom(s) are in excellent shape—often a major selling point—and that the interior and exterior look attractive enough for you to want to buy it.

The American Institute of Real Estate Appraisers has found that wallpapering, painting, and carpeting are generally the best investments you can make to increase the resale value of your home. For every $100 you spend on these improvements, the price of your home will go up by about $90. Painting the outside generates a 60 percent return—or 1,000 percent, if you do the work yourself. Other useful improvements include remodeling the kitchen (73 percent), adding central air-conditioning (72 percent), adding a garage (57 percent), converting an attic (55 percent), and adding a room (53 percent).

Refinancing Your Home

Refinancing is something to consider if interest rates drop substantially from what they were when you obtained your mortgage. If five years ago you obtained a mortgage at an interest rate of 12 percent, and now the prevailing rate is 8 or 9 percent, you could refinance your house—obtain a loan to pay off the outstanding balance of your original mortgage and get another mortgage at a more favorable interest rate. It is generally not worthwhile to refinance if there is only a small disparity between the current interest rate on your mortgage and the rate prevailing in your community. As a rule, the gap should be at least two percentage points before it is advisable to refinance your home. Even then, the expenses you incur may exceed your two-point savings. If you plan to spend a long time at your current address, it becomes more appealing to refinance, because the fees will be spread over a longer time period and the savings from the interest rate differential will last longer.

When you refinance, you normally have to pay closing costs

again, because you are applying for a new mortgage. These costs can sometimes be reduced if you are refinancing with the same financial institution that holds your original mortgage (see chapter 3).

The same bank may also waive certain fees, such as an appraisal fee. And if your original mortgage imposes a prepayment penalty, which is typically from 1 to 5 percent of the unpaid principal balance, it may also be waived if you refinance with the same lender.

Some lenders allow you to negotiate interest rates and points. Generally, if you intend to stay in your home for at least four or five years, you are better off paying the points and getting the lower interest rate. For tax purposes, even if you pay the points yourself rather than borrowing an additional sum in your loan to cover them, you must deduct them over the entire term of the loan. That is, if you pay $3,000 in points for a 30-year loan, you can deduct only $100 a year. By contrast, with a first-time mortgage, you may deduct the points entirely the first year if you paid for them out of your own pocket.

One way to arrive at a rough estimate is this: First, add up all the up-front costs of refinancing, including appraisal fees and points. Then subtract the projected monthly payment under a new loan from your monthly payments with the present loan. Divide that result into the refinancing costs, and you will have an idea of how many months it will take you to recoup the costs of the loan and start coming out ahead.

For example, if up-front costs for refinancing add up to $2,000, and the difference in monthly payments is $50, it will take you 40 months, or three and one-third years, to begin coming out ahead. (This method does not take into account the impact on your taxes or the amount you could have earned on the $2,000 if you had invested it.)

When refinancing, you may want to switch from a 30-year to a 15-year mortgage. You can thus save an appreciable amount in interest payments, and since you are receiving a lower rate on your new mortgage, your monthly payments may change very little, if at all. With the new lower tax rates in effect, the deduction for interest payments is worth less than it was, so you may want to pay off your loan sooner.

SELLING YOUR HOME

The Role of an Agent

While it is possible to sell a home on your own, the task is usually made easier by employing a real estate agent.

An agent advertises your home in appropriate markets, shows it to prospective buyers, screens buyers, and handles the details of the sale.

The first task of an agent is to help determine a realistic selling price for your home. (Some, particularly in cities where property is expensive, may offer out of the blue to appraise your home free of charge, even before you put it on the market. While it does not hurt to accept such an offer, be aware that it is often followed by an attempt to coax you into putting your home up for sale.) When appraising your home, the agent can suggest ways to improve its appearance before it goes on the market.

Once your house is for sale, an agent arranges to show it to prospective buyers at a time convenient for you—usually during the day on Saturday or Sunday. You will not be directly involved and need not be present. The agent should be able to answer all questions about the property.

The agent almost always works for the seller, and thus will not divulge any information you have provided that could work against you when negotiations begin, such as your deadline for selling. By law, however, your agent cannot withhold any information pertaining to defects in your home without incurring legal liability if problems develop.

A good agent, when interviewing serious prospects for buying your property, should be able to ascertain whether or not they have sufficient financial resources to buy the house without the danger of falling into serious financial difficulties in the future. Choose a broker who is well versed in the financial facets of a real estate transaction and knows about current mortgage rates and area financial institutions.

Once you have chosen a real estate agent, follow his or her efforts to sell your house. While respecting your agent's expertise in representing you, do not leave everything up to him or her. Pay attention at all times. And if you do not understand something as well as you would like, ask as many questions as you deem necessary. If you do not get satisfactory answers, choose another agent. Considering that a broker who sells a $100,000 house (not an unusually large sum today) stands to make an average commission of $5,000 to $7,000, you have the right to expect a completely satisfactory performance level.

On residential transactions, the typical commission amounts to 5 to 7 percent of the price for which the property is sold. The commission increases, usually to 10 percent, for the sale of land. By law, commissions are negotiable; they usually reflect the market conditions in a given area at a specific time.

Several types of arrangements can be made between a seller and a real estate agent. The most common one gives the agent an *exclusive* right to sell. In this situation, you the seller agree to pay the commission to the agent who lists the house, regardless of whether he or she or someone else actually sells the property. It's a good idea to modify the agreement to state that no commission is owed if you make the sale yourself. The advantage of the exclusive listing arrangement is that the agent may work harder.

An *open listing* allows the owner to list the property with more than one broker simultaneously. Only the agent who makes the sale receives the commission. If the owner sells the property directly, no commission is due. An advantage here is that more people may be working on selling your property.

Another widely used arrangement is the *multiple listing*. In a particular community, agents participating in a local listing service share information. The agent with whom you sign such a contract agrees to disseminate details about your home, such as its appearance, condition, size, features, and asking price. Often, a book including photographs is sent to the participating agents, who may show it to clients. The agents also learn how large the commission will be and how it will be split between the listing agent (the one you signed with) and the selling agent (the one who actually sells your house). You pay only the commission you agreed to in your contract. You may specify that the listing agent always be present when the house is shown, but customarily that doesn't happen; your house may even be shown by agents unfamiliar with it. You also may need to coordinate showing times. On the other hand, your house receives very wide exposure with this kind of arrangement.

Listing agreements of any sort are customarily in effect for 30 to 120 days (even 180 days in a slow market)—the period varies. The agreement also usually says that if, within 30 days after the agreement expires, the homeowner sells the property to a person who learned of the house through the listing, the agent is still entitled to receive a commission.

No matter what sort of arrangement you make with a broker, you should obtain a written brokerage agreement and have your attorney review it. It should include a clause stating that the commission is due when and if the title passes to the new owner. This protects you if you change your mind about accepting a contract from a specific buyer, or decide to take your home off the market.

Everything in the brokerage agreement is open to negotiation, including its length of term and the commission. Check the different types of agents. More and more frequently, there are new variations. Some charge a flat fee; others offer discounts. Such flat-fee or discount brokers may not provide as many services. Most often, they require that you show the home yourself to prospective buyers. However, usually they will run ads for you and help to negotiate contracts. They may even list you with the local multiple listing service, although you probably would have to pay an additional commission if your house were then sold by an outside agent. To determine whether to use a discount broker, weigh the cost against the type of service provided, and consider whether you think the discounter will bring in as many potential buyers as a more conventional broker. The longer your home is on the market, the less attractive it becomes for potential buyers who are aware that it has gone unsold for a while.

Selling It Yourself

If you choose to sell your house yourself, you'll have to compensate for the missing expertise a broker usually supplies in assessing market value, considering financial options, and screening potential buyers. The county clerk's office usually has a listing of recent home sales in any neighborhood, which can bring you up to date on the true market value of your house. Even better, have a professional appraisal made. Expect people to offer less than they would if you had an agent, because they know that you will save money by not paying a commission.

Advertise your home through newspaper ads, brochures, and bulletin board signs. In some areas, homeowners' service agencies or consultants will help you, for a fee, with some of the technical aspects, such as screening prospective buyers, arranging appointments, and negotiating a contract. Inform yourself about the options concerning financing, because the potential buyer will want to know. If an offer is acceptable, ask your lawyer to draw up a binder, and then a contract. Obtain some concrete evidence that the buyer in fact can afford to buy your house. You may ask for a copy of a federal tax return or W-2 form. Ask the buyer to fill out a financial statement, which you can get from a bank or mortgage lender.

Whether you use a broker or sell your home yourself, you will incur costs. These include appraisal fees, the cost of a termite inspection, and legal fees. You may also owe capital-gains tax unless you reinvest your profits in a new house within two years.

If you buy a new house before getting paid for your old one, you may need a bridge loan, which provides the funds for the down payment and other costs before you sell the old one. It is secured by your old home in the form of a second mortgage or equity loan. If you think you will need such a loan, shop for one while you are arranging a new mortgage. Try to get one with no points or origination fees; and take out a loan that will charge interest only as long as the loan lasts. Avoid charges for a fixed period of time, such as six months, regardless of whether you have already paid back the principal.

RENTING

About 35 percent of Americans prefer not to buy a home, or cannot afford one, and rent instead. Renting is not as complicated as buying, but there are important considerations nonetheless.

- Your monthly costs—including rent, utilities, parking, and insurance—generally should not exceed 35 percent of your monthly take-home pay.
- When comparing rents charged for different apartments, make sure that you know what each covers. Many people overlook this basic advice, only to be surprised by unexpected

charges for utilities, electricity, or maintenance, for instance. Make sure these details are spelled out clearly in your lease.

· In most areas of the country, it usually is not difficult to rent an apartment without an agent. Major newspapers have a wide selection of listings. Ask friends about which neighborhoods you should consider, especially if you are new to the city or town. Be prepared to spend a great deal of time looking at different apartments. There is no other way to ascertain what is best for you.

· If you can, check with current tenants of a building under consideration about frequency and amount of rent increases. (Be aware, too, of any state or local laws that may limit rent increases.) Is the building noisy at certain times, especially late at night and on the weekends? Does the landlord make necessary repairs promptly? Is the building well maintained? Is security adequate?

· You probably will be required to put up a security deposit of one or two months' rent. Ask whether the amount can be put in an interest-bearing account. Some areas require this; check the local laws. Make sure the lease states clearly under what circumstances you would not get the deposit back. Some landlords arbitrarily try to withhold the deposit when you move. If the apartment is damaged, or an appliance does not work, insist on getting everything repaired before you move in. If that is not done, make sure that the deficiencies are specifically spelled out in the lease. Otherwise, you may be held accountable later.

· All leases are negotiable. Bargain to include clauses you desire, such as length of the lease or types of alterations you want. The lease should state when the rent is due, to whom it is to be paid, under what conditions it may be increased, and the conditions for renewal of the lease.

· Never agree to verbal promises. For example, if you expect your apartment to be painted periodically, or certain services to be provided by the landlord, spell them out specifically in the lease.

· Scrutinize the lease and make sure you understand it completely. It is a formal contract, and if you do not understand it, consult an attorney. Note any restrictions; children and pets are often not allowed. Try to include a clause allowing you to sublet, and a provision allowing you to terminate your lease prematurely—for example, if you are suddenly transferred to a new job in a different community.

· Even though you are not a homeowner, you should get insurance to cover your personal property and liability in case someone should be injured in your apartment (see chapter 14).

22

Other Real Estate

Aileen Jacobson

As we saw in chapter 21, owning your own home can be a wise investment. But real estate affords other opportunities for significant financial benefits besides those found in your primary residence. In this chapter we'll take a look at these other types of real estate investments—from second homes to raw land, from REITs, RELPs, REMICs, and unit trusts to real estate CDs—and examine the financial and tax considerations of each.

With the Tax Reform Act of 1986, the days of investing in real estate primarily for its tax benefits ended; the long-term capital-gains tax is higher, the advantages of owning rental properties are fewer, the old tax shelters are gone. But real estate can still be a sound investment, and many deductions remain available. The potential for generating income and resale profits with the right investments is also good.

THE SECOND HOME

Many people share the dream of owning a second home. To some, a second home promises a hideaway for weekends and vacations, perhaps paying for itself through occasional rental. To others, it suggests an attractive investment, one that could reap a steady rental income and generate a profit when resold eventually.

In general, the financial benefits of owning a second home today are not what they were before the 1986 Tax Reform Act eliminated or reduced many of the tax deductions second-home owners were allowed. Buying a second property is not the most secure way to invest money; other investments offer greater liquidity, less risk, and more certainty of an adequate return. Buying a second home for personal use is a different matter, since the benefits are not measured strictly in financial terms.

Only a small percentage of American families own a second home—less than 4 percent, as compared with 5 percent several years ago, according to the National Association of Home Builders. Second homes have been bleak investments in recent years, dropping dramatically in price in many parts of the country. Although a rebound is likely with economic recovery, vacation homes will probably lag behind the primary market.

Your purpose in buying a second home, and the use to which you put it, influences almost everything about that purchase—particularly the criteria you use to evaluate the location and property and the tax benefits and liabilities you incur. Most people who purchase second homes do so primarily for personal use, whether or not they rent out the house some of the time. We'll examine that situation first. Then we'll look at owning a second home for investment purposes.

Second Home for Personal Use

While buying a second home may not, at first glance, seem as important as acquiring your primary residence, it is clearly a major purchase, requiring a commensurate amount of preparation and attention. Just as with the purchase of your primary residence, you'll want to do a great deal of research before buying it and enlist the expertise of a real estate attorney.

To begin with, you should be very certain about what you want, and why. If you are looking primarily for a vacation retreat or an eventual retirement home for yourself, then your choice of home may be very different from what you'd want if you were looking for an investment. When you buy a vacation home for personal use, such considerations as accessible parks and other public facilities, the quality of neighborhood schools, convenient public transportation and shopping, and easy access to major arteries will not be as critical as they would be if the house were intended to be your primary residence or if you were buying it as an investment to rent out to others as a primary residence. With vacation properties, the lakefront house that's less accessible from the main road can still be acceptable; the mountain chalet won't be ruled out just because it's a trek to the nearest shopping center.

Just as important as clarifying your goals is carefully calculating what you can afford to pay. As with a primary residence, you will use some of your own funds to make the down payment. Usually, the major proportion of funds will come from a financial institution that will lend you the money at a certain interest rate. As a rule of thumb, mortgage lenders conclude that you can afford to spend up to 28 percent of your gross monthly income on a home. Most will not make loans in amounts that require you to spend more than that figure in monthly payments of principal and interest.

Be careful about borrowing on your own home to finance the down payment—usually 10 to 20 percent of the purchase price—on the second home. This is a common practice, but usually not a wise one. You're better off if you can make a down payment from savings. If you insist on borrowing for the down payment, be very sure that you can carry the extra debt—which will include the mortgage on your second home, too.

It is better to take out a mortgage on a second home than to obtain a home equity loan, particularly if you plan to rent it out, because the mortgage interest is deductible against the rental income.

Some final points to note before signing the contract for the purchase of a second home:

- If the builder is offering financing, compare the terms with those at other lending institutions. Consult a lawyer and/or accountant before you complete the purchase arrangements.
- Use the same care in selecting a second home as you would in choosing a first one. Hire an engineer or building inspector to inspect the property.
- When buying a vacation home, do not sign the contract at the vacation site. Everything might look better in that setting.

Take home the contract and any available prospectus. Peruse them; let your attorney and accountant read them carefully. Unless one of you discovers a serious flaw in the contract, the property, or the financing, chances are you will still buy the property; but by taking the time to scrutinize the proposal in familiar surroundings, you'll be more secure about your decision.

· Check the laws of your state and the state in which you are buying. Some states require a "cooling-off period" of several days during which you are allowed to reconsider your decision before the contract becomes final. It gives you time to analyze fully what you are doing.

· Be cautious. Don't get in over your head. If you can't afford a luxury lifestyle, stick with a smaller property and affordable carrying costs.

Part-Time Rental of Your Second Home If you buy a second home for personal use and decide to rent it out part of the time, don't lose sight of the fact that the primary goal of owning it is to enjoy it yourself. Many real estate professionals believe that you should not treat your vacation home as an investment. They don't mean that you shouldn't try to rent it out and gain income from it, if you can; they mean that you shouldn't count on that income.

When you rent out your second home, whether the IRS considers it your personal residence or a rental business will determine the kind and extent of tax deductions allowable. We'll examine the tax implications in detail later, but be aware that the IRS considers your second home a residence if you use it more than 14 days a year, or 10 percent of the time that it is rented out, whichever is greater (see p. 462).

As you might expect, you must keep very detailed records regarding the rental of a second home; this is imperative, not only for reporting the direct income on your tax return but also for documenting the allowable deductions.

If you rent out your second home fewer than 14 days a year, you need not report income received for the rental. Most owners of second homes who rent at all, however, rent them out for more than two weeks (the average being 90 to 100 days per year), so they become part-time landlords, subject to both the headaches and the tax benefits that are the lot of landlords.

Many Americans of modest means are able to buy a relatively inexpensive second home and realize a steady rental income when they are not using it personally. Being a landlord, however, can impose considerable strain on your time and energy.

As a landlord, you are responsible for finding and selecting new tenants, setting rules (such as whether or not pets are allowed), maintaining the property, making repairs, collecting rents (and evicting those who don't pay or are otherwise not adhering to your rules), paying the mortgage and taxes, and seeing to it that local zoning laws are obeyed.

If you do all the tasks yourself, you must plan on devoting many hours to them. You will be on call virtually around the clock to respond to emergencies. Hiring a management company or other representative to handle the collection of rent and general maintenance of the property will cost you money but save you time. If you are handy—and if your second home is close to your main residence—you can save money by performing some of the maintenance chores yourself.

Obviously, it is easier on you as a landlord if your second home is relatively close to where you live. You can respond promptly if a tenant calls you at an inopportune time with an emergency. Periodic inspection of the property and tracking of property values and zoning regulations are easier if you live nearby.

If you must buy your dream house 100 miles from where you live, you will probably have to hire a property manager to oversee it if you rent it out.

Second Home as a Business Investment

How does a second residence fare as a business investment? Can you receive enough income from year-round rental of a vacation home or residential house, co-op, or condo to make the investment risk and the responsibilities of being an absentee landlord worthwhile?

Buying a home strictly as an investment can provide a steady stream of income and some tax breaks, even though these are limited now. In addition, it can provide capital gains if the house appreciates in value. As an added bonus, rather than a primary goal, some properties might also afford a place for you to vacation rent-free a couple of weeks a year.

Be forewarned that no matter how much expert advice you receive or homework you do, investing in real estate is never a sure thing; it is neither liquid nor guaranteed to increase in resale value. If you should find your property dropping in price, you cannot pick up the telephone and instruct a broker to sell it as you can with stocks, since there may not be a buyer who wants to take the property off your hands, especially at the price you are asking.

While all the investment caveats about second homes purchased primarily for personal use apply to properties purchased for investment purposes, you must be even more careful with investment homes that the property you buy has the greatest chance of appreciating in value and of being rented at profitable rates.

Before you buy an investment home, calculate whether your rental income will cover the annual upkeep, interest, and tax expenses. Check with local real estate agents or read newspaper advertisements to see what kinds of rents are being charged for comparable houses or apartments. If you can make your property more attractive than average in an upscale neighborhood, you may be able to charge a bit more. But use an average when figuring out the economics of such a purchase, and do not exceed by an appreciable amount the rents charged for comparable homes in the same or similar neighborhoods.

At the very least, the rent you charge should cover all costs of maintenance, mortgage payments, future repairs, and property, state, and federal taxes. Even if it barely covers those expenses, you'll probably still come out ahead, because if the property is defined as a business, you may be able to take a tax deduction for depreciation and other expenses. And if you've made a wise buying selection, you'll have a capital gain when you sell. No matter what your income, you'll be able to deduct all the expenses up to the amount that you receive for the rent.

Beyond those financial matters, there are many practical questions to consider.

If you buy a long way from home—say, a Wisconsin lakeside retreat when you live in New York the rest of the year—you will have to hire an agent to oversee its rental. It's usually very difficult to find a property manager for just a single home. Sometimes the real estate agent who sold you the property may take care of it for a limited time. But be sure to do the decision-making yourself. If you find a property manager, you may have to pay 10 percent or more of the rental income to him or her.

Some jurisdictions, especially cities, have stringent rules regarding the number of unrelated people allowed to rent and live in the same apartment. The same often holds true for rental houses in vacation communities as well. Be sure to check.

If you decide that you would like to divide a house into many separate apartments, find out whether the zoning laws allow it, and determine the maximum number of units allowed. Do not exceed that limit, or you may incur costly fines or have your building shut down.

Resort Homes Buying coveted and popular beachfront property virtually assures steady appreciation in value and income from renters who seek vacations at exclusive locations. But such properties are the exceptions, and far too costly for the average wage earner. As a rule, vacation houses in resort areas are not dependable as predictable, long-term investments for income production.

Vacation rental homes in resort areas are usually questionable investments because they are dependent on such changeable and unpredictable elements as the price of gasoline, the fashionability of an area, and the general economy, which dictates what sort of vacations people take. Net rental income tends to be lower with these vacation rentals because they usually are some distance from your home, so you probably will need to depend on a rental agent or property manager at the site. As a result, your control and your profits won't be as great as they would be with a property closer to home.

As a rule, except for certain anomalies in the choicest locations, vacation properties do not appreciate as fast as primary homes located in choice communities. First, the resort property is usually already being sold at a premium. Second, people are fickle, and they may decide for various reasons that they no longer want to rent or own property where yours is located. If gasoline prices escalate substantially, for instance, people may be less willing to drive to a vacation spot 100 miles from the city in which they live. And if the vacation area becomes unpopular, or if the economy goes a bit sour and people start canceling vacations, resort homes are likely to be hit harder than residential ones.

Plan for the future. Try to avoid buying in an area that is especially "hot" at a specific time but that may not remain that way for a long time. Time-sharing arrangements in trendy resort areas offered appealing investment opportunities only a few years ago, but in many parts of the country such rental units sit vacant during most of the year. Moreover, they can be virtually impossible to sell, if that's your choice.

The more seasons in which your home appeals to renters, the better you will fare financially. Your best buy is property that can be rented at least three seasons each year.

As with vacation homes purchased for personal use, don't sign anything at the vacation site. Insist on taking home a contract and prospectus to review with your attorney or financial adviser. Reconsider the idea yourself when you are no longer dazzled by the scenery and the sales pitch.

Apartments and Small Apartment Buildings Yet another sort of second-home investment is the purchase of a condominium or co-op apartment already occupied by a renting tenant. Usually, a developer has bought a building and made it into a cooperative in which some tenants own and others rent their apartments; and usually the tenants who rent would prefer to buy but cannot afford to do so. In such cases, outside investors may have the opportunity to buy an apartment or several apartments in the building from the developer. The tenants in those apartments, as long as they meet the requirements of their leases, are allowed to remain until they choose to leave.

Anyone contemplating such an investment should be very careful about several points.

There may be local laws or legal arrangements that put a ceiling on how much tenants' rents can be raised. As owner of the apartment (or of shares in the co-op building), you are responsible for paying the monthly maintenance fee in addition to your mortgage. If that fee increases rapidly and precipitously, and you are precluded from raising your tenant's rent as your maintenance fee rises, you may find yourself paying out more than you're collecting in rent. You are responsible for any difference.

Make sure you know the rental laws governing the jurisdiction where the property is located. This rudimentary advice is often overlooked by landlords, and many landlords who do pay attention to local laws fail to keep abreast of changes in them.

You can assume that if you buy one of these apartments as a

potential investment, chances are others will do so. If most of the buyers are, like you, absentee landlords, you may find that you have invested in a building owned primarily by people with little firsthand knowledge about the condition and maintenance of the property. Even payment of the monthly maintenance fees may be no guarantee that maintenance is up to par. If the apartment and the entire building deteriorate, you will have to pay more money to correct these conditions, and when the time comes for you to sell your shares, your property will be worth less because of its run-down condition, or it will not have appreciated as much as it would have if proper maintenance had been carried out.

For all these reasons, it is best to avoid investing in these types of arrangements, especially in locations that you cannot conveniently reach in order to inspect the property carefully and talk with local experts who know the reputation of the people involved in the transaction.

Going into Partnership You might consider going into partnership with other family members or friends to share the expenses and time commitment of owning an investment home. By pooling your resources, you may be able to buy more than one house or apartment, which spreads your risk but, of course, requires a greater amount of total capital. Be careful. Do not overextend yourself, even in conjunction with other investors.

Never rely on verbal agreements with friends and relatives. The best intentions among close friends or relatives can turn into disasters. Have a formal, written contract drawn up by an attorney. In particular, spell out what happens if one partner wants to sell but another does not. Are your other partners offered first refusal if you want to sell out? Do all partners have to agree before a share can be purchased by a new partner? You may want to designate one person, who has the time and inclination, to be in charge of the property or properties, perhaps for some extra compensation.

These arrangements can be profitable—and less risky financially than going it alone—if you have the right group of people. But beware: you could lose your friends or damage family relationships if things don't work out. One potential source of disagreement is how much money to put into maintaining the property. You should all discuss your philosophy and goals about rental property beforehand.

Get-Rich-Quick Schemes and Government Sales Do not fall for "get-rich-quick" schemes that you see advertised on television or in the newspaper or promoted in seminars and some books. Beware of deals that promise to buy property low and sell it soon at a much higher price. Also, do not be fooled by deals offering an opportunity to buy property with no money down, or those offering bargains at foreclosure sales or government auctions. In most foreclosure sales, the properties are in such disrepair that the repairs required to restore them cost more than you'll ever earn back on your investment.

Government sales often involve property that is in poor condition, and the prices are not bargains. At sales involving tax liens, the original owner often has the opportunity to buy back his or her home simply by paying off the taxes. That puts you at risk of losing your investment. These types of sales attract professional speculators, who spend a lot of time and effort pursuing such opportunities. Since they may have access to more capital, they can be formidable competition.

Some observers had hoped that a great many low-income individuals would be able to purchase inexpensive housing which wound up in government hands as a result of the savings and loan crisis. However, although a program to facilitate this effort was set up in 1989, very few homes have actually made it to the intended recipients. Bureaucratic inefficiencies and difficulties getting financing have made the program a disaster in the eyes of many.

Undeveloped Land and Custom Building

Buying undeveloped land is risky and may be a poor investment. You may have to pay relatively high carrying costs; you cannot rent the land, but you are still required to pay the taxes; and, even if you eventually want to use the land for business purposes, you cannot depreciate it. The purchase ties up your money without giving you any current returns.

If you buy land from a developer with visions of a thriving community and large profits coming your way in a few years, be aware that this is an area that has garnered numerous consumer complaints in many states. Check with consumer agencies and with the state's attorney general's office to see whether there have been any problems with the developer or the property. Make sure that any land you contemplate buying, whether undeveloped or about to be developed, is buildable. It must be accessible to major area roads and water and have essential services such as sewer, electric, or gas hookups available. The soil must have proper drainage and not be excessively rocky. Hire an architect, engineer, or builder (unconnected to the firm selling you the land) to look at the land before you buy it. For candid assessments of the resale value of your property, you might check with rental and real estate offices not involved in your specific transaction. Countless potential delays can arise before raw land becomes an active development; throughout the process, you will have to continue making tax, loan interest, and possibly other upkeep payments.

It's best to buy in an area where all the homes are completed and the necessary amenities have been installed. You are taking a big risk if you buy after looking only at a model. Do not fall for a promise of a swimming pool on the property, for example, if you see only a hole in the ground where one is supposed to be dug. Some developers are gamblers, depending on other deals being completed before finishing yours. If those projects are not finished, or they do not bring the expected return, your project might never be completed.

If you are contemplating buying raw land on which you plan to build, an understanding of local zoning laws is crucial. If a jurisdiction does not allow you to build on your parcel of land, your return on investment may not measure up to your expectations. Check with local zoning agencies to make sure that you may build on the land without undue restrictions, and keep abreast of environmental and zoning restrictions; they may change before you build.

Once a home is completed, you can take out a mortgage loan, or the construction loan can be changed to a mortgage loan, which can be deducted if it is on your second home. Usually you cannot take out a mortgage on a house that is not yet built.

For more information, get in touch with the National Association of Home Builders, 15th and M Streets NW, Washington, D.C. 20005. Tel. 800-368-5242, ext. 463. A general guide to building your own home, *Dreams to Beams,* is available for $9.95 (with a $3 handling fee). Ask whether other booklets or pamphlets are available.

Tax Considerations on Second Homes

The Tax Reform Act of 1986 and subsequent tax acts drastically altered the tax benefits of owning real estate. We will discuss the major changes, but keep in mind before you engage in a specific real estate transaction that you should consult an attorney and an accountant to address the issues relevant to your situation.

Mortgage Payment Deduction   On the plus side, the law still allows you to deduct your interest payments on a mortgage for a second home if you use it rather than rent it out as a business investment, as long as the total mortgage interest on both your first and second homes does not exceed $1.1 million. Of course, that tax benefit means less now that the top tax rate is 31 percent.

The $1.1 million limitation applies to loans obtained after October 13, 1987, and used to purchase, construct, or substantially improve a principal or secondary residence. You may also deduct up to $100,000 on loans using your home as collateral (such as home equity loans) in which the proceeds are used for these or other purposes.

Capital Gains   On the minus side, when you sell your second home, you don't receive the same tax benefits that are allowed when you sell your principal residence. You can't defer the tax on the capital gains by reinvesting in another home, as you can with the home in which you live. That is, you must pay taxes on your profit. Most homeowners avoid taxes on profits from their principal residences by reinvesting the money in their next home.

Nor with a second home can you ordinarily use the once-in-a-lifetime exclusion for those who are 55 or older. This exclusion permits you to avoid paying taxes on up to $125,000 in profits from the sale of a home, without having to reinvest the sum (or $62,500 for married taxpayers filing separately). But the home must have been your principal residence for three of the previous five years, and you can only use this tax-free maneuver once in your life. Some older homeowners may wish to consider moving to a vacation home for three years before selling it, if it has appreciated far more than their principal residence.

Only one spouse has to meet the age requirement. The $125,000 profit must be realized on a single sale; that is, if you realize $70,000 in profit in selling your house, you are not allowed to sell another house and gain $55,000 in profit tax-free. If your profit is greater than $125,000, you must pay taxes only on that portion that exceeds $125,000.

Most people don't have that choice when it comes time to sell a second home, and they must pay tax on the capital gains. Unfortunately, as of this writing, that is taxed at the same rate as your regular income except if you're in the 31 percent bracket.

Because you will have to pay tax on a gain, it is extremely important that you keep accurate records of all the expenditures you make on capital improvements to your second home. Capital improvements include adding rooms, putting up a fence, installing new plumbing or wiring, putting on a new roof, or paving your driveway. It doesn't include general repairs or painting, unless they are done as part of an extensive remodeling or restoration. All of these capital improvement costs can be added to the original purchase price to reduce the amount of taxable gain.

Deductions for Repairs If you are using the property only for yourself, the repairs are not deductible. But if you are using your property as a business by renting it out—and you must keep impeccable records to prove that you are—you may deduct the cost of repairs from the rental income you receive. Repairs, along with other expenses of running a rental property—such as costs of advertising for new tenants, legal fees for drawing up contracts or rental agreements, and depreciation—are deductible as losses within certain limits.

Deductions for Losses The tax law now states that losses from "passive" investments—which include most partnerships and all rental real estate, with an exception explained below—can only be used to offset income from "passive" investments and not to offset income from wages and dividends. With tax-sheltered partnerships and some rental real estate, people had been using the losses generated by depreciation and other costs to offset their other income, thus often reducing their overall tax bills to almost nothing.

Congress did, however, make one exception to the passive rules for what is sometimes called a "mom and pop" rental operation. The exception is for the person of relatively modest means who owns a second home (which may include a home in a vacation area, a home in one's own neighborhood that is used to provide extra income for the family, or other rental real estate) and is "actively" involved in managing the property. (The taxpayer must own directly at least a 10 percent interest but need not own the home outright. However, limited partners don't qualify.) Though neither tax court cases nor regulations have yet firmly established what exactly is meant by "actively" involved, the law does say that you do not have to knock on doors for the rent or repair the leaking roof personally. You should, however, be involved in management decisions, such as approving new tenants, setting rental rates, and approving expenditures for capital improvements or repairs. You should keep receipts and other records that demonstrate your active involvement. Keeping a log or diary would help, too. Pending legislation may further clarify this issue.

The exception is not limitless. First, the amount you may deduct from other income may not exceed $25,000. Second, the exception is only for couples who have less than $100,000 in adjusted gross income. (For a married person filing separately, the income level is $50,000 and the allowable deduction is a maximum $12,500, so there is no advantage in filing separately. To claim any loss, a married person filing separately must live apart from his or her spouse for the entire year.) After that, the allowable loss is phased out at the rate of 50 cents for each dollar that your adjusted gross income exceeds $100,000. That is, if the combined income for you and your spouse is $130,000, you may deduct up to $10,000 in losses against other income (50 percent of $30,000 is $15,000; subtracted from the maximum $25,000, that leaves a deductible loss of $10,000). By the time your adjusted gross income reaches $150,000, the loss allowance phases out completely.

If your income is greater than $150,000, your losses can be used only to offset your rental income from that property or from other passive investments you might own. Likewise, if your income is less than $150,000 and you have more losses than you may deduct, you may use them only that year to offset gains from other passive investments, such as a limited partnership or another rental property. (For instance: if your adjusted gross income is $100,000 and your losses from your rental business are $40,000, you may deduct $25,000 against your ordinary income—wages, dividends, and so on—and the remaining $15,000 only against income from other passive investments, such as limited partnerships.)

You can carry the losses forward to future years and claim any unused portion if you generate passive income from other sources. Any unused losses may be claimed when you sell the house. For instance, if you had accumulated losses of $30,000 over previous years, and you sell the house for $50,000 more than your purchase price plus improvements (less depreciation), you will have to pay taxes on only $20,000 in profit. Of course, you cannot be certain what your eventual sale price will be, so the losses could conceivably exceed any profit realized from selling the house. In such a case, you may deduct the net loss in the year of sale.

In sum, if your combined income is less than $100,000, renting your second home as a business potentially provides you with a nice tax advantage—deductions from your ordinary income. This is true to a lesser extent if your income is up to $150,000. But if your combined income exceeds this latter figure, you reap no tax advantages from renting it out as a business; you may find that owning a second home purely as a business does not make sense unless the rental income clearly exceeds the costs of owning and maintaining the home. In such a case, you may want to use the home often enough to make it qualify as a second personal residence. Then you may be able to deduct all the mortgage interest and property taxes on your personal income tax return. You still would be able to deduct portions of the costs of operating the house against income from rental during part of the year if the rental income exceeds the taxes and interest attributable to your rental use.

A long-standing personal-use rule applied by tax law to determine whether your property is a second personal residence or a business is generally based on the number of days that you reside there. If you use the house more than 14 days a year, or at least 10 percent of the time that it is rented out, whichever is greater, then the house is considered your second personal residence and not a business. That is, if you rent the house out for 200 days, you must use it yourself at least 20 days for it to be considered a personal residence. If you rented it out over the summer season (some 90 days), you'd have to live there yourself at least 14 days for it to be considered a personal residence (14 days being greater than 10 percent of 90 days).

If your property is used primarily as your second residence, you must generally prorate your expenses between rental use and personal use. You must deduct your expenses attributable to rental use in the following order: (1) interest and taxes attributable to rental use; (2) operating expenses; and (3) depreciation. However, you may deduct operating expenses and depreciation only up to the amount by which your rental income exceeds the interest and taxes attributable to rental use, even if your adjusted gross income is less than $100,000.

You may also deduct the taxes and interest attributable to your personal use (assuming the interest is deductible under the new mortgage interest rules). Suppose you rent your residence out for three months of the year and use it one month. In that case, you may deduct three-quarters of your maintenance costs and depreciation, but only to the extent that you have rental profits after deducting taxes and interest attributable to your rental use.

The tax law does retain an attractive exemption: if you rent your vacation home for no more than 14 days a year, you do not have to report the rental income on your federal tax return.

Which way to go—business or personal use—can be decided only by working out the arithmetic, perhaps with the help of an accountant. Your choice may also be determined by how much time you want, or are able, to spend at your vacation home. If its location is remote or you have limited time off from your job, it may not be feasible to use a vacation home more extensively.

If you have more than two homes that you use as personal residences, mortgage interest on the additional homes is considered personal interest, and is treated in the same way as debt resulting from use of your credit cards.

For the most up-to-date information, consult your accountant or tax attorney. Your local IRS office may also be of help with appropriate publications. Public libraries, too, often have copies of IRS publications. Among the IRS's relevant booklets are Publications 527, *Rental Property*, 530, *Tax Information for Owners of Homes, Condominiums, and Cooperative Apartments*, and 936, *Limits on Home Mortgage Interest Deduction.*

LIMITED PARTNERSHIPS (RELPs)

In limited partnerships, investors pool their resources in order to purchase a variety of properties, or sometimes one large one, that they would not ordinarily be able to afford themselves. Partnerships are intended to give a steady rate of return to investors, who must often commit themselves for 10 years.

The overwhelming majority of limited partnerships invest in

real estate (RELPs), although some choose heavy equipment, live-stock, and oil and gas drilling.

A *private* limited partnership may generally be offered only to investors who meet certain income and asset requirements or who are financially sophisticated. It is typically formed to construct or operate a commercial building or buildings. A *public* partnership usually includes many more investors and is registered with the Securities and Exchange Commission, and often with state agencies as well. It is similar to a mutual fund and requires moderate sums of money for investment, often no more than $5,000. Public partnerships typically invest in more projects than do private partnerships. Like private partnerships, they entail a commitment of several years.

Before the 1986 tax revision, limited partnerships and tax shelters were almost synonymous. Nearly all partnerships—except those intended for Individual Retirement Accounts—held appeal because they provided significant tax benefits. They tended to invest in property that offered generous write-offs, in the form of mortgage interest, depreciation, and other costs. Those write-offs could then be taken as deductions against other types of income, such as salary, thus reducing the investor's overall tax bill. Sometimes the deductions were worth far more than the actual dollar amount invested.

Most people who invest in RELPs today do so to produce income rather than to obtain tax deductions. Public partnerships attract far more capital than do private partnerships, partly because private partnerships had historically offered greater tax benefits and thus suffered disproportionately under the revised law. Sales of private partnerships in real estate have declined even more than sales of public partnerships since 1986. The major exception to the overall decline in public real estate partnerships is in those that are unleveraged—that is, those that have no mortgage interest and thus are purely income- or gains-oriented.

RELPs as Tax Shelters

If you currently own a real estate limited partnership that was oriented toward use as a tax shelter, you should consider trying to find an additional passive investment that generates passive income. The losses generated by your shelter can then absorb that income, or balance it out, so that you end up paying no taxes on the extra income from the second partnership.

Publicly traded partnerships can no longer be used to generate passive income, a change made by the Revenue Act of 1987. Income from public partnerships is now generally treated as portfolio income—the same as income from stocks, bonds, and savings accounts. Losses may be used only to offset income generated by the same partnership, although the loss may be carried forward to a year when the same partnership generates income or the interest is sold.

Selling a partnership interest is difficult and may result in a big tax bill. Furthermore, you will probably have to sell your partnership at a discount, perhaps at around 20 percent less than what it is actually worth, because there isn't strong demand for loss producers, and there are middleman fees. Before selling, you should confer with a tax expert. This is a good idea, in fact, for any partner who wants to learn the intricacies of the current tax legislation. Clearly, if you are likely to need the proceeds from a partnership before the partnership is to dissolve, you should be considering more liquid investments.

RELPs as Income Producers

Many limited partnerships, of course, have served not only as tax shelters but also as income producers. Generally, income- and profit-producing partnerships were invested and marketed as IRA-type instruments before the tax law revisions. Now, most partnerships stress their moneymaking possibilities, whether or not they are aimed at retirement accounts.

Partnerships designed to provide income and profit might involve the ownership of shopping centers, apartment buildings, office complexes, or even parking lots that generate steady income. These partnerships usually have small or no mortgages; when they are sold at some prearranged time several years after they were formed, the whole arrangement dissolves, and investors, with luck, get back their original investment with a profit. Sometimes part of the income is "internally sheltered" so that it comes to the investor tax-free. That is, depreciation and other costs are deducted against the income from rents or leases, thus providing income that is at least partly sheltered from taxes.

Despite the seeming allure of these investments, we recommend that you approach them with extreme caution. First, be aware that brokers often receive high commissions or other incentives for selling their firm's own partnership product. Second, you should not have such a risky investment in your retirement portfolio.

As for investing in a partnership outside a retirement fund, you would have to consider it among your riskier investments—more like stock investments than Treasury bills—since you don't know what will happen to the real estate market in an area in which you've invested, or what might happen to the type of real estate in your partnership, if it's concentrated in something like miniwarehouses or parking lots.

A partnership may end up being a very fine investment for those with the know-how to read and evaluate a prospectus carefully, or for those who are knowledgeable and astute about the prospects for real estate in particular parts of the country.

As with any other investment, do your homework before investing in a real estate partnership of any kind. Obviously, you should check on the success rate, as well as the reputation for integrity, of the firm that sells you a share or shares in the partnership. Before choosing a specific partnership, also follow these rules:

- No more than 16 percent of your investment should go into upfront costs, including the usual 8 percent commission that the sales agent receives and the management fees that go to the general partner who oversees the investment.
- Invest only in partnerships that identify in their prospectus the properties that they have purchased and intend to purchase; then, ask an independent adviser to evaluate those properties and the prices that are being asked for them.
- Be sure to read the section of the prospectus called "risk factors," as well as the accountant's notes. Again, it's wise to enlist the aid of your own accountant and/or attorney. Their fees may save you a lot more money in the long run.
- Ask whether your investment adviser has bought into this partnership for himself or herself; if so, ask to see proof of the purchase. This request, of course, may cause a problem, but remember that you are considering investing a great deal of your money, so you want to have as much assurance as possible that everything is being done in good faith.

- The prospectus should state unequivocally that the sponsor will not receive his or her share of the profits upon the sale or refinancing of the properties until all limited partners receive their initial investments plus a stated return.
- Look into investing in real estate limited partnerships that still can offer you deductions or credits; these include low-income housing in rural areas and certified historic buildings. But check very carefully with an expert before investing primarily to receive a deduction. As with all criteria involving investments, this one may not be important enough to determine your final investment decision.

Limited partnerships are not investments for the casual or very conservative investor, but they can be a good addition to an already diversified portfolio.

RECENT VARIATIONS IN REAL ESTATE INVESTMENTS

The last few years have seen the establishment of other types of real estate investments in which people pool their resources and buy shares for as little as $1,000. We'll examine the most important and common types of these.

Master Limited Partnerships (MLPs)

Hybrids between limited partnerships and stock, master limited partnerships are traded in units—often from $10 to $20—on the major stock exchanges or over the counter. They are liquid investments, because you can sell them when you wish. There are no guarantees; since they do trade in the open market, they are subject to the same fluctuations that affect other publicly traded investments, and indeed their fluctuations are often even more pronounced.

With stocks, corporations pay taxes on their profits before distributing dividends, on which investors again pay taxes. With some MLPs, only the investor's distributions are taxed; there is no tax levied on the MLP. Real estate MLPs enjoy the benefits of depreciation, so when you file income tax, your depreciation losses may offset some of the income that you receive from the same MLP. However, the 1987 Act limited the ability of investors to use income from MLPs to absorb losses from other passive activities, as it did with other publicly traded partnerships (see p. 464).

Real Estate Investment Trusts (REITs)

Real estate investment trusts, which you can buy from a stockbroker, are similar to mutual funds. A REIT shareholder benefits from the collective or pooled ownership of properties that produce income, just as mutual fund shareholders benefit from the pooled resources of many other coinvestors. REITs are traded, like stocks, on major exchanges, with their values fluctuating depending on supply and demand and other market forces. Since they are not heavily traded, it could take awhile to find a buyer, as it does with over-the-counter stocks. REITs can offer a good income-producing vehicle because by law they must distribute 95 percent of their earnings to investors each year.

Equity REITs have income-producing properties, while mortgage REITs offer short-term construction loans and permanent mortgages. Hybrid REITs do both, with no more than 75 percent of their assets invested in either category.

When you invest in a REIT, you do not have a say in or knowledge of the way your money is used. The manager of the fund determines what projects the investments are used for, without consulting investors. It is wise, therefore, to conduct a careful check of a REIT management's performance record before investing.

Because they own a wide variety of properties or hold secure mortgages, REITs are safer than many other real estate investments. Nevertheless, they do fluctuate as the real estate market moves up and down. In the 1970s, when real estate investments soured in many depressed areas of the country, REIT returns followed suit. Between 1972 and 1974, the average share price dropped 66 percent. From 1981 to 1984, however, as the real estate market started to boom again, the average annual return reached 20 percent. In April, 1991, the average yield for REITs averaged 9.4 percent.

Perhaps because managers are more cautious with investments

after the fluctuations of 1974 to 1984, REITs today are a safer, less speculative investment than they were several years ago.

Income from REITs, which can be partially or wholly sheltered from taxes because of deductions for mortgage interest and depreciation, is considered portfolio income, similar to dividends. The earnings are *not* "passive income," and thus cannot be used to offset passive losses.

Real Estate Mortgage Investment Conduits (REMICs)

REMICs are entities that issue a series of securities with varying maturities from a pool of existing mortgages. REMICs were created by the 1986 tax law, in part to ensure a larger mortgage pool for homeowners.

REMICs are issued by financial institutions, investment bankers, and mortgage bankers and are given safety ratings (just as bonds are). Their performance, however, can be affected if homeowners pay off their mortgages before maturity. Investors would get their money back earlier than expected.

REMICs are structured differently from other mortgage-backed instruments (see chapters 18 and 20), and they may prove to be more attractive to investors than these other older instruments.

In general, earnings of REMICs are higher than those of U.S. Treasury securities, although their track record is not long enough to warrant any definite conclusions about their performance as investments. Because they are complex instruments, they are more suitable as part of a pooled investment than as an individual purchase by an investor from a broker.

Real Estate Mutual Funds

Real estate mutual funds invest primarily in securities such as REITs and other real estate–related ventures. The general diversity of mutual funds offers advantages to the potential investor. However, because of the skimpy track record of real estate mutual funds, you should check carefully with an expert before investing in one.

Real Estate Unit Trusts

Real estate unit trusts are instruments similar to mutual funds. They are more static, however, than mutual funds: while mutual funds dealing in real estate offer portfolios that change frequently as the manager's opinion of certain investments changes, the unit trusts offer a fixed portfolio of varied real estate–related investments. You must choose whether you prefer the flexibility of the mutual fund or the fixed, known-entity real estate unit trust.

Real Estate Certificates of Deposit

Real estate CDs are offered by some commercial banks and savings institutions. They are backed by federal insurance, and the investments are in real estate instead of the customary money market instruments that back the bank certificates of deposit. Usually they guarantee a specific rate of return, but you retain the possibility of even greater earnings. Often these instruments mature in 10 years and require a minimum investment of $1,000 or $5,000. They offer little liquidity but have proven to be rather safe and predictable investments.

As with any real estate investment, be judicious when investing in real estate CDs. Know in advance what your needs are and whether or not you will need the money before the CD matures.

VI

RETIREMENT PLANNING

23

How to Plan for Your Retirement

Aileen Jacobson

PREPARING THE 30-YEAR PLAN

Planning for retirement is a task few people relish. And no wonder. For many people, the topic is associated with such discomforting possibilities as reduced physical and mental capabilities, infirmity, or boredom without the stimulation of a career. Others, of course, welcome retirement as a time when they can finally relax, travel, or pursue other leisure activities to their heart's content. Even for these people, however, planning is work—and long-term work at that. Potentially unpleasant sacrifices—such as putting away $2,000 or more into a retirement fund instead of spending the money on a vacation—are part of the planning process.

If you are young, you may think that the many years between you and retirement provide an excuse for postponing planning. But, in fact, the earlier you start to save, the easier your retirement planning will be. With increasing longevity—average life expectancy of a 60-year-old now stands at 80.5 years—a person who "retires" at age 60 will likely have another twenty years ahead of him or her. Proper planning can transform that span from a dark and dismal nightmare into a period of financial security and comfort. Indeed, with the aging of the Baby Boom generation, comfortable retirement is already becoming a new American Dream.

Retirement, as we use the term here, is not intended to mean age 65 or even that period when one stops working for a living. We use the term broadly to define the later years of life, when work activities tend to decrease (but do not necessarily end altogether), and when the potential for more leisure activity increases. By federal law, companies can no longer impose mandatory retirement, and many people prefer to continue working beyond age 65, the popularly defined retirement age.

This chapter describes the many factors that go into making a good 30-year plan for retirement, including such elements as the following:

- Calculating the income and expense requirements of your new lifestyle
- Making sure you are adequately covered by health and life insurance
- Learning which pension, Social Security, Medicare, and other benefits are due you
- Building an adequate savings and asset base from which your retirement will be launched
- Managing your assets and investments according to the needs of your stage in life

The above information will be presented broadly in this chapter; additional details that appear in other chapters of this book are cross-referenced.

EARLY PLANNING (AGES 20 TO 50)

Although planning for retirement should begin with your first paycheck, practically speaking, most people do not have the foresight or the inclination to start that early in life. During the early adult years, the focus of attention is largely on career and family. A young adult should never, for example, stick with a job that provides excellent retirement benefits if another employer provides better chances of career advancement and income but a poor retirement package. For most young people, such matters as saving for a house or laying the financial groundwork for a family must take precedence over building a retirement nest egg.

The difference between starting to plan for retirement early in life and starting late can be dramatic. If you start in your twenties, you may only have to save about $1,000 a year to reach your goal of a comfortable retirement. If you start in your forties or fifties, you will have to start putting away enormous sums of money to accumulate an equivalent nest egg—perhaps at some cost to your lifestyle in those years—or else resign yourself to some very meager years in retirement.

There are a number of valuable early planning steps you can take if you are able to do so.

Pension Plans

If your employer offers you a qualified pension plan, you should definitely participate. Often, you have no choice. If you are vested in a plan, when you leave a company you are allowed to take not only the money you contributed (which you may take in any case), but also the money that your employer contributed to the pension, including whatever income those contributions have earned. Whereas many employers previously had to provide vesting only for employees with 10 years of service, as of 1989 they must provide either 100 percent of vested benefits after five years, or else a sliding percentage beginning with 20 percent of vested benefits after three years and ending with 100 percent after seven years.

Although vesting is now faster, pension benefits still tend to depend on an employee's length of service and final salary. Typically, your benefit is determined by multiplying a percentage of your final salary (e.g., 1 percent) by your years of service.

When you are thinking about changing jobs, keep your pension rights in mind and calculate your pension benefits. If only a few weeks or months separate you from becoming vested, it may be worthwhile to postpone taking a new job, if that is possible. Once you leave, you should "roll over" the pension money into an IRA or into your new plan, if that is allowed, to keep the entire sum tax-deferred—and to keep it earmarked for retirement. Substantial penalties for premature withdrawal from a qualified plan make a rollover even more desirable. Don't spend the sum on current expenses. (See p. 507 for more on rollovers.)

Individual Retirement Accounts (IRAs)

Before the 1986 Tax Reform Act, most employed persons could make deductible contributions of up to $2,000 per year ($2,250 for an employee and nonworking spouse) to an IRA. Now, your ability to make deductible contributions may be limited. If you can make deductible contributions, you should. Even if you can't, you may want to consider making nondeductible contributions or exploring other retirement savings options (see chapters 24 and 25). And, as with other retirement funds, it's better to participate a little than not at all. If you can't afford to put away $2,000 a year, it is better to contribute $1,000 or less than to wait to salt away thousands a year at age 50. It's unlikely that you will have enough money then to make up for all the years of lost savings.

With any retirement plans, if you are not naturally a disciplined saver or if you don't have substantial assets, you should use the saving methods described in chapter 7. Make savings a regular outlay from each paycheck, instead of saving only what's left over. With a 401(k) plan, your employer usually takes a set amount out of your paycheck automatically.

Keogh Plans

If you are self-employed, you should set up some form of retirement plan for yourself, preferably a Keogh plan, which allows you to contribute—and deduct from current taxes—up to $30,000 a year (and in some cases even more), or a Simplified Employee Pension (SEP). Keoghs and SEPs are explained in greater detail in chapter 24.

When you are self-employed, you have much more control over your retirement savings than an employee does, since a Keogh is just one account that you and the trustee—not a corporate pension fund—control and manage. If you have a business on the side, as well as your regular job, you may be able to set up a Keogh in addition to your other retirement plans. However, the amount you put in is based on a percentage of your net income, not your gross, so it must be a profitable business for you to have a retirement fund.

Keogh plans are subject to the same comprehensive regulation as other qualified plans.

Cash or Deferred Arrangements

If you are eligible for a 401(k) plan at work, or its cousin in the nonprofit field, the 403(b) (both also known as cash or deferred arrangements or CODAs), you should definitely take part. This is especially true if your company matches your contribution partly or completely.

These plans, which are described in greater detail in chapter 24, allow you (1) to exclude the amount you contribute from your gross income, thus reducing the amount of income on which you must pay current taxes, and (2) to defer taxes on any interest or dividends until the funds are withdrawn, usually after retirement. While the Tax Reform Act of 1986 changed the rules for Individual Retirement Accounts (IRAs), making many people ineligible to deduct the $2,000 maximum annual IRA contribution from their federal income taxes, the 401(k) deduction survived the tax revision process. Now, however, an employee is limited to a maximum 401(k) contribution of $8,475 a year (in 1991), a ceiling that will be adjusted for inflation in subsequent years.

The advantage of investing before-tax money is that if you are in the 28 percent tax bracket, and you contribute $1,000 to such a plan, you are able to save $280 in taxes currently (though you must pay taxes when you withdraw the funds after retirement). Had you invested that money in a way that immediately incurred taxes, you would only have had $720, after taxes, to invest. Thus, you would be starting out with a larger contribution to your nest egg by using the deferred arrangement. (The trade-off is that you can't get the money out before age 59½, except under certain limited circumstances, without paying a penalty.)

Not only is your initial contribution to a nest egg larger when taxes are deferred, but income generated by the investment of the funds is not currently taxable and so goes back into the account; your money will grow faster, since you are not removing part of your profits each year to pay taxes. (This is the same principle that makes IRAs, Keoghs, and SEPs attractive.) If the account holds investments in bonds, bank accounts, or other interest-paying assets, the interest will compound free of current tax; if it is invested in stocks, any dividends it receives can be reinvested intact; and if it includes appreciated assets, such as stocks or fund shares that have grown in value, they can be sold without a tax on the profit (although any losses will not be deductible). In addition, if your employer is matching the funds you contribute dollar for dollar, you will be getting a further and immediate 100 percent return on your money. (At 50 cents on the dollar, you would be getting a 50 percent return, and so forth.) Whatever the percentage, it's hard to beat the return on an employer's contribution of matching funds.

You can participate in these plans even if you can't afford to put in the full amount you are eligible to contribute.

The rules on withdrawing money from a retirement plan are stringent. With a few exceptions, most withdrawals by persons under 59½, including those made when changing jobs, are subject to a 10 percent early withdrawal penalty. If you are under 59½ and withdraw your money, you usually will be subject to regular tax and the penalty tax unless you roll over the withdrawal (p. 507). If you are leaving a company after age 55, however, you may generally withdraw your retirement money without incurring a penalty.

During the years when your priorities are saving for a house or paying for a child's college education, you may not be able to contribute very much to retirement plans. But, if at all possible, you should contribute at least a little each year, since you will probably need to supplement either Social Security or private pensions if you want a comfortable retirement. Saving for retirement on a tax-deferred basis is one very good way. Another alternative is to use a regular high-yield savings plan such as investing in bank CDs or U.S. Treasury securities, or, depending on your tax bracket and investment preference, tax-exempt bonds, bond funds, or money market funds.

If you don't choose a tax-deferred method, you will have more flexibility and easier access to your money, and you may have more investment choices. However, there are drawbacks beyond the tax disadvantages: You are more likely to use those funds from time to time for other reasons, and then you won't have money when you retire.

Investing Strategies

The younger you are, the more aggressive your investments can be, whether or not they are in a tax-sheltered retirement plan. However, you should reserve your most aggressive investments for those outside your retirement accounts. Such investments may include growth stocks, aggressive growth stock mutual funds, or real estate. There are two reasons you may consider taking on more risk with part of your retirement portfolio. First, when you are young, you have many years to recoup a loss should you incur one. Second, and perhaps more important, unless you take some risks, your investments miss the chance to grow significantly. Many safe, conservative investments often provide an annual yield only a little better than the annual inflation rate, and sometimes the returns actually lose ground to inflation. You will never build a sizable retirement fund if the $1,000 invested today is still only worth $1,000 (adjusted for inflation) 40 years from now. That's preservation of capital, but not growth.

As you approach your fifties, you should take fewer risks, simply because you do not want to lose the assets you will need for retirement. Also, if you do take a loss, you will have fewer years to make it up as retirement approaches. Preservation of capital thus becomes more important than ever. To accomplish that, as you grow older, you should gradually shift your portfolio (both inside and outside a tax-deferred plan) into more conservative investments such as government securities; bank certificates of deposit; blue-chip stocks; certain long-term growth, growth and income, and income mutual funds; and income-oriented stocks, which provide high dividends rather than significant capital appreciation. Typically, more conservative investments are held in IRAs and qualified plans. Stocks should usually be held directly, since taxpayers may be able to use capital losses, if any, to offset other income. Moreover, it is possible that tax-law revisions will reinstate some special benefit for capital gains.

SERIOUS PLANNING (AGES 50 TO 60)

For most people, the sixth decade of life marks the beginning of serious retirement planning. By then, usually, you are at your peak earning years and thus have a good understanding of the kinds of assets you are capable of accumulating over the next 10 to 15 years and of the lifestyle to which you can aspire or want to maintain. By then, also, you will likely have paid off all or most of your home. You finally have more funds—and free time—to spend on yourself.

However, there are other factors that can and probably will complicate this simple picture. If your family's childbearing years were finished by the end of your twenties, the youngest child will still be in college. If the first child was put off until your early to mid-thirties—and depending on the size of family you created and the amount of responsibility you believe you should shoulder for your offspring's college costs—the fifties could only be the beginning of an expensive spending period that might involve some erosion of your assets to meet the cash needs.

Another factor, meanwhile, could be your own aging parents. If they were unable to plan their own retirement successfully, or if they are infirm or require a nursing home, you may have to help support them. Alternatively the death of both parents and distribution of their estate may significantly improve your financial picture.

It should therefore be clear that by age 50 you should be taking a total financial account of yourself and those around you who can influence that picture. You will want to review where you have been and where you expect or want to be going. One aim is to assess whether and how you will be able to retire when you wish to do so. You may find that your dream of retiring by age 55, 60, or even 65 is just not feasible if you don't want to retire into poverty. You may need 10, 15, or even 20 more full earning years to establish yourself better. Unfortunately, in these days of corporate volatility, you may find that the 15 or 20 more years of earnings you need may not be available. Your employer may be absorbed or dismantled in a buyout or merger, or streamline itself by moving to a remote location; it may institute mass firings or policies encouraging early retirement. In any of these situations, you may find yourself unemployed and unemployable, or only able to find a much lower-paying job. Early planning is a safeguard against such possibilities.

Many considerations must be taken into account in deciding when, how, and where to retire, including such variables as physical health, family situation, and personal inclinations. It is crucial that both husband and wife make these decisions jointly, particularly since women tend to outlive men by as much as seven years, and they will need to understand all the details of the planning. Below are the major areas to consider, including the crucial financial accounting.

The first thing you will want to determine is your estimated income. Make a list of all the possible sources and research how much you may receive from each. Among the possible sources are the following:

Pension, profit-sharing, and other retirement plans. Check with your employer about the payout options and the estimates of what you would receive if you retired at various age levels.

Social Security. Contact your local Social Security office to learn how much you will be receiving, and how that would decrease if you started taking money out at age 62 instead of age 65. You should do this at least three years before your planned retirement, but you should do so earlier if you will be relying on those payments for a large portion of your retirement income. Call 1-800-234-5772, or call or visit your local Social Security office, to receive Form SSA-7004. Within six weeks after returning it, you should have estimates of retirement benefits—although they will not necessarily be accurate until you are at least 60.

Your assets. Account for all your personal sources of income. These may include income from investments, rental income from property you own, and the proceeds from selling a business or a professional practice when you retire. Don't overlook the value of your life insurance, if you own a whole life or universal life (rather than a term) policy, which you may want to convert to an annuity or cash in. You may not need life insurance coverage anymore, or you may need much less, since its main point is to protect your family in case your earning capacity ends. However, do not leave your spouse unprotected. Discuss your life insurance needs not with your insurance agent but with your attorney when you are drawing up or reviewing your will (see chapter 26) and planning your estate.

You may also want to convert some items such as jewelry and antique furniture into income-producing investments. If you are planning to donate items to charity, consider doing so while you are still employed, when your tax bracket may be higher, thus making a deduction for a charitable contribution worth more. Consult a qualified appraiser before selling or donating goods of substantial value. To claim a charitable deduction of more than $5,000 for an item of personal property (or group of similar items), you must obtain an appraisal.

Table 23-1 will give you an idea of how long your invested assets will last before being depleted. Ideally, you would keep your capital

TABLE 23-1   Number of Years Your Retirement Funds Can Last

This table shows, for example, that if you withdraw 8 percent of your retirement funds each year, and earn 6 percent on them, your funds will be depleted in 23 years.

	Return on Retirement Funds				
Annual Withdrawal Rate	**5%**	**6%**	**7%**	**8%**	**9%**
10%	14	15	17	20	26
9%	16	18	22	28	
8%	20	23	30		
7%	25	33			
6%	36				

Source: Israeloff, Trattner & Co.

or principal intact and draw only on the interest. However, if you are retiring at age 65 and can make your assets last for 25 years, you are very unlikely to outlive them—and you would still be receiving Social Security and pension income, even if you do.

Continued employment, part-time or full-time. As mentioned earlier, many people retire to self-employment; some pursue a new career they never had time for before; others continue in their previous line of work on a part-time consulting basis; a few are able to transform a hobby into a business. For some, this can be a significant source of retirement income.

Others may have to continue working in some capacity simply to make ends meet in retirement. Traditionally, retirement has been viewed as a three-legged stool—supported by Social Security, pensions, and personal assets. Now, because people are living longer, continued employment is fast becoming an essential fourth leg of the stool. That is not all bad, however. Continued employment helps to keep retirees from becoming shut-ins without much social contact, and it provides the challenges and rewards that are often the benefits of work.

If you do plan to continue working, be aware that your Social Security payments will be decreased if you earn more than a certain amount ($9,720 in 1991 for those aged 65 to 69; $7,080 under age 65). When you reach age 70, you can earn all you want without jeopardizing Social Security payments. Until then, however, for every $3 you earn above the limit, you will lose $1 in benefits; at ages 65 to 69, you'll lose $1 for every $2 earned before age 65. By increasing your income, you may also subject part of your remaining Social Security benefits, if any, to tax. (See p. 526.)

The other side of the ledger is expenses. Imagine yourself in retirement. You may want to travel more, which means you will spend more money than you do now for this leisure activity. On the other hand, you may spend less on clothes than you do now. You may be able to cut costs in other ways, too, by moving to a smaller house with lower utility bills, for instance, or by taking advantage of senior citizen discounts. Some other expenses will disappear on their own—commuting costs, for example, and other business-related expenses—while others will appear. The major increased expense most retirees face is medical expenses, which even with Medicare can be enormous.

If you have no clear idea of where your money goes now, keep a diary of every expenditure for a month or two. Then you can make adjustments geared toward retirement. (For more information on budgeting, see chapter 6.)

Remember, some costs that may have been picked up previously by an employer will be yours in retirement—primarily, the cost of health insurance. Some employers continue providing health insurance even after you retire. Others don't. By federal law, you must be offered the option of continued coverage under the company's group insurance. You'll have to pay for this continued coverage, but as a member of the group, you will pay significantly lower premiums than you would as an individual policyholder. Also, if you have an existing health problem, a new policy may not cover medical treatment for that affliction, whereas the continued coverage would protect you against everything the company plan covered when you were still employed. (For more details, see chapter 12.)

Your housing needs may be reduced during retirement, too. If your mortgage isn't paid off by age 50, it may be by the time you retire. You may also want to sell your house, if you own one, and move to a smaller one, a condominium, a mobile home, or a retirement community. If you sell after reaching age 55 and don't reinvest all the profits (thus deferring taxes on the gain), you can take advantage of a once-in-a-lifetime exclusion from your federal income taxes up to $125,000 of the capital gains (see p. 167). If you are widowed or divorced and remarry, and your new spouse has already used the exclusion, you will not be eligible. Thus, both you and your spouse-to-be may be wise to consider selling your homes to use up all $250,000 in exclusions before entering marriage.

You may also want to consider shared housing or renting out part of your home, if zoning laws in your area allow that. (In some cases, those over 55 or over 65 get special exemptions from zoning laws.) If you own a home, you should look into programs that give property tax breaks to the elderly. These vary from location to location. A local senior citizen office, a real estate tax office, your county clerk's office, or the local office for the federal Department of Housing and Urban Development should have details of programs offered in your area.

Life-care communities are another option. With these, you generally pay for a home that the community retains after your death. In exchange, the community promises to care for you until your death, either in your own home or in a nursing home or hospital if that becomes necessary. Some life-care communities require a substantial endowment—$50,000 to $100,000—for you to become a member. However, inherent in any such arrangement is the risk that after you've bought into the community, it could go bankrupt or be otherwise unable to deliver the promised services. Also, if you become dissatisfied with the community or simply wish to move somewhere else, getting out may be complicated, expensive, or impossible. Before entering any life-care community arrangement, have a trusted lawyer or other competent adviser carefully assess the community and its contracts. Then proceed with extreme caution.

You may also want to explore such strategies as a reverse mortgage, an arrangement in which the loan is taken out in monthly installments and paid back by the borrower's estate or when the loan matures (see chapter 3). Another innovative arrangement is a sale/leaseback, also called a life tenancy, in which the owner sells the home and is guaranteed lifetime tenancy, often with an annuity set up to pay the rent. A deferred-payment loan offered by some local governments to low-income persons is yet a third option in which repayment is deferred until the owner dies or the house is sold. But each of these arrangements puts your assets in jeopardy and thus should be avoided except as a last resort. If you do enter into a reverse mortgage arrangement, consult a lawyer and make certain you are protected in the event that you outlive the arrangement.

Finally, when figuring your needs, factor in some estimate for inflation. An accountant, a financial planner, a banker, or some other professional may be able to help you get a realistic reading. If you're doing this calculation on your own, you may want to use an inflation rate of about 5 percent per year, which is slightly higher than the average annual rate for the 25 years from 1960 to 1985.

Once you have two columns of figures—income and expenses— you should have a good idea of where you stand. Now you should assess where you want to go and when. If you're only 50 while doing this estimate, you still have plenty of time to maneuver.

You may find that if things proceed on the present course, you won't be able to retire when you want to—at least not without serious compromise to your lifestyle or excessive risk that you may outlive your assets. To accomplish your goal, then, you may have to make some adjustments. Here are some of the steps you can take:

- Consider starting a business at home while you are still employed. This may be a mail-order, consulting, selling, or crafts business. Entrepreneurship is very risky and bogus get-rich-quick schemes abound, but if you are able to start with minimal capital at a time when you are still earning money elsewhere, you may be able to establish a profitable and fairly reliable trade by the time you retire. You will probably need legal advice as well, and you may have to look into local zoning laws, depending on the kind of business you are contemplating. (See chapter 23.)
- Although most people who have established careers may be reluctant to change at this time, don't rule out a career change or midcourse correction. Such a move, if made with care and wisdom, can pay off handsomely in salary increases and better pension benefits. It can even vastly improve your outlook on work.
- Increase your contributions to retirement plans wherever possible.

- Save more in general to increase your assets. At this age, however, do not consider risky investments as a means of multiplying your income.
- Think about ways you can decrease spending, both now and during retirement. You may want to give up one car, or stop eating at expensive restaurants so often. Set priorities. These are personal decisions, and only you—or you and your spouse—can decide which trade-offs you are willing to make.
- If you didn't consider postretirement work before, consider it now. One increasingly popular solution is for a wife to return to work or continue to work (if she returned later in life) after her husband retires. Often, a woman who was out of the work force during her childbearing years looks forward to the idea of returning to the workplace or to staying in it. Again, this is a personal decision.

Once you have formulated your retirement plans, review them periodically. If more adjustments are necessary, make revisions in your plans. Take advantage of expert help, too. Many employers provide preretirement seminars. Attend them. Your employer's benefits or personnel department is another source of planning help. Ideally, they should be able to explain not only your options but also the tax implications of your choices. Additional help can be sought from an accountant, tax attorney, banker, or qualified financial planner with whom you feel comfortable. Better yet, consult with more than one person to get alternative views and ideas. At the very least, you should ask one professional whom you trust to review all your calculations to make sure you have figured the numbers correctly and that you haven't overlooked better options.

IMPLEMENTING THE PLAN (AGE 60+)

The two most important decisions you must make at retirement usually involve what to do with your pension and what to do about health insurance.

Your pension options may include taking a lump-sum distribution—which means that you withdraw the cash value of your pension all at once and reinvest it on your own—or taking monthly payments, also called an annuity. You may have several choices among annuities, too. One option is to receive a larger amount of money each month for a fixed number of years. The alternative may be to receive a lesser amount that will continue for the rest of your life. You may also be able to opt for an even lower monthly disbursement, but with the guarantee that your spouse will continue to receive payments if he or she survives you.

If you choose an annuity, we recommend that you consider taking the kind that covers your spouse, too, particularly if the spouse is female, because a woman is about three times as likely as a man to outlive a spouse of the same age. Continued pension payment is also important if the spouse is not covered by his or her own pension. Of course, if you have sufficient other assets to ensure a comfortable retirement for your spouse, you should elect the higher monthly disbursements. An earner is no longer allowed to cut out his or her spouse without the spouse's consent. As of 1985, federal law has provided that pensions must cover surviving spouses, unless that right is waived by the spouse.

We also recommend that you study two crucial elements if you are considering an annuity: the number of years covered and the guaranteed payment, rather than just the current payment. Make sure that there is some floor below which total disbursements cannot go, and that it is a reasonable amount. You may also want to consider taking an annuity for your life and buying an equivalent whole life insurance policy to protect your spouse should you die first. The cost of the life insurance policy may be less than the reduction in monthly benefits under the joint and survivor annuity option.

The choice between an annuity and a lump sum presents a more difficult problem, and it should be worked out with the help of an employee-benefits specialist or an accountant. The tax implications must be considered carefully.

If you take a lump sum—that is, the entire cash value of your plan—you can use forward averaging to lighten the tax load.

If you reached age 50 by January 1, 1986, and were already in a qualified (IRS-approved) pension or profit-sharing plan by then, you may opt for either 10-year forward averaging using the 1986 tax rate schedule or 5-year forward averaging using the current tax rate schedule, whichever is lower. Everyone else must use only the 5-year averaging.

Forward averaging, which you may elect only once during your lifetime, means that you are allowed to calculate your income as though it were spread over 5 or 10 years instead of being concentrated into one year. For example, if your lump sum is $100,000, you may handle it as though you were receiving $10,000 a year for 10 years. Although that reduces the tax rate, you still pay the tax in one lump sum, based on special tables. If you have the option of using 5 or 10 years, you must work out the taxes both ways to determine which is better. For people receiving a distribution of less than $473,700, 10-year averaging usually produces a lower tax. Certain taxpayers who accumulate very large qualified benefits may be subject to a 15 percent excise tax. Some taxpayers may have another option. Those who were 50 years old by January 1, 1986, may elect to have the portion of their lump-sum distribution attributable to their pre-1974 participation taxed at a special 20 percent capital gains rate.

The advantage of taking a lump sum is that you have full control over the money immediately for whatever kinds of investments you may want to make.

You can also take the lump sum and roll it over into an IRA within 60 days. If you do that, the funds continue to accumulate earnings that are tax-deferred until you withdraw the money. After age 59½, you may start withdrawing from the IRA without penalty. (And you must begin withdrawing by April 1 following the calendar year in which you reach age 70½; see chapter 24.) However, you lose the ability to use the 5- or 10-year forward averaging when you start to take out the money. You may not elect forward averaging for IRA distributions.

Your decision as to which of these two options to take will depend partly on when you think you will start needing the money. If you need it immediately, you should probably take the lump sum and pay the taxes on it. However, for most people, the rollover into an IRA is more advantageous, because the money can continue to earn interest on a tax-deferred basis, and because the taxes on withdrawals will probably be low if they are spread over many years.

After figuring your after-tax income with an annuity from your company, a taxed lump-sum distribution, and an IRA rollover, you must make some comparisons and weigh your own priorities.

If you are not anxious to do your own investing, you should probably take the annuity offered by your firm. Before you do, however, make sure that your employer is getting the best rate available for you. One way to find out is to compare annuity rates listed in the *Retirement Income Guide,* published by A. M. Best Company, which is available in libraries or costs $53 for an annual subscription (A.M. Best Road, Oldwick, N.J. 08858; tel. 201-439-2200).

The major disadvantage of an annuity, however, is that it provides a fixed income, even though your buying power may be eroded considerably in times of high inflation. Based on your past experience as an investor, you must decide for yourself whether you would be able to achieve a higher rate of return by investing the money yourself, either in or out of an IRA. (For more details, see chapters 24 and 25.)

If you are lucky enough to have an employer who will continue your health insurance benefits after you retire, you are among a minority of American workers.

If you must pick up the cost yourself, your best option will likely be to continue the group health insurance coverage that your employer provides.

You should also shop around for other policies. Even if you have reached age 65 and are eligible for Medicare, you will need extra insurance to supplement it. For more information about health coverage, including Medicare and Medicare supplemental policies, see chapter 12.

CLOSE-UP: EARLY RETIREMENT

Increasingly, companies are offering early retirement incentives to workers. Usually, early retirement means ending work around age 55, but age 60 is also considered early. A 1986 study by Hewitt Associates, a benefits research and consulting firm, found that 32 percent of the 529 small, medium, and large companies surveyed offered some type of early retirement plan, also called a voluntary separation plan. Often, the companies made the offer to avoid mandatory layoffs. Consequently, it's a good idea to account for the possibility and potential impact of early retirement when you are making your overall retirement plans.

Companies usually offer some kind of economic benefit if they want to encourage early retirement. Du Pont, for example, wanted to reduce its work force between 1985 and 1987, and offered five years' additional seniority to workers who were willing to quit early. For 9,200 workers, this was enough incentive to retire early.

If you are offered early retirement, consider it carefully. You can't start collecting Social Security payments until you are at least 62 (or 60 if you are widowed), and then they would be reduced by about 20 percent for the rest of your life. At 65, you could start collecting the full payments. However, if you stop work at age 55, the amount you will be entitled to collect probably will be less, because you will have stopped contributing 10 years sooner than normal. You also will not be able to cash in your IRA until you reach age 59½ without a 10 percent penalty. Your pension will be reduced because pension benefits are typically calculated at 1–2 percent of final salary times years of service.

What you must do is compare the bonus you will be receiving for retiring early against the monthly benefits that go along with it in most incentive plans. The question you must address is whether investing the bonus will give you sufficient income to overcome the financial disadvantages of retiring early. For example, if you can find an insurance broker who will sell you a single-premium annuity that would pay a return for the rest of your life equal to the early retirement reduction in your monthly pension, there's little reason not to retire early if you want to do so.

Another alternative is to invest the bonus and roll over any distribution you receive from a qualified plan (if you do not immediately need the money), and then take another job for the next 5 or 10 years—if you can find one that pays a salary equivalent to the job you are giving up. You may even end up with a second pension, though a much smaller one.

CLOSE-UP: HOUSING ALTERNATIVES

A number of housing options are available for retired people. Here is a closer look at some of them:

Home sharing. In some areas, local community groups or governmental agencies will help match up homeowners and those seeking to rent, or will match two renters and even find them an apartment. Often, zoning regulations that prohibit multifamily dwellings or rentals of part of a house make exceptions for those over 65 or for those living as one "family" instead of in separate apartments within the same house.

There are some drawbacks to home sharing. For example, if one person is eligible for food stamps, he or she may lose the allocation if meals are prepared and shared with an ineligible person. If food is not shared, even though kitchen facilities are, then eligibility is not affected. Receiving additional rental income may also affect eligibility for Supplemental Security Income (SSI), which is available to those with income limitations and to the blind and disabled. Some property tax benefits available to the elderly in some states may also be affected by increased income. You should check into these possibilities and assess their impact on your financial situation before entering a shared living arrangement.

Accessory apartments. This arrangement is somewhat similar to shared housing, but each dwelling space has a separate kitchen area. In some locales, such housing is known as a mother-daughter home, because often the older person is renting or staying in an apartment within a son's or daughter's home. The apartment gives parents independence and privacy they would not have if they were merely sharing their children's households.

If the elderly people own the home, having tenants often gives them a sense of security as well as added income. Although exceptions are usually made for relatives living in the same home, zoning ordinances may block the addition of apartments.

If you are interested in the idea but face zoning barriers, lobby your local government, with the help of a group for the aging or a religious organization, if possible, to change the laws. Some communities make exceptions for renters or homeowners over age 62 or 65, for relatives, or for apartments in homes occupied by the homeowner. If you are considering an accessory apartment, check with an attorney about liability, tax, and other possible legal issues.

"Granny flats." This idea started in Australia, where the Victoria Ministry of Housing installs and rents self-contained units that are placed in the side yard or backyard of an adult child's home. The units are removed when they no longer are needed. It's a lending-library approach to housing. In 1982, Australia had about 800 such units.

In the United States, the concept is known as ECHO housing (Elder Cottage Housing Opportunity). However, in this country, such dwellings must be privately purchased and installed, where they are permitted at all. Some manufacturers are beginning to make a market for ECHO homes, in the $14,000-to-$20,000 range. They are generally portable and reusable, but they require the payment of the purchase price and installation costs, so they are too expensive for some people. They often raise property taxes, and the additional utility costs may exceed those of an apartment. Neighbors may not welcome them, either.

On the other hand, ECHO units can be worth the extra trouble because they offer the older person a degree of independence he or she would not have in a shared-home arrangement, while still affording the closeness and safety of a family.

24

IRAs and Keoghs

Aileen Jacobson

IRAs

In 1981, when tax-deductible Individual Retirement Accounts (IRAs) became available to every employed American, they were widely hailed as the working-class tax shelter, the road to retirement riches, and a prudent backup against the possible failure of the Social Security system. They have indeed turned out to be a good tax shelter and a spur to retirement savings—although the 1986 Tax Reform Act, which imposed severe limits on deductibility, put the damper on IRAs for some taxpayers. Today, those IRAs that remain deductible continue to offer one of the most advantageous retirement plans available; those that are not deductible at least offer a way of building a retirement fund on a tax-deferred basis.

What is an IRA? It is nothing more than an account—a deposit of money, similar to the savings, checking, or brokerage accounts with which you are already familiar. You establish an IRA by investing money through a so-called custodian or trustee, an institution that has been approved by the Internal Revenue Service to receive such deposits.

Unlike the typical savings account, however, an IRA is governed by strict rules defining who can open one, the maximum amount you may deposit each year, and the times at which withdrawals may be made without incurring a penalty. An IRA is not a simple panacea for your retirement planning worries; it's a tightly regulated part of an overall strategy, one that requires careful record-keeping and attention to dates.

We'll take a look at the regulations governing IRAs, and then discuss the issue of deductibility.

Opening an Account

Eligibility You may invest in an IRA only if you or your spouse have earned income or receive alimony payments. The amount you invest each year may not exceed the total of wages earned and alimony received. "Earned" money, of course, can come from self-employment as well as through work for an employer. (Those who are self-employed have additional options similar to the IRA: the Keogh account and the Simplified Employee Pension, or SEP, which combines elements of the IRA and the Keogh account. Both will be discussed later in this chapter.)

Types of Accounts IRAs may be opened with a bank or credit union, a mutual fund company, a brokerage firm, or an insurance company. They offer a variety of choices, including CDs, savings accounts, Treasury issues, bonds, different types of mutual funds, annuities, and individual stocks. (Each is discussed in more detail beginning on p. 502.)

Making Contributions There is a limit to the amount you may deposit in an IRA each year. If you receive the earned income or alimony yourself, you may contribute up to $2,000 a year to an IRA (as long as you earned at least that amount); if you and your spouse both work, each of you may open an IRA and each of you may make deposits totaling up to $2,000 of yearly income. Finally, a worker and a nonworking spouse may each open an account; in this case, the couple's total annual contribution to IRAs is limited to $2,250, which may be divided in any ratio desired, provided that neither account receives more than $2,000 per year. You may open an IRA at any time up to age 70½.

You may maintain an IRA even if you also have a pension plan at your place of employment, a Keogh plan, or a 401(k) salary-reduction plan. There are no restrictions on the number of accounts you may have, provided that you abide by the limits governing total annual contributions. You may deposit your IRA contribution with a different sponsor every year, or you may divide your money among several different investments. But the amount of record-keeping an IRA entails, and in particular the amount of paperwork generated by a premature withdrawal (see p. 500), make an abundance of IRAs a prospect to approach with caution.

Tax Considerations

The Nondeductible IRA No matter what type of IRA account you open, it is tax-deferred; that is, you do not have to pay taxes on the income it earns until you withdraw money from the account. And since you normally don't make withdrawals until reaching retirement age (see p. 499), funds deposited in an IRA grow faster than do the same funds deposited in a regular taxable savings account. For example, if you invest $2,000 in an IRA whose annual yield is 10 percent, it will grow to $2,200 at the end of one year. If you invest $2,000 in a taxable account and your tax rate is 28 percent, you will have only $2,144 at the end of the year; a tax bite of 28 percent of your $200 interest earnings will reduce your $2,200 by $56. Your actual yield, then, would be only 7.2 percent. Naturally, it would also earn less money the following year. Even at the seemingly low levels of yearly investment to which an IRA is limited, the effects of compound interest over 20 or 30 years are substantially enhanced by this deferral of taxes.

Table 24-1 (reprinted from the January 1987 *Consumer Reports*) shows the effects of compounded tax-deferred earnings after 10 years and after 20 years, for various annual yield levels. As the table shows, assuming rates remain constant, you are *always* better off with a tax-deferred savings instrument than you are with taxable savings, given the same rate of interest on each—provided, of course, that you do not incur penalties for a premature withdrawal. Add to the guarantee of speedier growth of your retirement money the likelihood that you'll be in a lower tax bracket when you do start withdrawing from, and paying taxes on, your IRA nest egg, and you'll see that even a nondeductible IRA is an option deserving serious consideration.

TABLE 24-1 Investing Inside vs. Outside an IRA

The table below compares the result over two time periods—10 years and 20 years—of hypothetical investments made inside and outside a nondeductible IRA. Earnings of an investment outside an IRA are taxed each year, thus reducing the true yield. The taxes on earnings of an investment inside an IRA are deferred until you withdraw funds from the IRA.

❶ **Annual investment.** We assume a $2,000 annual investment in each vehicle made at the start of each year. We did not subtract any sales commissions or loads. In almost all cases, you can invest for retirement without such charges, either through a bank or through a no-load mutual fund.

❷ **Hypothetical annual yield.** Yields toward the high end shown are what you might aim for with relatively risky investments, such as mutual funds invested in stocks or corporate bonds. Yields toward the low end shown have been typical of more conservative investments, such as money-market funds, certificates of deposit, and mutual funds invested in Treasury bonds and notes. The yields shown for investments outside an IRA are the net after a 28 percent tax, since you pay tax annually on the earnings.

❸ **Accumulation.** We assume reinvestment of all earnings. For investment inside the nondeductible IRA, the part of this sum that represents earnings on investment is subject to taxation on withdrawal. The remaining portion, the sum of the annual investments, represents after-tax dollars and is not subject to taxation on withdrawal.

❹ **After-tax value.** Based on 1988 rates for a married couple filing jointly. The 15 percent rate might apply to withdrawals made in installments, the 28 percent rate might apply to lump-sum withdrawals and to periodic withdrawals made in years with substantial other income. This figure does not include the effect of any state and local income taxes that may be due on withdrawal.

	Annual investment ❶	Hypothetical annual yield ❷	10 yr. Accumulation ❸	After-tax value at 15% rate ❹	After-tax value at 28% rate ❹	20 yr. Accumulation ❸	After-tax value at 15% rate ❹	After-tax value at 28% rate ❹
Inside	$2000	12%	$39,309	$36,413	$33,902	$161,397	$143,187	$127,406
Outside	2000	8.64 net	32,449	32,449	32,449	106,769	106,769	106,769
Inside	2000	10%	35,062	32,803	30,845	126,005	113,104	101,924
Outside	2000	7.2 net	29,904	29,904	29,904	89,838	89,838	89,838
Inside	2000	8%	31,291	29,597	28,130	98,846	90,019	82,369
Outside	2000	5.76 net	27,568	27,568	27,568	75,831	75,831	75,831
Inside	2000	6%	27,943	26,752	25,719	77,985	72,287	67,349
Outside	2000	4.32 net	25,424	25,242	25,424	64,233	64,233	64,233
Inside	2000	4%	24,973	24,227	23,581	61,938	58,647	55,795
Outside	2000	2.88 net	23,485	23,458	23,458	54,619	54,619	54,619

The Deductible IRA If you are eligible to open a deductible IRA, you have access to one of the best retirement savings plans available—one that is effectively subsidized by the federal government. If your IRA is deductible, you may deduct the amount of your annual contribution from your gross income when you compute your tax liability, thereby reducing the amount of taxable income.

The amount of your "subsidy" from Uncle Sam will vary, depending on your tax bracket. For example, if your annual income puts you in the 15 percent bracket, every $1,000 you deposit in an IRA will save you $150 in taxes. By contrast, an equal deposit in an ordinary taxable account would dwindle in *net* terms (leaving aside accumulated interest, if any) to $850 when you factor in the tax bite. And if you are taxed in the 28 percent bracket, you escape $280 in taxes for every $1,000 invested in an IRA; a $2,000 contribution, the maximum allowable, in effect "costs" only $1,440 in real spending money.

Rules of Deductibility Two factors affect deductibility: your income level and your coverage by other pension plans.

If neither you nor your spouse is covered by a pension plan—defined to include a profit-sharing plan or a 401(k)—you may deduct the amount that you contribute to the IRA, regardless of your income level.

If you are eligible to participate in a pension plan, or your spouse is, you may deduct your IRA contribution only if you fall below certain income thresholds, as described below.

If you are single and covered by a pension plan, you may deduct all of your IRA contribution if your adjusted gross income (AGI), as it appears on your tax return that year, is $25,000 or less. You may not deduct any of it if your income is over $35,000. If you earn between $25,000 and $35,000, you may take partial, prorated deductions: Generally, for every $1,000 of your income under $35,000, you may deduct $200 worth of IRA contributions. Hence, you may deduct $200 if your AGI is $34,000, $400 if your AGI is $33,000, and so on.

If you are married, and *either* spouse is covered by a pension plan, you may deduct your IRAs completely if your joint adjusted gross income (AGI) is $40,000 or less. You may not deduct any of it if your AGI is over $50,000. If your joint income is between $40,000 and $50,000, you may generally deduct $200 for every

$1,000 of income below $50,000. A married couple living apart for the entire year would be governed by the limitations for single taxpayers.

A married individual not covered by a pension plan at work can still qualify for the deduction even if his or her spouse *is* covered by a pension plan—provided that the pensionless spouse earns less than $10,000 and files a separate tax return. However, since filing separately usually increases a married couple's taxes by imposing different tax rates and limiting deductions in other areas, it is often unwise to file separate tax returns just for the IRA deduction.

Clearly, it is important to understand the criteria used by the IRS to determine whether you are covered by a pension plan at work. What if you are not vested? What if your coverage ends midyear?

Even if you are not vested in a company pension plan, you are considered to be participating in it. The same is true if you do not have any choice about joining the plan, or are not required to contribute to it yourself.

If you are covered by a pension plan for only part of a given year, the IRS considers you to be "covered" for the purposes of that year's tax returns. For example, with many plans, if you leave a job, and your pension plan, in mid-January, you lose your right to deduct your IRA for that year (unless your total income falls below the thresholds previously cited). If you start a new job in mid-December, only then gaining coverage by a pension plan (usually after a waiting period), you also may lose your deduction for the entire year unless you fall within the income guidelines. You should consult an employee-benefits specialist at your place of employment to determine whether you are considered "eligible to participate" in the pension plan if you join or leave the firm at midyear.

Obviously, this may present problems for people who have no pension plan, make an IRA contribution early in the year, and then change jobs later in the year and begin receiving pension coverage. Similarly, people who end up making more money than they expected may also lose all or part of the deduction. IRS rules account for cases such as these. You may withdraw a nondeductible contribution from your IRA without incurring the usual early withdrawal penalty, provided you do so before filing your tax return for that year (by April 15 of the following year). You may still incur a withdrawal charge by the financial institution where you opened the IRA, however. Furthermore, you will have to pay taxes on the interest earned by the funds while they remained in the IRA. It must be included as income for the prior year, even if your withdrawal was made after December 31. Premature withdrawals may be made from an IRA without penalties in cases of death or disability or in certain other circumstances.

If you must decide between an IRA and a 401(k) plan at work—or a 403(b) if you are employed by a nonprofit organization—you are probably better off with the 401(k) plan if your employer matches your contribution to it in whole or in part. If your company matches half your contribution, for example, you have an instantaneous 50 percent return on your money. It would take a remarkable IRA to match that return. Also, your 401(k) contribution is guaranteed to be tax-deductible, while your IRA investment would be tax-deductible only if you fall below the income threshold.

Furthermore, your contribution to a 401(k) may help you become eligible for an IRA deduction. For example, if you are single and earn $36,000 a year, making a $2,000 contribution to a 401(k) will reduce your adjusted gross income to $34,000 and qualify you for a partial deduction on your IRA contribution.

To summarize, a tax-deductible IRA is one of the best retirement investments available, and if you are eligible to open one, you should. A nondeductible IRA has fewer advantages, but it should be considered and weighed against other possible retirement investments.

Withdrawals

As mentioned, strict rules govern withdrawals of money from your IRA. You *may* begin drawing on the account after you reach age 59½. You *must* begin withdrawing money by the April 1 following the year in which you turn 70½. But if you begin withdrawing money before age 59½ or after the April 1 after you reach 70½, you will incur a penalty, with the exception of planned early withdrawals (see p. 502). The penalty for early withdrawal is 10 percent; the penalty for late withdrawal is a hefty 50 percent of the amount you should have taken out but did not. In both cases, regular income taxes are still due on the distributions.

If you can afford to, it is to your advantage to defer withdrawals as long as you can, up to age 70½. The longer you can wait, the longer your account will continue to grow tax-deferred.

When you do begin withdrawing, the minimum amount you must take out is determined by the IRS, based on actuarial tables. IRS Publication 575 provides tables and a worksheet to help you figure out how much you should take out each year based on your remaining life expectancy.

Under rules that took effect with the 1984 Tax Act, an alternative method is available for calculating minimum withdrawals. You may choose to recalculate your withdrawal schedule each year based on a changing life expectancy. That is, with each additional year that you survive, your life expectancy climbs and your yearly withdrawal requirement becomes smaller. Using this method, you can avoid outliving your IRA—although it may be severely depleted by the time you enter your nineties.

If your spouse is younger than you are, another way of stretching out your withdrawals is by averaging your life expectancies. IRS rules also allow an IRA holder to use this joint life expectancy method with a beneficiary not his or her spouse, but limit the age spread to 10 years, regardless of the actual age of the beneficiary.

If you are seriously concerned about outliving your IRA funds, you should consider buying an annuity contract, which guarantees fixed payments for the rest of your life. However, keep in mind the costs of an annuity contract, which usually involve many fees and impose some limitations, as compared with the benefits of keeping tax-deferred funds in an IRA.

If you continue to earn money after you reach age 59½, you may continue to contribute to your IRA and withdraw the funds with no penalty (though you're unlikely to be doing both at once). For obvious reasons, therefore, an IRA remains an appealing type of investment for older workers. Of course, after age 59½ you may withdraw substantial amounts if you choose, in a lump sum or in installments. The portion that remains in the account continues to grow on a tax-deferred basis.

Taxes on Withdrawals How much of the amount that you withdraw from an IRA is subject to tax? That depends on what portion of your original contributions was deductible and what was not. If all of your contributions were deductible, all of your withdrawals are taxable as ordinary income. If you made nondeductible contributions, you have already been taxed on those amounts and need not pay taxes again when those funds are withdrawn (although you will have to pay taxes on the portion of each withdrawal that represents earnings on the contribution). If you made both deductible and nondeductible contributions, your withdrawals will be taxed proportionally, based on the relative amounts of each type of contribution (see below).

Early Withdrawal Penalties If you withdraw funds from your IRA before you are 59½, you must pay a penalty of 10 percent of the amount of the withdrawal that has not been taxed previously. You must also pay income taxes on that amount.

For example, if you prematurely withdrew $2,400 from an IRA to which you made only deductible contributions, you would pay a $240 penalty and owe income taxes on the $2,400 on your next tax return.

By contrast, a premature withdrawal from an account to which you made only nondeductible contributions would incur penalty and taxes only on the previously untaxed portion of the withdrawal—that is, the amount that the account earned beyond your original contributions. For instance, if you made nondeductible contributions of $2,000 to an account that subsequently swelled to $2,400, and then withdrew the entire $2,400, you would owe the penalty and taxes only on the $400 in earnings. Therefore, you would pay only a $40 penalty.

If you made both deductible and nondeductible contributions, then your tax situation becomes more complicated. (This holds true whether you are withdrawing funds early or after age 59½.) By law, you may not withdraw first those sums of money on which you have already paid taxes, thus deferring taxation even longer on your deductible contributions and on your earnings. Each withdrawal is instead deemed to draw on taxable and nontaxable funds in the same proportion as they make up your total IRA assets.

Let's suppose that you made $6,000 in deductible contributions and $12,000 in nondeductible contributions, and that your $18,000 has generated additional earnings of $2,000. Of your $20,000 in total IRA funds, $8,000 is taxable—the $6,000 deductible contributions plus the $2,000 earnings. Since that taxable portion represents 40 percent of the total in your account, if you withdraw, say, $5,000, you will owe taxes on 40 percent of $5,000—that is, on $2,000. And if you withdraw early, you will also owe a penalty of

10 percent of $2,000, or $200. If you have several different accounts at different institutions, they are considered in aggregate, and the percentages outlined above would apply no matter which fund you actually draw from.

Clearly, it is important to keep careful records so that you will know what portion of your contribution is taxable and what is not when you eventually compute your tax liability. Indeed, such record-keeping is compulsory for the nondeductible portion of your IRA, and it must be reported each year on Form 8606. Your IRA custodian should provide you with a statement (Form 5498) regarding your contribution. As you make your contributions each year, keep track of which contributions are deductible and which are not.

Planned Early Withdrawal Although you should not use your IRA as a tax-deferred savings plan for short-term goals, under some circumstances an IRA—even with the costs of early withdrawal factored in—may provide greater cumulative savings over the years than a savings account that is not tax-deferred. Whether you are better off with an IRA or with another savings account depends on the respective rates that the two accounts earn during their accumulation phase.

Under the 1986 Tax Reform Act, there is one way for you to withdraw funds early from your IRA (or any pension fund) without paying a penalty. Even if you are not yet 59½, you may make a series of substantially equal withdrawals based either on your life expectancy or on the combined life expectancies of yourself and a beneficiary without incurring a penalty.

Once you reach age 59½, if you have been making withdrawals for at least five years, may may then withdraw the balance in one distribution. You may continue making contributions to an IRA even after starting the withdrawal program. The financial institution that acts as trustee for your account should be able to assist you in calculating what your withdrawal schedule would be.

Investment of Your IRA Contributions

IRA funds may be invested in many different kinds of accounts, including certificates of deposit, mutual funds, stocks, bonds, and United States Treasury certificates. Since IRAs are intended to

serve as retirement savings, it is wise to stay with relatively conservative—and, once the total amount has grown, judiciously
diversified—investments.

As with any type of investment, the more risks you take, the
greater the potential return. With IRA funds, it's particularly
important to consider safety, long-range returns, and fees, since
many institutions charge extra fees for establishing and maintaining the custodial account required by an IRA.

Among the safest investments are federally insured certificates
of deposit at banks, savings institutions, or credit unions. Unless
you are close to retirement, however, you do not need such a high
level of safety for all your retirement savings. A range of mutual
funds (see chapter 20), including those that invest in stocks and
corporate bonds, is an appropriate addition for most people.

Certificates of Deposit Among the advantages of CDs are
that they are completely safe and that banks usually don't charge
any fees for maintaining the IRA account, as some other institutions do. CDs are also available in a variety of maturities, so you
may lock in a favorable interest rate for several years. On the other
hand, if interest rates rise, you usually can't get out of your CD
investment without a penalty.

Brokerage firms also offer CDs, often at a higher return than
that offered by a bank. But you have to pay brokers a fee, and brokerage firms generally charge annual maintenance fees.

Mutual Funds Mutual funds invest in a variety of vehicles
(see chapter 20), including stocks, corporate bonds, Treasury securities, and government agency securities. For a retirement account,
you should, of course, avoid those that invest in tax-exempt municipal bonds.

For the younger saver who has time to ride out the ups and
downs of the stock market, long-term growth funds that invest in
stocks or in stocks and bonds are possibilities to consider seriously.
Mutual funds that invest in Treasury issues or government agency
bonds and offer a high rate of return may be more appropriate for
the near-retirement worker.

It's always best to invest in a no-load fund, but even no-load
fund companies charge IRA maintenance fees. They are usually
smaller, however, than IRA fees assessed by brokerage firms,
which also usually charge a sales commission when you buy a fund.

Some groups of funds allow switching between funds, commission-free, which can provide greater flexibility in long-range investment planning.

Savings Accounts Banks, savings institutions, and credit unions also offer regular money market and savings accounts for IRAs. They may be convenient temporary places to keep your money liquid but still tax-sheltered while deciding what type of account you want for a longer term.

Government Bonds U.S. Treasury bills, notes, or bonds are as safe as a bank account and offer similar returns (see chapter 19). Zero-coupon bonds, which offer a higher interest rate because the interest is not paid out until the bond matures, are particularly well suited for IRAs or Keogh plans. You may buy these through banks or brokerage firms.

Government bonds generally offer a slightly higher interest rate than CDs of comparable maturity, and they are more liquid. But banks and brokerage firms charge transaction fees, and brokerge firms may also charge a fee for maintaining the IRA account.

Stocks Stock trading is risky, and you shouldn't consider it for an IRA account unless you are knowledgeable and experienced. Moreover, neither losses nor brokerage fees in an IRA account are tax-deductible. Although a stock mutual fund may be just as risky, at least it doesn't require commissions or the higher maintenance fees that brokerage firms often charge.

Self-Directed Accounts IRA accounts with a broker are called self-directed accounts. They usually are the most expensive to maintain, with an initial fee that may range from $10 to $50 and an annual maintenance fee of $20 to $100, or higher, in addition to transaction fees. But they offer the widest variety of alternatives within one account, since you can buy CDs, Treasury bills, mutual funds, and other types of investments. For a $2,000 investment, the fees are disproportionately high, but they could make sense in larger accounts. Aside from the convenience of having one account and one statement, self-directed accounts impose a single fee, which may turn out to be smaller than the combined fees of various mutual fund companies.

Annuities Insurance companies offer various types of annuity contracts that are tailored to retirement accounts. They always carry sales charges in some way (at the front end, when you buy, or the back end, when you withdraw, although the back-end charge usually diminishes the longer you hold the annuity). They also carry annual administration and management fees. Most annuities offer a guaranteed monthly payout when they mature. You usually have several options for the payouts, one of which is payments for the duration of your life—an advantage for those who fear outliving their retirement funds. On the other hand, the fees charged are often high, and you may end up with a smaller return than you would with other investments.

Coins You can invest IRA funds in ½, ¼ or ¹⁄₁₀ ounce U.S. Gold coins or 1 ounce silver coins minted by the Treasury Department beginning October 1, 1986. These are not rare coins and do not fluctuate in value as collectible coins would. However, since their value is tied to the price of gold and silver, they are rather risky for retirement investment use.

Fees

IRAs and other retirement accounts impose different kinds of fees. You should check carefully to find out what they are.

Most institutions—with the exception of most banks—charge a fee to establish the custodial account. This may vary from a nominal $5 or $10 up to $40 or $50. There is often an annual maintenance fee as well. As discussed earlier, it tends to be lowest, or nothing, at banks, and highest at brokerage firms.

If the institution allows it, you may pay these fees with money outside the account rather than having it deducted from your tax-sheltered fund. In this case, the fee may be deductible as a miscellaneous itemized deduction, subject to the 2 percent floor. You cannot, however, pay charges such as mutual fund management fees or brokerage commissions with money from outside the IRA. Thus, you diminish your IRA contribution every time you must deduct a sales charge or similar fee.

Timing of Investments

Instead of waiting until April 15 of the following year, as many taxpayers do, you might consider a weekly, monthly, or quarterly contribution plan. If you are investing in a mutual fund, for example, you can invest periodically and take advantage of dollar-cost averaging (see chapter 17). By investing a fixed amount at regular time intervals, regardless of share price, you cushion the effects of price fluctuations. Consequently, your average cost per share may be less than it would have been if you had invested all at once. You may also want to consider making your investment early in the year, so that the earnings are sheltered from taxes for as long as possible.

Investing early in the year can be extremely advantageous. Over the course of many years, the cumulative effect of earning tax-free income for up to 15 additional months each year (if you invest on January 1 of the tax year rather than waiting until April 15 of the following year) can be very significant.

Transferring Funds between Accounts

What if an IRA investment you made, such as a CD, has matured and you want to switch to another type of account? What if you hastily opened a savings account to meet the April 15 deadline, only to find out later that another type of account offers greater earnings?

Once you have made an IRA investment, you are seldom locked into it. There usually are several ways you may switch from one type of investment to another, or from one institution to another. But make sure you know in advance whether there are penalties. (Early withdrawals from CDs and annuities, for example, may incur penalties, or sometimes may not be allowed at all.)

Switching investments within the same company is the easiest way to gain mobility. For example, after a CD matures, you could invest the proceeds in a money market account at the same bank, usually with little effort. And when switching from one mutual fund within the same family to another fund, you can do so often with one telephone call. Be sure, though, that you are aware of any sales charge or fee that might be involved in switching to the new fund. You should also check with the company to see whether there is a limit on the number of times you may switch between funds during any particular period.

With a bit more trouble, you can usually transfer funds from one institution to another. For example, when your CD matures, you may direct your bank, in writing, to send a check to another investment at another institution. Expect to encounter slight delays, and make sure that the first institution knows that you are transferring your money to another IRA, so it does not report an early withdrawal to the IRS.

The IRS imposes no limit on the number of times each year that you can take advantage of these kinds of direct transfers; the funds are never in your possession. Nevertheless, you may incur a fee each time you set up a new account.

Rollovers Another type of transfer you may make is the rollover, which allows you to withdraw funds from an IRA and contribute them to another IRA. You have a maximum of 60 days to complete the transaction. A rollover is convenient when you need money briefly (although we highly recommend you tap other funds instead), or when you're considering a new investment and need more time to make a decision, or when a transfer from one IRA account to another proves difficult to execute. But a rollover may be used only once a year for each separate account. The one-year period begins on the date you receive a distribution. Thus, if you receive a distribution on May 1, 1989, which you roll over into another IRA, you must wait until May 1, 1990, not January 2, 1990, to roll over the funds in this second IRA account into a third IRA.

During the time the money is temporarily withdrawn from the account, any interest or dividends the funds earn from investing them elsewhere must be reported on your tax return. If you keep your money out of the IRA for more than 60 days, the transaction is considered to be a withdrawal, and you must pay the early withdrawal penalty as well as taxes if you are younger than 59½. Again, if you engage in this practice, make sure that the institution knows that you rolled the account over; otherwise, it will report your transaction to the IRS as an early withdrawal. If you want to transfer funds quickly from one institution to another, a rollover is often the simplest method. You need only to endorse the check to the new institution and you retain control over the timing. On the other hand, the direct transfer method, in which you do not have temporary possession of the funds, avoids some of the rollover's potential problems; there's no danger the IRS will consider it a withdrawal, and no once-a-year limitation.

A second type of IRA rollover is quite different, although it shares the same name. It involves taking money from another pension plan and placing it in a special IRA rollover account within 60 days. You would usually do this at retirement or after leaving a job and withdrawing from the pension plan, in order to defer receipt of taxable distributions from the plan. By putting the pension funds in a rollover IRA, you keep them tax-sheltered. It is preferable to paying taxes on the money and then spending it—and, if you're under age 59½, paying a 10 percent penalty. You may also roll over funds from a qualified pension plan into a Keogh plan, if you have one.

This type of rollover account should be kept separate from your regular IRA contributions. If you later rejoin a company with another pension plan, you may be able to place the IRA rollover fund in that plan, if the plan accepts it.

You may also choose the rollover option if you are retiring. Rather than accepting a periodic payment from your pension plan, you may want to take all or some of it out as a lump sum, and reinvest it in a rollover IRA. The money would stay tax-sheltered, but you would have more control over the investment options and over withdrawals. However, you should consult an accountant, attorney, or pension administrator before deciding what to do with your pension distributions. It may be advisable for you to take the lump-sum distribution and pay taxes on it immediately, using the 5-year (or, for those eligible, 10-year) forward averaging (see p. 486 and p. 511). The only way to find out what is best for you is to consider your own situation—how soon you'll need the money, how much you'll need, and what the tax consequences are.

In general, the longer you can keep your money growing on a tax-deferred basis, the better off you are.

KEOGHS

Keoghs (named after the congressman who sponsored the enacting legislation in the 1960s) are qualified retirement plans for the self-employed and for those who have an income-producing business outside their regular employment. Like IRAs, they are governed by regulations about who may open them, how much may be deposited each year, when funds may be withdrawn without penalty, and how much must be withdrawn. And also like IRAs, they are tax-deferred. Unlike IRAs, Keoghs are deductible for everyone, regardless of income level or coverage by another pension plan. In many respects, Keogh plans are more like corporate pension and profit-sharing plans than like IRAs. Moreover, the ceiling on contributions is significantly higher: In some plans, you can contribute up to $30,000 a year or 25 percent of the self-employment income (whichever is smaller). Other types of Keogh plans have smaller maximums. You may contribute to both a Keogh and an IRA.

Two disadvantages of Keoghs as compared to IRAs stem from their complexity. First, the rules governing Keoghs are fairly complicated; these accounts demand greater attention and care than do IRAs in order not to run afoul of IRS regulations. An accountant or financial institution should be able to help you keep within IRS guidelines. Second, if you have any employees and establish a Keogh for yourself, you must extend its benefits to them, in proportion to your own benefits. The contribution rules if you have employees are immensely complicated, and you must obtain professional advice. For instance, you may not have to cover employees who have not met minimum eligibility standards. Moreover, if eligible employees leave before they are 100 percent vested, they forfeit all or part of their benefits.

The biggest headache, for some Keogh holders, is having to file a 5500-C or 5500-R report by July 31 every year. However, the IRS has come up with an easier form for individuals who are the only members of their Keogh plans. Called the 5500EZ, it is available to plans that cover only one person, that person and a coowner spouse, partners in a partnership, or partners and their spouses. Be sure you file it on time, though, because the late penalties are steep: $25 a day up to $15,000. Moreover, if you have under $100,000 in assets in the Keogh, and have no employees, you do not have to file.

Opening an Account

Eligibility According to IRS regulations, the following are eligible to open a Keogh plan: sole proprietors who file Schedule C with their tax returns; partners who file a Schedule K; self-employed individuals who earn income from services rendered or products sold; freelancers; Subchapter S corporations; and members of corporate boards of directors. Only income from the above activities may be contributed to a Keogh, and only *net* income— the amount left over after you deduct expenses or losses from your business.

Making Contributions   A Keogh must be established by the end of the calendar year, not by April 15 of the following year. You may set up a Keogh in December, however, and delay contributing to it until the due date of your return the following year—April 15, or later if you have extended the date.

A Keogh may be set up at any of the institutions discussed previously for IRA accounts, and may use any of those investments.

The amount you may contribute to a Keogh varies with the type of plan you set up.

Types of Keogh Plans

There are two basic types of Keogh plans: defined-contribution plans and defined-benefit plans.

Defined-Contribution Plans   Defined-contribution plans are more common. With these, as the name indicates, the plan defines the level of contribution you make, with no regard to what the eventual payout may be. There are three different types of defined-contribution plans, each with its own rules.

Profit-sharing. This is the most flexible of Keogh plans, because you can decide each year whether you will contribute to your plan, and how much. If your profits fluctuate wildly, this is the best choice for you. The limit per person is 15 percent of earned income or $30,000, whichever is less. All participants must receive the same percentage of their earnings.

Money purchase. You may contribute a larger percentage of your earnings with this type of plan—up to 25 percent—but you lose some flexibility. (The actual limitation isn't exactly 25 percent, because the Keogh contribution itself is deducted from your self-employment income, which reduces the ceiling. For instance, if you have $100,000 in earnings, you may contribute a maximum of $20,000 to your various Keogh holdings. That leaves a net income of $80,000, of which $20,000 represents the maximum possible 25 percent.)

Paired plan. The IRS allows a hybrid of the above two options, too. With a paired plan, you can choose a base-level percentage that you must contribute annually to your money-purchase plan. Then, in addition, you may contribute to your profit-sharing plan on a fluctuating basis from year to year. The combined maximum is 25 percent of earnings. Using this approach, you get the higher limit of the money-purchase plan and some of the flexibility of a profit-sharing plan.

If you are an owner-employee, you will have to figure how to make contributions for your employees as well. Institutions that handle Keogh plans have tables that show the percentages at different levels of net profit, or they can figure them out for you. If you have employees, you also must use a plan administrator. This could be an additional cost to you, the employer, if you use a professional. In small companies, however, the administrator is often the owner or an officer.

Defined-Benefit Plan The defined-benefit plan is rarer than the defined-contribution plan, and it can be expensive to maintain. The defined-benefit plan is suitable primarily for those who are older (at least 45) and who want to shelter most or all of their income. With a defined-benefit plan, you may contribute as much as 100 percent of your earnings in order to reach a predetermined "benefit," up to $108,693 a year in 1991, when you retire. An actuary is required to review your account every year to determine what your contribution should be, based on the distributions you want and your life expectancy. This service could add several hundred dollars to the yearly cost of maintaining an account, so it's worthwhile only for relatively high-income people.

It is easy to overcontribute to a Keogh inadvertently. If you find at the end of a year that you have made a contribution greater than the amount allowed, you must withdraw the excess before the end of the plan year in which it was made if you want to avoid a 10 percent penalty on the overcontribution. In many businesses, you may not know your actual earnings until you review your expenses and deductions. Sometimes this requires the help of an accountant.

Although you must set up your Keogh account before the end of the year, you can wait until your filing date to fund it. By then you will know your net income.

Withdrawals

As with an IRA, you may not begin withdrawing money from your Keogh account without penalty before reaching age 59½. If you do, you must pay a penalty of 10 percent of the amount withdrawn in addition to ordinary income tax. You must begin taking distributions by April 1 of the year following the one in which you reach age 70½ if you reached that age after December 31, 1987 (older tax-payers may be covered by prior legislation). If you're still working by that time, however, you can also continue making contributions.

If you elect to take a lump-sum distribution after age 59½, you may be able to use forward averaging. Several requirements must be met for a payment to qualify as a lump-sum distribution: You must make the distribution during one calendar year; the distribution must represent the entire balance of your account; you must have been a participant in the plan for at least five years; and the distribution must be on account of death, attainment of age 59½, separation from employment (through retirement, quitting, or being fired), or disability (if you were self-employed).

Ordinarily, you must be 59½ to use forward averaging, and your only option is 5-year forward averaging. However, if you were 50 by January 1, 1986, but you have not yet reached 59½, you may elect to use either 5- or 10-year forward averaging. You must work out the arithmetic to see which is more advantageous, and you may need professional help to do so (see p. 486).

One caveat: You can use forward averaging only once in your lifetime, so if you have both a company pension plan and a Keogh, you may want to roll over your company pension into your Keogh and then withdraw it all at once. You may even be able to use a rollover IRA in the interim if you haven't established a Keogh yet but intend to do so in the future. However, there are restrictions on the use of rollovers, so you should check with an accountant or attorney before moving your funds around.

Investment of Your Keogh Contributions

The investments you may choose for a Keogh are similar to those available for an IRA. However, because Keoghs usually involve greater amounts of money, you may be more likely to invest in mutual funds or open a self-directed account with a brokerage firm. For the small Keogh plan, a bank CD with no custodial charges may be the most economical.

SIMPLIFIED EMPLOYEE PENSIONS (SEPs)

The Simplified Employee Pension Plan (SEP) combines some of the simplicity of the IRA with some of the flexibility of the Keogh. It is essentially an IRA, but one in which the employer, not the employee, makes annual contributions. While the employer pays, however, the employee establishes his or her own plan.

SEPs circumvent some of the red tape found in Keogh accounts and stretch the $2,000 contribution limit associated with IRAs. Unlike a Keogh, a SEP requires no outside help to establish if you have employees. You may obtain Form 5305-SEP from the IRS and fill it out yourself. Since each employee keeps his or her own account, you do not have to hire an administrator.

If you are a sole proprietor of a small business, you may contribute up to 15 percent of your net earnings minus the SEP investment itself from that business to a SEP (which in this case is your own IRA), up to a maximum of $30,000. If you have employees, you must contribute the same percentage of each person's salary to his or her SEP-IRA, yourself included. That is, if you contribute 10 percent of your compensation to your IRA, you must contribute 10 percent of each employee's salary to his or her own SEP-IRA.

There are two ways to fund a SEP. Either the employer can make contributions, in addition to the salaries he or she pays employees, or the employees can elect to have their salaries reduced by the contributed amount. The two methods can also be combined.

Generally, employees must participate if they have a year of service.

An employee who wants to make an additional contribution of up to $2,000 on top of the employer's contribution to the SEP-IRA may do so, but should be careful not to let the combined total exceed the 15 percent/$30,000 limit. A penalty is assessed if the contribution exceeds the limit and the excess is not withdrawn before the tax return is due the following year. The employee's contribution is not deductible unless his or her income falls under the thresholds outlined for IRAs on pages 497–99, Rules of Deductibility.

While the relative simplicity of a SEP may make it more appealing than a Keogh, there are drawbacks. With a SEP, you may not exercise the forward-averaging option when you withdraw the funds after retirement. Nor are vesting options for employees as flexible as they are for Keoghs; as soon as contributions are made to an employee's plan, the funds belong to the employee. With a Keogh, an employer may delay 100 percent vesting.

However, a SEP does hold an advantage for anyone who failed to establish a Keogh before the end of the tax year: It can be established anytime until April 15.

The 1986 Tax Reform Act modified the SEP regulations to provide for salary deferrals of up to $7,000 (that figure was increased to $7,627 in 1989) for employers who have 25 or fewer employees, if at least half of the employees in the plan agree to accept deferrals. This portion of the plan offers a tax break to the employees without requiring a contribution from the employer. While this seems to benefit the employer, he or she should check carefully to ascertain whether or not the costs of setting up such a plan exceed the benefits.

ALTERNATIVES TO IRAs AND KEOGHS

401(k) and 403(b) Plans

The 401(k) salary-reduction plan has become increasingly popular since it was first authorized by Congress in 1980. It benefits employers because it allows them to reduce pension costs by encouraging workers to save more themselves; it benefits employees because it offers tax-deductible savings—often matched in whole or part by employers—of up to $8,475 for 1991, with the maximum pegged to inflation each year.

With a 401(k) plan—or, in a nonprofit organization, a 403(b) plan—you are allowed to earmark up to $8,475 a year (the 1991 limit, but it can change each year) of your annual salary to a retirement fund (or $9,500 with a 403(b) plan). The employer establishes a trust. You, as the employee, designate the amount to be deducted from your paycheck, and it is deposited into a special savings/investment account. In some plans, you may be given several options of varying degrees of risk and may choose growth stocks and bonds, money market securities, or a guaranteed fixed-rate income fund. The amount contributed is deducted from your paycheck and isn't currently taxable. Essentially, the IRS is agreeing to postpone taxing you on that portion of your paycheck that you have chosen to put off receiving. Your earnings accumulate tax-free until you decide that you want to receive the money. There is a penalty of 10 percent for withdrawing funds before age 59½. A lump-sum withdrawal after age 59½ may be eligible for favorable tax treatment.

Many employers match, in whole or part, the contributions that an employee makes to a 401(k) or 403(b) fund. You would be hard pressed to find any other retirement savings plan as advantageous as the tax-deferred, tax-deductible 401(k) or 403(b) fund matched 100 percent or even 25 percent by an employer.

Annuities

For those who no longer qualify for deductible IRAs, annuities, sold by life insurance companies, might be considered as an alternative. Like nondeductible IRAs, such annuities accumulate earnings on a tax-deferred basis. Each year you may invest as much money as you desire; the IRA's $2,000 limit does not apply. But there is a sales commission, usually 4 or 5 percent, commonly charged when the annuity is paid out.

As is the case with all other retirement savings vehicles, withdrawing funds from an annuity before you reach age 59½ incurs a penalty of 10 percent of the amount withdrawn. In addition, many insurance companies impose a surrender charge, which can run as high as 7 percent of the amount withdrawn, if you withdraw funds before the annuity is six years old. Such charges usually decline after that, disappearing completely after you have held the annuity for 10 to 12 years.

The insurance firm usually guarantees you a certain interest rate for one to five years, and commonly invests funds in CDs, bonds, and Treasury bonds and bills. Therefore, yields tend to follow the money market interest rates, but changes in interest rates tend to hit annuities later than they hit the underlying investments. You may be able to select the type of investment by investing in a variable annuity. If you choose to invest your annuity funds in stocks or bonds, where those are investment options, the insurance company does not guarantee a return rate.

You are allowed to withdraw your money either in one lump sum, in installments or guaranteed payable over your lifetime.

Because the $2,000 annual limitation on an IRA does not apply, annuities might be attractive to people who have more money to invest for retirement than IRA rules allow. While insurance companies tout annuities, however, we do not see them as an attractive alternative to a nondeductible IRA. For one thing, they incur the same penalties as IRAs do; for another, the sales charges they impose cut into your total return.

Tax-Exempt Bonds or Bond Funds

The main advantage of tax-exempt bonds and bond funds is that they will never be taxed. With an IRA, in contrast, if taxes go up, you could end up paying taxes at a higher rate than the current one when it comes time for you to withdraw your deductible contributions and earnings from your IRA.

On the other hand, bonds have several disadvantages as retirement investments: little growth and therefore little protection against inflation; sensitivity to interest rates, which means that you may lose money if you must sell one before maturity while interest rates are higher than the bond's return; and greater market risk, unless you buy insured bonds (which reduces your return). For low-income (and therefore low-bracket) taxpayers, they offer little tax advantage.

Although the earnings of IRAs are taxed when the funds are withdrawn, they offer more diversity of investments than does a succession of tax-free municipal bonds. And, if invested in CDs or Treasuries, IRAs also offer more safety.

Tax-exempt zero-coupon bonds could be an attractive alternative to an IRA, but only as long as they are backed indirectly by U.S. Treasury securities. They should offer higher returns than other bonds of similar maturity dates and safety levels, because they do not pay interest until they mature. Since their maturity can be timed, they become ideal investments for retirement.

If you already have enough money invested in retirement funds and want to avoid putting your money in another restricted account while saving on taxes, a municipal bond fund may give you the flexibility you seek. You can liquidate it, if necessary, without incurring a tax penalty.

For more about bonds and bond funds, see chapters 19 and 20.

25

Social Security and Pensions

Aileen Jacobson

SOCIAL SECURITY

Although the Social Security system was established more than half a century ago, debate about its basic mission and its policies continues today. Those who believe that it is essentially a social welfare program designed to alleviate poverty in old age feel that the affluent elderly should not be entitled to payments. Indeed, Social Security payments are now partially subject to taxation for recipients who have certain levels of income from other sources.

Another group argues that Social Security is essentially a compulsory insurance program and that everyone who has paid "premiums" through a lifetime of wage withholdings is fully entitled to benefits on retirement.

Both groups share a concern about the future financial viability of the program, particularly when post–World War II "baby boomers" reach retirement age just as the number of active workers still paying into the system is likely to decline. Government forecasts indicate, however, that Social Security is likely to be preserved for the foreseeable future.

Currently, about 95 percent of the work force is covered under the Social Security system, and some 16 percent of the U.S. population is drawing benefits. With the exception of federal employees hired before 1984 and some state and local government employees, almost all workers must be covered. The few exceptions include some clergy and some Americans working abroad. Before 1988, a person working for a spouse's business did not have to be covered, but that is no longer so.

Scope of the Program

Many regularly employed people who view the Social Security system primarily as a source of retirement income are unaware of some of its other functions. In addition to providing old-age benefits to all who qualify, the system also makes payments before their retirement to disabled workers and their dependents and to the widows and children of workers who have died, either before or after retirement. In addition, low-income individuals age 65 and over, blind persons, and the disabled may be entitled to payments under the SSI program. (See p. 535.)

Medicare, a health insurance program to which all people over 65, retired or not, are entitled, and Medicaid, a supplementary health-care program for low-income people, are also managed by the Department of Health and Human Services, as is Social Security.

The retirement benefits are those most commonly associated with Social Security, however, and we will deal first with them. Later, we will discuss programs of concern to the disabled and the poor. Finally, we will explore pension plans, the other major source of income for the retired.

Qualifying for Retirement Benefits

The eligibility requirements for retirement benefits involve more than age (65, or 62 if the early retirement option is chosen) and some history of wage-earning. Your eligibility for benefits and the level of the benefits themselves depend heavily on your work history.

To become eligible for any benefits, you must have worked, during your lifetime, for a certain number of "quarters" for employers who withheld Social Security contributions from your earnings and matched your contributions with their own. If self-employed, you must have made contributions for yourself for those quarters. The minimum number of "quarters" required depends on your age. If you reached age 62 in 1987, for example, you needed 36 quarters—a total of nine years—of employment to qualify for benefits. If you reach age 62 after 1990, you will need 40 quarters.

Actually, the term *quarter* has been a misnomer since 1978. Before that year, it applied literally to a calendar quarter during which you worked. In 1978, however, a quarter was equated to each $250 of annual earnings, and four quarters could be credited to anyone who earned $1,000 in one year, even if it was earned in a single month. The Social Security Administration will increase this figure each year to keep pace with average earnings. In 1991, the figure rose to $540.

Employees of nonprofit organizations who were 55 years of age or older on January 1, 1984, may qualify for benefits with fewer quarters of credit, and should check on their status with their local Social Security office.

From one point of view, it is advisable to begin accumulating credits as early in life as possible in order to be eligible for disability benefits if you become disabled early in life. If, for example, you become disabled at age 24, you need to have worked for only one and one-half years in the preceding three years in order to be eligible for disability benefits.

Women who have not worked steadily throughout their lives may find it especially advantageous to acquire work credit as they approach their retirement years. But unless their earnings are substantial, married women may discover that the spousal benefits to which they are entitled automatically when their husbands retire (50 percent of their spouse's benefit) are higher than what they would get as a result of their own work history.

A special provision allows people who are self-employed but don't make much money to earn Social Security credits in years when they wouldn't qualify with their taxable income. Normally, you must have net earnings of at least $400 to qualify for Social Security coverage. However, if you are engaged in an agricultural trade or business and your gross income is $600 to $2,400, you may choose to receive credit and pay Social Secuity taxes on two-thirds of your gross; if your gross income is over $2,400 but your net income is less than $1,600, you may choose to receive credit and pay Social Security taxes on $1,600.

You may elect to use a similar "optional method" of computing your income if you are engaged in a nonagricultural trade or business as long as you earned at least $400 in two of the preceding three years. This computation can only be used five times in your lifetime. Check with your local Social Security office for details.

How Much Can You Expect?

In its pamphlet entitled *Your Social Security*, the Social Security Administration warns that old-age benefits "are not intended to replace all lost earnings," and it urges people to "try to supplement Social Security payments with savings, pensions, investments, or other insurance." This advice is sound indeed, because the elderly who now rely entirely on Social Security payments live close to the poverty level. A 1987 poll by Louis Harris & Associates found that among the elderly who live alone, nearly one-third had annual incomes below the federally defined poverty line. Yet even in the households of those over 65, of whom 92 percent received Social Security payments, only 45 percent had private pensions as well.

Benefit payments are, of course, lower for individuals who have worked only sporadically, or worked intermittently in jobs not covered by Social Security. But even workers who have had an uninterrupted employment history find themselves forced to lower their standard of living if they have no other source of income. In fact, the higher one's lifetime earnings, the smaller the proportion of earnings that Social Security benefits replace. Again, the implications of these economic facts are that retirement planning should assume that Social Security benefits must be supplemented by savings, investments, IRA accounts, annuities, and, if possible, employee pensions.

Opening a Social Security Account

Your Social Security account is opened as soon as you have been assigned a Social Security number, which you receive by filing Form SS-5, obtainable from your local Social Security office. Along with this application, you will be required to submit proof of your identity, age, and citizenship in the form of a birth certificate, baptismal certificate, newspaper birth announcement, passport, naturalization papers, or other documentary evidence.

Under current law, children must have a Social Security card by the time they are one year old because, although they are unlikely to work for pay during the next 10 years or more, their numbers must be used when you claim them as dependents on your income tax and they must also appear on any income tax return they file to report such unearned income as the yields on custodial accounts or securities registered in their names. An application for a child's Social Security number requires, in addition to the documentation listed above, proof of your identity and your status as parent or guardian.

Unless you are applying for a card after you reach the age of 18, you may request an application form by telephone or by mail and submit the completed form and supporting documents by mail. (After age 18, you must appear in person.) Because photocopies of some of the documents will not be accepted, however, you may hesitate to use the mails for such difficult-to-replace original papers as birth certificates or immigration documents. You may decide to go in person. If so, schedule your visit for late afternoon and for the end of the month in order to avoid what may be a long wait for service.

Throughout your lifetime, you should have only one Social Security number. If you change your name, through marriage or for some other reason, you should notify the Social Security office of the change rather than filing a new application. Although there is no penalty for having two numbers unless fraud is involved, such duplication can confuse the record of your lifetime earnings.

Your Social Security number is used by banks, stockbrokers, and other investment managers to report your unearned income (interest, dividends, and other investment gains) to the IRS. Because hospitals and other public facilities use it for identification purposes, you need to be careful about recording it accurately and wary about disclosing it to others.

Checking on Your Credited Earnings

Your contribution to Social Security is automatically withheld from your paycheck, and there is nothing you can do about that. But you ought to be continuously aware of its level, which is usually recorded on the paycheck stub. You should also be aware that your employer is required to match your contribution dollar for dollar—so that you can ultimately check to see whether your account has been credited properly.

Basically, your contribution is a fixed percentage of your annual earnings up to a specified maximum, and both the percentage and the maximum change periodically. For years after 1990, the percentage is 7.65 percent, and the maximum earnings from which contributions are withheld will be increased by a calculation based on the increase in national wage levels.

Your Social Security benefit will be directly related to the level of earnings reported each year. However, your earnings will be updated (indexed) so that amounts earned early in your career are stated in terms of overall wage levels prevailing at the time you become eligible for benefits. Earnings are indexed through the second year before a retiree turns age 62 or through the second year before the worker's death or disability. Earnings after that point are counted at their nominal value. For example, since economy-wide wages more than doubled from 1972 through 1989, actual earnings of $7,000 in 1972 would be indexed to over $19,000 in terms of 1989 earnings levels.

As the years go by, it's important to check on your Social Security account periodically to make certain that your earnings have been credited correctly to you. Your employer is required to provide you annually with a copy of your W-2 form, which indicates your total wages or salary for the year and the amount that has been withheld as your contribution. If you detect any discrepancies, inform your Social Security office before the expiration of the statute of limitations—three years, three months, and fifteen days from the date you earned the money. After that, a mistake generally will not be corrected unless your employer under-reported or failed to report your earnings, or unless you otherwise qualify for an exemption. Periodic checks become more important as you grow older, because your income (and hence your Social Security earnings) will be higher. But they're important at any age, because clerical errors are not uncommon.

Estimating Your Benefits

The Social Security Administration provides detailed information on your Social Security history and projected benefits upon retirement. You can get an accounting of your yearly earnings history, a total of how much you've paid in Social Security taxes, estimates of your retirement benefits at ages 65, 70, and an age that you designate on the form, and estimates of survivors' and disability benefits. You can obtain Form SSA-7004 (Request for Earnings and Benefit Estimate Statement) from your local Social Security office or by calling 800-937-2000. You must provide your name, Social Security number, current earnings, and an estimate of average future earnings. You should receive an answer within three to six weeks.

You may also want to do some calculations yourself to get an idea of how much you may be able to receive after retirement. Benefits are based on average earnings and it is extremely difficult, if not impossible, to accurately predict an individual's earnings very far into the future. As a result, it is difficult for an individual to estimate his or her own benefit amounts, unless the individual is close to retirement However, it is possible to approximate the percentage of your earnings that your benefits are likely to replace if you retire at the full-benefit retirement age (currently age 65) and had steady earnings at the same relative level throughout your life. In general, as we have noted, the higher your average earnings, the lower the percentage that your benefits will replace.

For example, a worker retiring at age 65 in 1991 with no entitled family members who has always had low earnings (45 percent of average earnings for all workers, estimated to be $9,530 in 1990) will get basic benefits equal to about 59 percent of his or her monthly 1990 earnings or about $460 a month.

The basic benefits of a worker who always had earnings at the average level for all workers (estimated to be $21,179 in 1990) will be equal to about 43 percent of 1990 earnings—$750 a month. And a worker who always earned the maximum level taxable under Social Security will have a basic benefit equal to about 24 percent of 1990 earnings—$1,020 a month.

The earnings-replacement percentages demonstrate that the benefit structure is weighted in favor of lower earners. Benefits are weighted because workers who spent their whole lives in low-paying jobs have had less opportunity than higher-paid workers to supplement Social Security with private savings and investments.

These earnings-replacement percentages are likely to change only slightly in the future. According to the 1991 Report of the Social Security Trustees, earnings-replacement rates for workers retiring at the full-benefit retirement age will decline very gradually from the year 2000 to 2030 and remain constant thereafter for the next 35 years at 56 percent for low earners, 42 percent for average earners. Earnings-replacement rates for maximum earners at full-benefit retirement age will fluctuate somewhat between 1995 and 2020 and then level off at 27 percent through 2065.

Married workers typically receive higher total benefits than single-workers—either because both partners worked in covered employment or because one is eligible for the 50 percent spouse's benefit based on the partner's covered work. If a person is eligible for both a benefit based on his or her work and a benefit as a spouse, the person receives an amount equal to the higher of the two benefits.

These modifications do little to remedy the numerous inequities in the system. For example, workers who retired in earlier years enjoyed a higher income-replacement percentage than those who retired later, and couples in which one member earned a high income and the other little or nothing receive a higher replacement percentage than couples in which both members earned similar salaries for many years.

The percentages cited here, of course, are very general and cannot answer the question that is most important to you: "Precisely how much can I get in benefits when I retire?" Before you reach the age of 60, any estimate will be only a rough approximation because it can't take into account your future earnings, the effects of future congressional legislation, and the periodic adjustment of benefits as a consequence of inflation. Once you approach the age at which you plan to retire, however, you can obtain a fairly precise estimate by mailing Form SSA-7004, as noted above.

Applying for Retirement Benefits

Applications for the various types of Social Security benefits—for retirement, for disability, for the support of dependent children—require somewhat different supporting documents. But since most of them may be needed on short notice in the case of such unpredictable events as your own or your spouse's death or disability, they should be collected as soon as possible and stored in a safe and accessible place—a bank safe deposit box or a fireproof security file at home. If these documents are not available, a Social

Security staff member can advise you about acceptable alternatives. The documents that you will need to present are the following:

- Your Social Security card or a record of the number
- Your spouse's Social Security card or a record of the number
- Original or certified copies of a birth certificate, baptismal certificate, or other proof of age for yourself and your spouse
- Your marriage certificate (and/or divorce documents) if you are applying for spouse's or ex-spouse's benefits
- Birth certificates (or adoption orders) for any children for whom you are seeking benefits (see p. 535)
- Copies of your W-2 form for the previous year or, if you are self-employed, copies of Schedule SE from your two most recent tax returns, along with proof of payment.

Alternatives for Spouses

A spouse who retires at age 62 or later is entitled either to the benefits she has earned through her own contributions or to spousal benefits (half of the retired spouse's benefits, reduced for months of retirement before age 65), whichever are higher. (For illustration's sake, we'll assume the spouse is the wife, as is more typically the case. But the following also holds true if the husband is eligible as a spouse.) If the husband is not ready to retire, she can take early retirement at age 62 based on her own earnings, and then, when her husband retires, receive in addition any difference between her earned benefits and her spousal benefits. If her husband should die in the interim, she can, after age 65, apply for a full widow's benefit. Reduced widow's benefits are available beginning at age 60 (age 50 if disabled).

A divorced spouse is eligible for a spousal benefit if the former mate is at least age 62 even if he is not yet collecting benefits, provided that the marriage lasted at least 10 years and the divorce predated the application by at least 2 years. If the husband was already collecting benefits before the divorce, but has returned to work, there is no 2-year waiting period. If the ex-spouse dies, the divorced spouse may be eligible for survivor's benefits as early as age 60 (or 50 if disabled).

A wife who is responsible for the care of her retired, deceased or disabled husband's child under the age of 16 or disabled and who is also receiveing benefits based on the worker's earnings (even if the child is not hers) can begin drawing benefits at any age. (The same holds true, of course, for a husband in similar circumstances.) There is, however, a limit on the total monthly Social Security benefits that any one family can receive.

Medicare

Whether or not you retire at age 65, you become eligible for Medicare at that age. Unless you enroll three months before your sixty-fifth birthday, you will have to wait until the next open enrollment period (January 1 to March 1), and pay a higher premium thereafter (an additional 10 percent for each 12-month period that you could have had the insurance but were not enrolled). Also, your protection does not begin until July 1 of the year you enroll. It is important to take advantage of all the insurance options available from Medicare when you enroll, because they offer better value than any commercial policies.

Taxation of Your Benefits

Prior to 1984, all Social Security benefits were exempt from both federal and state income taxes. Today, however, recipients whose income exceeds certain limits are taxed federally on half of their benefits. (Some states now levy taxes on Social Security benefits, too.) These income limits are $32,000 for couples filing a joint return and $25,000 for single individuals, but they drop to zero for married couples who file separate returns. These limits cannot be taken at face value, however, because they are calculated on a different basis from your regular tax return—by including, for example, interest on tax-exempt municipal bonds.

The calculation is done by adding to half of your Social Security benefits all income derived from wages, taxable pensions, interest, dividends, and all other taxable income *plus tax-exempt interest.* If the total does not exceed the maximums cited above, you owe no tax. If it does exceed them, however, you must pay taxes on 50 percent of the excess or 50 percent of the benefits, whichever is less.

An IRS worksheet included in your tax-return packet leads you through this calculation. In addition, the Social Security Administration sends you a benefits statement each January that includes a worksheet and a record of the benefits you received in the preceding year.

Although benefits are not directly subject to state income taxes, those recipients who live in states that base the taxpayer's liability for income tax largely or entirely on his or her federal tax return will, of course, feel the effects of the federal tax on their benefits.

The only way to avoid or reduce this taxation is by reducing your adjusted gross income. Your accountant, tax preparer, or financial adviser can suggest tactics tailored to your individual circumstances—among them investing in tax-free bonds or in Treasury bonds on which interest is deferred to maturity, contributing to an IRA account, or buying a single-payment annuity or life insurance policy. Reducing your adjusted gross income may have the further advantage of allowing you larger medical deductions, since they can be taken only if they exceed 7.5 percent of your adjusted gross income.

Before using any of these tactics, however, bear in mind that your major goal is to maximize income, not just to avoid taxes.

Early Retirement

Entitlement to full retirement benefits begins at age 65—and this age limit will rise to 66 by 2009 and to 67 by 2027. But retirement benefits at a permanently reduced level are available at age 62, and a significant percentage of the work force is taking—or perhaps being forced to take—early retirement.

Taking Social Security payments early does not, of course, require you to stop working; you can continue in your present job or take another one. In either case, however, earning more than a specified amount will automatically reduce your benefits.

If you contemplate leaving your job and taking early retirement, you need to consider the following questions:

· To what extent will my Social Security benefits replace my current income, and how will this affect my standard of living?
· To what extent will my employee pension be reduced if I leave my current job before the specified retirement age? (This is

especially important if your employee pension is linked to Social Security benefits.)

· If I continue to work until age 65, how much will the further earnings increase the benefits I can expect if I were to retire then?

· Since I will not be eligible for Medicare until age 65, can I provide for health insurance coverage in the interim?

Given the relatively low level of income replacement that Social Security benefits provide, you need to consider, if you contemplate leaving your current job and taking early retirement, not only your cost of living in the postretirement years but also your other sources of income. Such sources as investments and pensions are dealt with in chapters 18, 19, 20, 24, and later in this chapter. Here we will limit our discussion to two considerations: the level of Social Security benefits you will receive if you retire early and the limits that the Social Security Administration imposes on income you earn after you begin receiving benefits.

Benefit Reduction   Once you decide to retire early, you will receive for the rest of your life a benefit lower than what you would be entitled to if you retired at age 65, although this benefit, like the full benefit, will be adjusted for the effects of inflation. The reduction from full benefit is 20 percent at age 62 and diminishes, on a sliding scale, if you retire between 62 and 65. Your spouse's benefits should also be considered if he or she is not likely to get a higher benefit based on his or her own earnings. If you retire early but your spouse does not retire until age 65, your spouse will receive at that time 50 percent of what your full benefit would have been had you retired at age 65. The spouse who retires early, however, will also receive benefits that are permanently reduced. The reduction at age 62 is 25 percent.

Calculating the benefit reduction that early retirement will cost you and your spouse is not difficult. Once you have received from the Social Security Administration the estimate of your benefits at age 65 (see p. 522), you can use table 25-1 to calculate the reduction that early retirement will cost you. (The SSA will estimate your benefits for retirement at ages 62, 65, 70, and one other age you request, but not for all the levels in between.) Simply multiply your benefit at age 65 by the factor shown for the month in which you

TABLE 25-1   Social Security Reductions for Early Retirees

If you plan to start taking benefits before reaching age 65, multiply your estimated benefits at age 65 (as provided by the Social Security Administration)
by the reduction factor below for the month in which you plan to retire to see
approximately how much you will receive. (Those who qualify for spousal benefits should use table 25-2.)

Months before Age 65	Reduction Factor
1	.994
2	.988
3	.983
4	.978
5	.972
6	.967
7	.961
8	.956
9	.950
10	.944
11	.939
12	.933
13	.928
14	.922
15	.917
16	.911
17	.906
18	.900
19	.894
20	.889
21	.883

TABLE 25-1   Social Security Reductions for Early Retirees
(*continued*)

Months before Age 65	Reduction Factor
22	.878
23	.872
24	.867
25	.861
26	.856
27	.850
28	.844
29	.839
30	.833
31	.828
32	.822
33	.817
34	.811
35	.806
36	.800

plan to retire. A dependent spouse who retires early would also receive reduced benefits, as shown in table 25-2.

Despite the reduction of your benefits, early retirement may still be an economically sound decision. If you retire at 62, you begin drawing benefits three years earlier. In general, you would need to collect benefits at the full rate for 12 years to make up the difference.

Restrictions on Earnings   If you continue working after you begin receiving benefits, the Social Security Administration places some restrictions on the amount you may earn without losing some benefits. These restrictions apply only to income earned by your own labor; "unearned" income—from investments of any kind—is not considered.

TABLE 25-2   Social Security Reductions for Dependent Spouses
Who Retire Early

Months before Age 65	Reduction Factor
1	.993
2	.986
3	.979
4	.972
5	.965
6	.958
7	.951
8	.944
9	.938
10	.931
11	.924
12	.917
13	.910
14	.903
15	.896
16	.889
17	.882
18	.875
19	.868
20	.861
21	.854
22	.847
23	.840
24	.833
25	.826

TABLE 25-2 Social Security Reductions for Dependent Spouses
Who Retire Early (*continued*)

Months before Age 65	Reduction Factor
26	.819
27	.813
28	.806
29	.799
30	.792
31	.785
32	.778
33	.771
34	.764
35	.757
36	.750

Before age 65, you may earn up to $7,080 a year (in 1991) without affecting your benefits, but beyond that maximum, you will lose $1 in benefits for every $2 you earn. From ages 65 through 69, the maximum earned income that leaves benefits intact is $9,720, and beyond that you lose $1 for every $3 earned; from age 70, there are no restrictions.

During the first year of eligibility, a monthly test of your earnings may be used, rather than an annual one. That is, in 1991 a worker who retired between the ages of 65 and 69 was paid full benefits for any month in which he or she earned no more than $810 or was not substantially self-employed, regardless of total earnings. For workers who retired before age 65, the monthly maximum was $590.

On the other hand, if you continue to work beyond the full retirement age (currently 65), you will continue to contribute to your Social Security account, and your additional earnings may increase your annual benefits. For each month you delay receiving benefits, the annual benefit you eventually receive will be increased by a certain percentage, as indicated in table 25-3.

TABLE 25-3   Percentage Increase in Social Security Benefits for
Each Month or Year You Delay Retirement

Year You Attain Age 65	Monthly Percentage (of 1 percent)	Yearly Percentage
Before 1982	1/12	1
1982–89	1/4	3
1990–91	7/24	3.5
1992–93	1/3	4
1994–95	3/8	4.5
1996–97	5/12	5
1998–99	11/24	5.5
2000–2001	1/2	6
2002–2003	13/24	6.5
2004–2005	7/12	7
2006–2007	5/8	7.5
2008 or later	2/3	8

Source: Social Security Administration

Timing Your Application   Applications for early retirement
benefits cannot be filed more than three months before you want
your first benefit payment and must be filed no later than the last
day of the month in which you want your benefits to begin. If you
ignore this deadline, you will receive no back payments. If you are
65 or older, however, you may receive retroactive payments for up
to six months before you applied for them.

Other Benefits

Although people who are in good physical and financial health are
interested primarily in retirement benefits, the Social Security
program also provides benefits for workers who become disabled
before age 65 and their families and for the families of workers
who die before reaching retirement age. In addition, the Social
Security Administration is responsible for administering the SSI
programs to aid those who are aged, blind or disabled and have
limited income and resources. It is important to be aware of these
programs, even if you are unlikely to fall below the poverty line
yourself, because you may have a dependent parent or other relative who is or becomes eligible for assistance.

Disability and Survivor's Benefits Workers who are physically or mentally disabled are entitled to benefits, provided they can satisfy the Social Security law criteria for disability, i.e., that the disability prevents (or has prevented) employment for at least one year or is expected to result in death.

Benefits are also payable to the survivors of workers who die at any age. The child of a disabled worker is entitled to a benefit equal to 50 percent of the worker's basic benefit, and the child of a deceased worker, 75 percent. If there are several children in the family, each can receive 50 percent or 75 percent if the worker is deceased to a specified maximum which varies. These benefits continue until the child reaches the age of 18 (or 19 if the child attends a secondary school full time). If a child is disabled before age 22, however, the benefits can continue indefinitely unless the child marries.

Applications for disability benefits must be accompanied by the following documentary evidence:

- The names, addresses, and telephone numbers of doctors, hospitals, or clinics that treated you, and approximate dates of treatment. Be as specific as possible.
- The Social Security number and proof of age of each person eligible for payments, including unmarried children under 18 (or 19 if full-time high school students); children 18 or older if they were disabled before age 22; and a spouse 62 or older, or of any age if the spouse is caring for a child under 16.
- A summary of your work history for the previous 15 years.
- A copy of your W-2 or federal tax return for the previous year or two.
- Dates of any military service.
- Dates of any prior marriages if your spouse is applying.
- The claim number of any other disability check you may receive.
- The worker's death certificate and proof of marrige if you are applying as a disabled widow or widower. (If your disability started before your spouse's death or within seven years afterward, you may be eligible for benefits. If you were divorced but your marriage lasted 10 years, you may also qualify.)

It's important to file the application for Social Security benefits quickly. Unless they file applications within a month of the worker's death, survivors of a deceased worker who are age 60 to 65 will not receive payments dating back to the date of death. For survivors over the age of 65, surviving children, and spouses who care for child beneficiaries, this limit is extended to six months, but they will receive no benefits that were payable before they reached 65. A survivor who is already drawing a spousal benefit need not make a new application, and the limits on back payment are not applicable in this case.

Applications must be accompanied by the following documentary evidence:

- Your Social Security number and that of the deceased worker's
- Proof of your age
- Proof of your marriage, if you are applying as a widow or widower
- Death certificate, or other proof of death, of the deceased
- Deceased's W-2, or federal tax return if self-employed, for the previous two years
- Proof, if you are applying as a dependent parent or dependent grandchild of a deceased worker, that you were being supported by the worker
- Proof that you have a surviving child in your care

If your claim is denied, you have a right to appeal. There are four appeal levels. The first, called reconsideration, gives you an opportunity to submit new evidence. You generally have 60 days after receiving a denial notice to file an appeal. For more information, contact your Social Security office.

Supplemental Security Income The Supplemental Security Income program (SSI) provides benefits for low-income people who are 65 or older and those of any age who are blind or disabled. Although administered by the Social Security Administration, it is funded not from Social Security taxes but from general federal funds that are, in some cases, supplemented by state revenues to raise the benefit payments above the federal maximums.

Although some 6 percent of Social Security recipients currently receive SSI, a 1986 New York study indicates that only about 60 percent of those eligible actually received payments. The other 40 percent didn't apply because they were unaware of the program, had difficulty with the application process, felt that they would be stigmatized or lose their privacy, or feared that they would lose their homes or other assets. These people not only gave up payments to which they were legally entitled, but they were unaware that qualifying for SSI probably would have made them eligible for Medicaid and facilitate their eligibility for food stamps, emergency assistance, and other welfare programs.

Eligibility for SSI is based on the applicant's assets and income, both earned and unearned. The assets limitation is $2,000 for a single person and $3,000 for a couple, but these figures exempt a home, personal and household items, an automobile to a maximum value of $4,500, a burial space, certain life insurance policies, and a burial fund of $1,500 for each applicant which is offset by any excluded life insurance policies.

In 1991, the Federal maximum monthly SSI benefit was $407 for an individual and $610 for a couple, but this figure varies, depending on whether an individual has income and whether he or she lives alone, lives with others but pays his or her own expenses, or lives in an institutional setting. Some states pay additional benefits. The first $20 of an applicant's unearned income (from such sources as Social Security benefits and veteran's compensation) or $65 of earned income is excluded and, therefore, has no effect on the individual's benefit. Beyond these limits, the benefit is reduced $1 for every dollar of unearned income and $1 for every $2 of earned income. Thus an individual making $427 a month in unearned income or $899 a month in earned income in 1991 would no longer be eligible for any Federal SSI benefit. For a couple, the limits would be $630 in unearned income and $1,305 in earned income. Again, the limits vary state to state and by the person's living situation.

If your assets are too high for eligibility but you are otherwise eligible, you might consider reducing them by "spending down"— that is, by making large expenditures for your own use (such as travel) and keeping careful records of them. Since a home is exempt, you may want to make home improvements, pay off a mortgage, or even purchase a new home. An alternative is to give your assets to others—to your children, for example. You should be cautious about giving assets to your children unless you have a trusting relationship with them. And it is important to approach spending down with care, since you don't want to become destitute—and perhaps still not receive SSI.

The date on which you first call or visit the Social Security office is the date on which your benefits will begin if you are found eligible. You must file your application within 60 days of that date, and you are allowed a 30-day extension from the application date for presenting any supporting documents that you were unable to provide with your application.

The documentary evidence you will be expected to provide includes the following:

- Your Social Security card or a record of your Social Security number
- Your birth certificate or other proof of your age
- Your most recent tax bill or assessment notice if you own real estate other than your home
- The names of people who support you, and the amount of support they provide
- Bank books, stock certificates, bonds, and insurance policies
- Motor vehicle registration
- Proof of pensions and annuities, payroll slips, your most recent tax return, and other information about your income
- Medical records if you are blind or disabled
- Proof of citizenship of lawful-alien status, or proof that the Immigration and Naturalization Service plans to allow you to stay in the United States
- Information about burial plots or burial funds you own
- Information about your spouse's income and assets if you live together
- Information about your parents' income if you are under 18

You can appeal the decision on your claim if you are found ineligible. There are four levels of appeal: reconsideration at the local level, a hearing before an administrative law judge, and appeals to a council review and a federal court. You must exhaust each of these before proceeding to a higher level. Social Security Administration Publication 05-11008, *Your Right to Question the Decision Made on Your SSI Claim*, provides information on each step. Most people handle the appeals process by themselves, but if you feel you need help, your local Social Security office or an advocacy group for the elderly can help you find someone to represent you.

Medicaid   This health-care insurance program is available to low-income people regardless of age. Eligibility for SSI usually carries with it automatic eligibility for Medicaid, but you may be eligible for Medicaid even if you are not eligible for SSI (that is, if you are low-income but not over 65, disabled, or blind). In this case, you need to apply at a Medicaid office.

Lump Sum Benefit   Every covered worker is entitled to a lump-sum payment (currently $255) from Social Security to help cover costs associated with the worker's last illness and death.

EMPLOYEE PENSION PLANS

As we have noted, your Social Security benefits should not be your only source of income if you want to live comfortably during retirement. Although your own IRA or Keogh plan (see chapter 24) can supplement your retirement income, a pension that is included as part of your employer's package of fringe benefits can make your retirement more secure.

If you're working with a firm that has more than 250 employees, and you're making around $25,000 a year, your private pension with many types of plans probably will be 18.9 percent of your final pay after 20 years of service and 27.6 percent after 30 years of service, according to Labor Department surveys analyzed by the Employee Benefits Research Institute, a Washington-based non-profit research organization. If you make about $40,000, you would probably receive 19.2 percent of your final pay after 20 years of service, 27.5 percent after 30 years. If you work for a smaller firm, it's less likely that you'll have a pension at all, and if you do, it's likely to be less generous.

In addition to providing employees with a further measure of retirement security, pension plans benefit employers by helping them attract and retain desirable employees and thus reducing turnover.

Today, about 81 percent of employees with medium-sized and large firms (100 or more employees) have some kind of pension plan. Among those in smaller companies, about one out of 43 workers is covered by a pension benefit beyond the mandatory Social

Security contributions. In some situations, labor unions or professional associations establish and administer pension plans that may cover employees in several companies or organizations.

The number of retired people receiving private-sector or government pension income that supplements Social Security benefits is also growing rapidly. Within the past two decades, this group has more than doubled in size, and today about one-third of retired people enjoy income from this source. In comparison, about half of those who retired in 1987 are receiving a pension.

This general proliferation of pension plans has attracted the attention of both the U.S. Congress and the IRS. Congress has passed several laws to protect both the security of pension funds [including money in profit-sharing and 401(k) plans] and the rights of the participants. For example, the Employee Retirement Income Security Act (ERISA), passed in 1974, offers employers who establish "qualified" plans special tax benefits in exchange for meeting an increased number of conditions. Although the law does not specify the level of pension benefits that participants in a qualified plan must receive, the funding of such a plan is both specified and monitored to ensure that participants will receive what they are promised. In addition, some pension benefits are now insured by a federal agency.

Other federal legislation (part of the Internal Revenue Code) includes several provisions especially favorable to women who may need to leave a job to bear a child. It allows people not yet vested in a pension plan to have their previous years of work taken into account if they take a one-year break and then return, and it helps people become vested faster (see p. 540). It also helps divorcing spouses divide pension benefits, in accordance with state laws, by permitting a court to authorize the plan trustee to pay benefits to a former spouse. In addition, it makes the surviving spouse the automatic beneficiary of any pension rights (except the rights of military or railroad pensions) of a deceased participant unless the spouse files a notarized statement waiving such rights.

Understanding Your Pension Plan

Just as the Social Security Administration makes (and changes) the rules for benefits and allows you little flexibility, so, too, do many employers present pension plans to employees on a take-it-

or-leave-it basis, offering few if any options. Employers are required by law to provide employees with a description in writing of the company pension plan, indicating the eligibility requirements, explaining the formula used for the calculation of benefits, and describing any available options. Nevertheless, many longtime employees remain unclear about their rights or about the current accrued value of their pensions. And many job applicants are reluctant to inquire extensively about a company's pension plan for fear of making a poor impression on the interviewer.

It is usually unwise to choose a job primarily on the basis of the pension benefits it provides, except in the unlikely event that you are faced with a choice between two job offers that are identical in all other respects. (Of course, if you are close to retirement age, a pension plan might be a significant factor in deciding on a job.) Nevertheless, the terms and conditions of your pension plan may influence some of your important career decisions, not only about accepting a job offer, but also about changing jobs, timing your retirement, and making supplementary retirement-oriented investments. Hence, a clear understanding of what you can expect from your employee pension and when you can expect it may have a powerful influence on your entire career.

You should be sure that you will, in fact, be covered in a company plan, because employers can exclude some employees. It's also important to ask about whether your pension benefits will be reduced by the amount of your Social Security payments, a common practice that hits low-income workers particularly hard. Changes in the law no longer permit pension plans to reduce a retiree's benefits to zero, as was formerly possible.

In general, make sure you understand the pension plan so you won't be disappointed—or poverty-stricken—later.

The information that follows is intended to explain the several types of pension plans, some principles that underlie them, the legislation that protects their viability, the options that may be available to participants, and the tax implications of various plans.

Vesting and Job Mobility

One of the most important features of a pension plan of any type is the matter of vesting—that is, the transfer of pension rights to your personal ownership independent of your remaining employed. Vesting usually occurs not all at once but in several stages and according to a specific schedule. This schedule can be important to you.

If you are covered by a pension plan to which both you and your employer contribute, and you leave the firm, you are entitled to take with you every cent that you contributed. But having your pension vested—that is, being entitled to the money contributed on your behalf by your employer, as well as your share of the pension fund's earnings—requires that you remain on the job for a certain length of time.

Until changes brought about by the Tax Reform Act of 1986, most workers had to remain on the job for 10 years to vest. Today the law offers the private-sector employer two options: Either employees must be 100 percent vested on completion of five years of service, or they must be given 20 percent vesting after three years and full vesting, in graduated stages, after seven years.

This shortening of the vesting period which is effective for plan years beginning after December 1, 1988, is of particular benefit to women whose job continuity may be interrupted for child rearing, and for younger workers, who tend to change jobs more frequently than their elders. But every employee should be aware of the vesting schedule. If, for example, you are thinking about changing employers, the timing of the move may determine your entitlement to vesting. On the other hand, if a new job offer requires an immediate response, a loss of vesting may be used as a bargaining point in salary negotiations.

Government employees and those covered by multi-employer plans, as well as most people who work for organizations affiliated with religious groups, are not affected by this change. They still must work for 10 years or longer before being vested.

Vesting is not the only problem faced by mobile employees. Pension benefits under most defined-benefit plans are a function of your years of service and final salary. Typically, your benefit is determined by multiplying a percentage of your final salary (usually 1 percent) by your years of service. Thus, if you are thinking of changing jobs—particularly if you are older—you should carefully calculate your pension benefits before leaving. If you change jobs before "topping out," you may be worse off in the long run. This is particularly true in inflationary times.

Types of Plans

Although you are unlikely to have much choice with respect to the type of plan a prospective employer offers, an understanding of the principal features of the plan may influence your decision about participation (if it is voluntary) or about the level of your participation (if it is compulsory).

Pension plans vary considerably in their terms and their rules, as well as the timing and value of the benefits that accrue to the employee, but most of them belong in one of two categories: the defined-benefit plan and the defined-contribution plan. Although either type may perform as well as the other in terms of providing you with an adequate pension, they are based on very different principles and incorporate different features.

Defined-Benefit Plans   As the name implies, a defined-benefit plan promises to pay you, upon retirement, a specified amount of money for a specified number of years, or, more commonly, for life. The precise amount depends on your age, number of years of service, and wage or salary level. The formulas determining the benefits vary from one plan to another. Some plans base the benefits on your earnings during the three or five years immediately preceding retirement. Others base them on your average annual earnings over your entire career with the company. Thus, if the plan uses the formula of 1 percent of your annual earnings and you retire with 30 years of service you can expect an annual pension of 30 percent of your annual income—either your average annual income with the company, or your average annual earnings of the last few years, depending on the plan. Most union-sponsored pension plans base their formulas on years of service only, although some combine years of service with income in various proportions.

This type of pension plan is funded entirely by the employer, whose level of contribution to the fund will be determined not only by the benefits promised but also by actuarial data on the life expectancies of the employee group covered and by computations and predictions of the pension fund's future investment performance.

Because plans of this type specify precisely the levels of their retirement payments, their benefits (provided the plan is qualified) are at least partially insured through the Pension Benefit Guaranty Corporation, a federal agency. This, of course, is valuable protection for employees, but many employers, apparently finding the government regulations connected with this insurance excessively onerous among other reasons, are moving to pension plans that are less closely supervised. As a consequence, the defined-benefit plan is losing popularity.

Defined-Contribution Plans In contrast to the defined-benefit plan, the defined-contribution plan does not promise a fixed amount of retirement income. Instead, it specifies periodic contributions (often made jointly by employer and employee) that will be invested with the intention of producing the largest possible increase in value by the time the employee retires. Unlike the defined-benefit plan, which deals with all employees as a group, the defined-contribution plan establishes a separate account for each employee and often offers the employee some say about the growth and, in some cases, the management of his or her account. In some companies, such a plan is combined with, and supplements, a defined-benefit plan.

The defined-contribution plan can take many forms. Often the employer's contribution is supplemented by a contribution from the employee. In some plans, for example, the employer contributes a fixed percentage of the employee's income, and the employee is permitted to contribute a percentage of his or her own earnings. The size of the employer's contribution and the employee's maximum permitted contribution depend on the structure of the plan. In some plans, the contributions may be made with before-tax money, giving a great tax advantage to those who contribute.

Although the law does not require it, defined-contribution plans tend to be vested earlier than defined-benefit plans—a distinct advantage to individuals apt to change employers frequently in the course of their careers. In addition, some of these plans permit you to raise or lower the amount of your personal contribution as your cost of living changes, and to enjoy some tax advantage by deferring investment income until retirement.

There is, however, no certainty about the amount of accrued benefits that you can expect on retirement, because their value will depend on the performance of the economy, the level of interest rates, and the astuteness of those managing the investment of the contributions. In short, unlike the defined-benefit plan, which guarantees a specified level of retirement income regardless of how the employer funds it, the defined-contribution plan shifts the risk entirely to the employee. Over the past two decades, some participants in well-managed plans have accrued benefits that far exceeded their expectations. Others, however, might have fared better under a defined-benefit plan.

Some defined-contribution plans in common use include the following:

Subsidized-thrift plans. In these plans, your employer usually matches your personal contribution dollar for dollar (or 50 cents to the dollar), up to a specified maximum, and the combined contribution is invested—in a mutual fund or an annuity, for example—to accrue until you retire or leave the company. For the employee who can afford to make the maximum personal contribution, this can be an excellent plan, since the company's matching contribution produces an immediate 50 or 100 percent return on money contributed.

Employee stock ownership plan. In this plan, you are given stock in the company for which you work. You cannot vote with the stock, as most shareholders can, since ownership is controlled by a trustee. Usually, your share is proportionate to your salary. The plan can be advantageous for employees if it is used in conjunction with another pension plan. Used alone, however, it can be risky, since the value of the stock rises and falls with the success of the company. In many cases, employees have been able to build a healthy nest egg over the years, as their shares have increased in both number and value. However, a 1986 survey of ESOPs by the U.S. General Accounting Office found that many small companies with such plans had gone out of business, some of them by filing bankruptcy.*

Profit-sharing. Popular among small companies that cannot afford to commit themselves to a set percentage of contribution, this type of plan stipulates that the company will contribute a percentage (which may be variable but must be "recurring and substantial") of its profits. No contributions need be made during unprofitable years, and even during some profitable ones.

Although the investment of the contributed funds accumulates

---

*The GAO didn't record exact figures on numbers of companies that went bankrupt or out of business, since the survey was intended to look at matters unrelated to the employee side of ESOPs.

tax-free until it is withdrawn, the annual contributions made by your employer are taxable to you as ordinary income.

Deferred-compensation plans. These plans, known as 401(k) for the private sector and 403(b) for charitable and educational organizations, are growing rapidly in popularity, although the cost of setting them up is a deterrent for smaller firms. About 40 percent of employees at firms with 100 or more workers participated in a 401(k) plan in 1990. The great advantage of these plans, which involve joint contributions by you and your employer, is that your contributions can be deducted from your earnings, thus reducing your adjusted gross income—and hence your income tax liability until you begin receiving benefits. In addition, many of these plans offer you some degree of choice among a number of investment possibilities.

Even if you are eligible for a tax deduction on your IRA, contributing to a deferred-compensation plan is preferable because the ceiling for tax deductibility on IRA contributions is only $2,000 per year, whereas the ceilings for the 401(k) and 403(b) are, respectively, $8,475 (in 1991) and $9,500, and these ceilings are indexed for inflation.

Some of these plans permit you to contribute after-tax income. This is usually a less desirable option because it locks in the money until retirement without offering the advantage of a current income tax deduction, even though taxes on the earnings are tax-deferred. However, if you have enough available funds outside the plan, this lock-in disadvantage may not be important to you. The tax deferral on earnings may be more significant. At any rate, because of the obstacles to early withdrawal, you should use these plans only for retirement purposes and keep other funds more readily available for other uses.

The federal government allows withdrawals for certain hardships, such as paying medical expenses or college tuition, putting a down payment on a residence, or preventing the loss of a home. However, rules issued in 1988 make it plain that you must prove that you have exhausted all other financial resources, including borrowing from commercial sources at reasonable rates, liquidating assets, or, if your plan allows it, borrowing funds from the plan. Furthermore, a withdrawal is treated as regular income and is subject to a 10 percent penalty tax if you are under age 59 ½. (The penalty is waived if you are paying medical expenses amounting to more than 7.5 percent of your adjusted gross income.) You also may be suspended from the plan for a year and your future contributions limited.

If your plan allows loans, there's generally no limit to the amount you may borrow if your account contains $10,000 or less. If the account has more than that, you're limited to borrowing half the total, but generally no more than $50,000. Loans must be repaid within five years, unless they go toward buying a principal residence. Borrowed funds aren't taxed, but the interest you pay is not even partially tax-deductible if the loan is secured by your before-tax contributions or the income is attributable to them. And the funds you have borrowed against don't earn interest until you have repaid them. On the other hand, rates may be lower than at commercial banks.

Payment Options on Retirement

Some plans offer several options for payout on retirement: a lump-sum payment, or monthly or annual payments. If you choose the periodic form of payment, you may be offered an annuity plan, under which payments continue in one of three ways: until your death; until your death or that of your spouse, whichever occurs later, with full or reduced benefits going to the survivor; or for a stipulated number of years, with payments going to your heirs if you should die before expiration of the specified annuity term. The amounts payable under each of these alternatives will differ, since each will be based on different actuarial assumptions, but in many cases the differences are smaller than the retiree anticipates. The choice of option need not be made until you retire, and at that time it should be based on your family structure, the status of your own health, and your other sources of income.

Each of these options has different—and often complex—tax implications. If you choose the lump-sum payment, you are permitted, if you have reached the age of 59½, a one-time use of forward tax averaging for a period of five years; if, however, you reached the age of 50 on or before January 1, 1986, you are allowed to use a 10-year period for forward averaging, but in this case you must pay taxes at the rates in effect prior to the Tax Reform Act of 1986. The only way to choose the more favorable option is to calculate your tax liability for each of them.

The Tax Reform Act of 1986 has phased out, over a six-year period, the favorable capital-gains tax rate applicable to funds accumulated before 1974. Retirees who reached the age of 50 before January 1, 1986, however, may continue to use it, but younger retirees must treat all pension payments as ordinary income.

If a lump-sum withdrawal exceeds $750,000 (in 1989, but this figure is indexed to inflation each year), it may be subject to a 15 percent excise tax, which is also applicable to yearly withdrawals of more than $150,000 (in 1989, also indexed). The limits apply to your total (aggregate) withdrawals from all your pension plans, including IRAs. These rules are complicated, so it's best to consult a tax professional if you think you may be subject to the excise tax.

One way to postpone tax liability on a lump-sum withdrawal is to roll it over into an IRA account, where it will continue to generate tax-deferred income and can be drawn upon in any amount once you have reached the age of 59½. Of course, these withdrawals will be taxed in full as ordinary income, and you must start to withdraw from the IRA account when you reach the age of 70½ (see chapter 24).

Early Retirement

Not all pension plans allow you to start drawing benefits before reaching age 65, although some allow you to start as early as age 55. It depends on each plan's rules. Early retirements that are voluntary inevitably result in a reduction of pension benefits, but the amount of the reduction will depend on the plan formula, the employee's length of service and level of earnings, and the retirement age. Highly paid workers who retire early and are covered by a defined-benefit plan based on years of service will receive much less than the maximum of $108,963 a year (for 1991) to which they might be entitled if they remained at work until the specified retirement age, but this reduction does not apply to benefits they accumulated by 1986. (The maximum of $108,963 will be indexed to inflation, so the figure will rise each year.)

Not all early retirements, however, are entirely voluntary. In recent years, many employers intent on reducing their work force or cutting labor costs have offered incentives for early retirement, because older workers are generally more highly paid than younger employees. Incentives typically offered include pension benefits greater than what the employee would normally receive at his or her present age, an extension of health insurance coverage and other fringe benefits beyond retirement, or a cash bonus.

In recent years, the average retirement age has dropped significantly—in part as a result of the proliferation of retirement incentives during periods of recession. Early retirement has so many financial ramifications that some employers who offer it to large numbers of workers hire independent financial planners to counsel the workers about the offer. With or without such assistance, you need to consider not only your immediate financial situation but also your future sources of income.

You must first determine whether your pension benefits will cover your current cost of living. Although some how-to books on retirement stress that living costs drop after retirement, many retirees find that they do not drop appreciably, if at all. These same books are optimistic about opportunities for further earnings through work after retirement, but such opportunities cannot be relied on, since they depend not only on your qualifications but also on the needs and economic conditions of your community.

In estimating your future income, bear in mind that you will not be eligible for Social Security benefits until age 62, and that if you take them at that age, you must settle permanently for a reduced level of monthly payments. In addition, the incentive portion of any pension income offered by the employer is not eligible for insurance protection by the Pension Benefit Guaranty Corporation.

Finally, you must consider carefully your postretirement insurance coverage for health care, because the need for medical attention and prescription medications tends to rise with increasing age. Although you are eligible for Social Security payments at age 62, you do not become eligible for Medicare until age 65.

Even if you are in good health, there are social and psychological effects to consider. Many who retire early find themselves isolated from social activities that were largely work-centered, and they discover that the leisure activities to which they looked forward do not provide them with a full and satisfying life. The fact that a significant number of people who retire early find themselves seeking employment—often at lower income and lower status—indicates that early retirement has both economic and social drawbacks.

Checking Up on Your Pension

Unless your employer provides periodic statements about your accrued pension benefits, you should ask for one every few years, or even every year, because such a statement can help you estimate not only your retirement income but also the benefits you have earned if you were to change jobs or retire immediately—or the benefits you might earn if you were to stay on beyond the specified retirement age. You have a legal right to see this statement yearly. Sometimes it states only what you would receive if you left immediately. Ask also what you might expect by age 65 and by age 62 if that's not included, and ask how it's determined and what assumptions are being made about your future income.

Studying the statement can also help you determine the kind and amount of outside investment you feel you need. You may, for example, find on the open market an individual annuity or other investment that promises a better return than your voluntary contributions to your pension plan earn, but this seems unlikely. Because company plans cover large numbers of people and are carefully negotiated and managed, they are likely to be superior to those offered to individuals, and if your company plan allows for flexibility in employee contributions, you may decide that increasing your contribution is as good an investment as you are likely to find, even though it ties up your money for many years.

Again, be sure you understand whether your pension will be reduced by the amount you receive from Social Security (a practice called integration of benefits). If the reduction is significant, you may even want to change companies.

26

Wills and Trusts

Aileen Jacobson

PROVIDING FOR YOUR HEIRS: WILLS, TRUSTS, AND TAXES

Wills and trusts are instruments that enable you to pass your assets on to your heirs and to control the ways in which these assets are used. Yet, despite their importance, they are widely neglected by many people, for a variety of reasons.

About two of every three Americans die intestate—that is, without having made a will. Some of them procrastinate because of an unwillingness to face their own mortality; some because they have made no firm decision about the disposition of their assets; others because they feel that what little they own does not justify the trouble of making a will; and still others because they assume that their assets will automatically pass to their natural heirs. All these procrastinators, however, are exposing their assets and the welfare of their heirs to serious risk.

A trust is even less widely used than a will—apparently because many people believe that it is useful only for the very rich. But increasing numbers of people who are moderately well off but not rich are recognizing that a trust, as a supplement to a will, can protect their assets, reduce their tax obligations, and extend their control over their assets far more effectively than a will alone.

Because wills are essential for everyone who has either minor children or even moderate assets, whereas trusts are "optional extras," we will deal first with wills. The discussion of the limitations of a will may, however, spur you to establish a trust as well, which is dealt with later in this chapter.

WILLS

The crucial importance of drawing up a will can best be recognized by reviewing the consequences of dying without one. To begin with, if you die intestate and have minor children, the probate court will appoint a guardian for them. The court's appointment may coincide with your own choice—but it very well may not. Because the court assumes that "blood is thicker than water," it is likely to appoint one of your relatives, whereas you may prefer to choose a close friend whose style of child rearing is more compatible with yours.

If you die without a will, your assets will be distributed not according to your wishes but according to state law, and the result can be quite different from what you would prefer—and even somewhat bizarre. In some states, for example, your spouse would receive one-third of the estate and the children would share the other two-thirds, even though the spouse could have serious need for the entire inheritance. And if, for example, you have children by a previous marriage and none by your present one, your assets may not be divided the way you wish.

In almost all states, if you die childless and widowed, your estate goes to your relatives, and you can leave nothing to friends, charitable institutions, or your alma mater.

Yet another argument for making a will, even if your current assets are modest, is that it permits you to designate your executor, or personal representative—the person who will, on your death, consolidate your assets, pay your outstanding bills and taxes, and distribute the residue to your named beneficiaries. If you die without a will, the probate court will appoint an administrator to carry out these duties. This is likely to be costly, because court-appointed administrators must be bonded and must be paid a fee, whereas you can specify that the person you designate is to serve without bond and without fee, or for a very small fee.

Even if your assets seem insufficient to justify making a will, the guardianship function alone makes a will essential if you have minor children. But many people underestimate their assets—especially if they own a home that has increased in value. And there is always the possibility that you may die while holding securities that can skyrocket in value, or the winning ticket in a multimillion-dollar lottery. If your assets or your family structure should change, bear in mind that it is far simpler to revise an existing will than to make a new one.

No matter in whose names the assets of a married couple are held, both spouses should have a will; there is no way of knowing which partner will die first. For unmarried couples who enjoy a stable relationship, a will is especially important, because the law does not recognize the relationship as a marriage, so the marital inheritance laws do not apply.

Before you set about drawing up a will, it is important to make some decisions with respect to each of its three major functions. All of them require not only careful thought but also some preliminary investigation.

Designating a Guardian

If you and your spouse should both die, your minor children will not be permitted to register at school, participate in athletic events, or even receive medical treatment unless they have the authorization of an officially appointed guardian. As we have noted, in the absence of a will, the court will designate the guardian—usually a member of your own or your spouse's immediate family—but this may be someone you regard as unsuitable: an elderly parent, for example, or an uncongenial sister or brother-in-law. You, on the other hand, may prefer a close friend—the child's godparent, for example. If you specify a guardian, you may also stipulate that he or she is not required to make periodic accounting to the court of expenditures on the child's behalf.

Your choice of a guardian requires very careful thought, because the individual you name should be one whose lifestyle and child-rearing patterns are compatible with yours. On the other hand, unless you have assets or insurance policies sufficient to provide for the rearing and education of your children, guardianship entails very heavy financial responsibilities. Hence, it is essential to discuss all aspects of guardianship with the person you would like to designate and to make certain that he or she is genuinely willing to undertake the responsibility and is not simply yielding to the pressures and obligations of friendship.

Bear in mind that guardianship is purely voluntary and that no one can be forced to undertake it. Hence, it may be important to designate an alternative guardian in the event that your initial choice dies or experiences lifestyle changes—for example, divorce, childbirth, or economic reverses—that would make the guardianship difficult or impossible.

You can also specify in your will the names of persons whom you do *not* want to serve as guardian. If, for example, you are in a second marriage and have custody of your children, you may prefer the children's step-parent to be their guardian instead of letting custody revert to their biological parent. (However, your former spouse may challenge your designation in court.)

If your designation of a guardian is contested by members of your family who would like to have custody of your children, the court may decide in their favor, but your testamentary rejection of a specific person or persons is likely to be considered carefully by the judge. It is important to phrase the reasons for such a rejection carefully, because your will, when it is probated, becomes a public document, and derogatory remarks about potential guardians or beneficiaries may provide grounds for libel suits against your estate.

If your estate is modest, you may decide that the guardian of your children can manage the assets that you have passed on to your children through your will. But if your estate, including your life insurance proceeds, is substantial or consists of a variety of assets that require monitoring and management, the guardian may not have the acumen necessary to handle the assets efficiently. In such circumstances, you may want to designate another person, who will be responsible for managing your children's assets in cooperation with the guardian. Such a person can be an adult child, a friend or relative, a lawyer, banker, or accountant, or anyone else who is both trustworthy and reasonably competent in financial matters. Ideally, the guardian and the person managing their assets should have a close and congenial relationship, since the rearing of the children and the management of their assets are closely linked.

The major disadvantage of guardianships is that they terminate when a child reaches the age of majority, at which time the child is free from the guardian's authority and immediately entitled to all assets. Therefore, if you feel that your child or children are not likely to be able to manage their inheritance responsibly at the age of 18 or 21, you should consider establishing a trust (see p. 561).

Distributing Your Assets

Because your assets may change significantly in the course of your career, and your family structure is likely to change as your children reach majority, your decisions about how much to leave to whom are likely to change periodically. This is why your will should be revised at least every three years—and immediately after you experience a change in family structure through death or divorce. The fact that changes will inevitably occur should not, however, deter you from making a will immediately.

One way to avoid revisions that result from changes in your assets is to express your bequests not in fixed dollar amounts but in percentages. For example, you may decide to leave 75 percent of your total estate to your spouse and divide the remaining 25 percent among your children. This does not preclude your use of fixed dollars or specific bequests as well. You may, for example, bequeath $5,000 to your community library or $10,000 to your alma mater. And you can specify that a close friend is to receive your grandfather clock or your coin collection.

Because it is always possible that a beneficiary you have designated will die before you do, it's imperative that for each bequest you name one or more contingent beneficiaries. For example, if a daughter you have named as a beneficiary dies before you do, your bequest will go to her estate unless you have named her brother or someone else as a contingent beneficiary.

Your will can also specify persons to whom you do *not* want to leave anything. Although the law prohibits the disinheritance of a spouse, any of your children can be disinherited. In most states, children do not have the legal right to inherit, but it is probably wise to specify the disinherited child by name, because if you have made bequests to your other children, the disinherited child may claim that he or she was omitted inadvertently rather than deliberately.

In general, the legally correct wording of a bequest and the designation of beneficiaries are far more complex than they may appear, and this is why it is highly advisable to consult a lawyer for all but the simplest wills.

Designating an Executor or Personal Representative

In addition to naming a guardian and specifying the distribution of your assets to your beneficiaries, your will should designate someone to serve as an executor (called a personal representative in some states), who will be authorized by the probate court to consolidate your assets, pay your bills and taxes, and distribute the residue to the beneficiaries you have chosen.

If your estate is neither large nor complex, you may decide to designate the person you have chosen as guardian to serve as executor as well. But the settlement of a substantial estate consisting of real estate, securities, valuable tangible personal property, and other assets can demand considerable sophistication, time, and effort. In such circumstances, designating an executor different from the guardian may be preferable. For settlement of large estates, banks and trust companies often serve as executors—for a fee, of course.

The probate court requires that executors must be bonded and paid a fee, usually based on the value of the estate, but if you choose a friend or relative as executor, your will can specify that he or she can serve without bond. Unless the person you choose is sophisticated about asset management, however, the fee you pay a professional executor may help ensure that your estate will be managed properly.

Your criteria for selecting an executor should include trustworthiness, financial acumen, an orderly mind, and a sharp eye for detail. It may also be helpful if the executor lives in the same state. As in the case of a guardianship, you should name at least one alternative executor in the event that your initial choice is unable or unwilling to serve, and you may wish to authorize him or her to appoint successors or to transfer the executorship to a bank or trust company.

What a Will Cannot Do

Within certain limits, your will can dispose of your assets in any way you choose, but these limits need to be recognized. To begin with, you cannot disinherit a spouse, because under state law the spouse is entitled to a substantial portion (one-third to one-half) of your estate, regardless of what your will specifies. Some states require that household items and automobiles must go to the spouse or the children, and this requirement also overrides your will.

In addition, you can include in your will only assets that belong solely to you—not assets that you hold jointly with your spouse, such as your home or your securities, as is commonly the case. Similarly, you cannot will assets held in trust. The proceeds of insurance policies and pension payments cannot be willed unless you have designated your estate as the beneficiary. Otherwise, such assets go to the beneficiaries you have designated in the policy or the plan. The same applies to Series E savings bonds if, when you bought them, you specified that they were "payable on death" to someone specific.

In the so-called community property states (Arizona, California, Idaho, Louisiana, Nevada, New Mexico, Texas, and Washington), and in Puerto Rico, all assets except those acquired through gift and inheritance are considered to be owned equally by the two spouses. This fact may impose additional restrictions on what you can bequeath through your will. Community property laws differ from one state to another, so it is essential that you consult a lawyer in connection with your will and any other property transfers, especially if you have moved to a community property state and are unfamiliar with the law.

You cannot make a bequest based on a condition that the probate court would regard as contrary to sound social policy. For example, you cannot bequeath to your daughter a sum of money conditional on her divorcing her husband, and you cannot make a scholarship bequest to a university to be used for the benefit of white students only.

Finally, your will should not include instructions about your funeral preferences, organ donations, or anything else that needs to be done promptly upon your death. Often a will is not located and read until it is too late to carry out your instructions on these matters. They can be communicated far more effectively in your letter of instruction (see p. 567).

Drawing Up a Will

Although handwritten (holographic) wills, and even oral wills, are legally acceptable in some states in very special and limited circumstances, a will should be drafted formally in full compliance with your state's inheritance laws. Forms for simple do-it-yourself, "one size fits all" wills are widely available on both paper and computer software, but these are unlikely to cover all possible contingencies or comply with all the idiosyncrasies of the widely different state laws. A few states publish will forms that comply with their own laws, but even these may not cover some of your special needs. They may not, for example, indicate, as a lawyer would, that setting up a trust could save you substantial estate taxes.

Because the probate court may rule a do-it-yourself will invalid on the grounds of seemingly trivial technicalities, it is wise to have a lawyer draw up your will, or, if you use a do-it-yourself form, review it. The lawyer you choose should be one who is experienced in estate planning, not necessarily the one you use for other family or business problems.

A simple will should not cost more than $100. Since most lawyers base their fees on an hourly rate, you will save money on a complex will if you arrive at the lawyer's office with a list of your assets and liabilities, your proposed distribution to your beneficiaries, your selection of guardian and executor, and as many other details as possible so that the lawyer can devote his or her time to ensuring that your wishes are expressed in legally correct form. A lawyer is not a family counselor or an investment advisor; problems requiring these kinds of advice should be solved elsewhere. You are paying the lawyer to make certain that your will is legal.

Your signing of the will must be witnessed by two or more persons, depending on state law. This is usually done by employees in the lawyer's office. Bear in mind that the witnesses need only see you sign the will and need not see the contents. In general, the witnesses should be local people who are younger than you are, in the rare event that they may be called by the probate court to verify your signing.

The safekeeping of the will requires careful thought. If you file it in your lawyer's office, you may feel embarrassed to ask for it if you should change lawyers, or you may feel obligated to designate him or her as your executor, even though you might prefer someone else. Storing your only copy of the will in a safe deposit box is not a good idea: On your death, your box may be sealed by the bank to await a state representative's examination of its contents for tax purposes. Although special permission can be obtained from the probate court to open the box for the sole purpose of finding the will, this procedure may take valuable time. In some states, the will can be filed with the county clerk.

Making Changes

As previously noted, your will should be reviewed periodically and revised when a child is born or adopted or reaches majority, when changes occur in your lifestyle or assets, or when your family structure changes through death, divorce, or remarriage.

If the changes are major, writing a new will is advisable. But if they are minor—the replacement of a beneficiary, for example, or a change in the amount of a single bequest—they can be made by means of a codicil, a written amendment to the will that is witnessed and attached to the original. Preparing the codicil is less expensive than drawing a new will.

The Probate Process

Most states provide for transfer of assets to beneficiaries by the relatively simple procedure of affidavit or summary probate. There are numerous restrictions on these procedures, however, and the maximum value of the estate is subject to various limits, ranging from $2,000 to $60,000. If your estate cannot meet the restrictions, or if its value exceeds the statutory limit, your will must undergo the full probate process through the county probate court.

Through the probate court, the state ensures that your will is valid, that your assets are carefully protected against loss or theft, that your bills and taxes are paid, and that all your remaining assets go directly to the beneficiaries you have designated.

This process takes a good deal of time—often months, sometimes years. The executor must consolidate all your various assets; notify your creditors of your death; have your real estate and other property appraised and pay the taxes and mortgage on them until they are transferred or liquidated; decide whether and when to dispose of your business, your brokerage accounts, and your other investments; and have your other possessions appraised for purposes of federal estate and state inheritance taxes.

In addition, probate is a public process, and anyone curious about your net worth or your family relations can find out "who got what" from the public record. As a consequence, your beneficiaries may find themselves besieged by requests for philanthropic donations or, worse yet, by proposals for dubious financial investments.

Avoiding Probate

Recognizing the costs and delays inherent in the probate process, many people try to avoid it by arranging their affairs so that they own nothing in their own names at the time of their death. If they own nothing in their own names, there is no need for probate because a person cannot will assets that he or she does not own exclusively; hence, there are no probatable assets.

One tactic that avoids probate is joint ownership of your assets with rights of survivorship. Under this arrangement, the assets are owned jointly by two or more individuals; on the death of any one joint tenant, the ownership of the entire asset passes to the survivor or survivors automatically and without probate. For this reason, joint ownership has been called "the poor man's will," and it is very widely used by spouses in connection with their homes, their bank and brokerage accounts, and other assets.

But joint ownership is not restricted to spouses. It can be established between parents and children, grandparents and grandchildren, homosexual couples, or close friends. And setting it up requires nothing more than a change in the title of the bank account, the brokerage account, or the real estate deed from individual ownership to "joint tenants with rights of survivorship," usually abbreviated as JTWROS.

Joint ownership of a bank account can be a convenient way of making sure that your bills are paid if you should be absent or disabled, but the same convenience can be achieved by giving someone—your spouse or an adult child—a power of attorney with respect to the account.

Joint ownership is not, however, without its limitations. Because any one owner has the legal right to use the jointly held asset, it should be used only between or among individuals who have a stable relationship. It is possible for a deserting spouse to abscond with a jointly held bank account or similar asset; although this is illegal, recovery can be very difficult. On the other hand, since the disposition of jointly held real estate requires the signatures of both parties, the absence or disagreement of one of them can create serious problems. In addition, joint ownership, once established, is difficult to dissolve. It can be dissolved only by mutual agreement between or among the tenants or by a court as part of a divorce settlement, but in general it should be regarded as a permanent arrangement.

Moreover, an unexpected death can undo the intentions of joint ownership. If, for example, you place your summer cottage into joint ownership with your two daughters, intending that they share its use or its proceeds after you die, but one daughter dies shortly after you do, the cottage automatically passes to the surviving daughter, and the spouse and children of the deceased daughter lose all rights to it. In addition, giving your daughters joint ownership may subject you to federal gift tax (see p. 565).

The income tax consequences of jointly held assets must also be considered. If you hold assets jointly with your spouse and you file a joint return, the income derived from the assets is reported jointly. In theory, if you own a bank or brokerage account jointly with a child, you are liable for the income tax in proportion to your contribution to the acquisition of the joint asset—usually 100 percent. In practice, the tax is payable by the person whose Social Security number appears on the account.

In addition, although joint ownership may avert probate for you, it may create problems for your survivors. For example, if on your death your spouse becomes sole owner of a brokerage account that the two of you had held jointly, the account will be probatable on the death of your spouse unless he or she establishes joint ownership with someone else immediately after your death. In addition, if your spouse has no experience in managing assets, they may be exposed to all sorts of unscrupulous or risky investments or business ventures.

Joint ownership between spouses may also result ultimately in larger estate taxes, once the second spouse dies. Although no estate taxes are due when assets pass to the surviving spouse, they may be due—if the estate is large enough—after the second spouse dies. Having a proportion of the assets pass directly to the children or other beneficiaries, or setting up a trust, may reduce the total estate taxes due for those who have substantial estates.

For all these reasons, many people have concluded that their heirs and their assets can be better protected by the establishment of some kind of trust in addition to a will.

TRUSTS

A trust is a legal entity—in some respects like a corporation—that can own, buy, sell, or transfer assets. Just as the corporation is managed by its officers, the trust is managed by one or more trustees. When you transfer your assets into a trust, you relinquish legal ownership of them, but for some kinds of trust you can name yourself as a trustee and thus retain the right to do anything you like with the assets. A trust is especially important for the parents of a severely disabled child who will need lifetime custodial care. But there are many other ways in which it is far superior to a will, even though it is not a substitute for one.

If, for example, you plan to earmark money for a young grandchild's future college expenses, you might bequeath the money to the child's parents, but there is no guarantee that they will manage it carefully or resist using it for their own purposes. And if you were to deposit it in a custodial account, the child would assume control of it at the age of majority and might decide to use it for other purposes. On the other hand, if you place the money in a trust and specify its purpose, the money can be managed effectively, protected against misuse, and preserved to fulfill your original intent.

Inter Vivos Revocable Trusts

As its name implies, the inter vivos revocable trust, or "living trust," is set up during your lifetime and can be revoked at any time. Its immediate advantage is that it can circumvent probate. If all your assets are held in the trust, then legally you own no assets in your own name. Hence, because you have nothing to transfer through your will, there is no need for probate. Despite this legal transfer of ownership, you retain control of the trust assets and have the right to use them for any purpose you choose whether you serve as your own trustee or name your spouse or someone else as cotrustee.

This type of trust has many additional advantages, both during your lifetime and after your death. First, should you become disabled or unavailable for an urgent decision about the trust assets—about the purchase or sale of securities, for example, or about an unexpectedly high offer to purchase your home—your cotrustee can make any necessary decisions in your absence. Second, if your assets are valuable and numerous, you can appoint as trustee or cotrustee a bank, a trust company, or a financial adviser who can manage them if you don't have the inclination or the skill to manage them yourself. You can also appoint one or more successor trustees to manage the trust after your death.

On your death, the trust may provide greater likelihood that your wishes will be carried out effectively. For example, if your will leaves assets to your children, and if you die shortly after a child reaches majority, there is no way to prevent this immature child from using his or her inheritance in ways you might seriously disapprove of.

If, instead, you use a trust or include a trust in your will, the trustee has far greater discretion with respect to the investment of the bequest pending its transfer to the beneficiary. Perhaps more important, your trust document can specify all kinds of conditions about the disbursement of your assets. You may, for example, specify that no child is to receive his or her inheritance before reaching the age of, say, 30, or that the inheritance is to be doled out in annual payments rather than paid out in a lump sum. You may authorize your successor trustee to use discretion about the disbursements to your children, so that if one of them suffers a serious illness or financial reverses, he or she can receive more money than the others.

If the trust is named as the beneficiary of your insurance policies, the proceeds will be used at the discretion of the trustee instead of being paid outright to a beneficiary who may not be mature enough or experienced enough to use them wisely.

If your spouse is inexperienced in financial management, the assets bequeathed through your will may be eroded or lost through poor management or injudicious investment. A trust under the care of a sophisticated trustee, on the other hand, can maintain or increase the value of its assets without depriving your widowed spouse of their use.

It is often difficult to transfer every one of your assets into a trust. But if enough of your major assets are held in the trust, the residue—for example, a small checking account, an automobile, unused airline tickets, and other items of moderate value—may add up to less than the maximum permitted by your state for settling your estate through affidavit or summary probate procedure.

A revocable trust offers you no income tax benefit because you are responsible for tax on the trust's income. In addition, trust assets are subject to creditors' claims.

As is the case with joint ownership, transferring assets into the trust involves nothing more than changing the registration of the bank account, the real property, or any other asset. But in contrast to joint ownership, you, as a trustee, can do whatever you like with the assets and you can change the terms of the trust at any time and in any way you choose.

Because the wording of a trust document is highly technical, it should be prepared by a lawyer experienced in estate planning. A lawyer will charge you for the time involved, and, because a trust document is necessarily more detailed than a will, you can expect to pay $500, $1,000, or more for its preparation. It may not be worth the expense for those without substantial assets. As with a will, the more decisions—about the selection of trustees and beneficiaries and conditions of disbursement—that you make ahead of time, the less time the lawyer will need to spend with you.

Irrevocable Trusts

Unlike the revocable trust, the irrevocable trust requires you to part forever with whatever assets you transfer to it. Such trusts are usually used in order to obtain tax benefits and require special planning.

When you create an irrevocable trust, you are essentially giving away the assets you transfer to the trust, but the conditions you include in the trust document may give you significant control over their use. That is, you can not only specify the beneficiaries but also specify the purposes for which the income can be used, the rate at which it can be disbursed, and virtually any other conditions. The wealthy can use the irrevocable trust to reduce their tax burden, since income taxes may be paid by the trust itself or by beneficiaries on the income they derive from the trust.

In addition to the fact that you cannot use the trust income for your own benefit, you cannot, except under certain limited circumstances, act as a trustee. There is no reason why you cannot appoint a trusted friend as trustee, but irrevocable trusts are generally large enough to justify the use of a bank, an attorney, or a trust company in order to ensure that the trust assets receive continuous and sophisticated management.

Miscellaneous Trusts

There is a wide range of trusts with special uses. An attorney specializing in them should be able to tailor a trust to your personal circumstances and needs. Setting up a trust requires the services of a lawyer, who should be able to tailor a trust to your personal circumstances and needs. Trusts can be used in various ways for a wide variety of purposes, including not only the avoidance of probate but also the avoidance or reduction of the federal gift and estate tax (see below).

You can, for example, set up a standby trust, which may contain no assets at first but can serve as the sole beneficiary of your life insurance policies. Or you can direct, through your will, the establishment of what is called a testamentary trust, to be funded by your estate and thus take effect when you die.

POWER OF ATTORNEY

If you are not prepared to establish a trust and you hold assets in your name alone, it may be important that you give a spouse, adult child, or trusted friend a power of attorney—that is, the right to sign checks and conduct other business on your behalf if you should become incapacitated. This power can be revoked at any time or it can be written so as to be effective only when you become incapacitated. Forms for various types of power of attorney are available from banks, securities brokers, and office-supply firms. Or you may want to consult an attorney.

UNIFIED FEDERAL GIFT AND ESTATE TAXES

Because the united federal gift and estate tax applies only to estates whose value exceeds $600,000, until recently most middle-class persons disregarded it, considering it of interest only to "the rich." With the inflation of real estate values and other investments, however, an increasing number of people are likely to pay it. Since the ultimate value of your estate is unpredictable, you should give some thought to reducing your possible exposure, especially as you near retirement. Even though your probatable estate may be small, your taxable estate may be considerable. That's because your insurance policies as well as assets held in joint ownership, such as your home or your brokerage account, are not subject to probate but are subject to estate tax.

If your assets are sufficient to provide you with a comfortable retirement, you might consider giving away enough to reduce the estate value below $600,000 or $1.2 million for married couples. Doing so allows you to experience the gratitude of the recipients; more important, your gift may be far more valuable earlier in their lives than later.

You cannot, however, give away assets without the possibility of tax consequences. Gifts beyond a specified amount are taxable by the federal government—and you, the donor, are liable for the tax, not the recipient.

The system works as follows: You are allowed to give a maximum of $10,000—or $20,000 if you make the gift jointly with your spouse—to any recipient once a year without incurring any gift tax obligation. This can be a rather liberal allowance, because, for example, if you and your spouse want to give your married daughter $40,000, you can give $20,000 to her and another $20,000 to her spouse, who can in turn give it to her or use it for their joint purposes. In addition, you can give up to $10,000/$20,000 to each of your grandchildren. And since gifts are taxable on the basis of a calendar year, you can make one set of gifts on December 31 and a second one on the next day, January 1.

There is no limit on gifts between spouses. One way to avoid or reduce the estate tax is to give your spouse some of your assets to be held in his or her name, so each of you can take advantage of the tax benefits. If you place these assets into joint ownership with a right of survivorship, your spouse will receive them at your death without tax. Careful planning is needed to be sure that both spouses take advantage of their $600,000 "credit equivalent," no matter who dies first.

Although you must file a tax return for gifts of more than $10,000 (or $20,000 with the consent of your spouse), you need not actually pay the tax. The government establishes for you a $600,000 "line of credit," so to speak. If your total lifetime gifts plus the value of your estate do not exceed this limit, you pay no tax. If the total does exceed the limit, your estate will be taxed.

In calculating the value of your estate for tax purposes, the government includes the following assets:

- All assets owned by you alone
- One-half of the assets you own jointly with your spouse
- All assets you own jointly with a person not your spouse unless you can prove that the other person contributed to their acquisition
- Your life insurance unless the policy is owned by someone else
- Life insurance payable to your estate
- Assets in a custodial account for minors if you are the custodian
- Assets in a revocable trust

You can sometimes reduce the tax liability of your estate by transferring ownership of your insurance policies to someone else (who then becomes responsible for paying the premiums) or, as we have noted, setting up an irrevocable trust and making periodic gifts to it that do not exceed the annual $10,000/$20,000 limit.

Because the government provides an unlimited marital deduction, you pay no tax if you bequeath your estate to your spouse. But this may merely postpone the problem, because it leaves a heavily taxable estate following your spouse's death. One way to alleviate the future tax liability on your spouse's estate is to create a trust that takes advantage of the $600,000 credit. You may create a $600,000 trust that pays the income to your surviving spouse for life and the principal to your children. The assets in this trust are included in your estate but sheltered by the $600,000 credit. They are excluded from your spouse's estate because he or she has only a limited right in this trust.

Another type of trust is called a QTIP (qualified terminable interest property) trust. Its purpose is to obtain the marital deduction but still ensure that your children will inherit your estate after your spouse's death. Income must be payable to your spouse for his or her life. Your executor must elect to claim the marital deduction for the assets of the trust, thus excluding them from your taxable estate. However, the assets will be included in your spouse's estate even though he or she may not have power over the trust principal.

If your estate is so large that the suggestions made here are insufficient, an estate planner can suggest a number of alternatives.

LETTER OF INSTRUCTION

As noted, your will is a formal document that requires careful preparation. To revise it each time there is a change in the nature and value of your assets would be expensive and inconvenient. Hence, your will should dispose of your assets in rather general terms and should not attempt to dispose of every stock, bond, bank account, or other possession individually.

For this reason, it is extremely important that you maintain a current record of everything you own and everything you owe, so that your survivors will not overlook something because they are not aware of its existence or its whereabouts. Your spouse, of course, may be fully aware of everything you own individually or jointly, but should you both die simultaneously, your survivors may have great difficulty in assembling all your assets and liabilities without this record.

This inventory of your assets, known as a letter of instruction, can serve three further purposes. First, it can specify your wishes as to the distribution of personal possessions not mentioned in your will: antiques, jewelry, mementos of various kinds. Although the letter of instruction does not have any legal force, your family members are likely to feel morally bound to comply with your wishes. Second, it can specify your preferences with respect to funeral arrangements and organ or body donations. Last, it can include any personal wishes or messages to your survivors that you do not wish to be made public, as will inevitably happen if you include these in your will and your will is probated.

There is no set form for a letter of instruction. It can be maintained in any way you prefer—for example, in loose-leaf or index-card form so that you can make changes easily each time you acquire or sell an asset or incur a liability. If you have been solely responsible for handling your personal business affairs, the record should include specific information on your life, homeowner's, and automobile insurance policies; your tax records; your employee pension plan; the location of your safe deposit box key; and anything else that your executor or your survivors need to know in order to settle your affairs.

Unlike your will, which may be filed with the county clerk or your lawyer, the letter of instruction should be in a place known and immediately accessible to your survivors. If you update it regularly, you will not only protect your assets but also save added stress on your survivors.

YOUR LIVING WILL

Although you may plan to bequeath substantial assets to your survivors, these assets can be severely eroded or entirely wiped out by the costs of a terminal illness—especially if your last weeks or months are spent in a comatose state, maintained by life-support machinery. Technological developments in life-support systems have made this situation increasingly common and have created legal and ethical dilemmas about "pulling the plug" on patients who have no hope of recovery but can be maintained indefinitely in a vegetative state.

Within the past few years, however, at least 42 states and the District of Columbia have passed laws which in one way or another support the legality of living wills, which permit the withdrawal of life support when a patient is terminal or in a persistent vegetative state. And even in those states that have not yet passed legislation, there is an increasing willingness to respect such wishes.

To make your wishes known, you need to execute what is called a "living will," specifying that you do not wish to continue on life support when your condition is terminal. You do not need a lawyer's assistance in writing a living will; forms usually are available from your physician or your local hospital, or they can be obtained from the following organizations:

- Concern for Dying, 250 West 57th Street, New York, N. Y. 10107
- Society for the Right to Die (same address as above)

Your living will should be witnessed by at least two adults and notarized, and a copy should be filed with your medical record. You can, of course, revoke the will at any time if you change your mind.

Index